Chapter
HUNG[...]
339

Chapter 20
CORRECTIONS
353

Chapter 21
MY TERTIARY YEARS
365

Chapter 22
THE SOCIALIST EDUCATION MOVEMENT
381

Chapter 23
ACTIVITIES IN THE GREAT CULTURAL REVOLUTION
423

Chapter 24
AN INTERPRETER AT THE GUANGZHOU TRADE FAIR
467

Chapter 25
THE END OF MY SCHOOLING
481

EPILOGUE
493

CHRONOLOGY
494

ACKNOWLEDGEMENTS

Special thanks goes to everyone at New Holland Publishers who helped on *Jade Eye*. I especially wish to thank Anouska Good, Publishing Manager, for her efforts and support, and Monica Ban, Senior Editor, for her patient and strenuous editing.

I am grateful to Lynk Manuscript Assessment Services for acknowledging the value of *Jade Eye* and for giving me frank suggestions to improve my story and offering me continued encouragement for its publication.

Heartfelt thanks also goes to Dr Virginia Lowe and Robyn Sheahan-Bright, who both initially edited *Jade Eye*. Their efforts enabled me to overcome many of the barriers between Oriental and Western ways of thinking.

Many thanks also to my Moonee Ponds neighbours—readers and advisers of *Jade Eye*. In particular I wish to thank Mr and Mrs John Fraser and Bernadette Bartels, who all offered me valuable advice and sustained encouragement.

It would not be possible for me to have concentrated on my writing without the ever-present support of my wife, Lu Huan-qin, who was my first reader, my ardent adviser and my frankest assessor.

chapter 1

MY VILLAGE, MY HOME AND MY PARENTS

A son never questioned the ugliness or beauty of his mother. A dog never left his master's poverty-stricken family. A Chinese peasant never left his village—being born, growing, raising children, toiling and dying on the same land.

The Paradise Palace

During the prime years of the Qing dynasty (1644–1911), there lived its long ruling emperor, Qian-lung (enthroned in 1736, abdicated in 1795) who loved hunting. One day, flanked by his lackeys, he hunted at a place twenty-five kilometres south of his palace—the Forbidden City. When the setting sun crimsoned the western sky he reined in his horse to the edge of a bank of a small river. The bank was covered with wild chrysanthemums and lined with poplar and willow trees. A refreshing breeze caressed his face. He felt very happy and his zest for hunting was very high. He ordered his men to camp for the night by the river. He noticed a small village on the opposite bank, partly camouflaged by the poplar and elm trees.

The emperor was still in high spirits during his dinner. Putting a piece of meat into his mouth, he suddenly paused in his chewing and asked a eunuch the name of the village. The eunuch had earlier learned that the place was called 'Village Shi'. The answer was on the tip of his tongue when he realised that the village name *shi* had the same pronunciation as the word for human faeces. If he uttered the word *shi* while the emperor was eating, he would be asking for trouble. He was a clever eunuch and could handle all situations nimbly, otherwise how would it be possible for him to wait at the emperor's table? His eyes rolled and his brain worked quickly. He did not wish to dampen the emperor's mood and he did not want to lose his own head. 'Why?' he thought, 'wherever the emperor stays is a palace!' He was happy with this revelation. Humbly, he told the emperor that the village was called the 'Paradise Palace' and the river was called the 'Paradise River'. The emperor was very pleased at hearing the name of the village. He thought that coming out of the Forbidden City and camping at the Paradise Palace was a fortunate coincidence. He laughed merrily and finished his dinner happily.

This story was passed by the village elders of one generation to another and another and another and the village has been called 'The Paradise Palace' and the river 'The Paradise River' ever since. This was the origin of the name of my home village. Whether the story is true or not, none of the villagers ever questioned it; however, I believe it is true. My argument is simple: quite a few neighbouring villages also have names connected to the same emperor. For example, the village about five kilometres to the north is called the 'Royal Horse Well' because the emperor had water fetched from that well for his horse, while another is called the 'Front Camp' because it was once a camp for his guards.

The Paradise Palace, by the time of my birth, had several hundred houses with a population of about one thousand. Villagers with the family names of Li, Ma, Guo and Wang were the majority. Maybe I was different to the other one thousand; at least I felt so when I was old enough to know more about the village. While I travelled the world, generation after generation never moved to other places; they only toiled, suffered, hoped and expanded the population of the Paradise Palace.

The village, which had Beijing twenty-five kilometres to the north, was about ten kilometres from Yong Ding River to the west. The river, which was about one kilometre wide, had 'an iron head, a copper tail, and a bean curd middle section'. The riverbed's middle section was called 'bean curd' because of its vulnerable bank, which was much higher than the houses of the surrounding villages. A long, high dyke was constructed to tame its water, which flowed more than ten metres above the rooftops. It was a constant threat to the village during summer downpours. Gigantic sand dunes lay less than two kilometres to the north of the village. In winter, the roaring wind from Siberia carried a considerable quantity of sand into the air and scattered it onto the village and its fields. A creek, which the villagers also called the Paradise River, flowed through the village. A highway, which was called the Beijing–Kaifeng Highway ran parallel to the creek heading south. A temporary bridge, which was merely a few logs placed on bricks, connected the tip and the main body of the village.

The Paradise River, when I was old enough to play in its shallow water, was still flanked by poplar and willow trees and its banks were still carpeted with wild chrysanthemums. Yet in spring when the villagers needed water badly, it was dry. When it rained for successive days in summer it raised the level of the brimming river higher than the fields, making it impossible for the villagers to drain excess water from their land into it.

Land around the village was sandy and mostly in the hands of a score of families who lived in grandly constructed grey-coloured compounds of quadruple houses (square houses with each side considered a wing), which looked like very strong citadels. Most of the villagers had only small patches of land which were called 'manger land', with the middle of the patches being much lower than the sides. These patches were created by the wintry wind, which carried the top sandy soil to the bottom of the trees and groves around each field and settled there year after year. Manger lands could never give a full harvest. When there was drought, only the bottom of the fields would produce a harvest and when there was a lot of rain, only the slopes of the fields would produce a harvest. Such a small piece of land could not support a family. The male villagers had to be casual or long-term farmhands to big landowners in the Paradise Palace or in the villages nearby to gain extra food.

My Birth and My Home

On Lunar 26 July (the old generation of peasants counted the days and months by the moon) in the year of the snake, Buddha delivered me to one of the Li families in the Paradise Palace, as a special favour or perhaps as a random choice. I know little about the details of my birth. I am certain of the date because my parents told me of it but they never told me in what year I was born. They just told me how old I was each year on New Year's Day. When I was in primary school, my teacher worked it out from my age and told me I was born in 1941.

I was born when the peasants of the Paradise Palace and the villages nearby were groaning in dire misery and astounding hardship. The puppet soldiers of the occupying Japanese and roaming bandits haunted the villages. The secret undercover Kuomintang agents (recruited from the villagers) and the secret undercover Communist Party members (also recruited from the villagers) were vying for the support of the peasants. Natural calamities, such as floods and drought, also besieged the villagers constantly. It was the period when peasants were in 'deep water and burning fire'.

I was born, like millions of Chinese rural babies at the time, not as a product of two people deeply in love but as a product of my parents' being brought together by a matchmaker and married by the order of their parents. It was just like growing corn—sow the seeds and the plants will come up, later giving birth to new pieces of corn. The word 'love' was something my parents had never heard of. Frankly, I might have been the product of my parents' boredom, as was the case with most babies, for besides lovemaking peasants had no other entertainment available except their daily toil in the fields.

Two families, my father's and his older brother's family, shared a small house. They did not inherit the house from their own parents because their parents had never had a house. They lived, as my father told me, in a dugout until my father and his brother inherited the house. Prior to my father and his brother, no one in our family had ever owned a house. My father and his brother inherited the house from another Li family that had no heir after the death of the old couple. The two of them, my father and his older brother, were the closest nephews of that family, so the house was given to them. The house was made from pieces of half-bricks and was more than sixty years old. In every aspect it showed its age. It had three rooms—the middle room, the left bedroom and the right bedroom. The right half of the middle room and the right bedroom belonged to my father; the left half of the middle room and the left bedroom belonged to my uncle Yong-jiang. The entrance door of the middle room was the only entrance into the house and was shared by both families. The middle room had a left and right door, each leading to the left and right bedrooms. The house was called a 'one common and two privates' house. The three rooms were of the same size; each measured more or less twelve to thirteen square metres. The middle room provided a space for the activities of both families and was called the 'common room'. A cloth curtain draped from the lintel of each bedroom door to separate it from the common room and provide a bit of privacy to each bedroom, hence the description 'two privates'.

When pushing open the entrance door, the first thing that met the eyes was a shrine on a big, rickety square table against the back wall. The table, whose black lacquer had long lost its original glossy smoothness and brilliance, stood in the centre of the common room. Sitting on a pedestal in the shrine was the deity Guan-gong. He was a famous general in Xi Shu (West Shu State) during the three kingdoms of Wei, Shu and Wu, and was declared a deity by the emperors after his death. (Rulers of all the succeeding dynasties worshipped him, but I have no idea which emperor actually deified him.) He was the common deity worshipped jointly by our two families. Between the black laquer table and the partitioning wall on each side of it was a vat, which was used to store drinking water. Each family had an unbaked clay-brick cooking range either side of the entrance door, directly under the windowsill. A printed picture of a kitchen god was glued above each one. When my aunt (who I called Da Ma, meaning 'big mother' because she was older than my mother) and mother, squatting back to back by the cooking ranges, were cooking at the same time, it looked as though the passage was impassable, otherwise this common room was quite spacious, even though it was shared by two families and a deity. Guan-gong, who sat in the shrine overlooking this common room bare of any other wooden furniture, was already blackened by the cooking smoke and covered in dust, despite protection from a curtain. Guan-gong just sat there—he never commented, never complained and never helped.

The front half of our bedroom was occupied by a rectangular *kang*, a clay-brick bed for the whole family. The *kang* was a combination of vertically and horizontally placed clay bricks, the top surface being a layer of clay mixed with chopped straw. A mattress woven from reeds was spread over it to serve as our bed sheeting. We slept with our naked bodies on the mattress, without even shorts, because the body was tougher protection against wear-and-tear than clothing. If the mattress was worn out and my father could not afford to buy a new one, we had to sleep on the bare clay surface—we did this a couple of times over the years. On this *kang* slept all six members of my family, our heads lined along the rim of the *kang*, like sardines in a can. Two quilts, which were made when my parents married, were the only coverings owned by the family at the time.

The floor of the bedroom was unpaved but had a clay surface, which was spread by my father over the original sand floor. At the right corner against the back wall were two porcelain vases, the only valuables in the room. They were the only things of a dowry my mother received from her mother, who had them as a dowry from her mother. They must have been passed down many times from mother to daughter as a dowry, for they could not be less than two hundred years old, being products of the early Quian Lung period of the Qing Dynasty. The walls, whose cheap paper was plastered on at the time of my parents' wedding, was blackened by smoke and had neither pictures nor any other decorations. Pits and cracks on the walls were covered with stains of darkened blood left by bed bugs killed on the spot either with a thumbnail or with a stick.

The front yard, divided from the centre-line of the doorway into two equal halves, was about ten metres deep, ending at the back wall of a house of another Li family. (The Paradise Palace had about twenty-five Li families. I called the different generations and members 'uncle' or 'granny' as my father instructed me). Against their wall were partitions for a toilet for our family and a space for stacking our firewood. In front of our window was an awning erected from tree branches. An unbaked clay-brick cooking range was beneath it for cooking in summer. The rest of the yard, apart from a narrow passage, was used for growing vegetables such as beans and cucumber and bottle gourd for making ladles.

I was the first baby born to this Li family and I was born on the very day that my Da Ma was carried to the house in a sedan chair to be the spouse of my uncle Yong-jiang. (My uncle married late. He was about fifteen years older than my father.) As my birth and my uncle's wedding were regarded as occasions of great joy and happiness for the family, my parents gave me the name of 'Shuang Xi', meaning double happiness. However, I cannot recall any moment of their being happy in my early memories, and I never heard them talking about happiness.

Some of my uncles (those of my father's generation who were neighbours were all uncles to me) nicknamed me 'Yu Yan' (Jade Eye), because the white of my left eye was actually bluish green. I never knew whether they used Yu Yan as my name to remind me I was different or because they thought 'Shuang Xi' was too good for a poor family. It is through my jade eye that I am telling you the things I saw and experienced as a Chinese peasant boy.

My father had only two *mu* (one *mu* = ⅙ acre) of land from the same family from which he and his brother had inherited the house. The soil of this land was sandy, not fertile, and it was not big enough to sustain the family, even with a bumper harvest. My father had to hire himself out as a casual or as a long-term farmhand when the land was not sown with watermelon or sweet melon. My mother was as strong as a man, as able as a man, and worked like a man. Most years, she had to tend the two *mu* of land almost entirely by herself.

Some things about my childhood are clear. I know that before I could walk I was often left by my mother to lie in a bag half-filled with sand, which was the customary nappy used for babies in our part of China. I do not know, though, how my parents kept me alive during the 1943 famine. The year 1943 was considered 'a stone roller that did not turn and roll' because there was no harvest. (The peasants used the stone rollers to crush wheat and other crops for kernels in the big yard of the village. When there was no harvest, the stone rollers lay idle.) During the Japanese occupation (1931–1945), *hun he mian*, a mixture of acorn flour and flour, whose other ingredients were unknown to the villagers, was sometimes available at the local market. It was mouldy and smelly and remained as heavy as lead in the stomach, making people constantly run to the toilet. Even this smelly mixture was out of reach for most of the penniless villagers, who had only peanut shells and the crushed core of corn to fill their stomachs. 'When you stood up,' my Da Ma once said to me, 'your dung was blown away by a gust of wind before it dried. You felt so weak that it was very hard for you to stand up after squatting to relieve the bowels. Some people never stood up. You never knew whether you would be able to get up from your bed the following day! You never knew when you squatted down to relieve yourself whether you would be able to stand up again or whether you would just kiss the ground and go to the other world.'

Normally my uncle Yong-jiang and Da Ma's life was better than that of my parents because of my uncle's trade of making harnesses, whips, ropes, and so on; a trade that suited life in the countryside. If life was so difficult for my uncle and my Da Ma, it must have been much worse for my parents. My parents never told me how they survived that famine.

This was my home, to which the Buddha of Mercy delivered me.

My Father
My father, whose name was Li Yong-mao (Yong-mao means 'ever prosperous'), was born on Lunar 16 August 1918, the year of the horse. He was a small man—small because he was below the average height of the male villagers; small because he was sinewy and not robust and he was shorter than any one of his sons; small because he was unknown to the world outside his village and he had not been well-known within his own village; and small, perhaps, because malnutrition during his childhood and teenage years had hampered his growth.

At the age of nine, he was sent to a carpet manufacturer's workshop in Beijing to be an apprentice. An apprentice, at this time, was the equivalent of a servant—a servant not only of the owner of the workshop, but also of his own teacher and the other master weavers. He had to wait upon them at every meal, fetching food for his teacher and the master weavers before he could eat himself. Every time he took up his bowl and had a mouthful of food, a master weaver would call him to refill his bowl. All master weavers ate their food very quickly, a habit formed when they themselves were apprentices. When his teacher and all the master weavers finished eating, my father had to stop eating too, partly because he had not enough time to eat and partly because when he had time to eat there was not much food left for him. Consequently, he was always only half fed.

The experience of eating during his apprenticeship, as well as his years of being a casual or long-term hired labourer to landowners, compelled him to form the habit of eating quickly. Even today, at over eighty years of age and his life easy, he still eats very quickly, as if he is afraid that if he eats slowly he will go hungry for the rest of the day.

The owner of the workshop required my father to weave one square foot of carpet per day. My father was only a small boy and he was slow. At the end of the day he could only finish eighty per cent and had to complete his work in the evening under the light of a lamp. Little food and working overtime daily made him as thin as a bag of bones and his eyesight worse. At the age of thirteen, when he had nearly completed his apprenticeship, he was not far from being blind. The owner of the workshop gave him one silver dollar coin and told him to go home. He was sacked. He only had a silver dollar and a small bedding roll. He did not want to pay for his trip home with the one coin, which he had earned through more than three years' hard work, so he just 'legged it' all the way. His clothes were so infested with vermin, my uncle Yong-jiang, my father's only brother, had to make a fire and shake the clothing over it when my father returned home. The cracking of the vermin in the fire was as intense as the cracking of sesame seeds under a grill, making them feel sick.

My father was too small and too sick to be hired to herd pigs for other people, so my grandfather and my uncle managed to have him enrolled in school, hoping that he might gain a better life through schooling. But the family was too poor to continue supporting his study for long; and he had to quit after a little more than one year.

Not as strong and big as other peasants, my father was not suited to casual work. When he was a casual hand during the wheat harvest, my mother had to lend him a hand in order to keep pace with the other labourers. But he was valued as a long-term hired labourer because he was honest and never shirked his responsibility. He never stopped working, whether the owner was supervising or not. 'Neither the hard-working nor the lazy labourers will get the blame, only those who take their eyes off the job and take no heed of the approaching master get the blame,' my father always said. 'I was hard working and I never worried whether the owner was present or not. I just worked. So I never got the blame.' And so he never had any difficulty in finding someone to hire him.

My father was a man of few words. 'Bludgeoning him three times will not knock a word out of him!' my mother often complained. 'One cannot even quarrel with him!' she would add. They rarely quarrelled. I noticed them quarrelling only once and it did not consist of fighting or of any exchange of undesirable adjectives. Their quarrel was just silence, in which they competed to see who could remain silent the longest. And during that one quarrel which I remember clearly, they remained silent for a whole month.

'When you were two years old,' my mother once told me, to show the temperament of my father, 'you walked on the clay bricks of a neighbour. The clay bricks were still wet and you destroyed them all drying in the sun. Your father did not say a word. He just remixed the clay and remade the bricks for the neighbour!'

When somebody taunted my father with cruel jokes, he would not even comment about it. If somebody gave him a slap on the head for fun, he would not scold them. Nothing could make him speak in retaliation or make him angry. 'He is just like a lump of dough! Anybody can knead him!' my mother would say. But my father once told me, 'Boxwood is soft, but it is used for carving figures of gods, and people will kowtow to it. The mulberry tree is hard, but its timber is only used to make shoulder poles, and it will break some day in the end. The tongue is soft and the teeth are hard. When all teeth disappear the tongue is still there.' So he never quarrelled with anybody.

Whatever mistakes I made he never corrected me with his palm or with the broom handle, as my mother did. He just told me it was not good to do that. His eyes were very soft and he never spoke to me, my mother or to anybody in a raised voice.

One early, rainy summer day, he took me to our 'north-western land' to sow lentils in places where peanuts grew. He carried about two-thirds of a gourd ladle filled with lentil seed. 'When we finish the seed, we shall go home,' my father told me. Then he added, 'four or five seeds in one hole, not too many'. My father tilted the hoe, raised it up about two feet from the earth, thrust it down, pulled the hoe horizontally sideways, and thus made a hole with a pyramid-like small pile of soil next to it. I would throw four or five lentil seeds into the hole and sweep in the pile of soil with my right foot, and press the soil down hard. By and by, I got tired of the work. I remembered that my father told me that as soon as we finished the seed, we would go home so I began putting three or four times more seeds into each hole. Well before noon arrived, we finished the seed and returned home.

A couple of days later, when my father came back from weeding in the field, he carried home a full basket of lentil shoots.

'Where do you get them?' my mother asked in surprise.

'Your son grew them for us,' my father replied.

'You are already five years old and you still don't understand a thing!' my mother scolded me.

'No need to blame him. We can now have a treat of lentil shoots. If he had not done it, we would not have been able to have such a treat till New Year's Day!' my father pacified my mother, whose eyes were belching fire.

My father was intelligent. He was good at mathematics for practical use in the countryside. When measuring land, the dung-heap, or a pit, he would have the answer before the most learned villager using an abacus, and he was always right. If somebody read stories from a book to him, chapter by chapter, he could relate the stories in the long winter evenings to other people, without any omission, though not entirely word for word. Even the person who read the stories to him liked to listen to him re-telling them, because the stories became more colourful from his lips.

My father was slow with his hands in almost everything he did. When my mother and he were weeding the peanuts with hoes, my mother was already at the other end of the field while he was just a bit over halfway. When we shelled peanuts, he could only do ten kilograms a day without doing anything else. My mother could do fifteen kilograms while she had to cook three meals and feed the pig. However, when he completed the weeding, not even a tiny grass blade would be left. What others achieved, he attained by taking more time, and with superior quality.

During the coldest winter days when the ice was about a half a metre thick and when the soil was frozen as hard as rock, my father, when he was not hired, would collect firewood. Actually I should not call what he retrieved firewood, I should call it fire materials, for he just used a piece of tree branch to beat the dried grass off the ground and then scooped it together with a rake. He never touched tree branches for firewood.

Honest, mild of temperament, reticent, tenacious and hard working; these were the qualities of my father. Small, ordinary and unknown as he was, he was great in my mind.

My Mother

My mother was born in 1923—the year of the pig—but I do not know on which day. Unlike women before her and women of her own time, my mother had her own name and was not just called by the family names of my father and herself (if so, she would have been called Li Wang Shi, meaning the person named Wang in Li's family). She had her own name, which was Wang Qing-rong (meaning to rejoice in prosperity)—a very good masculine name. She could not be classed as small, as she was slightly above the average height of peasant women in our village.

Although my mother was uneducated, she seemed to be ahead of her time. When she was still a child, all girls had to bind their feet with long bandages to have all four small toes of each foot under the sole, leaving the big toe as it was. All the small toes would be broken as they walked on them. This restriction was so their feet could become 'three-inch golden lilies'. Her older sister had her feet bound and cried bitterly during the day but mostly during the night. But she dared not touch the bandages; she just suffered. Warnings such as 'if you have large feet you will not get married, for no man likes to marry a girl with large feet,' frightened her. However, my mother was different. When my grandmother bound her feet, she tore off the bandages and cut them into tiny pieces. 'Nobody will marry you if you don't bind your feet!' my grandmother scolded her. 'If nobody wants to marry me, I will not marry anybody,' my mother answered back. She teased her older sister when she tottered about the house or yard. Her older sister would be in tears but never dared to touch the bandages; she envied my mother when she ran freely about the yard, but never dared to liberate her own feet.

My mother's family was wealthier than my father's. My grandfather had a three-room house with a big yard of more than one acre in size, which was used to grow corn or sweet potatoes or peanuts. He also had two acres of land, sandy but good for growing anything. I could not understand why he married his second daughter, my mother, to my father who was so poor. Neither my mother nor my father ever mentioned it. Was it because of her unrestricted natural feet? Was it because my grandparents feared it unsafe to keep her at home because of the 'Japanese Devils'? The peasants called the Japanese invaders 'Japanese Devils' who looked for 'flowery girls' to satisfy their lust wherever they roamed. If a girl had been raped by the Japanese Devils, no family would accept her willingly as a daughter-in-law. (The Japanese called beautiful girls 'flowery girls'.)

My mother was only eighteen when I was born. Often parents married a girl from fourteen to seventeen years of age to rich families, but it was very rare that parents would marry a girl of seventeen to a poor man like my father. When I was old enough (at the age of four) to remember things, she looked just like a girl. Poor as our family was, her oval face was always rosy due to her physical labour in the field. Her hair was bountiful and very black. Her shabby clothing could not hide or spoil her healthy beauty. She never worried about whether she was beautiful or not. She never took up her only mirror unless she combed her glossy hair to twist it into a bun behind her head just above the collar.

The only time of the year when my mother applied make-up to her face was before the Spring Festival. (The New Year in China is called the Spring Festival, perhaps because New Year's Day is always the beginning of spring. Other countries called it the Chinese New Year). My Da Ma and my mother would sit opposite each other and clean one another's face, in turn. Either my Da Ma or my mother would have one end of a piece of thread held in the mouth by the teeth, with the other end held by the left hand. They would twist the thread and keep the loophole of the thread wide open with the right thumb and forefinger. The thread loophole would then be pressed hard against the face, with a backward jerk of the head, and the twisting of the thread would pull the 'sweat-hair' off the face. This was repeated all over the face. When this was finished, the face became very clean. Then they would trim each other's eyebrows. During the Spring Festival, though she had no new dresses, my mother did look different.

When at home, my mother would weave a belt for my father, or she would weave inch-wide long laces for binding the lower open ends of trousers in winter. She would spin strings with hemp fibre for stitching together the shoe-upper and the shoe-sole. She would make cloth plasters so that she could make shoe-soles later. She would also, of course, cook three meals a day. Her hands were never for a moment idle, and she utilised her hands nimbly and quickly.

When working in the field, my mother used the hoe quicker than my father, and during breaks she would stitch a shoe-sole or a shoe-upper. When collecting leftover peanuts below the ground in the fields of big landowners, she handled the small rake, which we called 'the small four teeth', so quickly that her hands seemed like the hands of a machine. She also used her hands to correct me if I did silly things.

'Shuang Xi, come over here,' she would call.

I would stop playing, approach her, and stand at a distance from the reach of her hand.

'Come closer, didn't you hear me?' she would demand.

Reluctant as I was, I had to move closer, to the spot she indicated with her left pointing finger.

'Where are my hemp strings?' she would ask.

'I used them as bowstrings.' I replied, watching her hand, and ready to bolt away at the slightest sign of movement from her.

'What? I spent so much time to spin them! You are already five. Can't you learn a thing? I must give you a good beating to make you remember!' she would hiss.

I was on the point of dashing away to avoid the beating because she flared up instantly, but her anger was always short-lived. If I could get away, she would forget the correction when I came back later. But nine times out of ten I could not get away. Before she finished the word 'beating', her left hand would get hold of my lapels or one of my arms, pull me towards her, and her right palm would slap my buttocks like raindrops on broad pumpkin leaves. If a broom had been available nearby, she would smack my buttocks with its handle like beating a drum. Fortunately, she seldom corrected me when I needed no correction. She was a fair 'judge'.

When I went with her to weed or harvest, she would pick up twigs or manure on the road and place them in her basket. Wild asparagus or mushrooms in the woods lining both sides of the road could never escape her eyes, for she needed them to give the family a better meal. She never seemed to care about the taste or quality of food at meals. She swallowed the food made from a mixture of more wild vegetables and a little flour simply to fill up her stomach. When there was not enough food to eat, she would go about her work with a half-filled stomach without complaining and without slowing down her hands.

Never holding a grudge in her breast against anybody; never leaving a word unsaid; never not working; never wasting a thing; never complaining about life; and never being afraid of any difficulty were the qualities of my mother.

I inherited my temperament and character from my mother!

chapter 2

MEMORIES OF MY CHILDHOOD

Natural disaster, running away from battles, the bullying soldiers, shortage of food—these are my childhood memories. In July 1937, Japan launched an aggressive attack on China. In retaliation, the Kuomintang Army (the Nationalists) began a series of battles and relentless blows on the Japanese invaders. The Eight Route Army and the New Fourth Army, under the leadership of the Communist Party of China (CPC), fought the Japanese on their soil and thus played the decisive role in the victory against Japan. The Japanese occupation of northern China came to an end when the CPC forces defeated them in a series of battles. The Kuomintang Army then launched an attack on the liberated areas occupied by the CPC and civil war broke out between the Nationalists and the Communists.

The Young Watchman and the Hailstones

When I started to learn in life, I discovered how to please myself very quickly. I kneaded clay into tiny pots, cups and saucers and hardened them in the cinders and hot ashes after my mother finished cooking. I made a bow with a thumb-thick young willow tree stem, and arrows with the reedy, long smooth part of sorghum stalks under the ears. I played hide-and-seek with the neighbours' children. My childhood activities were quite diversified and flourished until I was harnessed to trudge along the rut of my parents; the rut of battling peasants.

One early summer morning in 1945 when I was nearly four years old, my father shook and awoke me. He told me to go to our sweet melon plot to be a watchman there. This was the beginning of my working life and the premature end of my childhood frolics and freedom. Sweet melon is different from rockmelon or honeydew melon—it is white in colour and one just needs to wash it, cut it open to get rid of the seeds and the pulp, and eat the skin and flesh. It is crisp, fragrant, and sweet.

Our sweet melon plot was the two *mu* of land my father had inherited. It was about one kilometre away to the north-west of our village and in our family was called 'the north-western land'. It was in the small hours of the morning when I got up. The crescent moon was not peeping out yet. The sky was dusted with bright twinkling stars—they seemed to wink at me in praise, admiring me for being given such an important role at such a young age. They would not jeer at a boy who got up so early to watch the sweet melon field, or at least I felt so in my childish mind. As I walked, a soft caressing breeze was fondling my face and my head, which was shaved like that of a monk. Crickets and cicadas were still asleep, not chirping away like they did at noon and in the early evenings. Now and then a dog's bark was carried to my ears by the breeze.

The cart road was compacted sand so that the wheels of the carts and the hooves of the horses could not leave prints unless it rained. The dry sand felt very soft under my bare feet. I had often been on this road to our sweet melon field, but it was the first time I had travelled on it alone in the quiet of the early morning. It was very familiar to me, though. I walked, hopped, jumped and pranced along with confidence while I brandished a stick in my hand in bold imitation of the sword dance by the village's martial arts dance team.

Halfway to our 'north-western land' the road was flanked by rows of willow trees and thick willow bushes on both sides. Branches on one side of the road kissed those on the other side—this section being very much like a darkened canopied lane. I became goose-fleshed and a chill ran down my back. The morning air, so fresh and friendly a while ago, now seemed full of mysterious voices and murmurs. I dared not run or shout, for fear that I would show the white feather (the Chinese would say 'don't be a hen's feather', meaning not to be a coward). I wanted to look back to see what was following me but stopped short, because I recollected Granny Li-Ma Shi's words (my father's mother, whom I called Granny). 'A small boy has three magic lanterns,' she told me, 'one on top of his head, and one on each shoulder. The three magic lanterns protect the boy from devils or ghosts or spirits. When walking in the dark, never touch the top of your head or look back. When you touch your head, that lantern is put out. If you look back over your right shoulder, your breath will blow out the right lantern. If you look back over the left shoulder, your breath will blow out the left lantern. When all three lanterns are out, you will be left unprotected.' So I did not look back. My legs became a bit weak and sweat trickled down my face. I grabbed my stick tightly, ready to strike if needed.

I got out of the festooned lane of trees and bushes without anything happening to me. I felt relieved and happy. 'The three magic lanterns must have protected me!' I said to myself. I arrived at the sweet melon field and propped up the window flaps of the watchman's hut whose roof could be lowered or raised up like the flaps of a winter hat. My father had erected the hut just a few days ago. I felt safe then.

All of a sudden I heard animal cries, which were very similar to the sound that Granny made when imitating a hungry wolf's cry when she told me stories about them. Wolves were not devils or ghosts or spirits. This time the three magic lanterns could not protect me. I bolted up instantly to put down the flaps of the hut to shut myself in the dark. I stood fully alert and was ready to strike if the wolf dared creep in to get me. I could not remember how long I stood there, I just remembered that a strong light woke me. I opened my eyes and found my father grinning at me.

'Shuang Xi,' he said, 'why did you shut yourself in the dark? You would not know even if all the melons were stolen!'

'Wolf!' I replied. 'I hid myself from a wolf!'

'What wolf? How did you know there was a wolf?'

'I heard the cries of a wolf!'

'How did the wolf cry?'

I mimicked the cry of the wolf.

'That's the cry of an ox,' my father laughed. 'Look over there in the field.' He pointed to a neighbour's field where a peasant was whipping an ox with a stick to plough the land for late sweet potatoes.

'We have no wolves in this area,' my father explained. 'In winter when the Yong Ding River is thoroughly frozen a wolf or two may come from the western mountains, but so far I have not heard about a wolf coming to our area.'

I was ashamed of myself but the feeling vanished quickly. The sight of a piece of *bing tzi* split into two halves with the inside coated with salt and sesame oil, delighted me. (*Bing tzi* is a dough of corn flour pressed onto the cauldron wall for grilling. It is as big as a man's hand, about two to three centimetres thick and oval-shaped.) It was a rare treat. Such a thing could only be had when my mother or father thought I had done something good. Normally, we could not afford to have pure corn *bing tzi*. My mother always mixed at least half the quantity with wild vegetables. I was overjoyed and devoured it greedily.

'Don't choke yourself,' my father warned me. 'Nobody will rob you of it.'

I just grimaced and ate my food without slowing down. When one has food mixed with wild vegetables every meal, slightly better food makes one happy. When one has good food every meal and every day, he complains of 'having no appetite'.

In our area there was a saying, 'The first son, a harnessed ox; the first daughter, a house maid.' I was the first born and I was the first son. Probably, my parents gave me the treat to mark the start of my becoming a young harnessed calf!

My father spent a lot of time in the plot trimming, weeding and fertilising. He seldom straightened up for a break. He knew each individual melon as he knew his fingers. He could tell exactly how many days a particular melon had already grown. When he did step out of the melon field, he would check around the edges of the field for spots to grow beans. Land was precious and he could not allow any of it to be wasted. He grew beans near the trees, because they were very tenacious and could grow well, even in the poorest soil...and the flour from such beans made good, tasty noodles.

When my father was working in the field, I would walk around him, very much like an overseer or a supervisor. Sometimes I would squat beside him, watching him work and learning from him. When I became a nuisance he would tell me to look for cicadas in the surrounding bushes. That was enough to get me off him instantly. Cicada meat was the thing I liked most in my childhood.

My father was on this field every day, not hiring himself out as a casual or as a long-term farm labourer, because melon growing was work that needed more experience and skill. He could not trust the job entirely to my mother. Sweet melons, when in season, could bring enough money to supply the family with grain for the year, so he gambled with the weather and devoted himself entirely to this 'north-western land'.

As it became warmer and warmer, the sweet melons grew bigger and bigger. I was no longer the lonely morning watchman in the field. My father remained in the field day and night. He slept in the hut, with me by his side. It would have been very nice to sleep in the field without the attacks of mosquitoes—it was a pity there were so many of them to spoil my sleep.

My father got up very early in the morning to walk among the plants in search of worms on the leaves. He could detect them at first glance, because not even the slightest change of a leaf would escape his notice. The sweet melons were his babies and the plot his treasure. He loved the plot—his only land—so fondly, that his face was always beaming when he was in or near it. My mother and father had invested all their hopes and expectations in the sweet melons. They had built their dreams on a good harvest. The sweet melons had grown as large as beer mugs. In another fortnight or so, they would be ready for the market being the earliest sweet melons in the area. The realisation of their dreams was not too distant now. Their knitted eyebrows became relaxed and they began discussing their plans.

One day, the sun had just begun to descend, when dark clouds came rolling swiftly towards us from the north-western sky. Faint thunder rumbled in the distance. Ink dark clouds swiftly engulfed the sun and, in a twinkling of an eye, cloaked the sky above our heads. It turned dark, very much like the evening dusk.

My father became very nervous. Fear showed in his eyes. My mother looked even worse and dared not look into my father's eyes. Something catastrophic seemed to be looming above us in the air. I was a bit scared, but could not understand why. Lightning split and tore apart the dark clouds with silvery blinding brilliance. Thunder cracked ominously, deafening and heart piercing. My mother pulled me to her and held me in her arms. Big raindrops shot the earth, pitting the sandy soil like bullets. A sudden gust of strong wind rose, bending the trees and rocking our hut. Sweet melon leaves were blown upwards and many of the vines of the plants rolled on top of the leaves. They might be pulled off their roots by the wind at any minute. A few peasants from nearby fields came running to our hut for shelter.

Rain came down like a sheet as if Heaven were pouring 'the silver river' upon us (the Chinese call the Milky Way 'the silver river'). The north side flap of the hut was lowered, the wind and rain coming from that direction. Then the wind carrying the rain, like a whirlwind, spun round to lash into the hut. The south side flap was also pulled down. We were all shut in the dark, huddled on the raised platform, which served as a resting place. We were very crowded. Everybody knew what the others were thinking but nobody uttered a word. Silence reigned. Wind and rain raged, whipped, and slapped the hut violently, threatening to blow it away. The mat roof started leaking. Rain dashed in through gaps between the flaps and the side supporting posts. Everybody in the hut was wet. A while later we felt the rain and wind abating, and something like bullets began drumming the hut. 'Hailstones!' somebody exclaimed, desperately. His words announced the arrival of what my parents had feared. The hut flaps were propped up in an instant. Hailstones, some as large as peanut kernels, but mostly as large as soybeans or sorghum seeds, rushed down from the sky. The lush green leaves of our sweet melons were holed like sieves at first, and then were tattered like beggars' clothing. Sweet melons, concealed by the leaves, now lay exposed in the field. The whole plot was scattered with sweet melon pieces! The hailstones pebbled the sweet melon field for as long as 'half a meal' (time was always estimated by the peasants as 'a meal' or 'half a meal', not in terms of minutes or hours.) Hailstones carpeted the field like snow, chilling the air and our hearts. It turned cold and I shivered. The faces of my parents had turned ashen. 'My watermelons!' a man shrieked hysterically and dashed into the hailstones. Though the skin of watermelons was thicker, they became rotten after they were pitted by the hailstones. 'My watermelons are also destroyed! I am finished!' another man commented, sighed, became silent, and started smoking his pipe. The hut was evacuated as soon as the hailstones stopped. Everyone hurried out into the wind and rain.

Thrusting me to the ground, my mother ran into the field. 'Why? Buddha of Mercy! Why don't you have mercy on us!' she shouted repeatedly to the sky. My father wobbled into the field, as if he was drugged. He picked up a melon. His hands trembled, violently. His lips quivered. 'We needed just another half month!' he faltered, and each word drew tears from his eyes. White sweet melons, thousands of them, lay helplessly on the ground, exposing their wounds to my father. The hailstones had pitted every sweet melon, big or small. The raw wounds of the melons were oozing juice, like tears from eyes!

My father sighed, so despondent that his sighs struck my heart like a hammer. My mother cried out loudly. 'Ma, don't cry.' I tried to comfort her and joined her crying. I cried so loudly that I felt the world had come to an end for us. 'Stop crying. Let's get the melons together,' my father said in a shaky voice. 'The wounds make the melons rot quickly. We must be quick if we wish to sell them for a bit of money.' My mother understood that. She immediately began ripping melons off the vines. With each melon, she shed fresh tears. I'd never seen her cry before—she was too strong-willed for that. My father also commenced picking up the sweet melons with his still trembling hands. As I helped, I stole glances at my mother and then at him, as I cried and shivered.

A great heap of sweet melons was piled up in front of the hut. My father went back to the village to borrow a donkey cart. (The donkey cart is narrower and lighter than a horse cart. A man can pull a donkey cart, but not a horse cart.) My mother and I continued to collect the remaining melons as well as to clear the plot of the plants. Tears welled and trickled down her face all the time, as if from a never drying fountain.

My father arrived with the donkey cart and we hastily loaded it. My father and I, with him between the shafts, transported the cartload to the village for sale. With me as a megaphone to shout continuously 'Big sweet melons, five cents a catty (1 catty=½ kilogram), good for making salted vegetables!' we hawked along the village street.

'What big sweet melons!' people said as they shook their heads. 'What a pity the melons were destroyed by the hailstones! I am so sorry for you!' others would say to my father, sympathetically. Each comment brought a fresh tremor to the corners of his mouth.

Rain covers a vast area but hailstones strike an area like a belt. Crops outside the belt would not be damaged. That was the reason why some of the villagers could offer their sympathy for us. Their fields were untouched by the hailstones.

We sold two cartloads of the melons before evening. When we dragged our tired limbs to the hut, the sun was already long behind the western mountains. My parents were fatigued, devastated and despairing.

Before sunrise, we transported another cartload to the village and had it sold before long. The last cartload of melons was transported to the town seven kilometres from our village where we sold them quickly amidst sympathetic comments. Though too small to understand the magnitude of the full damage, my heart sank each time I heard the customers' remark, 'Gold is sold as copper!'

But our trouble did not end there. The previous year, my father borrowed seed from his uncle, who lived just a few houses away from our house. My father had to pay him back at the end of that year with an exorbitant interest. His uncle insisted that a contract in writing be signed. My father was desperate to get the seed, but he did not expect to be cheated by his own mother's brother and so he signed the contract.

Not a single seedling came out of the ground. My father dug up some seeds and found that they were already rotten. He suspected the seeds had been cooked. He went to the house to ask his uncle why. His uncle would not admit to having cooked the seeds. My father was very angry with him. 'You want to have my land by tricks!' he said quietly.

'How dare you say that!' his uncle protested. 'You are treating my kindness as the liver and lung of an ass!'

My father never approached his uncle again for anything and there was nowhere he could go to seek justice. His uncle did not press him for payment that year, but, now that our sweet melons were destroyed, he came to my father with the contract, demanding payment. Like a dumb person tasting bitter roots (a Chinese way of saying that the misfortune was so bitter in the mind, that the person was not able to speak about it), my father was not able to utter a word about his bitterness. He promised to pay in a few days.

'What your dirty uncle wants is our north-western plot!' my mother cried.

'I know,' he replied.

'If we do not sell the land, how can we pay him back?' she asked.

'No, we cannot sell the land. I will hire myself out, try to get a bit of an advance, and borrow from my old friends.'

My father left to be hired as a farmhand and as soon as he had paid his uncle, he got the contract destroyed. The relationship between them ended on that day. The work on our only land became entirely my mother's job. And she had to manage to feed us on her own.

Ambushing a Japanese Tank

On 15 August 1945, the Japanese invaders declared unconditional surrender. The eight years of resisting the Japanese invasion and occupation finally came to an end, but the Japanese refused to surrender to the Communist armies and guerrillas. At the time, the Communist guerrillas were very active in our area. Here is the story I heard many times about how the guerrillas forced a Japanese tank crew to surrender.

It happened in the latter half of 1945, in the season when dates were already as big as glass beads, though not yet ripe for eating. Word passed from one child to another that a labyrinth of tunnels and trenches had been dug out under the sand ridge, which was covered with trees. The ridge bordered the southern edge of the Paradise Palace. We children found those tunnels and trenches most suitable for playing hide and seek.

The Beijing–Kaifeng Highway, the main road in our district, was made of cement. One night, under the direction of the County Guerilla Brigade (the organisation of guerillas in our county, which was called Xian Da Dui), all the peasants from the surroundings villages worked together to sabotage the Beijing–Kaifeng Highway. Without using explosives, for fear of making too much noise, the peasants dug beneath the large concrete slabs of the highway making them sag or drop into the cavities below. The highway was so damaged that it was impossible for even a donkey cart to use it.

My father was away working as a hired farm labourer. My uncle Yongjiang's family was away in the town five kilometres to our south, visiting his mother-in-law and relatives. So only my mother and I were at home.

One morning when the sun already bid farewell to the treetops to climb higher towards noon, an intensive volley of guns broke out suddenly, seemingly very near. Bullets whistled over our roof and loud booms like thunder frequently came to our ears.

I darted into the bedroom like a frightened rabbit from the yard. My mother and I squatted behind the *kang*, trembling with fright.

Babies howled, children cried, women shrieked, and men's hoarse barking mingled with thunder-like footsteps that rolled north through the open field between our house and the high walled quadruple houses of a big landowner to our east.

'Shuang Xi's mother,' somebody from the fleeing crowd shouted to my mother. 'Come out and run! A Japanese tank is fighting the guerillas!'

Guns raged. Explosions were ear-splitting. My mother picked me up under her right arm and dashed to the front door. Just as she stepped over the threshold, one tile from the eaves was hit by a whistling bullet and fell near her toes, cracking into pieces. Scared, she withdrew back into the bedroom to hide behind the *kang* again. All the time the crescendo of the symphony of the battle boiled. My eyes never left her face. I was more confused than scared.

A short while later, for the second time, she picked me up and clamped me between her right arm and body, mustered up her courage and darted to the front door. Just as her feet touched the ground, the date tree on the edge of the open ground and our yard was hit by a cannon ball. Dates were falling upon us like hailstones. Thank goodness, among the raining dates there were no shrapnel fragments. My mother retreated into the room behind the *kang* for the second time. Her teeth chattered, violently.

There was no sign of the fighting abating. The whistling of bullets and intermittent explosions shook our nerves. Gritting her teeth to stop trembling, she clasped me up and bolted out of the door for a third time.

The strip of open ground was deserted, except it was covered in footprints. She raced north, in the opposite direction to the fighting. She pressed on without stopping until we got to a field surrounded on all four sides by dense willow bushes and trees on high sand ridges. The place was about one kilometre from our village. Dropping me to the ground, she slumped onto the sandy slope of the ridge, too fatigued to utter a word. We were well concealed and felt safe.

Time dragged on and the sun was approaching the western mountains. No guns could be heard anymore. Quietness reigned. My stomach groaned. My mother did not dare venture back home, not until it was fairly dark. When we returned, our door remained open as we left it. Tired and terribly hungry, I waited patiently for her to cook supper.

The following day exciting news passed quickly among the villagers: 'A Japanese tank was caught by the guerrillas. The tank was blown to pieces and the Japanese were taken prisoners.' Some villagers talked boastfully as if they had been present at the battle themselves. But we all felt proud of the outcome of the battle; for the first time the Japanese had been defeated here.

Life returned to normal, but the battle left me with a dreadful, unfading, and unforgettable memory.

Babysitting My Baby Brother

It was on Lunar 14 August 1946 that my younger brother was born. Nobody, neither my father, nor my mother, nor my Da Ma ever told me the date or the month, but I remember the day very well, definitely without mistake. Was it because of my good memory? Of course not! I remembered because the following day, Lunar 15 August, was the mid-autumn moon festival. It was the day for peasants to worship the moon and to pray for a bumper harvest the following year. It was the day for children to look forward to enjoying the sacrifices offered to the moon.

It was difficult for our family to celebrate the moon festival with good food, however, my father did manage to buy a pig head, a few catties of fruit, such as pears and apples, and four moon cakes for each of us. He would offer all this food to the moon as sacrifices and, after that, the whole family would enjoy them. Supper, shared around the table by Granny, father, and myself, had been finished for quite some time. My mother could not join us as she was in bed with my baby brother. My father was still taking his time preparing the moon worshipping ceremony. I had shuttled many times between the room and the yard to see whether the moon had peeped out. Finally I urged him to be ready.

'Baba,' I said, 'don't you think everything should be ready by now?'

'Still too early,' he replied. 'The moon will not be out within a mealtime.'

'Better a bit early than missing the rising moon.' I insisted.

He capitulated. He took our meal table into the yard and put it in the middle of our half. He then placed the pig head in the centre of the table, fruit on both sides of the pig head, and an incense holder in front of it all.

'Sit here and make sure that no dog approaches the table,' he said.

I obeyed, playing the part of watchman. Sitting on top of the entrance steps, I cupped my chin in my hands, happily waiting for the moon to rise. I waited patiently, for how long I could not tell. Then the moon shyly showed its face.

'Baba,' I shouted excitedly. 'The moon is out.'

My shouting was so loud that the baby was woken. He started crying very loudly. (Babies of poor families always cried very loudly, either complaining about being born to a family so poor, or showing the strength with which they would survive the poor life. In later years, when I carried my baby brother around to play with the babysitters from the neighbours, I witnessed a lot of such crying.)

My father came out into the yard. He kindled a bunch of incense, raised and lowered it three times before he secured it in the incense holder on the table. He knelt in front of the table, prayed and kowtowed. It didn't take long for him to complete the ritual.

'Finished?' I asked.

'Yes,' he replied.

Smiling, I stretched my hand for a pear.

'Not yet, son,' he said. 'We must wait for the moon to enjoy the offerings first.'

'But the moon will not touch them!'

'Don't say such things! The moon will not be happy!'

I waited. Meanwhile, he told me the story of the moon cake:

'In the old times, people were ruled by the Mongols, who treated them very badly. One time, ten families were using one kitchen knife to prepare food for cooking. The knife was attached to an iron chain and was guarded by a Mongol. The Mongols were afraid of giving knives to the peasants for fear of an uprising. The ten families had to provide for the Mongol supervising them. One day, some people offered cakes to each family. A note was wrapped inside the cake, telling people to kill the Mongols on Lunar 15 August. On that day, many Mongols were killed. From that time on moon cakes were used for the celebrations.'

My father never told me why the moon was worshipped for a bumper harvest. This was a pity as I have never been able to find the reason since, either from books or from stories told by other people. I can only guess that the reason for the Chinese peasants worshipping the moon was because they determined their sowing and harvesting time by the number of moons elapsed in a year.

At last, the moon had had its feed and my father handed me a pear, an apple and a moon cake. 'Don't eat too fast,' he warned. 'If you finish too quickly, you can only watch others eating later.'

I didn't care. It was the first time that I had ever seen such things and I attacked them greedily. That is why I can remember my second brother's birthday so clearly.

My brother was born in the late morning—forenoon to be exact. My Da Ma was boiling water in the big cauldrons on our cooking ranges. She sliced a *bing tzi*, dusted the two halves with a tiny pinch of salt, sprinkled a few drops of sesame oil, ground the two halves against each other to have the salt and oil evenly spread, pulled them apart again, and handed them to me.

'Go play with the other boys,' she said to me. 'Don't come back till dark.'

I was surprised and happy. Surprised, because the instructions I got were always for me to do something, never for me to play. Even that very morning my mother, who lay in bed, had instructed me to fetch clean dry sand for her. I had placed a big heap of sand on the *kang* and near the cooking range, as instructed by her. I was happy, because I could play with other children as I pleased. When boys and girls played together, the favourite game was 'opening the lock'. We would hold one another's hand to form a long line and then sing in chorus:

'Open the lock,
What lock?
It is a gold or silver lock.
Open the gate and let me through.'

The first two people at one end of the line would raise their linked hands high, signalling that the gate was open. The other end of the line would start to go through the 'opened gate'.

Around sunset, my playmates all went home for supper. I delayed returning home a while longer. When it began to get very dark I went home, not quite sure whether it was time for me to go back or not. I was on the point of calling 'Ma' when my Da Ma appeared on the steps to hush me with a finger to her lips.

'Your father brought home a baby brother for you. The baby and your mother are sleeping. Don't wake them up,' she whispered to me. I tiptoed into the room and saw a tiny black head by my mother's side. I felt very happy to have a baby brother. It did not matter whether he was brought home from the field or not. He was named Xiao Bao, meaning 'the young treasure'.

When a baby was born to a family, the older children were always told that the father happened to come across the baby when he was working in the field. Children were never told that it was the mother who gave birth to the baby. Children were never told how a mother could give birth nor that a baby was the creation of the sexual activity of their parents. So I believed that my father brought my baby brother home from the field. However, a grandmother would teach her grandson or grand-daughter the following children's song:

'A small boy sat on the block supporting the door.
He cried and howled for a wife.
Why do you want a wife?
I can talk to her under the lamplight,
And she can keep me company after going to bed.'

I saw my mother with protruding bellies a couple of times, and I saw the big belly become flat every time I had a brother or sister brought home by my father. I saw my Da Ma's belly protruding and I had seen her belly become flat each time my uncle Yong-jiang brought home a male or female cousin for me. I saw many of my aunties' bellies protruding and sagging, but the idea that babies were born from mothers never entered my head. (Altogether I have three brothers and one sister. Before I went to Beijing in 1959, my third brother was born.)

Once when I was sent to collect manure on a winter morning, I asked my mother and Da Ma why, while on the road every morning, I did not come across a baby. They laughed vociferously till tears filled their eyes, but they did not reply to my question.

When my baby brother was a few days old, my mother got up from her bed. She scraped from under the *kang* sand cakes tainted dark red with dried blood, put them into a dustbin and told me to tip them into the toilet pit. My mother would not venture into the yard until the thirtieth day after the birth of my brother according to Chinese tradition. It became my daily routine to tip the caked sand and to sieve more dry and clean sand for her.

When I grew older I came to know two things which were common in our area: firstly, a woman never went to hospital to give birth to a child. Peasants could not afford to send wives to hospitals to give birth. A sister-in-law would act as a midwife to help deliver the baby of a pregnant woman. Secondly, the woman who gave birth to a baby used dry and clean sand. It was unheard of to use paper tissues, and anyway they would not have been able to afford paper tissues, had they ever known about them. Strangely enough, I never heard of any woman becoming infected through sleeping naked on sand to soak the blood discharged after the birth of a child.

The following morning after the birth of my brother, a strip of red cloth was pinned to the curtain of our bedroom door. This served as an announcement that intrusion by visitors, males in particular, was not welcome due to having a newborn baby. The villagers believed that if a man entered a place where he might find evidence of a mother's postnatal discharges, he would have bad luck. The strip of red cloth on the curtain served to warn visitors that they should not blame the owner if bad luck fell upon them due to entering the room. Once the strip of red cloth was pinned onto the curtain, no visitors would dare to enter the room. Thus mother and baby could have undisturbed rest.

When the baby was thirty days old, my mother cooked two *shao bing* (a round-shaped bread fifteen centimetres wide and two centimetres thick, which was grilled on the cauldron), which she would eat without being seen by anybody. This was called to 'satisfy the mouth'. (Actually I had seen my mother cooking the two *shao bing* and I had seen her hide in the bedroom eating it but I pretended not to notice by going stealthily into the street to play with other children.) It was a customary practice in our area for women to 'satisfy the mouth' with *shao bing* on the thirtieth day after giving birth to a baby, before starting to work outdoors again. This custom probably came from the fact that they ate only millet porridge with a bit of brown sugar in it as it was very hard to get food made from wheat flour. When a woman was pregnant, she would save a little bit of wheat flour for this occasion. They could not afford to have much of such food, because the only way a poor family could have wheat flour was to collect the leftover wheat from the field of the rich during wheat harvest season.

My mother sewed three or four cloth bags, to hold sand and these were called sandbags. My mother filled about one-third or half of a bag with sand, put it flat on the *kang*, and then stuffed my baby brother in it to lie on the sand. She would then cover the baby and the bag with a quilt. The head of the baby was not covered and the bag had enough room for the baby to straighten or curve his legs. The opening had laces to tie together like shoulder straps. This kept the baby lying on his back, unable to turn onto its sides or stomach. This had several advantages—the baby remained dry as any wetness was absorbed by sand; cleaning was easy and simple, you just had to empty the soiled sand into the toilet pit; and the bag could be washed and re-used after being dried in the sun. Nappies were not used, at least not in poor peasant families.

The day my mother started outdoor work again was the day that I commenced babysitting. Before setting out to our 'north-west land', my mother would put a bowl of porridge and a piece of corn bread in the cauldron to keep them warm. The food was reserved for me. When the baby cried and I could not stop his crying, I cried with him. He often cried himself to sleep. Later, I found that food helped to calm him. I would get a small quantity of porridge and put it into his mouth bit by bit with my finger. His crying would soon stop. The baby of a poor peasant family is tough and easily raised. My mother only came home at noon to suckle the baby and to have a piece of *bing tzi* for lunch. She would also put the baby into a fresh sandbag and then go to work in the field again.

I would lie on my stomach to watch my baby brother and to attract his attention when he was awake, but he could not understand and would not purposely look in my direction. When he was asleep, I would play with a lump of clay in the yard. I always knew how to create ways of entertaining myself.

The sun rose and set, set and rose. My mother shuttled between home and our 'north-western land'. With the arrival of mid-autumn, the harvest of peanuts and sweet potatoes began. She had already harvested our own plot and was in every way ready to collect the leftover sweet potatoes and peanuts from the fields of the big landowners. Since our own land was small and could not supply the family with enough food, collecting peanuts and sweet potatoes was particularly important to our family and to many other families as well.

Peanut or sweet potato picking was like fighting a battle, though there was no actual fighting between pickers. One had to be quicker than most if one wanted to get more. Sweet potato or peanut pickers were numerous. Each picker dug the earth in a frenzy with his small rake (the 'small four teeth'), anxious to get as many sweet potatoes and peanuts as possible. The rolling out of one big sweet potato after another under the 'small four teeth' of one picker would drive the surrounding pickers mad. The air was filled with heavy and oppressive urgency. The upper body was bending and the 'small four teeth' was rising and falling, while sweat trickled down the face of each picker. Nobody had time to wipe the sweat off his or her face. Each one tried hard to get in front of the other with the view to getting more sweet potatoes. Each pair of eyes followed the soil dug up by his 'small four teeth' attentively and fixedly in order not to miss a single sweet potato or peanut. Urgency, expectation, exaltation and fear shone in their eyes.

A picker also had to compete with pigs. Well-off families always hired teenagers to herd their pigs into the fields from which peanuts or sweet potatoes had been harvested. Such families relied on this period of the year for their pigs to grow quicker and fatter. At the cracking of the huge whip of the head herdsman, pigsties would be opened and pigs trooped willingly by themselves into the street to join the others. When the horde of pigs approached the exit of the village, the flow of them would make it impossible for anything to pass. On the road, one herdsman would lead the pigs at the head of the horde, another two would flank the horde on each side, and the head herdsman would be at the rear. The horde of pigs would trot towards a sweet potato or peanut picking field. The high pitched 'hou hou' of the herdsmen rose and fell like singing a monotonous folk song. The dust stirred up by the pigs rose high, signalling to the pickers the arrival of the horde.

The herdsmen, being from poor families, would usually give the pickers some time before they drove pigs into the field. However, the pigs were more skilful than the pickers in finding the sweet potatoes or peanuts concealed underground. Their muzzles, which seemed to be equipped with special devices, ploughed the earth more effectively than a picker's 'small four teeth'. Now and then, at very short intervals, a pig would raise its head, chewing a big piece of sweet potato contentedly, proudly and noisily. His eyes would always focus fixedly on a picker nearby, seemingly to demonstrate his skill. The 'ka cha, ka cha' cracking noise of the pigs' chewing compelled the pickers to strive harder for more sweet potatoes. Once the pigs, which usually covered the whole width of a field at one end, pressed ahead of the pickers, the pickers would not have much luck in getting more. Once the pigs had cleanly scoured a part of the field, there was little hope for a picker who tried his luck there. To a picker and his family (a poor family like ours), the quantity of sweet potatoes or peanuts picked determined how difficult their survival would be. So, it became a battle for food between all the pickers and the pigs.

One day, my mother cushioned a piggyback basket on her back, put my brother and his sandbag into it, gave me a 'small four-teeth' to carry, and tied a towel, which contained our food, to the basket. She embarked on the journey of sweet potato collecting. Accompanying us was Granny Li, a widow who lived in the house by the end of our lane, bordering the main street. Her husband was dead and she was on her own. She had a big yard in which there was an apricot tree. I was the only child she gave plenty of her apricots to. She would not even give any to the grandsons of her next of kin. She loved me very much and she loved to listen to my babbling. I also loved to be with her, because she would always carry some nice food for me.

We were not a lonely group. There were a great many sweet potato collectors on the road. Some were ahead of us and some were behind. We just followed the flowing stream of people.

When we arrived at the site of the sweet potato harvest, the morning sun had already climbed over the treetops. The site was about three kilometres from our village. It was a vast piece of land, stretching to the horizon lengthwise and about seventy or eighty metres wide. The sweet potato vines were already cut, bundled and piled along the edges of the land.

There were at least fifty to sixty hired peasants digging the sweet potatoes with big rakes, which we called 'the big four teeth'. The work went very fast. The vines were used to circle the platform of the carts and the sweet potatoes were put in the middle. The top was covered with vines, too. Large sweet potatoes were piled into heaps and loaded onto four or five horsecarts to be transported away. They looked nice, arousing my appetite. My childish mind could not imagine how big the landlord was.

Many sweet potato collectors like us, women and children, were waiting along the borders of the land. Children were playing by their parents—whatever the situation children will play. The sweet potato collectors were not merely from our village but also from the surrounding villages.

Noon arrived. We started to wash down our cold lunch with cold water. Mine was *bing tzi* made of corn flour mixed with sweet potato leaves. It was halved and coated with salt and sesame oil, which I liked the most. Granny Li gave me a piece of her own *bing tzi*, pure corn flour *bing tzi* without sweet potato leaves or husks. It tasted much better.

'You always save food from your mouth to give Shuang Xi,' my mother said to her. 'It will be late today before we can go home.'

'Never mind,' Granny Li said. 'He is young and he needs something better.'

My mother had the same kind of *bing tzi* as mine. She was suckling the baby while she had her lunch. She never had any good food even though she had to suckle the baby. She never complained.

The sun was already descending. The harvesters were tiny spots, far away at the other end of the field.

'Don't leave your brother alone here,' my mother told me. 'I will come back for you at the end.' She guessed that very soon people would be allowed to look for the leftover sweet potatoes.

'Ma,' I whispered to her, 'look over there, under the vine piles. There seems to be a small heap of sweet potatoes there.'

She whispered back to me, 'Dash to the heap and sit on it when permission is given, I will join you there.'

The sun was already very near the western mountains when permission was granted to the collectors to dig for the leftovers. Sweet potato collectors, hundreds of them, raced into the field from all sides, with baskets and rakes, digging madly. Such urgency and hurrying was more intensive than anything I had ever seen. 'I got a big sweet potato!' shouted children here and there, with such happiness, joy and triumph, that those who lack nothing cannot comprehend.

I darted to the vine heap before my mother could get up. She joined me, carrying her basket, rake, and the baby, a few seconds later. Nobody worried about us or even looked at us. It was a small heap of sweet potatoes. My mother ripped the big ones off their roots to fill our basket. When the basket was nearly full, she placed the sweet potatoes vertically against the rim, thus increasing the capacity of the basket. She weighed the basket and found it was already heavy enough for her. She gave the rest to Granny Li, whose basket was also full.

That was pure luck. It seemed that the 'Buddha of Mercy' gave us help to alleviate my mother's difficulty. None of the other hundreds of the pickers had such good fortune. But everybody got sweet potatoes, some getting more and others less. They all started leaving. The sun was already behind the western hills and twilight had set in.

'Shuang Xi's mother,' Granny Li said to my mother, 'let's go.'

Eyeing the baby, the basket, and me, she replied. 'You go first, I'll come soon.'

We were alone in the field by then. My mother was racking her brains to solve her dilemma. The basket was so heavy that it was already an almost impossible job for her to carry it home; the baby was definitely an impossible job for me to carry, because he was too soft for me to hold properly without hurting him. She sat there in the dark, feeling frustrated but not cowed. Nothing, no matter what kind of difficulty, could intimidate her. She had guts, more guts than even some men had. Finally she had the solution.

'Come with me,' she said to me as she picked up the baby. We hastily walked along the road towards home for about fifty metres.

'Why do you leave our basket behind?' I asked, worrying I would have no sweet potatoes to eat if the basket was lost.

'Sit here with your brother,' she instructed. 'Don't move.'

She then went back for the basket. I heard her coming towards us. Her basket creaked and squeaked loudly, rhythmically, as if saying 'too heavy, too heavy'. She walked past us without stopping. It was dark and I was alone with the baby, who began crying and I cried with him.

She came back, picked up the baby and suckled him while she walked quickly homeward. I ran to keep pace, afraid to be left behind. We passed the basket and continued for some distance. She then put the baby on my lap and went back to fetch the basket. She came, passed the baby and me, and pressed on. I wanted to go after her, and to catch up with her. I tried to hold the baby under his arms so that I would not hurt his back, but I could hardly lift the bottom of the sandbag off the ground, being short for my age. The baby was made uncomfortable and started crying loudly. I sat down again and had him on my lap, but he would not stop crying, no matter how hard I tried to soothe him. I was crestfallen and hated myself for being neither tall enough nor strong enough to carry the baby or the basket. I opened my eyes very wide to see whether my mother was on her way back to fetch us. I strained my ears to catch the sound of her footsteps.

She came back and repeated the cycle of transporting the baby, then the basket, then the baby and then the basket, again and again. We thus inched nearer and nearer to home.

When we finally arrived home, it was already very late. And when she had the sweet potato and porridge cooked, I was already asleep on the *kang*. My mother had to shake me violently to wake me up. I could not fully enjoy the booty of our hard labour and exertions of the day—I was too sleepy.

The following day when Granny Li called for my mother to go to the sweet potato field, she said to me, 'Stay home with your brother, I will be back as quickly as possible.'

I refused, arguing, 'We shall not have the same good luck as yesterday.'

She agreed and we went sweet potato collecting again.

Sure enough, such good luck did not repeat itself all through the autumn. Each day we would get half a basketful or a basketful or somewhere in between. Now my mother could carry the baby and the basket simultaneously. We also spent a lot of time picking peanuts, which was a bit different from sweet potato picking. Patience was the most important thing in peanut picking. One would sit or squat while digging with the 'small four teeth' and the eyes had to remain alert so not to miss any peanut uncovered.

My brother suffered malnutrition. He was always sick until the following autumn. By then he could already crawl and I was taller and stronger. I no longer followed my mother and I carried my brother to the nearby field where people were collecting peanuts. I would look for peanuts from the surface of the field. I unshelled them, chewed and put them into my brother's mouth with my forefinger. I also ate them myself.

My mother did not notice any change in my brother and myself at the beginning—nobody did. Only my father noticed the changes when he came back from his job in a rich peasant home.

'Our young son gets stronger and bigger,' he remarked to my mother. Only then did she realise that my brother had not been sick for a long time and that my brother and I had not touched lunch for a while.

'What did you have for lunch?' she asked.

'Peanuts,' I replied.

My second brother was almost entirely my responsibility. We were together all the time. He grew well and got bigger and stronger. Wherever I went, he went. Whatever I did, he mimicked. He became so attached to me that he seemed to be my shadow. This lasted until I went to junior high school.

The White-necks

'Here come the White-necks!' This could silence a crying child immediately. The fear of the White-necks was profound and real.

What were White-necks? How did they come into being?

My father told me that there were two land reforms by the Communists in our area. The Communist-led guerrillas conducted the first land reform sometime in 1946. The Kuomintang (the Party set up by Sun Yet Sen in 1912, but which was under the control of Chiang Kai-shek soon afterwards) formed forces to grab the land back from the poor for the big landowners in 1947. These forces were called the 'Home Return Corps', and each of the soldiers wore a white towel around his neck, and so were called the 'White-necks'. This, of course, was not the only reason they were given that nickname. They were also called White-necks because of their similarity to a kind of crow which had a white ring around the neck and which was detested by the peasants.

One autumn night, I was suddenly woken by an intense light on my face. My baby brother cried when the light moved to his face. My mother was already up, and so was my uncle Yong-jiang's family. I sat up and watched in fright as the beams of three or four flashlights darted here and there in the room. They were also in the common room and in my uncle's bedroom on the other side of the common room. Two soldiers probed here and there with their bayonets, which were fixed on to their rifles. Earthen jars were tipped. Flour was spilt. One soldier crushed a jar with the butt of his rifle. Another soldier took a small bag containing one or two kilograms of wheat flour and secured it to his belt. Our night basin was turned upside down, making muddy puddles on the floor.

'Pauper devils,' a soldier muttered with disgust.

'Don't take my wheat flour!' my mother cried, trying to snatch back the small bag.

'Stay still and be quiet!' the soldier snarled, with dark menace.

As the Chinese saying goes, 'on encountering a soldier, a scholar will receive no justice no matter how sound his arguments are.' In front of a soldier, especially in front of a soldier who was like a mad dog, a peasant woman could get no justice, no matter how sound her arguments were.

Sensing the imminent danger, she withdrew her hand and moved back away from him. Such soldiers were like wild, hungry wolves. They never hesitated to kill, even for no reason. One soldier raised his gun butt, threatening to hit me. I started to howl like my baby brother. They all laughed boisterously, like the crowing of the white-neck crows!

In the yard, hens squawked like mad. A commotion of stamping feet, of sickles cutting things, curses, shouts, all came to the ears at once. The same was also heard from the neighbours, but we did not dare go out to check. We all huddled on the *kang*. My mother looked out through the window glass, which was as small as two palms of the hands. That was the only glass we had. Our big window with latticed frames was covered with window-paper, a special kind of paper, tenacious and strong to stand the wind.

'Let them eat bullets,' my mother whispered (meaning let them be killed by bullets).

Dawn came and my mother and Da Ma were forced by the soldiers to a neighbour's house, without breakfast. Each was ordered to take with her a wash basin and a washboard. Many women were already there, washing soldiers' bed sheets, clothing, and leg-laces (the bandages soldiers used to bind the trouser legs to the calves) around the well in the yard. My mother and Da Ma were ordered to do the washing immediately. Two soldiers guarded the gate with rifles and bayonets, preventing any women from leaving the yard.

I had cold *bing tzi* for breakfast. I had nothing for my baby brother as he was too little to eat such food. He was still sleeping in a sandbag. I went into the yard and the sight made me cry.

The White-necks had cut all the sugar cane to feed their horses. The sugar cane looked very much like sorghum, which my mother grew for me to enjoy during the coming Spring Festival. This we learned from a neighbour in whose yard the horses were fed. Sugar cane leaves were scattered everywhere in the yard. Their very sharp stubble squinted up at the sky. Beads of juice adhered to the stubble like tears on eyelashes. This drew tears from my eyes again and I hated the White-necks so much that the scene remains just as vivid today, as I am writing about it.

Noon came and went. My mother did not come home—nor did my Da Ma. My baby brother awoke several times, and each time he cried himself to sleep. Finally he awoke, cried hoarsely and would not stop. He was hungry. I chewed a tiny bit of cold *bing tzi* for him but he refused to be pacified. I called my mother to come back from our fence, but she failed to appear. The two guards still stood by the gate, not permitting anybody to leave.

Without breakfast and lunch, my mother was hungry and tired. So were my Da Ma and the other women. She emptied water from her wash basin and stood up.

'Let's go home,' she said to my Da Ma.

With the basin and washboard in hand, she left. She walked past the guards at the gate without looking at them. The guards looked at her but did not stop her. They were not conscious of the situation yet. My Da Ma followed in the wake of her, but not very closely. When she saw my mother had left without any trouble, she quickened her steps. This time the guards were fully aware of what my Da Ma wanted to do. They glared darkly at her. She was cowed and retreated back to the other women to resume washing bed sheets. All the other women were frightened, too. No one dared to try and leave again. They remained washing till dark, without food, without rest, without the courage to complain.

My Da Ma returned home late and was so fatigued that she had not the strength to curse the 'White-necks'.

'The damned White-necks,' she cursed when she and my mother were cooking breakfast the next day. 'Let them eat bullets!' Then, she added, addressing my mother, 'You are brave!'

'Brave? Not a bit!' my mother said with chagrin. 'I had to feed the baby.'

Both used strong adjectives to curse the White-necks and prayed that the guerrillas would eliminate them. The White-necks departed the following day but a bad memory remained. For a long time thereafter, the villagers cursed whenever the White-necks were mentioned. Fortunately, they did not create widows in our village, but they did create widows in other villages not too far away from ours. The barbarous behaviour of the White-necks, as I see it, was one of the reasons that caused the quick collapse of the Kuomintang regime.

My Story about Redeployment and Wild Shooting

In about December 1948, more than one million Liberation Army forces started a campaign to encircle Beijing, Tianjin and Zhangjiakou, which were under the control of the Kuomintang Army. About 600,000 Kuomintang troops were surrounded within those cities. First Zhangjiakou and Tianjin were liberated, then Beijing, which was called Beiping at the time, on 31 January 1949. The Kuomintang troops were redeployed to different areas and pressure was exerted on the Communists to make them part of the Liberation Army.

Trenches, which stretched for many kilometres away from our village, scarred and marred the fields. They seemed to appear overnight by magic. I hadn't noticed any of them until they were suddenly there, even though I went into the fields to collect firewood almost every day. They were not utilised as they were originally intended, because the Kuomintang troops had surrendered peacefully. We children made good use of them playing hide-and-seek.

Company-sized or battalion-sized groups of Kuomintang troops roamed the countryside aimlessly. When they saw a peasant in the field, who had a white towel turban on his head, an officer would approach the peasant, while the other troops waited at the roadside, asking, 'Can you tell me where we can find the guerrillas for us to surrender to?' The guerrillas wore the towel turban in the same way a peasant did so as not to be identified by the enemy. The Kuomintang troops were unable to recognise a real guerrilla and so asked the peasants who had a towel turban on their head if they knew the whereabouts of the guerrillas, but the peasant would not expose their location, for fear of bringing trouble on them.

During those years, one of my uncles, Song-lin, told me that the peasants risked their own lives to protect the guerrillas. One day under the Japanese occupation, some Japanese soldiers entered his yard. My uncle immediately hurried into the yard to meet them (uncle Song-lin lived in the house in front of ours).

'Are there any guerrillas here?' one of the Japanese soldiers asked him in pidgin Mandarin.

'No guerrilla is in the house,' uncle Song-lin said. 'We are docile people. If we hide guerrillas, you can kill us!' He put the edge of his palm against his neck, mimicking the killing. Some guerrillas were in his bedroom at that very moment and had the Japanese ventured into the room, the 'raising door curtain' combat would have broken out at once.

The peasants sided with the guerillas again when the Japanese were replaced by the Kuomintang troops. The peasants definitely would not reveal the locations of the guerilla, because his own son or the son of a neighbour might be one of them.

One day, mid-morning, in 1949, Liberation Army personnel with guerrillas as guides, who were known by the villagers, came to be billeted in the village. Half of each house had to be reserved for the army's use. Courtyards and open spaces in the village were also marked for the army's use. The village chairman informed the peasants that the 94th Army Corps of the Kuomintang armed forces would be reformed in our village to become soldiers of the People's Liberation Army.

A few days later, trucks full of soldiers, pulling long-stemmed cannons on wheels, horses with cavalry soldiers on their backs, and long lines of foot soldiers, streamed into the village, and were channelled to their respective billeted house, yard, or open space. The village was so full of soldiers and villagers that it looked like a busy fair.

The soldiers had no badges on their caps and collars, the old 'blue sky and white sun' badges had been torn off the caps, and the new 'red star' of the People's Liberation Army badges had not been given to them yet. They were Kuomintang soldiers being redeployed after the peaceful liberation of Beijing. It was said that those clad in faded yellow clothes were officers of the Liberation Army and those in new khaki uniforms were the newly liberated Kuomintang officers. It must have been true, because we now saw red star badges on the caps of the former, but not on the caps of the latter. (It was the first time the villagers heard and used the expression 'the Liberation Army'.) Bayonets or hand grenades were attached to their hips.

The soldiers were rough, wild and restless. They gambled, among themselves or with the peasants. Almost every room they occupied was a gambling site, including the one in our house. Our two families were crammed into my uncle Yong-jiang's room.

On one occasion, a soldier, who was the loser, had no more money to continue gambling. He put his hand grenade in the middle of the gamblers, muttering thickly, 'This is my stake!' He looked around for those who dared say 'no'. 'At the gambling table, everyone is equal. Don't blackmail others,' some watching soldiers chimed in, and grabbed his arms and pulled him away.

Quarrels were frequent, and always among the soldiers themselves, for the peasants would not dare to displease them. Onlookers would fuel the quarrels. However, when the quarrelling parties were about to resort to guns or hand grenades, the onlookers would pull and push them apart. Probably the soldiers wanted to break up their dull life with arguments or perhaps they quarrelled for fun, because I never heard of them settling any quarrel with bullets. Probably the responsible commanders thought it not right to mix with the villagers for too long. The soldiers moved out of the peasants' houses except those with more spare rooms. Smaller courtyards were also evacuated.

Soldiers used whatever they had to swap cooked peanuts with the peasants. This happened more and more frequently. A soldier exchanged with my uncle Yong-jiang a small bag of rice for a dustbin of cooked peanuts. Another exchanged a blanket made in the US for cooked peanuts. It was said some soldiers bartered for peanuts with two new wheels of a jeep, which turned out to be true, because that peasant used the wheels to rig up a brand new horse cart after the departure of the soldiers. Stationery made in the US was also used to exchange for peanuts, and quite a few students used it in school later.

One day as I was playing near the wall of the big landowner, (who was later classed as a landlord) a soldier popped his head out from the other side of the wall. He called to me loudly, 'Hello, small devil', and raised in his hands an army overcoat lined with white sheepskin. 'Take this overcoat home and bring me a basket of cooked peanuts.' The expression 'small devil' or 'little devil' was not used in our part of the country and I thought he was cursing me. His whiskered face looked sinister to me. I was frightened and started running home.

'Damned little rascal,' he shouted after me and threw a hand grenade towards me. It exploded with a big bang but it did not hurt me. I was almost scared to death. In those days, if the soldiers killed a person, it was just like killing an ant. No peasant would dare to ask for justice from the army. My mother, therefore, cautioned me to be careful—better to remain at home and not to wander outside.

Homesickness spread like a plague amongst the soldiers. Everyday we heard of soldiers deserting the army. My uncle Song-lin said that one day a soldier came to his house. He knelt in front of my uncle's mother, whom I called Granny Zhang, and begged.

'Please take me as your son. Allow me to stay in your house. I am a good peasant. I can do anything,' he pleaded. 'I was taken into the army by force. I never blackmailed the peasants before.'

'I am very sorry, I cannot adopt you as my son and I cannot keep you in my house. The army can find you easily,' Granny Zhang said.

'Well, please give me some of your son's old clothes,' he sobbed and begged. Clothes were given to him and they fitted him well.

That night he was the sentinel. When the next soldier came to replace him he had gone. His gun was placed against a fence and his army overcoat was hanging from the bayonet fixed to the rifle. He had become a deserter.

One morning, my mother had just sat on the *kang* at the meal table, ready to have a breakfast of corn meal porridge and *bing tzi* with Chinese cabbage. An officer in a long army overcoat swaggered into our yard and came into our common room. A leather belt hung from his left shoulder slanting to his right hip. A leather case attached to the belt rested against his hip—it had a Mauser in it (peasants called this 'the twenty-sound pistol'). He went to push my uncle's door but it had been bolted as soon as my Da Ma saw him coming into our yard. He then turned to the entrance of our room, which had only a curtain but no door. He came into our room and stood in front of us, saying nothing. He simply fixed his stare upon me. The man had a broad-rimmed officer's hat on his head. His face was whiter than that of the villagers. He had the features of an educated man. He was in his mid or late thirties. On his face was a look of confusion, perplexity, melancholy and sadness. He was of average height, slim and neatly dressed. His stare was straight, fixed like that of a mentally sick man.

My mother did not know why he came into our room or what he wanted to do. She did not want any trouble. She had to do something.

'Sit on the *kang* rim and have some breakfast,' she said to him, her voice quivering, though she tried hard to sound normal.

He did. He took up a bowl of porridge and started to eat. The porridge was hot—scorching hot. He blew over the bowl to cool the porridge but his stare still fixed upon my face. Now and then he puffed over the rim of the bowl at me. I felt a bit nervous and shifted away from him. Whenever I looked at him his lips would split slightly, an indication of a smile. The indication was so tiny that my mother could not possibly have noticed.

Having had two bowls of porridge and a piece of corn *bing tzi*, he stopped eating. He never took his eyes from me. He sat there, not moving, not speaking, but just looking at me. I seemed to see water welling from his eyes but he managed to contain his tears. He looked down, only once, at his pistol and sighed deeply.

'Now that you have finished your breakfast,' my mother said to him, 'go back to your own place.'

He slipped off the *kang*, gave me a final stare and walked out of our room, out of the house, out of the yard, and was gone. My Da Ma opened their door immediately and came over to talk to my mother.

'You are courageous!' my Da Ma praised. 'I was terribly scared. He had a gun!'

'I was also scared,' my mother said, 'but what could I do? I had to protect my two children!'

'We did not hear him say anything,'

'He did not utter a word!' my mother said. 'His eyes never left Shuang Xi's face.'

'Why?' my Da Ma said thoughtfully, 'I think he has a son of similar age. He is missing his son. He is missing his home.'

He never returned to our house. Eventually the whole army departed from our village. I did not have the chance to ask him why he looked at me all the time. He must have been very homesick. Now that peace was in sight, whoever on earth would not be homesick in such a situation?

Not all the soldiers behaved like that officer. The army was like a wild tiger in the process of being tamed. On the one hand it would show it had started to adopt human nature but on the other hand it would show the ferocious ugly nature of a wild beast.

Gradually the presence of the soldiers in the village became a part of our daily life. We no longer shunned them. Two grooms sometimes would entice us children to walk the horses for them. In return they would offer to take us for a ride in a jeep. We had never seen a jeep before and it was fascinating for us to ride in one. We all competed for such a chance.

Sometimes they would lift us on horseback for a ride. My mother warned me to stay away from them, as did other mothers. But we were children and could not resist the temptation of riding on horseback or in a jeep.

There was a child soldier among them, too. He stayed in a house not far away from our part of the village. He was only twelve years old, three years older than me. He was taller than me but shorter than most peasant boys his age. His face looked like that of a ten-year-old boy. He was very thin, and his arms looked like thin sticks, which could be broken easily. His cap was much too large for him. His padded yellow khaki jacket was too wide and too long and he had to roll his sleeves up at the cuffs. His jacket draped below his knees like an overcoat. His padded trousers were also rolled up, a very thick rim at each ankle.

He liked to join us playing hide-and-seek or in our other games. One day he suggested that we have a game of 'war fighting' in the trench. He said one side should play the People's Liberation Army and the other should be the Kuomintang Army. No children wanted to be on the Kuomintang side and so he alone was it, and ten boys or so formed the People's Liberation Army. Our weapons were frozen sandy soil lumps, breaking easily when landing on somebody. Our 'shooting' was too much for him to return fire. He would back away along the trench. We chased him and our 'bullets' rained on and around him. Then half of us would get through other trenches to intercept him. When he was caught in the pincers and being pelted from the front and the back, he would kneel down and raise both arms high above his head, 'I surrender!' But we, the peasant children, did not understand what that gesture meant. We continued throwing 'hand grenades' at him. At first he would hold his head with both arms and then he would flare up and shout at us.

'The People's Liberation Army never hit a surrendered soldier!' We felt proud and pleased and we stopped 'shooting' at him. We would then sit together for a break or go home.

'The PLA treated the surrendered soldiers very well,' he once told us. 'Lots of our soldiers are prepared to cross over to the PLA if we are ordered to go into battle against them.' We could not fully understand what he said. To us, a soldier was a soldier and that was it.

Sometimes, he would seem very sad. 'I have never played with children so happily before,' he said. 'When I leave I don't know whether I will be coming back alive to see you.' And on other occasions he told us, bit by bit, about his own life. He did not know the name of his home village. His parents were dead. He was herding sheep for a family to pay for his debt incurred from burying his parents. The master did not give him enough to eat and the son of his master always beat him, so he ran away with the passing army. He was not included but just followed until the kitchen squad accepted him.

'Our army is no match for the PLA because many want to go back home to get land and be good peasants,' he said, sighing like an adult. It was said that the guns, the cannons, the jeeps, the trucks, the blankets, the boots, everything were from America, and that some officers and soldiers were not willing to surrender. Resentment loomed over their heads and they wanted to vent their anger.

On Lunar 2 February, the day when 'the dragon raised its head' and where people cooked pancakes with a thin batter of mixed green lentil flour, dawn was ushered in by an intensive shooting of rifles, Mausers, pistols, and machine guns. We were so scared that we thought a battle had broken out in and around our village. Then we learned that the disgruntled soldiers were shooting for fun.

Putting on my dome-like winter cap and pulling down the two flaps, I ran out to have a look. My mother tried to catch my arm to pull me back but failed. This was so exciting! I ran along the street to the temple and I found an officer firing his Mauser into the air. I stooped to pick up the copper shells that had popped from his gun. I bared my head to use the cap to hold the shells. The officer looked at me, reloaded his Mauser, and started shooting into the air again, adjusting the angles so that the shells would drop on my head. I tried to avoid the falling shells but could not. He adjusted his shooting angle so accurately! If I tried to move a bit away from him, he followed. I simply could not avoid the shells falling on my head. The officer laughed merrily. Human beings are like that. The suffering of one person can be fun for another.

My cap was full to the brim with cartridge shells and I ran back home. I then went to the edge of the village. Three or four soldiers were firing a Maxim at an elm tree as thick as a telephone pole. I went over but found two or three teenage boys already there, fighting for the cartridge shells. I had to look for shells elsewhere. Later we found the tree was horribly damaged. Had it been a bit smaller, the tree would have been cut into two halves by the bullets.

The shooting did not die off until noon. We later learned that had it not been for a manure picker, our village would have been wiped off the face of the earth. There were four or five PLA army corps positioned some distance from our village as 'security' to see that the redeployment was carried out smoothly. At the Royal Horse Well village, a great number of cannons raised their barrels to point at our village, ready to fire at the signal of the commanding officer. The noise of the shooting from our village aroused suspicions of a mutiny of the 94th army. Scouts were dispatched to check what was happening in the Paradise Palace.

One of the scouts met a manure collector from our village mid-way between our village and the Royal Horse Well. The scout asked him what was happening in the Paradise Palace and he said that the soldiers were shooting for fun. He was taken to the commander.

'Lao Xiang,' the commander asked. 'What is happening over there?' (Lao Xiang means fellow-townsman or fellow-villager. It is similar to 'mate' in Australia. The PLA men used it to address peasants so that they would regard them as fellow-villagers and not soldiers.)

'You mean the shooting?' the manure collector asked. 'Soldiers in our village are shooting for fun.'

Other scouts came back. It was confirmed that the shooting was only for fun. Thus the Paradise Palace avoided the fate of being wiped out by bombardment.

It was said that there were two casualties that day. The first was a boy. He and a few other children were squatting in a tight circle rolling glass balls. The boy was in the inner circle. A stray bullet hit him and he died instantly. No one heard the bullet or knew where it came from. None of the others was hurt. The dead boy was the son of a rich peasant. He was a bright boy at school. The second casualty was a regimental commander of the army. A few drunken soldiers, whose eyes were bloodshot, chased the commander along the street. The soldiers shot at him with their rifles, swearing and chasing him. He fired back at the soldiers with his pistol while he was running towards a jeep. He reached the jeep, opened the door and placed one foot on the step when a bullet caught him. He fell to the ground, dead. The soldiers laughed vociferously and dispersed. Nothing was done to the soldier. There was not even any gossip about whether his widow demanded justice. Later the army departed and headed south, it was said, to take part in the Huai Hai Campaign. One story says that when they crossed a mountain pass, an officer standing by the roadside spoke to the unit to which the drunken soldiers belonged, 'Dear soldier brothers,' he shouted, 'whoever killed the regimental commander step out please. The widow of the commander does not wish to go any further with the army. Give her some money from each of you and let her go home.' The soldiers stepped out of the marching lines. They were led away by the officer, and punished with death. Was this true? I never knew. I just heard it from the villagers.

On my very first day at school, the already reformed army departed our village for the south. I never learned how the army was reformed but I saw their departure. Before they left, plenty of pistols, hand grenades, and boxes full of cartridges were thrown away in the woods or in the wells. The army also buried several hundred tons of cannon balls in a courtyard, which was in the very middle of the village. If they exploded, the whole village would disappear from the face of the globe. These cannon balls were dug out in 1958 after all the villagers had been evacuated.

Children collected the boxes of ammunition. I myself found four boxes without the knowledge of my parents. I dragged them to one corner of our yard and buried them there, protected by dried grass. I prised open one box and found that the cartridges were well greased and their bullets, painted red, looked beautiful.

We children created ways to use those cartridges for fun. We would sit around in a circle on the sand, each having about twenty cartridges in his pocket. First we would bury the stone slab about fifteen centimetres into the ground, then we would put the bullet of the cartridge on the slab and secured it vertically with sand. Next we pressed the point of the independent bullet tightly against the percussion cap of the cartridge and held it upright with the left hand. We would strike the thicker end of the bullet with a stone in the right hand. With a muffled bang, the explosion came and the cartridge would be blown into beautiful shapes, such as a spoon, or a flower, or a claw. The bullet of the cartridge would dive deep into the soil and could not be retrieved. I tried almost every time but I never was able to find the bullet. When I got tired of those cartridges, I would throw them into a basket and start to make new ones. Such split shells as well as the shells I collected during the mad shooting by the soldiers were used in later years to barter for matches. One copper shell was bartered for one box of matches. These matches lasted for quite a few years, right until 1958.

Cartridges were also played with in risky ways. One day, four or five of us boys, went into the field. Each brought twenty cartridges with him. We collected some twigs, branches, and dry grass to build a fire. Then we threw the cartridges into the fire and took shelter in a trench. In a very short time, bullets whistled over the trench, into the air or along the surface of the ground. In a word, they flew around us with no fixed direction and with no fixed height. We did not dare to move until long after the bullet whistling stopped. We then jumped out of the trench to look for shells in the cinders of the fire.

About fifty metres away was a cart road linking our village with another village. A man stood up from lying on the ground of the road. He was scared into lying on his stomach by the whistling bullets. He must have been confused, the army having already been gone. When he saw us children, arses pointing to the sky, clustering there boisterously fighting for something, he understood what had happened immediately. Slipping his shoulder pole off the ropes, he began running towards us with the pole in his hand.

'You nasty rascals,' he shouted. 'The war did not finish me, but now you children want to send me to hell!' He came nearer and nearer. 'I must give you a sound lesson and you will never do such a thing again!' he blabbered. We felt confused a bit at first. Then we realised he wanted to revenge himself upon us. We were frightened and fled at once. The man, who turned out to be a hawker, came to the cinders of the fire and stopped. He did not continue to run after us but simply confiscated all our remaining shells from the ashes.

The older boys taught us to make fireworks with powder from the cartridges. We would collect saltpetre from the lower part of the toilet brick walls, pick out the charcoal from our mother's cooking cinders, grind the charcoal into powder, get broken glass and crush it into tiny bits. We then mixed them together. We placed this mixture on a piece of paper and ignited them. They would spurt beautifully! Big boys from school made much more beautiful fireworks. Adults put the meal-like cartridge powder to better use. They would swallow the powder to treat their stomach complaints.

Some children from an adjacent village threw hand grenades at dead tree branches to knock them down for firewood. After repeated use, some of the hand grenades exploded and injured three of them. We stopped playing with these when we heard that news. Still it could be called fate that I was not hurt nor injured nor killed!

Some soldiers, after the mad shooting, fired American carbines into an empty sweet potato storage cellar dug out in the yard of a neighbour. We thought there must be plenty of the dome-shaped bullets in the cellar, so one day, about four or five of us jumped in to dig for those bullets. Unexpectedly, the manhole was blocked. A boy looked up and saw that the muzzle of a carbine was pointed down through the manhole.

'Don't shoot,' he screamed.

'Don't shoot,' we chorused.

The gun disappeared and the manhole was clear. Quickly we climbed up and found a soldier sitting by the manhole wiping sweat off his face.

'What are you doing in the bloody cellar?' he shouted at us. The soldier, ash-faced, made a cross with his hand touching his forehead, breast and belly. Thereafter, we never visited the cellar again.

One day I put a big firecracker inside an empty cartridge shell, placed them on the brick, and aimed the cartridge at my mother's only hen. I ignited the firecracker and retreated to a safe place, afraid to be hurt in the event of an explosion. The firecracker exploded and the empty shell was expelled, quicker than an arrow, to the hen, and hit her on the side. The hen spread her wings, squawked, and ran madly around the yard. My mother came into the yard at the commotion and immediately saw what I had done. Picking up the broom lying against the awning post, she intended to give me a good beating. I ran swiftly away down the street.

Witchcraft among Peasant and Peasant Doctors

Throughout my entire childhood, I had seen, and I had been treated by, the countryside 'witch' and the peasant doctors.

I was four years old when my first illness occurred. My temperature was so high that my skin felt as if it was on fire at the touch of fingers. My parents were worried.

'Shuang Xi has lost his soul somewhere,' Granny told my parents. 'We must get his soul back as quickly as possible. If we do not do it soon, he may lose his soul forever!' Granny and my mother pulled a broom covered with my jacket around the yard for my soul to recognise, calling, 'Shuang Xi, please come home!' They called and called. Their voices were sweet and enticing. They thought, as other peasants thought in similar cases, my soul would follow the broom home and return to my body. But my temperature refused to come down and Granny became more worried.

'Go look for your uncle Li,' Granny instructed my father. 'He can do "chasing the soul with the fastest horse".'

My great uncle Li lived by the end of the lane on our right, bordering the main street. I called him 'Lao Yie' because he was one generation above my father. Lao Yie is the equivalent of great uncle. I had never heard that he could chase the soul with the fastest horse. He came to our house in the evening when the moon was nearly at its zenith. He carried me with his left arm while he stood on our steps under the eaves. He turned his face towards the moon and chanted incantations. He raised his right arm towards the moon and grasped at the air, thumped his right foot loudly on the step, and moved his right hand to my head, gesturing to inject my soul back to me through the top of it. He repeated the procedure three times before stopping.

'Shuang Xi is all right now,' he told my father. 'Let him sleep. He will be normal in the morning.'

I was better by the morning. But whether it was because he 'chased' my soul back for me or because of my own natural recovery, it is hard to know.

Once, when I was still small, I was sick, feeling on fire one moment and frozen the next. People said I had malaria. When I felt cold, no matter how many quilts my mother put over me, I still shuddered and my teeth chattered. When I felt hot, no matter how I bared myself, I still felt I was on fire. I felt that I would be burned to death.

At the time, peasants in our village had not yet heard about quinine. People thought the devil was playing tricks with the sick and if the sick could hide away, the sickness would leave him. If somebody told the peasants that mosquitoes carried and spread malaria, they would not believe it.

'Mosquitoes carry malaria? You must be joking!' they would have said. 'Catch some of those mosquitoes and let them bite me to see whether I shall have malaria!'

Granny believed that the devil was playing tricks with me. She told my father to get a man called Ma to look into his almanac to check why I was sick.

'Go home and check under the pottery jar by the eastern corner in your room for a big green worm,' the man told my father. 'Throw it away! Don't let Shuang Xi come home during the day so he can escape from the devil!'

When my father told my mother to look for the worm, she did find a big green one under the pottery jar holding the flour. She threw it away.

'The devil turned out to be a green worm!' she exclaimed.

My parents could not understand how a big green worm could hide there and they could not imagine how Ma could have known there was a big green worm there through the almanac. As a result they believed him and told me not to come home during the day.

'Go and play with the other children. Don't come home until sunset,' my mother told me. 'I will look for you in the street to give you something to eat at noon.'

I played with friends in the street. When they went home for lunch, I remained in the street waiting for my mother to give me something to eat. When playing, I was not conscious of whether I had the fever or the chill. I was not conscious of it in the afternoon when I played with my friends again. No matter how serious the sickness was, when playing, a boy would forget everything.

I returned home for supper. Nobody asked whether I suffered during the day, for fear of having the devil back again. I was put into bed immediately after supper and I had a good sleep.

The next day, I was well, though still a bit weak. The whole family believed that I was successful in hiding away from the devil.

Once the right arm of my cousin Xiang became swollen at the elbow. My uncle Yong-jiang took him to see the doctor in Beijing and his arm was fixed with gypsum plaster. When the plaster was finally taken off after three months, the elbow of his right arm had become rigid, beyond cure. His forearm and upper arm remained at a permanent right angle.

My Da Ma suggested Ma look in his almanac for my cousin's condition. She went to him, asking why the elbow joints of my cousin's arm had become useless. Ma looked into the almanac.

'Look, in the past, carts passed through your field in which your ancestors are buried. Now you have blocked the passage to make carts pass along the edge of your field. That's why your son's arm became bad, it resembles the right angle turn of the road.' My uncle Yong-jiang immediately redirected the road to let it pass through the field again. Still this did not help.

Then my Da Ma suggested a she-witch would cure Xiang. The she-witch came and ordered a big bowl of spirit to be placed in front of her.

'When I am inviting the deity, don't speak to me. Just do as you are told,' she told my uncle and Da Ma.

The witch sat on the pile of quilts against a wall of the room. She put her hands, palm against palm, together and raised them in front of her eyes. She tucked in her legs, as monks did. In front of her was a table my uncle Yong-jiang had placed covered in sacrifices and a batch of burning incense. The witch closed her eyes, stretched out her arms, and yawned, as if just waking up. She started speaking, meaningless at first, then she started to order.

'Kindle the spirit! And wash the elbow of the boy with the flaming spirit.'

My Da Ma did so accordingly. All the time the witch gestured with her arms and hands as if without her own effort and control.

'I am leaving!' She finally said after about one mealtime and she fell from the quilt pile onto the *kang*. It was something of a wonder in itself that the witch, who was about fifty years old, did not hurt herself in her fall.

'What deity have I invited?' she asked my Da Ma.

'I did not hear the name clearly.' my Da Ma replied. 'It seemed to be the "Cripple Li".'

'Good,' the witch said. 'It must be him!' She collected her fee and left. The arm of my cousin Xiang was never cured.

However, we did have good peasant doctors in our village and in the villages nearby. It would be more accurate to call those peasant doctors 'barefooted doctors', which was the term later used during the Great Cultural Revolution of the late sixties.

The first vivid memory of a real peasant doctor in my childish mind was an old man from a neighbouring village about two kilometres from ours. I was four or five years old when I saw him coming into my uncle Song-lin's courtyard, the house just in front of ours. He came to the house regularly because the place was convenient for patients and because my uncle's mother was a well-known peasant eye doctor.

The man came on a donkey's back, with his legs dangling, his feet just twenty or thirty centimetres from the ground. He just rested near the rear tip of the donkey's back, and I thought he might fall onto the ground any minute. His body swayed but his eyes were closed, for the donkey knew which yard to carry him into. He had to be very old, judging from his beard and whiskers, which were silvery, shiny, lengthy, and bushy, swaying in the breeze against his breast. His face, which had an air of authority without artificial pretension, was radiant with a rosy colour, not creased parchment paper like other old peasants. Benignity was always on his face. His hair, thin and silvery white, was plaited into a finger-thick long pigtail draping behind his back. That was the last symbolic vestige of the last dynasty shown on a peasant head. (The Qing dynasty demanded every man have a plait. When China became a republic, it demanded every man cut his plait. But some old peasants retained their plaits in memory of the Qing dynasty.)

It was summer. A meal table, which also served as a consultancy table, was placed in the yard under the awning rigged up by tree branches. A round straw mattress woven with wheat stocks was placed near the table for him to sit on. Another mattress was placed on the opposite side of the table for patients. He sat there with his back very straight and with his long legs tucked in on the mattress, just like a monk.

'Doctor, I have a headache and…' a middle-aged woman from the East Street began speaking.

The old man opened his eyes, fixing his penetrating stare on her face.

'I know you have a headache and I know you have suffered bodily pain! Do I need you to tell me how you suffer?' He closed his eyes again and kept on feeling her pulse.

'You caught your pain because you were not careful enough after you gave birth to your child. You caught the chill then!' The doctor said and began making a prescription.

The woman watched the doctor with her eyes wide open. The surprise in her eyes showed that the doctor was absolutely right. He never asked any patient to tell him what ailed them. He just closed his eyes to feel the patient's pulse. Sometimes he would check the patient's tongue or look into the patient's eyes. He would tell the patient how he suffered and how he caught that sickness before he used his silver needles to give acupuncture on the spot or make a prescription. When he performed acupuncture, he never requested a patient to roll up the sleeves or to take off the shirt or jacket. He just did it by piercing through the clothing!

'Doctor, please have lunch in my house,' a patient would offer him. That was the only compensation he got, for he never charged a fee. When he had lunch in a poor peasant house, he never complained that the quality of the food was not good. When he had lunch in a landlord's house, he never showed any pleasure or delight in having a banquet-like lunch or supper.

'The doctor is coming!' Whenever he was seen coming toward the village on his donkey's back, children would broadcast his arrival with shrill shouting. He was a blessing to all the villages around, which had no other doctor as good as him.

When he died shortly after the New China was established, the villagers mourned him by offering drapes made from an entire bolt of black cloth to hang in his house. On the drapes were the words in memory of him. There were so many drapes offered that the fences of the streets of his village were all covered up! The peasants missed him, for they needed doctors like him.

My uncle Song-lin's mother, Granny Zhang, lived in the house in front of ours. She was an eye doctor, but not the kind of eye doctor seen in a hospital. She was an eye doctor accepted by the peasants. She had only simple tools: a pair of tiny sharp scissors, a small hook she made by herself from a needle, a big batch of the file-like long needles made from wheat ears, and a normal needle.

Granny Zhang was small in height. She was slim and her feet were the real 'three-inch golden lilies'. Her hands were small, too. But her eyes were sharp and her hands were quick, nimble, steady, and sure. She was an expert in curing people suffering from eye diseases. In summer, young and old, male and female, all that suffered from eye ailments, would come to her for treatment. Some would come from villages far away, some came on donkey's back, while others came on foot.

One of the most common eye problems was where the inside surface of the eyelids were covered with blood-red rotten flesh. Granny Zhang just instructed the sufferer to sit quietly against the wall. She would up-turn the upper eyelid and use the file-like needle to scrub the red flesh away. When she had cleared all the red flesh, the operation was complete. The sufferer would then go home. The eyes became normal from the very moment the operation finished.

Another common case was the pupil being covered with a layer of white film. Granny Zhang would instruct the patient to sit tightly against the wall. She would ask two men to hold the head of the patient against the wall, not allowing it to move. Then, hook in one hand and scissors in the other hand, she would watch the eye of the patient, waiting for the correct moment, then, quick as a flash, she would catch the white film with her hook and cut it off with her scissors. Immediately, the patient was cured. The patient would be able to see as normal.

Granny Zhang never erred, not even once all her life. Eye patients cured by her were numerous. She never charged a fee and she never rejected a patient. For her, to operate and cure patients was to let them see again. She never regarded it as a means of making a living—all the old peasant doctors were like that. She stopped operating on people when she was eighty years old.

'To do the operations, my own eyes must be good. I must see clearly,' she said. 'I cannot make even the slightest mistake. It is the eye on which I am operating. A mistake and the eye will be destroyed! I am too old to do it now.' So, when Granny Zhang stopped performing eye operations, the skill and knowledge could not be passed on. There was no longer such a good eye doctor in the village or in the villages around.

She was not a qualified eye doctor and yet she achieved much more than many modern eye doctors in the large hospitals. It would not be proper to class a peasant as a doctor. One peasant might just have one particular skill but, putting them together, they could relieve the peasants of quite a few ailments and it was very handy. Every villager knew which person had what skill. When anyone suffered, he or she could always find the person with the skill to cure the particular complaint. For example, one peasant not far from our house was good at fixing bone problems. When somebody had his leg or arm bone crushed to pieces, he could put each tiny piece into the original place with his hands through the feeling of his fingers. Then he would secure the damaged section with a wood clipper and the patient would be normal again after three months. Several ladies could cure 'fan' sufferers. The word 'fan' meant to roll one's body over. I therefore thought the pain of such suffering was so great that the sufferer turned his body over and over again. Once when I was thumbing through an old almanac, I found illustrations of seventy-two different 'fans'—one showed a person who had loose bowels and vomited at the same time, one showed a person rolling on the ground, and another showed a person holding his belly with both hands. I do not know what these sufferings are called in the West. I only saw three kinds of 'fan' being cured by old women.

One time, Granny's stomach ached terribly. She lay on the *kang* but she could not lie still. She groaned and rolled over and over on the *kang*. An old woman from our neighbourhood was called.

'She is suffering from "sheep fleece fan",' she told my father when she saw Granny. 'Get some buckwheat flour and make a dough with it.'

When my father borrowed some buckwheat flour and made a piece of dough, she began rolling the dough on the belly of Granny, around and over the navel. She continued to roll until Granny stopped groaning and moaning completely.

'How do you feel now?' she asked.

'I am all right,' Granny replied.

She took the piece of dough and broke it to show to Granny, my father, my Da Ma and my mother. There were four or five pieces of long wool-like grey fleeces in the dough!

Once my cousin, Xiang, suffered indigestion for a long time. He went to the county hospital several times but he still suffered. Then my Da Ma took him to a neighbour to our west. The old woman looked at him and said that he suffered from 'fan'.

'If you look at the underside of his tongue, you will find two dark blue blood vessels. If you look at his anus, you will find a few blisters with dark blood,' she explained.

'Open your mouth,' she said to Xiang. Sure enough, the blood vessels under his tongue were a very dark blue. She had a triangle needle in her right hand. With the speed of a flash, she pierced the blood vessels under Xiang's tongue. Dark blood came out before my cousin Xiang could scream! She then asked him to bare his buttocks. Sure enough there were a few dark blood blisters around his anus. She pierced them, too. Then she put a kind of Chinese pungent wild pepper into a piece of cloth and crushed them with her teeth. She pressed the crushed pepper into Xiang's anus.

'He will be well in a few days!' she said. And sure enough, my cousin did become well within three or four days.

One day my belly ached and I had to run to the toilet every now and then. My mother took me to the old woman living just two houses away from ours. She pressed the middle finger nail of my right hand. She watched the white mark made by her pressing for a moment.

'He is suffering from "fan".' she told my mother.

The method to cure me was to pierce the dark blood blisters from my anus and to put crushed Chinese wild pepper into it. The ache and the loose bowel were immediately cured!

In northern China, many people suffered from chills. When the chills accumulated on the shoulder, on the back, or on the legs, one suffered greatly. This was called *liu* and my father was very skilled in treating such ailments. The treatment was simple. He just used the free end of a Chinese writing brush to press hard on the aching area, with the outer edge first. When the whole area was covered with tiny purple-blue spots made by the hole of the brush (there was a very tiny hole in the middle of the stem. The stem was as thick as a small finger and the hole was as big as a millet seed), he would prick the area with a needle, but not pierce the skin. Then he would rub the area with Chinese salted soy condiment sauce. The treatment was thus completed and the patient would be relieved from any pain.

I also heard about a medicine to cure indigestion. 'My digestion is no good,' an old woman complained. 'I need to have a scavenger beetle to help my digestion!' She would ask her grandson to look for a few scavenger beetles for her. There were several kinds of scavenger beetles. She just needed the kind called 'officials in the court'. This referred to the scavenger beetle with three horns on the head, which looked like the hat of an officer. She would burn them into charcoal and grind them into powder. She then swallowed them and her indigestion would be gone.

In our district there was a kind of mushroom called the 'medicine mushroom'. It was round and brown in colour, similar to the shape of the dropping of a donkey. I was taught at a very young age to keep it in mind. Actually, each year I would come across one or two. The mushroom was kept in a safe place, waiting for use. The powder of the mushroom was good for stopping bleeding. Once I cut my hand and when I applied mushroom powder to the cut, the bleeding and aching stopped instantly. Though the cut was deep and large, it healed in a couple of days with no inflammation or infection. The peasants regarded this mushroom as 'treasure for the house'.

The pity is that young people today do not believe in such cures and there are no more peasants with such skills to perform traditional treatment. Peasants used to know which herbal plant or simple medicine was readily available to them, and they knew how to use them, and without much cost or any cost at all. Peasants in all parts of China had their own methods to treat people but I have never heard of anyone collecting or studying the old peasant methods or skills used to treat people.

chapter 3

THE GREAT CHANGES

The Communist Party of China won the civil war and China once again had a central government. Mao and his comrades set about forming a China that would empower peasants and workers and limit the influence of landlords, capitalists, intellectuals and foreigners. People were taught that struggle, revolution and change were good. Wealth and power were redistributed. The Communists called what they did during and after the civil war 'land reform'.

Land Reform

The first land reform, according to my father, was carried out in 1946. I had not the slightest idea or knowledge of this reform, because I was only five years old. It was, I believe, partly the reason why the White-necks were considered to be such pests. The second land reform took place in late 1948. I heard a lot about this one from the conversations between my parents.

Land reform was also called the redistribution of land. In our village, the big landowners had so much land that they had to hire long-term labourers to till it and they still tried to acquire more land. The poor peasants had only small pieces of land or none at all. When there was a natural disaster or when somebody in the family was sick, the small piece of land, which was all a poor peasant had, would probably be sold. Hence land reform was needed to equalise the share of land between the villagers.

The Association of Poor Peasants, in which my father was a member, was set up mainly for this purpose. Land redistribution was actually carried out by this Association, which was under the direction of the guerrillas in 1946 and the Communist government in the newly liberated area (all the cities, towns and villages around Beijing) in 1948. The first reform was done in secrecy and the latter was carried out noisily in the open. First, members of the Association had to measure the total land belonging to the village, then they had to classify the land into categories such as good, average, or arid. Likewise, they would also classify the villagers into categories such as landlord, rich peasant, upper middle class peasant, middle class peasant, or poor peasant. This had to be done using the criteria of the governing policies. Then they would check the total number of villagers. The total land was divided by the total number of villagers. Since it had already been done in 1946, it was not a difficult thing to do this time. Thus, any extra land of the landlords and rich peasants was redistributed among the poor peasants. The land reform was not to confiscate all the land owned by the landlords and rich peasants, it was to equalise the ownership of land, which had been dreamed by the Chinese peasants for thousands of years. The Association of Poor Peasants had to discuss, on a family by family basis, such matters as the location of the land and the size of each piece of land.

In 1946, prior to the land reform, my father was working for a rich peasant, named Ma, as a long-term labourer. His pay was twelve bags of corn kernels for the whole year. Each bag could hold about fifty kilograms. By the end of the year, the owner offered my father an option that he could have either twelve bags of corn kernels or ten *mu* (one *mu*=⅙ acre) of land. The land offered to my father, as an option, was about one kilometre to the south-east of our village. At this time, my father only had his two *mu* of land, the north-western land. Land to him was something he could only have in his dreams. To him the option was too attractive to refuse. It was not a piece of good land, it was manger land—low in the middle and high on all sides. Drought or inundation, the land would only give a half harvest. My father calculated that he could level the land to get a good harvest within two or three years—being young, strong, and energetic. My mother also entertained this idea. With her help the land could be turned into good land very soon and through their hard work, they could have sufficient grain for the family. So my father decided to take the land, fully prepared to have more wild vegetables for food till he could get a good harvest from it.

His boss made a very good bargain, which became apparent only when land reform began. If my father had not taken this ten *mu* of land, the owner would have been classed as a 'rich peasant'. 'Rich peasant' was a status that would make him and his families suffer for quite some years until the end of the sixties. He released some of his land, probably, on the advice of his brother who was a soldier in the Liberation Army. My father made the worse choice, a very expensive choice. If he had not chosen the land, he would have had it from the land redistribution, anyway, and our whole family would not have had such a bad food situation if he had taken the twelve bags of corn kernel instead of the ten *mu* of land. In this world, if one received a very attractive offer from others, one had to think twice, nay, one had to think ten times before taking the offer. No offer was made without a purpose behind it.

We had four-and-a-half members in the family at the time of land reform: my father, my mother, my little brother, myself, and Granny who was considered as half of our family and half of my uncle Yong-jiang's. My father was entitled to have nine *mu* of fertile land—the best category of land. But he was a timid man, better with his brains and hard working, but not good at taking any risk. As a result, he would not compete with other poor villagers for the best land.

The seesaw of battles between the Kuomintang troops and the Communist guerrillas before 1948 were frightening. When the White-necks arrived, they killed and looted many villages, though they did not kill in our village. The final victory of the Communists was not yet in sight and with Beijing still in the hands of the Kuomintang, my father decided to ask for the poorest land from the Association of Poor Peasants because he did not know what the future held.

About two kilometres to the west of our village was nine *mu* of alkaline land belonging to a rich peasant bearing the same name of Li. In winter and spring, it was covered with a thick layer of white alkali. The owner had not grown much on this land. It was that piece of land my father asked for.

'This land cannot produce anything,' members of the Association of Poor Peasants said to him, 'why do you ask for it? You can have nine *mu* of good land.'

'That is waste land,' my mother also argued with him, 'we cannot harvest anything from it even if we work hard.'

'But what about the White-necks?' he asked in a whisper. 'Are you sure that they will never come back? As long as we have land, we can make it grow well!' That silenced her. She could not be sure. Nobody in the village could be sure. It was beyond the peasants to predict the final victory by the Communists throughout the country. Fear and a dash of good conscience made my father maintain his insistence. The Association of Poor Peasants would not mind as my father's decision only helped them have less difficulty in pleasing others. My mother, however, did mind but she could not bend my father's will. And so he was given the 'waste land'.

My father was also entitled to get a three-room house from the same rich Li family. Again he refused. Instead, he asked for half a *mu* of construction land. The Association of Poor Peasants was surprised but agreed to satisfy his will. My mother was taken aback, frustrated and exasperated. She demanded why.

'It is embarrassing to live in the same yard as the owner and see each other daily,' my father argued. 'We both have the same family name as Li. If you trace back a bit you will find that we do belong to the same Li family.'

'Why don't other people feel embarrassed?'

'They are what they are and we are what we are. We can work hard and build our own house in the future.' But the construction land was turned into a vegetable garden and he was not able to construct a house until all his sons grew up and built their own houses.

However, except for the few landlord families and the rich peasant families, everyone was pleased with the new government. Later, when they came to know that it was the Communists who gave them everything, the peasants became unswerving followers and supporters of the Communists.

The land reform carried out in northern China at the time was the key factor in destroying the morale of the Kuomintang troops, owing to the fact that most of the soldiers were from poor peasant families. It would not be wrong to say that the land reform had won the whole country for the Communist Party.

Distribution of Moveable Belongings

The distribution of moveable belongings was carried out simultaneously with the second land reform. After leaving a reasonable quantity of grain, clothing, furniture, farm tools, live stock and other daily necessities in storage, the Association of Poor Peasants would carry all their moveable goods to the open yard in front of their gates and distribute them among the peasants. I myself was a small witness to this glamorous, boisterous, and excited movement.

It was a clear winter morning, nearly noon. The air was not very chilly and the sky was blue, like blue silk fabric, and there was not a single patch of cloud to spoil it. The sun was benign, beaming upon everybody. Quite a few male peasants had shed their winter jackets, wearing their autumn lined jackets instead.

My mother, with my brother on her back and myself beside her, headed for the site of the distribution of moveable belongings. My father was not with us—being a member of the Association of Poor Peasants—and was already at the site to help keep things in order. Several other families were heading in the same direction. They exchanged a few happy greetings with my mother and advanced towards the site. Smiles were on every face.

The site was actually a big yard, which was used to process wheat, peanuts, soybeans, and other agricultural products. It was about the size of ten basketball courts. On its northern edge was the big quadruple compound house. On the other edges were houses, much smaller, but all belonged to the same family name. Strips of green, pink and yellow paper with Chinese ideograms written on them were glued to the walls of the houses bordering the yard. They carried slogans that read 'Down with the landlord! Liberate the whole of China! Long live the Communist Party!' I had heard school students read such slogans aloud. In front of the gate of the quadruple house were placed a couple of black lacquered square tables, at which sat executives of the Association of Poor Peasants. On the tables were books containing name lists and blank books for recording as well as a few pieces of other things such as an abacus and writing brushes. A couple of cleanly dressed men were also at the square tables—they were teachers from the school to help keep the records correct.

Wooden furniture, such as chests, tables, wardrobes, benches and chairs were placed in one part of the yard. Each piece had a slip of paper attached to it, numbering the item. Gunnybags and canvas bags full of corn, millet, wheat, black beans or sorghum were clustered in another part of the yard. Horses, oxen, donkeys, mules, and so on were tethered to posts separately in another part of the yard. Clothing and fabrics were in yet another part of the yard. The furniture, clothing, grain and animals were all guarded by members of the Association of Poor Peasants.

The yard was seething with people. Male peasants clad in black padded jackets with cotton bursting from the elbows and shoulders, grouped around the animals, commenting on each of them. Women clad in black jackets and trousers like the men, clustered around pieces of furniture, appreciating and guessing who would get which. Children chased each other through the crowds or through the furniture pieces. One thing was common with everybody—smiles! Smiles were on each and every face.

It was the first time that I had been in this part of the village. This quadruple compound house on the edge of the yard was much higher, larger, and grandiose than the one next to our house to the east. Its main entrance opened to the south. It had two huge steel sheathed doors painted dark red. A screen wall was inside the entrance, blocking prying eyes from seeing the inside of the compound house. The gaps between the main north house, the east and west wing houses, and the south house, were all connected with brick walls to form an integral structure. The walls were all higher than the roofs. The top of the walls were latticed in flowery patterns with tiles, at once making the houses stylish and serving as parapets in case of an emergency. The outside appearance of the compound house was that of a castle. I was so astonished by the size, the style, and the grandeur of the houses that when I grew up and visited the Forbidden City I was not so amazed. The master of the house, a colonel in the Kuomintang army, had retired here because of ill health. In this house, after the liberation of the country, he spent his jail term, also due to ill health. Whether he had done anything bad, nobody knew; at least I never heard about it. But this man was very ambitious, no doubt. To express his own aspirations and ambition, as well as to show his expectation of his children and his siblings, he gave everyone a special name. Connecting the last word of each given name of his sons and nephews in the order of age from the eldest down to the youngest, it formed a complete sentence, reading: to administer the country, to unify the country, to stabilise the country, and to rule the country.

Poor peasants churned in the yard, eyes darting over the articles of furniture, tools, animals, and clothing. Sweat trickled from their faces. Expectations and impatience filled the air. Distribution started shortly before noon.

The chairman of the Association shouted at the crowds, 'Folks keep silent and listen carefully. Come forward to the table when your name is called.' One teacher stood up to sing out the first name, as well as what he should receive. The man went to the table, pressed his thumb on the red ink pad and then pressed on the record book in a place indicated by the teacher. He left, smiling broadly. 'Take good care of the mule,' an executive said to an old man who was given a healthy young mule. It was tall and of brown colour. Its hair and mane showed an oily lustre. Its muscular breast showed strength. 'I will, I will.' The old man bowed repeatedly, his features were contorted by his hearty smile.

The crowd thinned out quickly.

At last the name of my father was called. 'Take care of your brother,' my mother said to me and hurried to the table. My father was already going over the formalities at the table. They carried a big wooden chest over to the place where my brother and myself were waiting for them. Then they carried to us a square table, a bedside chest, some farm tools, grain, and seeds.

'Wait here,' my mother said to me. 'Your Baba and I must carry the grain and tools home first.'

My brother and I played on and around the big wooden chest. It was lacquered red. It was about three metres long, one metre wide and one metre high. It had three compartments, each of which had its own lid. I opened the lids one by one to check the inside and found two marble eggs. I jumped in to get them out. They were so cool and smooth to the touch and they looked so real that if they were mixed with real ones, it would be hard to distinguish them without touching them. My brother and I played with them happily.

It was already mid-afternoon. The sky was as blue as it was in the morning. There was not a stir in the air. The sun was spreading warmth unselfishly to everyone. It seemed like spring. It seemed to enjoy the happiness with the villagers.

When my parents had the big wooden chest, the last piece to move, on their shoulders, I followed them with my hand holding that of my brother.

'Ma,' my brother called, 'I am hungry!'

My stomach also began complaining. Yes, I was hungry, too.

That supper we had pure corn flour *bing tzi* and porridge to celebrate. I was sure that many families in the village were celebrating the occasion with a special supper that day.

The Communist Party had again won the hearts of the peasants.

Joining the Army

'Good men never join the army; good iron is never used for nails.' This had always been what the villagers said, but now things had changed.

Shortly after the land reform in 1948, young villagers were called upon to join the People's Liberation Army to liberate the country and to protect the 'fruits of victory'. My cousin, Quan, joined. Like my father, my cousin was a man who liked to use his brain.

One day he came back home and declared, 'I have enlisted in the army.' Everybody was flabbergasted. My Da Ma and mother were strongly against the idea. They cried a lot and tried to persuade him to give up the idea.

'If nobody joins the army, who can guarantee that our land will not be taken away by the White-necks?' he argued.

'Yes, you are right,' they said, 'but we still don't want you to go.'

His departure day arrived. The end of our lane was packed with the women from our family: grannies, aunts, my mother—all were there. I was also there with my mother. We waited.

A contingent of horses and men came from the direction of the cross street. The man on the first horse was a soldier in army uniform. Behind him were other young villagers. Two wide red silk laces, from the left and right shoulders down to the waist, crossed each other at the breast. A big artificial red satin flower was pinned to the silk lace cross at the middle of the breast of the young men on the horsebacks. My cousin Quan was somewhere in the middle of the line. He sat upright on the horse. He looked very handsome and proud. He peered towards us and nodded but said nothing. My Da Ma and mother were immediately in tears. They wiped their tears with the front of their dresses, which were now so wet, that if they had twisted them, water would surely be wrung from the material. Long after the horses disappeared out of sight, they still wept.

My cousin Quan was assigned to the County Guerrilla Brigade. Others were assigned to the field army. Some went to fight in Korea later in 1950. My cousin was discharged and came back in 1951 or 1952 and he became an active leader in the Co-operative, the Senior Co-operative, and the Brigade of the People's Commune.

From 1948, young men from our village were active in joining the army. Several even came back from Korea with medals for good deeds. A man, who lived in the north half of the village, came back from Korea with a medal. He was a cook in the cooking squad of the army. He said that one day he carried food with a shoulder pole uphill for his platoon. On his way back to the cooking squad, he saw a few Americans clustered in a valley. 'I could not run. If I did, they would see me and shoot me down with their guns. I unhooked my buckets and dashed to them, brandishing my shoulder pole. The two pieces of iron chains and hooks made loud noises as I did this. "Hands up!" I shouted. The three Americans, without knowing what was in my hands, raised their arms above their head. As I reached them, I picked up a gun and pointed it at them. With the muzzle of the gun, I motioned them to move away from the other guns and from me. I then picked up the other guns and marched the Americans back to our cooking squad. The high commander of our army gave me this medal as an award for my heroic deeds.'

No villager ever questioned the truth of his story about his medal. They liked to feel proud for his brave deeds.

The old saying of 'good men never join the army; good iron is never used to make nails' was replaced by 'good men should join the army; good iron should be used to make nails.' Enlisting in the army became a praiseworthy act for young men, from that time onward.

chapter 4

MY EARLY SCHOOL DAYS

It was something the children of poor peasants never dared to dream—that they might go to school to receive professional education. As soon as the Communist government was in place, it courageously opened the school gate to those poor children. Despite the difficulties the new government faced, it encouraged, helped and persuaded the parents of those children to send them to school. Yet the peasants were still very poor. Though the school fee could be exempted, they still could not afford to pay for the notebooks, pencils, slates, and many other things necessary to a student. Unless a poor boy could find money himself to supply his needs in the school and assisted his family with the same amount of help on the land as before, attending school would still be just a dream to him. The memory of how I succeeded in going to school is still poignant.

Going to School

It was the spring of 1949 and still months before Mao declared the founding of the People's Republic of China. The second land reform and property redistribution had been completed. The poor peasants were planning what to grow on their land, which had been recently given to them. The village chairman came to my home one evening for a chat with my parents. He did not come to discuss the spring sowing with them; he came to discuss my schooling!

'Yong-mao,' he said to my father, 'Shuang Xi should go to school this year when school starts.'

'Go to school?' my father was surprised. To him going to school was for children from rich or well-off families, not for children from families like ours.

'Why not?' the chairman said. 'In the past, we were not able to go to school even if we wanted. Now, the new government intends to have all children educated. Going to school will be compulsory very soon.'

'But we are too poor to pay the school fees,' my mother said.

'Shuang Xi can be exempted from paying his school fees,' the chairman replied.

'It's still costly,' she insisted. 'What about a school bag? What about books, notebooks and pencils?'

'That you have to pay for,' the chairman answered candidly.

'You see,' she turned to my father, 'where can we find the money? And we need him to look after Xiao Bao and to collect firewood.'

'In the past the school gate never opened to children from poor families like ours,' the chairman tried patiently to persuade her. 'Don't spoil Shuang Xi's future.'

'You are right,' my father agreed, 'we need our children educated, hard as it is.'

'Do you still remember the story about the "Vulture"?' the chairman asked my mother.

'Of course I do,' she replied.

'Do you wish to have the same joke played on our children?' he asked. 'How difficult it is even to have our couplets written for the New Year!'

She was silent.

Even children like me could tell the story about the 'Vulture', which was the nickname of a man in our village, who was considered a glutton. Once he bought two catties (one kilogram) of pork for his family to celebrate the Spring Festival. He was asked to slice it into thin pieces and grill them. He did this willingly. The sizzling of the pork in the pan was so tempting that he picked up one piece to taste whether it was cooked. He tasted the pork again and again and when he finished doing the grilling, he had eaten four-fifths of the meat. He then thought it was not worth keeping the remaining one-fifth for the whole family for the Spring Festival so he swallowed the rest of the meat. Thereafter, he was nicknamed the 'Vulture'.

One time he bought a large piece of red paper, cut it into proper sizes, and asked a man to write couplets for him. The couplet writer decided to play a joke on him, and so he wrote two sets of couplets. He gave the Vulture the one set, telling him where each was to be glued. He told the Vulture to put what should be on the wall inside his room on the wall of the pig's shed and vice versa. The Vulture was not able to read but he was able to follow the instructions he had been given. Visitors to the Vulture's house laughed aloud. As we Chinese describe it, the visitors held their bellies to roar with laughter. Of course many of the visitors were as illiterate as the Vulture. They came because they heard that the Vulture had put the couplets for a pigsty in his room. The Vulture became suspicious and asked why they all laughed. A man told him that he had put 'fat pigs fill the sty' on his bedroom wall, and 'raise your head to see fortune' on the wall of the pigsty. (It was the custom that 'raise your head to see fortune' was glued to the bedroom wall, as a good wish for the New Year. It was also customary to glue 'fat pigs fill the sty' on the pig's shed, wishing to have more fat pigs.) The Vulture became embarrassed and angry. He went back to the couplet writer to demand an explanation. But before he opened his mouth, the couplet writer handed him the other set and told him the correct places for him to glue them on. It was a joke and he could not make a row about it. Had he been able to read the Chinese ideograms, such a joke could not have been played on him.

I was very attentive to the discussions between the village chairman and my parents. The chairman's arguments made me the happiest boy one moment and my mother's words reduced me to the most depressed boy the next. The chairman raised me to happiness again and my mother threw me into the abyss once more. My mood fluctuated quickly, falling and rising with their discussions.

I longed to go to school so much! When students boasted of their knowledge learned from school I envied them. When they talked about the strictness of one teacher and the leniency of another teacher I felt it was terribly attractive and fascinating. When they wrote on the ground the words they learned, I inched as near as possible to watch and memorise how they wrote. When they recited multiplication tables from one times one to nine times nine, I could recite them fluently in my mind while some of them were still faltering. I was confident that if I was given the opportunity to have schooling I could do better. My father might be poor in material wealth but he made me rich in having a good brain.

That night it was hard for me to fall asleep. I worried about my mother's attitude. She was practical and not interested in the distant possibility of a better future for me. Though I was not big enough to toil in the land, I could look after my brother so that she could have more time in the field. If I went to school, I would be a 'money spender'. The chairman alone might not be able to persuade her to send me to school. I had to do something myself.

The key factor to consider was how to pay for my books, notebooks, pencils, and other things. How could I earn enough money to pay for them? First I recollected that one day when I took Xiao Bao to play along the river, I saw shrimps trooping upstream along the water edge. I could find ways to catch them for money. Then I thought that I could pick peanuts during autumn vacation and I could ask my father to sell them for money. When I grew a bit older, I could find other ways and means. Small as I was, I could see that my road to schooling would be a long and arduous one. I made up my mind to persuade my mother that I was determined to go to school, whatever happened. The following morning at breakfast I spoke to my parents, very solemnly.

'Baba,' I said, 'I want to go to school.'

'But we have no money,' my mother interrupted.

'I can earn money for my own books and pencils,' I replied.

'How?' my mother questioned me impatiently.

'I can catch shrimps,' I said, 'and Baba can sell them for me.'

'How would you catch shrimps?'

'I will find the ways and means.'

'Suppose you can catch shrimps,' my mother drove on. 'Can you sell them for enough money?'

'I can,' I said very positively.

'All right,' my father said, 'you can go to school. If we find it too hard to provide for your schooling, you will have to quit then.'

I agreed. Reluctantly, my mother also agreed. Schooling for poor children, a good and kind effort by the government, was not easy for the poor peasants to manage.

That night I woke to hear my parents still arguing about my schooling.

'It will be very, very hard for us to support him at school.' my mother said.

'I know,' my father replied. 'But soon life will change for the better since we already have land! Do you still remember what my father told us about the words of the fortune teller?'

'I don't know what you mean.'

'My father carried Shuang Xi for a stroll in the street when he was only two years old. A fortune teller came by, and feeling Shuang Xi's back he told my father that the boy would not be one who toiled among the villagers. He said Shuang Xi would go away when he grew up. If he does not go to school, how can he find his future elsewhere?' my father told her.

'Let him go to school, then. We shall see whether we can continue to support him.'

Summer vacation was nearly over and school would soon start. My mother had to manage time to make preparations for me. She had to 'cook without edible materials'.

She fumbled in her basket and found a piece of blue cloth. She sewed it into a rectangular bag and lined it. She attached to it a long shoulder strap. When she finished, she asked me whether I liked it—my first school bag. I liked it very much. Though most of the students had school bags bought from town, I always regarded my own bag as not a shade less beautiful than that of the other students. It served the purpose and I carried it till I went to junior high school (middle school) when a school bag was no longer necessary.

Next my mother sold a few eggs to buy a slate for me. It was a slate with a wooden frame. I would copy words from our Chinese language book on it with a slate pencil, as all the students did. I loved it so much that I would touch its smooth surface many times a day, and before going to bed, I would put it in a place where Xiao Bao was not able to reach or touch it.

Next, my mother had to make some lye water to wash material for making an autumn jacket for me. Washing powder or washing liquid were not yet heard of. Soap was something the poor peasants could not afford to use for washing. She scooped ashes from the cooking range, put them into a basket, sprinkled water in them, and pressed the ashes hard to make a small reservoir in the centre. She placed a basin underneath the basket and then poured water into the reservoir. Water seeped through the ashes and dripped into the basin, already a light coffee colour. When she had enough lye water she soaked my padded jacket fabric and lining in it for some time before she washed them on her washing board. When the fabrics had dried thoroughly under the sun, she mended the holes. She then cooked some pure corn meal porridge, skimmed the starchy watery surface into a basin, in which she soaked the mended fabric. When the fabrics were half dried, she placed them on a very thick, heavy duty stone slab and beat the fabric with two spindle-like date wood bludgeons. After this she was ready to make a lined autumn jacket for me. When the jacket was finished, though patched here and there, it was very clean, and it fitted me well.

To complete 'furnishing' me, my mother planned to make a pair of shoes for me. She went into action immediately. She sold eggs to buy fabric for the shoe uppers. She then applied starch to the surface of our meal table, glued cloth rags smoothly on it, applied starch again and then put more rags on it again. She did this alternatively until the thickness satisfied her. When the rags were completely dry, she cut shoe soles out of them. The outer edge of these was wrapped with white fabric. She then stitched quite a number of layers together—hard, tough, and strong—with hemp strings. The shoes were called 'shoes with a thousand-layer soles'. Such shoes were handsome looking and comfortable to wear. (At the time, all poor peasants had to make their own shoes. Only the few well-off families could go to Beijing to buy shoes.)

My younger brother Xiao Bao envied me greatly. He babbled that he would go to school with me. He cried when nobody heeded him. I had to pacify him, not being able to stand his crying.

'Don't cry,' I told him, 'when you are my age, I will give you my slate, my slate pencils, and my school bag. Mother will make new clothes and new "thousand-layer sole" shoes for you.'

He was pleased. 'I will go to school when I grow up,' he sang happily.

The word 'school' occupied my childish mind completely. My mother told me that I was babbling about school in my dreams. Now and then I would take out my slate and slate pencil to write the words I learned from students who wrote them on the ground. My brother would eagerly help me to wipe them off the board.

Now and then when Xiao Bao and I sat on the sand playing, I would write those words on the sand with the index finger of my right hand. Xiao Bao also tried hard to copy them.

The night before the first day of school, I checked and re-checked whether all my things were in the school bag. First, I thought I should hold the bag in my sleep. I gave up the idea for fear of breaking the slate pencils and the slate. Then I placed them on the square table not far from my head when I lay down to sleep. Later I thought better of it. I moved it quite a few times until my father assured me that nobody would touch it.

'Ma,' I said to her, 'don't forget to wake me up in the morning. I must not be late!'

My mother assured me of that; my father assured me of that; and Granny assured me of that.

I felt so excited that I could not fall asleep as quickly as before. I tossed and turned, like a piece of grilled corn flour bread, which my mother turned over and over again until it was fully cooked. If it had been a wooden bed or a spring bed, I would have robbed everybody of their sleep by the squeaking of the bed. But our mud-brick *kang* was hard and didn't squeak and so everyone slept undisturbed.

Bugles blared, loud and clear, to call the reformed soldiers up. Unlike other mornings, noises of horses, men, jeeps, and trucks were in the air, awakening all the villagers. My mother was cooking breakfast and I was checking my school bag. When breakfast was ready, I hurried through it.

'You have had too little breakfast,' Granny said to me. 'You will be hungry before lunch.'

'No fear,' I said, 'I've had enough.'

My mother, finally, was ready to take me to school. We walked along the street side by side with a steady flow of soldiers towards the cross street. Holding her hand, I jumped, skipped, and hopped as happy as a lark. At the junction where the streets merged, soldiers, horses, and trucks joined into a bigger, stronger, steadier flow to the highway and headed south. The redeployment had ended and they were headed south to join the Huai Hai Campaign, which was on the lips of the villagers.

We could not get across to the other side through the advancing army. We had to get to the other side because the school was on that side on the north-eastern edge of the village. It was already mid-morning and we were still blocked on the opposite side of the school. More children came together with their parents or just with their mother or father. All were blocked on our side. Like me, all the children were excited and nervous but a bit frustrated by the waiting.

Shortly before noon there were only foot soldiers, four columns abreast, marching along the street, their bayonets flashing under the sun. Now we could not wait any longer and we broke through the marching columns to the other side. A short while later, we arrived at the school.

A male teacher with very thick glasses greeted us and I had my name entered. He told my mother to leave me to him and she could go. From that moment on, I was a student! I belong to the category of students 'born in the old society but brought up under the red flag'.

My First Days at School

Our school was on the very edge of the village's north-eastern tip. It was a grand quadruple house compound owned by the Guo family, who fled before the liberation of our village. The main gate opened to the south, at the corner starting from the east wall westward, and was wide enough to let in a horse and cart. The big doors of the gate were sheathed with a very thick steel plate, which had a shallow dent from when it was hit by a cannon ball. The gateway was paved with grey bricks. The front yard was about one foot lower than the brick-paved passage under the gateway. A side entrance was sandwiched by the western wing house and by the south house. Its door was also sheathed with a steel plate, which was painted black. The second gate in the middle of the high wall connecting the east and west wing houses divided the yard into the front and the main yards. The main yard was also paved with grey bricks, and was on the same level as the front yard. The main yard also had east and west wing houses. From the main house, which was the north house, to the line of the west and east wing houses' northern walls, the yard was about one foot higher than the main yard. It served as a platform. Walls as high as the houses connected them all. Looking from the outside, it was merely a square shaped castle.

The villagers said that foxes frequented the houses in the compound. Foxes, through many, many years of praying to the God, could succeed in assuming human forms, such as beautiful girls. The inhabitants of the house were scared and had moved away. The houses therefore were used as classrooms and offices for students and teachers. No ghosts, demons, or devils would ever haunt a place occupied by students and teachers. Neither would foxes dare to visit the place again.

A basketball court bordered the eastern wall of the house. From the basketball court to the western bank of the Paradise River was the main sportsground. This side of the riverbank was lined with willows and poplar trees. Underneath was wild chrysanthemum. Bordering the southern edge of the sportsground was a piece of agricultural land belonging to a peasant. Against the south wall of the compound house was a three-room lean-to, which was the kitchen for the teachers.

That first day of school I joined a few children from my neighbourhood and we played on the southern edge of the sportsground. I wanted to pee urgently, and, just as I did in the open when collecting firewood, I did it there and then. One or two other boys also joined in. None of us thought it improper to piss at the edge of the sportsground until a bigger boy, who was a senior student, came running to us, shouting, 'You must not pee here. You must go to the toilet!'

'But where is the toilet?' we asked in unison.

'Over there,' he pointed to the place behind the north wall of the house. 'I will not report you to the teacher this time. But if I catch you again, I will.'

That was the moment when I realised that we could not just pee anywhere we liked, as we had before. That was the very moment I realised that to pee in the open was shameful.

The bell rang. We did not know what to do at first, then we ran in the wake of the senior students into the main yard. The teacher wearing glasses was calling 'New students line up here'. The queues of new students were much longer than those of the senior grade students. Our queues looked like undulating waves, the result of a random mixture of shorter and taller students. The teacher swapped the positions of the students so that the shortest was at the beginning of the queue and the tallest at the end. Thus our queues looked similar to those of the students of the senior grades. We gathered in the yard for the school opening ceremony. The principal expressed his welcome to the new students and urged the senior grade students to care for the new ones. His speech was not very long but, nevertheless, I could not understand most of it. I could only remember the following: 'New students,' he said emotionally, 'you are lucky! If it were not for the new government, most of you would be unable to stand here at all. The new government cherishes you children very much. The new government has so much to do, but despite this, it pays attention to your education. Cherish this opportunity and study hard!'

A student standing on the raised 'platform', holding a piece of paper in his left hand, shot his right fist in the air and shouted, 'Long live the new government!' Other students, and also the teachers, shouted after him. We new students also shouted after him. Later I learned that this was called slogan shouting, which we had to do for many years to come. We were then dispersed to our classroom, which was the south house. It was cold in winter and hot in summer. The villagers always said, 'Don't live in the south house if you have money. It is not warm in winter and it is not cool in summer.' Inside, a huge blackboard was hung in the middle section of the east wall and about one metre or so above the floor, which was paved with grey bricks. Rows of desks and benches stretched from near the window wall to the bottom wall, leaving a lane between the window and the desks as an access aisle. The desks were wooden planks half a metre wide placed on brick supports, the height of which differed so that the row behind was a bit higher. Benches were rigged up in the same way, namely wooden planks placed on brick supports. The height of the benches allowed the legs to tuck in under the desks. Each row had eight students.

The teacher allocated a seat to each student. We were so tightly arranged that the movement of one student would disturb the ones on either side of him or her. Later, when we became familiar with each other, we drew lines as borders between us. If one crossed the 'border' with his or her elbow, the 'invaded' would knock that elbow back to the other side of the 'border'.

There were more than eighty students in our class. Our ages ranged from six to seventeen years. The wide range of ages in one year was due to the fact that parents could not afford to send their children to school before the liberation of our village. Now that the new government was established, children were indiscriminately encouraged to come to school regardless of age. The older they were, probably, the more embarrassed they felt to come to school. Some would not come at all. Finally, students in the senior years would go to their respective houses and push them to come to school. Unfortunately, many of them quit school a couple of years later.

Our teacher introduced himself as Zhen and so we called him Teacher Zhen. He was about fifty years old and a bit taller than the average villager. His hair, parted at the middle, was neatly combed, stylish, not like the monk's heads of the male villagers. He had glasses with lenses that appeared as thick as the bottom of a glass bottle holding oil. He wore a long, grey robe, typical of the Chinese intellectuals of the time (before 1949, he discarded his long robe and wore a grey jacket, which was called Mao's style jacket). His robe reached down to the top of his leather shoes, which were polished to shine. In the village we seldom saw people wear leather shoes. A beaming smile instantly creased his benign face when he started to speak. His smile was natural and warm, winning immediate trust. His tone was soothing, like that of a mother.

Teacher Zhen requested everybody tell him their name, one by one from the front row. 'My name is the puppy dog,' the first boy of the first row reported. The teacher was surprised. The children were not. 'My name is the ugly girl,' the second one said. The teacher was wide-eyed because the girl was not ugly at all. 'My name is the brown ox.' More names were given, such as 'the big fool' or 'the big ram' or 'the black ball' and so on. Very seldom was a good name heard because parents thought an ugly name would make the child survive and enjoy longevity. Those names given at birth were called a 'small name'. The teacher stopped us and said that each of us should have an official name (those names were called a 'big name' or 'formal name'). He then gave us each a name and wrote it on our books. Since all my cousins had the second word of their name as 'chun' (spring), I was given the name Chun-ying (meaning spring flower, extraordinary person and the essence). Teacher Zhen wrote my name beautifully on the fly page of my book. The name was not bad except a bit girlish as the word 'Ying' was often given to a girl. After that, the teacher explained the rules and regulations to us.

'Students, now that you are in school, you should learn discipline, good manners and behaviour. At school, when you meet a teacher, bow to the teacher as a greeting. At home, when you see your parents, uncles, aunties, and grandparents, bow to them as a greeting. When the teacher comes into the classroom, you all must stand up, bow to the teacher, say, "good morning teacher", and sit down at the call of the monitor. In class, when any of you wish to ask a question, raise the right hand and ask the question after being acknowledged by the teacher. In class, sit upright with both hands behind the back.'

He nominated a teenager as our monitor. Then he explained the procedure, 'When the teacher comes in, the monitor should say, "Stand up". When the teacher is on the platform, the monitor should say, "Bow to the teacher!" When everybody bows, the monitor should say, "Bowing finishes! Sit Down!"' He wanted us to practise. He went out of the classroom and came back in.

'Stand up!' the monitor ordered.

We all stood up.

'Bow to the teacher!' the newly nominated monitor chanted as the teacher stood on the platform before the blackboard.

We all bowed.

'How do you do, students?' Teacher Zhen asked.

'How do you do, teacher!' we replied.

'Bowing finishes! Sit down!' the monitor declared.

We practised until the teacher was satisfied.

About mid-afternoon we were dismissed from school. We marched in double lines, branching off at each street, and a student would step out in front of his home. Villagers looked at us appreciatively.

Arriving home I bowed to my mother and Da Ma when I saw them. I was looking everywhere to see if there was anybody else at home to whom I could bow. I was so excited. They all praised the fact that I had learned such good manners at school. I was very pleased and proud. My brother Xiao Bao copied me bowing to everyone in the two families. Everybody laughed, boisterously and happily. My first day in school was thus completed.

Initial Classes and After School Activities

Our first two classes the following morning were the Chinese language. The first text contained three Chinese characters: *ren* (man), *ge* (single or individual), and *yi* (one). The text was *yi ge ren* (man, a single man, or one man).

Teacher Zhen asked us to read after him several times and then he told the monitor to lead us in reading. He demonstrated on the blackboard how to write the words correctly. Thereafter we were instructed to copy the text ten times on our slate. I was fascinated by the look of the words. The word *ren* looked like a man standing with his legs wide apart and his hands flat against his hips. The left side of the word *ge* looked like the side of a man standing straight with his arm stretching a bit forward. The right half of the word was a square enclosure with something inside. It looked very much like the shape of the walls of our school, square and solid, but Teacher Zhen said it resembled a man in full armour. No matter how I looked at it I could not imagine it was a man in armour. The word *yi* simply looked like a straight stick on the ground. Thus I memorised the three words in a short time.

The second text was: *shou* (hand), *zuo you shou* (left and right hand) and the third text was: *yi ge ren you liang zhi shou* (a man has two hands). Here, Teacher Zhen, probably suspecting that his students thought the texts were too easy, told us a story:

'A long, long time ago, there was a very, very rich family. It had only one son who was eight years old. The son was very much treasured by his parents, who were illiterate and getting old. They decided to send the boy to school so that he would not only be rich but also have bookish knowledge.

On the first day, he was taught *yi* (one)—a horizontal bar only.

On the second day he was taught *er* (two)—one short horizontal bar over a longer horizontal bar.

On the third day, he was taught *san* (three)—two short horizontal bars over one longer horizontal bar.

On the fourth morning, the boy said to his parents, "Father, there is no need for me to go to school anymore. I can teach other people and earn some money."

"Are you sure you can be a teacher now?" his father asked in surprise.

"Very sure!" the son replied.

Thus he quit school and opened a private school to teach. He only accepted students from rich families because he could charge more money, and the rich families were glad to send children to him, for they also wished their children to learn as quickly as he did and bring more money home.

The first student came. He asked the student's name so that he could write it for him. "My name is Wan Bai Qian." (*Wan* is ten thousand, *Bai* is one hundred, *Qian* is one thousand.)

"Wait for me here," he told his student. He ran back home.

"Mother, give me your comb," he asked.

"What do you want that for?"

"To write the name of my student."

He took the comb and ran back to the school. He dipped his comb into the inkpad and started to draw horizontally on the notebook of the student. When there was no more blank pages left, he handed it back to his student.

"What are they?" his student asked.

"Your name."

All the students quit and demanded refunds of the fees they'd paid him.'

'Now, students,' Teacher Zhen said, 'we have finished three texts.' He looked at us to see whether we were all attentive before he continued, 'We have to start from the simple words in language and simple additions in mathematics. It will gradually become more difficult. Don't be like that boy in the story. Study hard. Understand?'

'Understood!' we chorused affirmatively.

In the past children were taught the following:

'One way distance two or three *li*,
From the cooking smoke appeared a village of four or five houses,
Six or seven pavillions,
Eight, nine, and ten flowers.'

If we were given such a text, no student would think it too easy. Twenty words for students to begin the first class would definitely be enough for them not to regard it as too easy. But I did not treat the texts as easy, because I had not been taught to read or write by my family before going to primary school. What Granny taught me were only stories such as Gong-yie Chang:

'Gong-yie Chang was a man who could understand the language of birds. Once when he was working in his field, a crow stopped on a tree not far from him.

'Gong-yie Chang, Gong-yie Chang,' the crow called at him.

He looked up at the crow, which continued to speak:

'Gong-yie Chang, Gong-yie Chang,

There is a big sheep in the southern hill

You have the meat and I will have the intestines.'

Gong-yie Chang went to the southern hill and checked and surely there was a sheep there. He took the sheep home and greedily kept both the meat and the intestines. The crow was displeased. When Gong-yie Chang went to work in his field the following day, the crow planned to give him a lesson.

'Gong-yie Chang, Gong-yie Chang,

There is a big sheep in the southern hill

You have the meat and I will have the intestines'

Again Gong-yie Chang went to the southern hill. He was caught and flogged by the owner of the sheep and the crow laughed at him.'

Equipped only with such stories, I had not the slightest advantage in my study. I therefore had to study hard.

We had outdoor activities in the afternoon. Teacher Zhen taught us to play the 'lose and find' game with a handkerchief. He taught us to dance the *yang-ge* introduced from the liberated areas. He stood at the head of the class and dipped his head, his left foot jerked forward, his right foot followed and then he jerked back with his left foot following, his arms moved like wings of birds. Each step had to keep in time with the beat of a drum and a small gong and cymbals.

Then the 'flower stick dance' came to the school. The flower stick was a piece of wood about five centimetres thick and a bit over a metre long. It was painted with blue and red zebra stripes. Both ends had a rectangular eye cut through the stick. Copper coins were secured inside the eyes with steel wires. Colourful tassels were fixed to both ends. The dancer held the middle of the stick with the right hand, and swinging it would knock the left shoulder with one end of the stick and then knock the right shoulder with the other end. The coins would clatter noisily and musically. This dance could be performed by one person or by a great many people at the same time. Teacher Zhen usually led the whole class dancing. When all the classes were over for the day, the physical education teacher would lead the whole school dancing. Villagers came to watch when they had time.

The 'waist drum dance' was introduced to our school immediately after, and a waist drum team was formed. About thirty boys and the same number of girls were selected from all classes. Each person had a drum tied to the left side of his or her waist and each hand held a drumstick. Sometimes both hands would beat the same end of the drum and sometimes they would beat each end. Sometimes the right leg kicked high in the air and the right hand beat the drum from under the leg. There were quite a few tricks for the dancers to learn and demonstrate. Our physical education teacher commanded at the head with two big cymbals. When waist drum teams from all primary schools competed at the district centre, our school usually came first.

I was not very involved in such activities because I had to get home early to help and I had to make money to support myself. I had little time for games. I had to work!

Other children noticed my 'jade eye'—that my left eye was different from theirs—yet nobody ever referred to it. Every student understood the saying 'never scratch the opponent's face in a fight; never mention the defect of another person in a conversation.' If another student called me Jade Eye, he or she would be corrected by the teacher.

Shrimp Catching

'Catching fish or catching shrimps delay the growing of crops!' Such was the opinion of the peasants in our part of the district. They never held a very high opinion of a man wandering with a fishing net, neglecting his crops in the field.

I was the first to catch shrimps with the view of raising money for my schooling. It was already late autumn in 1949 so a padded jacket and trousers had to be worn in the mornings and evenings. I had checked in the evenings that schools of fat small shrimps trooped along the water edge upstream. The river was only less than knee deep now. The water flowed slowly so it was a good time to catch shrimps.

Finally I had an idea of how to catch the shrimps. I had to do it in secrecy, for, if my mother knew, I would not be allowed to lay my hands on the particular tool I needed most—her sieve. It had a drum-like round frame with a diameter of about 40 centimetres and a depth of about 20 centimetres. The frame was a wooden board about three millimetres thick. We called the frame the wall of the sieve. I grabbed the sieve and put it into the piggyback basket with three half-metre long sticks, which were sharpened at one end, one basin, two bricks, and one oil lantern, which I made myself. I went to the riverside as soon as I finished my supper.

I chose a spot that was flat with clean sand. I had checked the spot a couple of times. First, I made a shallow recess at the water's edge. Then I knocked two sticks into the riverbed just in front of the recess, about thirty centimetres apart. The third stick was hammered into the sandy bottom about a palm length behind the other sticks but also about a palm length away from the water's edge. Next I put the sieve on its wall, with its opening facing downstream, behind the two sticks, which prevented it from being carried away by the flowing water, and with the third stick preventing it from getting into the deeper water. One piece of brick was placed on top of the sieve-wall. The last thing I did was to kindle the lantern and put it on the other brick placed half a metre behind the sieve. I did this because I had heard from grown-ups that shrimps and fish tend to head for light.

I sat back to wait. Now and then I would peep into the sieve. Blocked by the fine mesh of the sieve, shrimps charged forward, withdrew a bit and charged forward again. They never tried to turn back or to look for other routes to swim forward. Fish were smarter, never staying in the confinement of the sieve for long.

When I had caught a handful of shrimps in the sieve, I would, with one hand holding the sieve in place and the other hand removing the brick on top of the sieve, tip it backward and the opening upward and take it out of water with both hands. Shrimps skipped and jumped madly in the sieve but could not get out. I would knock the sieve against the rim of the basin to empty the shrimps into it. There was a small quantity of river water in it and so the shrimps, once inside, would stay quiet. The sieve would be rigged up in the water again.

The night was quiet and there was a bit of a chill in the air. The night sky seemed higher and the stars were bright and twinkling. Now and then there was a splash in the river. Sometimes a horse and cart went by along the highway on the other side of the river, its safety lantern dangling and swaying under its shafts.

I waited patiently. I knocked more shrimps into the basin and the knocking sound pleased me. Now and then I tried to recite my Chinese texts, for reviewing the old texts helped to learn the new ones. The waiting time was thus not too dull.

The basin was full of shrimps within three or four meal times. When I got home the first evening, my mother scolded me severely, blaming me for using her flour sieve. When I showed her the basin of shrimps she became less severe but warned me not to damage the sieve, and requested that I let her know whenever I wanted to use anything.

My father sold the shrimps the following morning for four thousand yuan, an amount my mother could only get by selling fifteen eggs. (This was the old yuan used after 1949 when our village was liberated. Ten thousand old yuan was equivalent to one new yuan called *ren min bi* (RMB), which replaced the old yuan in 1955. One yuan (RMB) had one hundred cents.)

When the third basin was sold, my cousin Shan, who was six years older than me, saw the basin of shrimps and asked how they were caught. My father told him to ask me about it, and I told him how. He had the same equipment prepared and came with me on the fourth evening. He found a place about thirty paces downstream from my spot. Within the length of two or three meals we both had our basins full and returned to our respective homes together. With my cousin's company, I found I was more relaxed, no longer fearing anything.

On the sixth or seventh evening, we were joined by more boys. Competitions began. Each one wanted to position downstream of the other, because shrimps come from the lower reaches of the river. Each one feared that the one downstream of him might catch all the shrimps. The selfishness of the peasants was nakedly betrayed. However, I stuck to my old spot all the time, catching the same quantity every night.

By then, it was quite an interesting sight at our shrimp-catching site. Lantern lights, spaced about thirty or forty paces apart, stretched from my spot a long way downstream. Now and then one boy would run to another one to check how much he had caught. Conversations with each other were conducted in loud voices, since we were some distance apart. My quiet tranquil evenings never returned again during the next few years of noisy communal shrimp catching!

Shrimp catching stopped once ice began to form along the river. The last two basins of shrimps were cooked for our own consumption. Everyone—Granny, my father, my mother, and my brother, all liked the cooked shrimps to go with their porridge.

I made sixty or seventy thousand yuan from shrimp catching. My parents were happy for me and did not have to worry about my education again until some years later. When I grew older, I found other ways and means to pay my fees as well as lend my parents a tiny amount.

The Couplet and the Letter Writer

We were taught how to write with a brush from Year Two. The practice of writing and doing our homework was always done under an oil lamp in the evenings, and was handed to the teacher the following morning.

My father judged my progress neither from experience nor from his knowledge about brush writing because he had none, but he did it from looking at how many circles the teacher made on my paper in red ink. The circled place was where the teacher confirmed the work was passable. When I entered third year, I got more red circles.

'This year we do not need to ask other people to write the couplets for us,' my father said. 'Chun-ying can do it now.' (After I entered school, my parents stopped using my baby name, Shuang Xi. They used my formal name given by Teacher Zhen.)

My father bought a very large piece of red paper, cut it into the required sizes and put them aside, waiting for another few days to let me write on them with the brush. I was a bit nervous. I knew my writing was not good enough for such a task and I could not think of any beautiful verses yet. My father did not worry.

'For the entrance door frame posts, you just write "never forget the Communist Party for the new life and never forget Chairman Mao for the happiness",' he said to me.

My great uncle, who lived alone at the end of our lane, heard that I could write couplets. He also came with red paper already cut to the required sizes.

'Grandson,' he said, 'write these for me, too.' (In Chinese there is no expression 'grand nephew', so he called me grandson.)

'But I am not able to write beautifully!' I told him.

'They must be beautiful!' he said, 'especially when they are written by our own child.'

He then said that he had been poor for so long that now he would be able to have a good life. So he asked me to write, 'Saying goodbye to the old year, Chairman Mao kicked out the poverty devil for us. Welcoming the New Year, the Communist Party brought in good fortune for us.'

The saying, 'Driving the duck onto the rooster's perch' described a situation when somebody was set the task of doing something beyond his ability. Now I became the duck. I had to do it. When our own couplets were written, my father posted them up at different places and he appreciated them. My great uncle posted his up and also appreciated them. Two more neighbours came asking me to write for them. One wanted me to write, 'We worshipped Buddha for life but we never got help. We supported the Communists and we got a good life.' And the other neighbour requested, 'Chairman Mao pulled me out of poverty. The Communist Party gave me good life.' I knew they came to me mainly because 'it is difficult to ask help from lettered people'. To them, my brush writing could be as good as the best calligraphy of the ideograms of any of the great artists.

'Grandson,' my great uncle said to me, 'after New Year, bring your quilt and come to sleep in my house. You can review your lessons without interference. And you can keep me company.'

I was reluctant to join him, for I had a big boil on my head. It had already become soft but the pus could not seep out yet. It hurt so badly that I had to grit my teeth not to moan during the night. It ached with each beat of the blood vessels. But my parents encouraged the idea, so I went to sleep in my great uncle's house. By then the boil hurt me so much I could not stand it any longer. I found a rusty nail and pricked it open. Pus gushed out. The aching was greatly relieved. But the next day, it was full of pus and again I pricked it open to release it. By and by my father recalled a man who suffered a breast ulcer which no doctor could cure. An old man told him a simple medicine: 'Look for a big poplar tree (this tree has very smooth skin and very big round leaves. The leaves clatter in the wind. In spring its flowers dangle like that of children's snot.) If its bark is cracked on the northern side and its reddish fluid has dripped on the sand below, get a lump of that sand. Buy two ounces of sesame oil and mix the sand

and oil together. Apply the mixture to the boil with a feather.' The man did this accordingly and was cured. My father made the same mixture for me to apply to my boil. It cured me within ten days. As a result, I no longer disturbed my great uncle's sleep with my groans.

Every evening, I would either practise the Chinese brush writing or copy my texts or work on the mathematics homework assigned by Teacher Zhen. My great uncle would sit on the opposite side of the table, watching. He never uttered a word until I had finished.

'Grandson,' he would say, 'study hard and get a job in the town or in the city. Don't be like us, with our backs to the sun, and our faces to the yellow sandy soil!' He dinned this into me almost every day.

One evening, as soon as I finished my homework, he carefully took a letter out from under the mattress.

'I have a letter from your uncle,' he said, 'from Korea!' With trembling hands he withdrew a piece of paper from the envelope and handed it to me:

'Your Excellency, Father:

'I have not written to you for many years, not because I did not want to write to you but because I kept on moving with the army to fight one battle after another and I was not able to write.

'Now I am writing to you from Korea. I am the battlefield assistant doctor. I married a Chinese Korean girl last year and now you have become a grandfather. You have a grandson now.

'Your daughter-in-law, your grandson and I are all very well. But I miss you very much. Please write to me as soon as possible.

Your son.'

The letter had quite a few new, unfamiliar words that I could not read fluently and the handwriting was difficult for me. I copied down the words I did not know so that I could ask Teacher Zhen the following day. Anyway, my great uncle could understand most of the letter with a dash of guessing.

He showed me a photo that had my uncle, his wife, and their newborn son in it. I had never seen this uncle before. At the age of thirteen, he had hired himself to a landlord as a shepherd to graze the sheep and when the guerrillas were passing he ran away with them. He had not been heard of since and this was his first letter home. That was why my great uncle was so excited about the letter.

'Write the answer to him for me,' he said to me, putting a piece of paper in front of me.

I was a bit nervous. What should I do if I was not able to write the words? My great uncle saw the hesitation.

'Don't worry,' he said, 'leave the word out if you don't know. Ask the teacher tomorrow.'

So we started to toil over answering the letter. It was like dictation. Whatever my great uncle said I put down in writing. It read as follows:

'My Dear Son:

'To read my letter is as good as you see me. Your sister and myself cried so many times when you disappeared from home. We hoped and hoped that someday we could see you back home. We never forgot you even for a moment.

'It is all right now that you have written to me. You will not be able to imagine how happy I am to see you, your wife, and your son from the picture. Everything seemed to be falling on me from heaven!

'Don't worry about me, now we are liberated. I was given a piece of land. My quilt and my clothing were all newly bought. Your sister is already married to a man in our village. I am healthy and I am happy. I only hope that some day in the future you will bring your wife and son back to see me.

Signed.'

When we finished, he brought out an envelope, but I did not know where to write the address of my uncle and where to write the address of my great uncle. As I had quite a few words to fill in the letter we agreed to continue the following day. I could not sleep well, worrying whether the letter would be understood by my uncle. My great uncle did not sleep well either. He was too excited to sleep.

The letter did reach my uncle and his answer came some months later. Unfortunately, his reply brought back very bad news. My uncle's beautiful wife had been killed. She was a dancer who went to the frontline in a truck to dance for the soldiers. An American bomber hit the truck and it was blown to pieces. So was his wife. My great uncle cried hysterically and I cried with him.

I was the couplet and letter writer for many years for my great uncle, for my father, and for my uncles.

chapter 5

NEW LIFE

Land had been given to the poor peasants and the Communist Party led them to make the first step towards collective farming. It promoted communal order where everyone worked together for the common good. The party sent cadres or students to villages to cultivate relations with the peasants and to assign potential leaders. Villagers were classified as either landlords (those who lived off the rents of tenants), rich peasants (those who rented out a portion of their land and worked the rest themselves), middle peasants (those who worked their own land), poor peasants (tenants and owners of small plots who also rented or worked for wages) or hired hands (those with no land who worked for wages). Farmers were encouraged to form mutual aid groups where they temporarily shared their labour, tools and animals with local peasants. Hard as it was, life changed gradually for the better. Peasants started to enjoy a bit of life—a new life.

The Mutual Aid Group

The spring of 1949 was the first time that many villagers had worked their own land. The grain, which was allotted to the poor peasants during the movement of 'distribution of moveable belongings', had already been consumed. The government sent relief aid to the villagers but that seemed like 'using a cup of water to extinguish the fire of a cartload of firewood'. Aid could only address the emergency, but it could not help banish poverty. No external forces could be relied upon to create a better life.

Like many others, my father was simultaneously happy and worried. Happy, because he now had enough land to work on; worried because he had neither a horse, a mule, an ox nor a donkey to help him plough and sow the land. It was almost impossible for my parents to sow in season their twenty-three *mu* (nearly four acres) of land with just the farm tools they owned. The vegetable garden would consume most of their time, too. Unless something was done, many peasants, including my parents, would be in great difficulty, even though they now had land of their own.

'Forming mutual aid groups and being self-reliant!' became the slogan spread by the village cadres among the villagers. The cadres said that only through a 'mutual aid group' could they all have a bumper harvest in the coming autumn. The villagers jumped at this idea and formed mutual aid groups very quickly. In times of difficulty, peasants were quick to accept good proposals. Practical and smart, the Chinese peasants knew what was good for them.

My father's mutual aid group consisted of four families: my uncle Yongjiang's family, two neighbours (who were on good terms with our family), and our family. My uncle had an ass. One neighbour had a brown mule and a donkey as well as a rubber-wheeled cart. They also had two strong labourers—the father and son. The other neighbour had a black ass and a donkey-cart but was short of a labourer. My father had no animal or cart but he was young, strong and hard working. My mother was a good farm labourer as well. My father had always worked for the second neighbour as a part-time farmhand, and was trusted for his honesty and careful work. My uncle, though not a good farmhand, had the skills to make harnesses, ropes and whips—whatever a cart needed. My father would borrow an animal from either of the neighbours, even before the mutual aid group existed. And the second neighbour would usually seek his help, anyway. So it was natural that our four families form one mutual aid group.

More mutual aid groups sprang up in the village, almost at the same time, like 'spring bamboo shoots after a drizzling rain'. The pattern was usually a mixture of families with or without animals, and families with or without strong labourers. Not many were left out of the mutual aid groups unless a family was lazy or hard to co-operate with.

Ploughing and sowing followed a hierarchy, without argument, according to the combined strength of the labour, animals and farm tools of a family, if all the families grew the same crop. Thus, in our group the family with two strong labourers, a mule, a donkey, a cart, and complete farm tools had the first priority. My uncle's family, because of his special skills, enjoyed the second priority. The other family, which had a donkey and a cart, became the third in the sequence. Our family was the last in the group to have our fields sowed. Sometimes this pattern might not be followed. Sowing would be done according to the requirements of what a family grew. So, occasionally the last might be the first to have the land sown. Otherwise, the sequence would remain unchanged. My father never wanted free help. He would always try hard to make up for owning no animals or tools by helping them to weed and to care for their plants. That was why the neighbours always welcomed him.

When spring sowing started, all hands of the group were required, especially during and after any rain. 'The spring rain is as valuable as oil,' so rain could not be wasted. The more land sowed during and immediately after rain, the better the harvest would be. My help was needed as well. In the country, two weeks of spring holidays were given to students so that they could help their parents with the spring sowing.

Spring sowing was hard work. Two ploughs, one ahead and one in wake, would furrow the field, very much similar to a ship cleaving the sea. One labourer, with a round basket full of seed, would throw the same number of seed into the furrow at similar intervals. This labourer had to have his steps well controlled—each step had to cover the same distance, to guarantee seed the same distance from each other in the groove. This demanded great skill. Another labourer would seed the other groove. Women would spread manure into the grooves. They would hold big bins with both hands jerking the bin so the manure would always come to the same corner and flow into the groove steadily. Manure heaps were spaced so that when one bin was empty, the other manure heap would be just at hand. It was bad work if a person jerked and spread manure outside the groove. My job was to cover up the grooves and press down the soil. I used a device, which consisted of one wooden frame with a piece of brick fixed to it to give it some weight, and another wooden frame fixed with a stone roller. These two frames were secured to the end of two parallel ropes—the one with the brick was ahead of the one with the stone roller (we called it the small stone roller). The other ends of the ropes were connected to sticks, the top ends of which were connected with strips of leather. The sticks would be secured to a donkey's neck ahead of a leather collar. I would take the rein to lead the donkey. The donkey walked in the groove pulling the two devices along with it. The one with the brick swept soil into the groove and the roller pressed down the soil. The difficulty was at the end of the groove. While turning the donkey into another groove, I had to pull the devices to make sure they went into the groove without leaving the very end uncovered.

To keep up with the sowing season, there were no breaks between breakfast and lunch, nor between lunch and supper. Nobody complained no matter how tired he or she was, because everyone was working not only for himself, but for the group. Tiredness in spring meant more harvest in autumn. There was no need for anybody to be a leader. Whoever's land was being sowed, the master of that family would make the decisions. All the others were helpers or assistants. Everybody knew his or her own role. Co-operation was smooth and efficient. There was one aim in all hearts, to have everyone's land sowed as quickly as possible.

In difficult times, the selfish side of the peasants ebbed, or even disappeared. They helped each other without reserve. When life became better, their selfishness grew and the help dried up. Strange, but I have watched this happen.

The mutual aid group also co-operated in harvesting. Wheat, in particular, had to be harvested by all members of the mutual aid group collectively in order to get it dried out while the weather remained sunny. During harvest time, rain might come any day and at any time. If the wheat got caught by the rain, it could get mouldy. Our land was not suitable for wheat growing, yet my father would always be present to help if any of the members of the mutual aid group had wheat to harvest.

The harvesting of peanuts was not collective, but the two carts were used to transport the harvested peanuts for every family of the group. Three families could finish the peanut harvest early and almost at the same time. Only one family, which had an ass but no strong labourer, would lag behind. My parents were the first to help. Then the other families would join in as quickly as possible. Sweet potato harvest was done collectively, too.

There was no need to have meetings with the group members. In the evenings, the males of the group liked to take the fresh air together. They seemed to be isolated from the rest of the country and yet they seemed to know what was happening everywhere in China. They talked about the stories of different dynasties, about the wars between the Kuomintang and the Communists, and about the war in Korea. If any family needed help with any work, they mentioned it then.

The mutual aid groups were vital for the peasants. The groups won the new government credit. Without it, land reform would not have had such quick and positive results. With it, the countryside economy recovered fast; without it, the peasants might not have admitted the greatness of the Communist Party. Mutual aid groups made the Communist Party invincible and they made it possible to set up junior co-ops in 1953—for the peasants had seen the advantage of limited collective farming.

Make Our Alkaline Land Grow

My father had his nine *mu* of alkaline land on his mind all the time. He could not afford to let the land be wasted. From snatches of discussions he had with my mother, I knew he was racking his brain to solve the problem.

'As long as the seeds can germinate and grow out, the alkaline land can produce,' was what he thought, said, and believed. He told this to my mother.

'Look,' he said, 'the seeds can germinate but they cannot break the hard layer of alkaline earth. Some may break the layer and come out, but the rain would carry alkali into the grooves and make the layer harder, thus the seedlings are killed. If we make the seeds germinate and grow without hindrance from the hard layer, they will be strong enough when the rain comes.'

'But how can we do it?'

'We shall use sand instead of manure and we shall not cover the grooves with the roller.' My mother could not argue because she had not his experience.

That winter, whether it was fine or windy, when my father had nothing else of more importance to do, he carried sand into our field with our water buckets. On Saturday afternoons and on Sundays I went with him to carry sand with a basin. We could not take sand from any field, we could only take it from the road. Anyway, sand was plentiful on the road and the supply was not short. It was backbreaking work. When it was fine, sweat trickled along the spine inside my padded coat. It got cold and uncomfortable when we had a break. When it was windy, sand would blow up and whip the face like a knife cutting and it was hard to keep one's eyes open. Sometimes it was so cold that my hands cracked and bled. The sores hurt badly. In the evening my father would burn some black putty, like asphalt, on the lamp and drip it onto my sores to stick the flesh and skin together. It hurt terribly but it would stop the pain quickly. The next time, there would be more sores and more black putty sticking. We never stopped the work unless it snowed.

My father spaced the sand in small dunes as people did with manure. He would rig up a small screen with millet stalks on the north side of each sand dune to prevent sand being carried away by the wind. The screen would also help to accumulate the sand carried by the wind, thus lending us some assistance.

'Sowing without manure, one muddles along all year round without getting any harvest!' some people said when they saw my father and I carrying sand.

'Li Yong-mao is doing silly things again!'

'Li Yong-mao is the cleverest. When he asked for the alkaline land, he already knew he needed no manure in his field.'

Villagers seeing us carry sand thought we were wasting our energy and time. Sarcastically, they would make comments about my father. 'If sand can replace manure, why do we bother to have more and more manure accumulated?' My father never replied. He just smiled and continued working. He was adamant in his determination. Such jokes reached my mother's ears and she became doubtful, but my father would not budge. He pressed on with his work, believing it was the way to deal with alkaline land.

Spring sowing came. The mutual aid group found it easier to sow our millet. Sand was easier to spread into the grooves. Two donkeys and two children did not have to work due to the fact that the grooves didn't need to be covered. It rained shortly after the nine *mu* millet was sowed. The rain came as if Buddha was rewarding my father's effort in carrying sand for the whole winter. A few days later, my father went to the field and was overjoyed. All the seeds had germinated and shot out of the soil.

'It worked!' he said to my mother.

My mother looked at him without understanding.

'Our millet germinated!'

My mother was very happy. Carrying sand throughout the whole winter had not been a waste of time and energy! That autumn a good harvest was the reward my father received, and needless to say, more sand carrying would be done the following winter.

The harvesting was done with a hand knife. The knife was as long as the width of the palm and the edge was very sharp. It had laces at its back for the harvester to put the right hand through. I had learned how to use it. I would hold the stalk under the millet ear, with the stalk between my palm and the edge of the knife. A tiny jerking movement would have the ear off the plant. The job was light at the start but became harder and harder when I worked without rest.

The following year, sorghum with ears of black husk and white kernels was sowed. The seed germinated well but over half of the plants died. My mother was downhearted. She cursed the alkali. My father was not so pessimistic. He said to my mother, 'If it does not rain continuously in June, we shall have big worry!'

At first I did not understand why he talked about rain in June. But when the non-stop rain did come and when he asked me to get a few days leave from the teacher, I began to understand. He sharpened two sticks, each about an inch thick. He pushed one corner of a gunnybag into the other corner to make a hood and put it on my head. Then he made another for his own head. Sticks in hand, he led me into the rain.

About one-third of our nine *mu* of alkaline land grew well. The sorghum plants were already knee high. The leaves were a lavish dark green. He pulled out some plants and gave them to me.

'Make a hole with the stick, put a plant into the hole, but don't cover it up.' He demonstrated how to do it. 'Go and plant quickly! We must have the land planted before the sun comes up.'

I hastened away to do the planting as quickly as I could. My father was spreading the plants at regular intervals as the southern Chinese did to their rice seedlings. Rain had soaked through the gunnybag. Sweat and rain mingled, trickling down my face. The mixture tasted a bit salty. My back ached but I had no time to straighten up. I had to help him finish the planting as fast as we could manage so that I could return to school as quickly as possible.

My mother brought us lunch. Though we chewed and swallowed quickly, the corn *bing tzi* became soggy before we could finish. 'Does your back hurt?' she asked me. I nodded. Then my father told us a story:

'A father and son were harvesting millet in the field. The son straightened up and exclaimed, "Oh, how my back aches!"

The father snapped, "A child has no back!"

"But what should I call it?" the son asked.

"The middle."

When they set off home, the father asked, "Where is your sickle?"

"In the middle." the son answered.

His father went back to the field. After a long while, he caught up with the son, his face was ominously cloudy.

"Where did you put your sickle?" he hissed.

"In the middle."

"I fumbled all the stalks in the middle of the field but could not find it."

"In the middle here," the boy showed the sickle inserted between his belt and trousers waist.

"That is the back! Why did you tell me 'in the middle'?"

"A child has no back. You told me that it is called the middle.'"

My mother and I laughed. To adults, a child's back would not ache after working for a long time. If a child said his back was aching, his father would think the boy was asking for a break. As we had to finish planting the sorghum that day, and my father could not afford to give me a break, he told us the story, because he knew I was sensitive and could understand his real meaning. He successfully stopped me complaining about my aching back.

We three continued to plant the sorghum in the rain. It drizzled one moment and it poured down the next. The gunnybag was almost too heavy for me. I wanted to take it off but without it the rain was colder. My hands were an unhealthy white from being wet for so long. My teeth chattered and my back ached, but I could not slow down. In case we did not finish that day, I had to be absent from school the following day. I never liked to stay away from school.

My mother went back home a bit earlier to cook supper. My father and I finished the planting at dusk.

It rained for three more days before it finally stopped. All the sorghum we had planted was happily alive and already growing! That year the harvest of sorghum was very good. Sorghum became our only victual. Sorghum porridge, sorghum *bing tzi*, and steamed sorghum were the various dishes my mother tried to make so the sorghum would be attractive to eat. Although I was fed up with sorghum after that, I never regretted having planted it with my father on that rainy day. My father could make the 'waste land' productive, a fact I have admired to this very day.

While sand fetching was a backbreaking job, sorghum planting depended too much on the weather. So on the third year my father wanted to grow something different. He noticed that a kind of weed called tares or darnel grew well in rice fields and in alkaline fields. He decided to grow that.

Tares or darnel grew like 'mad', which was our term to describe the excellent growth. Neighbours were surprised to see that my father had grown 'weeds'. 'Why do you grow weeds?' they would ask. Because my father had already made two good harvests in the 'waste land', villagers stopped jeering at him, but curiosity remained. They were interested to know what he was doing.

'Selling it as pig's fodder.'

After harvest that year, he did sell the 'weeds' as pig's fodder, and the stalks as horse, mule or donkey fodder. He bought corn and a pig with the proceeds. As long as a person used his brain, he or she could make any land produce a good harvest.

Having had a couple of years of good harvests, the peasants turned their mind to the Spring Festival of 1951.

The Spring Festival of 1951

Spring Festivals came and went but never left any impression upon me—not until the Spring Festival of 1951, when, for the first time in my childhood, my parents discussed how to celebrate a good festival (the Spring Festival lasted for fifteen days from 1 to 15 January). In the other room my uncle Yong-jiang and Da Ma were also discussing how to celebrate a good Spring Festival. My parents discussed, rediscussed, adapted to the circumstances, and finally came to a happy mutual decision on how to celebrate the festival.

Life had changed for the better for the villagers since 1948. They were in the mood to celebrate the Spring Festival now. Every family was preparing for it. As Lunar December approached, my father went to town to sell several gunnybags of peanuts and brought back wheat, white corn, sticky millet, brown sugar, pork—all sorts of things for the coming Spring Festival—and many of which I saw for the first time. He bought red paper for the festival couplets and, to the surprise of everybody in the family, he bought a very big picture of Mao. Mao had on his head a cap with eight corners. His face looked very kind.

'Why did you buy this?' my mother asked in surprise.

'Do you know who he is?' he asked.

'No,' my mother shook her head.

'This is Mao Zedong!' he said proudly. 'Our land and our good life, all were given by him!'

'Are you sure he is Mao?' my mother asked.

'Yes, I am sure!' he said. 'We worshipped Buddha all our life and Buddha did not do anything to help us. Mao came and he gave us land. From now on, we must worship Mao.'

My Da Ma came into our room to look at Mao when she heard my parents talking about him.

'Yes,' she said. 'We are better off worshipping him than any deity!' She told my uncle Yong-jiang to buy one for their room. I did not know how it happened but I heard that many neighbours bought a big picture of Mao of their own free will as well.

My mother was pleased with what my father had brought back, which was not abundant but enough for a good Spring Festival.

The wives of all the neighbours queued to wait for the grindstone or millstone to grind their wheat, white corn, and millet to make the flour used during the Spring Festival. The 'grindstone' was a device which had a very big round marble slab supported by bricks underneath. A vertical post was secured into the hole at the very centre of the slab. A solid timber square frame was secured to the middle post, which served as an axle. In the frame was a big marble roller with a diameter of about seventy to eighty centimetres. A hole was on the outer end of the frame for putting in a wooden bar. People pushed the bar to make the roller roll, or an animal could be harnessed to it. The millstone was a device that had a big platform made from either wood, brick or stone. In the centre of the platform was a big flat stone. It had grooves on its top surface and an iron stud was in its centre to serve as an axle for a similar slab on top. The lower slab was fixed firmly to the platform, which was not moveable. The top slab had two holes called the 'eyes'—these were the grain feed holes. Pulled by animals or pushed by human beings, grain would be crushed into flour in between the slabs. There were about five or six such devices amongst our neighbours. It was hard to find any of them idle during the day. My mother had to watch for periods when they weren't being used. She would have her wheat and millet crushed into flour during these breaks.

It was customary in our village, as well as in our area, that from 1 January to the last day of the month, that no knife or scissors be touched, let alone used. Women who used them would become a widow. Mothers-in-law, even the most vicious mother-in-law, would not like her daughter-in-law becoming a widow and so forbade her from using a knife or scissors during that month. During that month, women could have an easier time. (This custom died when the People's Commune was established.)

Food had to be cooked in Lunar December. We had no refrigerator to store the food already cooked but we had the open air. My father wove a very large storage basket, its height reached his breast and it was larger than my parents could hold with their arms spread out and fingers linked. It was placed on top of the roof—our half of the roof. The other half also had a big basket—my uncle Yong-jiang's storage basket. Almost every family stored their food on their rooftop, but I never heard of any family losing any food. There seemed to be no thieves in the countryside at the time.

When Lunar December arrived, my mother started cooking two varieties of *man tou* (steamed bread-like buns). One was made from pure wheat flour and the other was a mixture of wheat and white corn flour. *Man tou* made from mixed flours cracked, while pure wheat flour *man tou* was smooth and without cracks. She also cooked wheat flour twisters and sugar triangles, which I had never seen before. Sticky millet cakes were also steamed. They would be eaten like 'the donkey rolling over its back', a food I had never heard of. My mother grilled a full bin of soybeans, ground them into flour, and then added brown sugar to the flour. When eating, one yanked a mouthful of sticky cake with chopsticks, turned it over in the sugar-flour mixture until it was fully covered, like a donkey does when rolling on its back on the ground, and put that into the mouth to eat. Thus it was called 'donkey rolling over its back'. It was sweet and fragrant.

Bing tzi, *wo tou*, and sweet potatoes were also cooked. *Wo tou* was a pyramid-shaped corn bread steamed in the cauldron. Because it was made with one thumb in the middle to make a hole but with all nine fingers outside to shape it, it was also nicknamed 'one middle nine outside'. When eating good things for days in succession, one wanted to have *bing tzi* and *wo tou* and sweet potatoes as variety and as appetite sharpeners. But in the latter half of the month, the main effort was to make dumplings. Dumplings were a popular food in northern China for the Spring Festival. The Chinese name for dumpling is *jiao zi*. *Jiao* means the junction and *zi* means the start of a day. *Jiao zi* actually means the change of the last minute of the old year into the first minute of the New Year. Dumplings, either as far as the dough or filling was concerned, had two varieties. The two kinds of dough were white and red—the white dough was made from pure wheat flour, while the red dough was a mixture of wheat flour, corn flour and elm root skin powder. The two kinds of fillings were a mixture of meat and vegetables, or just pure vegetables.

Dumplings were placed on round flat trays, which were made from the reedy, smooth part of the sorghum stalk under the ear. Granny was very skilful at making them. She stitched two layers of them together and then would fix one stalk with a pin to the middle and cut the ends off with this stalk as a measuring stick, just like drawing circles with a compass. Different sizes of such trays were made. The largest one was used as a cover for the cauldron. The slightly smaller one was used as a cover for the water vat. Smaller ones were used as covers for jars and as trays for food. Such trays, when filled up with dumplings, would be stacked into the storage basket.

Dumpling making was the work of the whole family. My mother would knead the dough and cut it into tiny lumps. I would roll them thin and round with a rolling pin. My father and Granny would put fillings in and wrap them up. Fillings were usually mixed and blended by my father. He always said he made the best fillings. While making the dumplings, he or Granny would tell a story.

'Once upon a time,' Granny would say, 'a daughter-in-law was cooking dumplings for the first breakfast of the New Year. She scooped the cooked dumplings from the cauldron into basins and other containers. All the basins, bowls, plates and dishes were filled up with cooked dumplings. But there were still plenty in the cauldron. "I had not cooked that much," she reasoned with herself in her mind, "so why are there so many dumplings? What is happening?" Just then her mother-in-law scalded, "Why did you cook so much?" "I did not cook so much," she replied. As she said this, the dumplings in the cauldron disappeared.'

'What happened next?' I asked.

'Nothing!' my Granny said. 'But you must remember, during the first breakfast on New Year's Day, don't say anything or make any comments.'

My father was a pious son. The stories he told were always about a daughter-in-law being bad to the mother-in-law and later, through some lesson, becoming good towards the mother-in-law.

'Once upon a time,' he would say, 'a daughter-in-law served her mother-in-law's food in their night soil basin. The mother-in-law dared not complain, because if she did, she would receive still worse treatment. She could only weep in secrecy.

"Grandma," her grandson's wife said to her, "stop crying. I will do something for you."

That day her grandson's wife was instructed to take food to her in the night soil basin. She smashed the basin to pieces in the yard. She began crying loudly.

"Don't howl like that," her mother-in-law said. "It is not worth much. We can use another one."

"I am not worrying about the basin," she sobbed. "I am crying because I am wondering what I will use to feed you when you get old."

The mother-in-law was afraid. She realised that her own daughter-in-law was learning from her. To avoid the same fate, she had to be good towards her own mother-in-law.'

I saw my father wrapping a copper coin, which had a square hole in the middle, into a dumpling, and I asked why.

'This is the lucky coin,' he explained. 'Whoever gets it at the first bite when having the first breakfast of the New Year has the best luck. He should just put it in his pocket and make no comment or mention of it, and the good luck will stay with him. I will make sure that this stack of dumplings is cooked first.'

'What if nobody gets it at first bite?'

'If someone gets it later he still has good luck, but not as great as at first bite.'

Lunar 23 December was the day to send the kitchen god to heaven. The kitchen god was a picture printed on paper. My mother offered sticky sugar balls to the kitchen god as a sacrifice, and burned incense. My Da Ma did the same to their kitchen god. The sticky sugar balls were offered to the kitchen god so that his lips were stuck together and could not report anything bad about the family he protected. Then a new picture of the kitchen god was glued in place, which was on the wall about half a metre or so from the front window and always behind the door. It was a metre or so above the cooking range. Then couplets would be glued to both sides of the picture. On the right was 'Ask favour for us in Heaven'. On the left was 'Protect us back on Earth'. Horizontally was 'Safe and sound every year'.

It was said that the kitchen god decided the happiness or misfortune of a family. Probably that was why peasants always asked the kitchen god for help when they had troubles or when they wished to know something in advance. That also explained why both families agreed to remove the figure of Guan-gong (the common deity worshipped by our two families) on the last day of the year but kept the kitchen god. To them the kitchen god was a god to protect each individual family. If they had the cooking range, they had to have the kitchen god. The kitchen god was something like a member of the family. When the printed kitchen god was no longer available (when the thinking of the peasants became more and more revolutionised, printers stopped printing them completely to avoid trouble), couplets were still put into the place where the kitchen god had been.

On Lunar 24 December, which was called the 'house sweeping day', my mother, with my help, moved everything from the room into the yard—pots holding flour, quilts and so on. She would occupy half the yard and my Da Ma would occupy the other half. My mother then tied a towel to her head as a working cap to prevent dust falling on her hair. She bound a broom to the end of a long pole and started to sweep the ceilings and the walls. Spider webs and dust were all removed with the broom. Dust filled the room like the dust stirred by the howling wintry wind. I had to sprinkle the room with water to settle the dust, but it would take some time before it finally settled down. Then the chests, the benches, the table and other utensils would be mopped clean. Old window papers would be torn off the window stiffeners and frames. New white paper which was strong, tough, and slightly elastic, was glued onto the stiffeners and frames. Then both my mother and Da Ma began preparing flower sticks, which were used like candles from New Year's Eve to Lunar 15 January. They would cut either dried reeds or sorghum stalks into pieces about a foot-and-a-half long. They then cut the white window paper into strips about an inch wide, which we called 'fine teeth' which were glued onto sticks. I would help my mother to glue the toothed paper onto the sticks to make them look flowery. My mother would bundle them up and put them aside, ready for use.

The last day of Lunar December was a very busy day. My mother and Granny cut quite a few patterns, which in Chinese is called 'window flowers', such as 'silver carp jumping through the dragon gate', 'a rooster ushering in the morning', the character for 'double happiness', 'bumper harvest', 'a boy kindling a fire cracker', and so on. This was a custom in northern China. Each family would buy large pieces of red paper for cutting patterns to glue on the windows as decoration. Peasant women were very skilful in cutting such patterns; some could make very complicated ones such as 'the eight deities crossing the sea', 'the Monkey king', and so on. My mother glued them to their proper positions on the windows—red paper patterns on a white paper background, which looked very beautiful. Together my parents glued the couplets to the door frame posts. The right-hand side read 'Never forget the Communist Party for a better life' while the left-hand side read 'Never forget Chairman Mao for happiness'. Horizontally on the door lintel was 'Think of the fountain when drinking water'. On the window stiffeners was 'The lucky star shines high'. On the ladder was 'Each step gets higher', meaning life becomes better each day. The inside walls had 'Seeing happiness when raising the head'. On the bedroom door frame was 'Entering the New Year, life is beautiful and sweet. Remember forever to think about the fountain when drinking water.' The word *fu* (meaning fortune, happiness and luck) was posted on walls, jars, vats, doors, and so on. All were glued upside down, which means '*fu* arrived.' (The pronunciation of 'upside down' and 'arrival' is the same.)

'Where do we put up the picture of Mao?' my mother asked.

'In the bedroom, on the wall facing the window,' my father replied. 'It is convenient for us to worship him and we can see him as we open our eyes every morning.'

'Good idea!' my Da Ma said. 'We shall put ours also in our bedroom, in the middle of the wall.'

'What about Guan-gong and the shrine in the common room?'

'Simple, just remove them!' my Da Ma said. And so the shrine and Guan-gong, the common deity of the two families, were removed.

Ceremoniously and piously, my parents glued the picture of Mao to the middle of our bedroom wall, facing the window. After the picture was in position, they knelt down and kowtowed, murmuring something to show their thanks.

The Chinese always had to worship something. Now that they willingly removed Guan-gong from their common room as the common deity, they began worshipping Mao. They put up Mao in their respective bedrooms, I guess, in order to seek a special favour from him. If they had nothing to worship they would feel empty at heart!

'The deity figures, the candleholders, and the bell, all are mine,' Granny declared, and she collected and stored them away. Later, she sold the copper figure of Guan-gong, together with the tin candleholders and the bell, for a small sum of money to buy herself snacks.

In places outside the house that were frequented by the family members 'Tai-gong is here, all other deities must retire' was posted. This was to order any deity or ghost or devil to avoid the place. Sesame stalks were spread all over the yard. They cracked loudly under your feet. The cracking noise was a warning to Tai-gong to move out of the way. Tai-gong was a Chinese deity who was a character in the novel *The Name List of Canonised Deities*. He was the favourite student of the God of Dao, who gave him a name list and authorised him to deify every person on it. Tai-gong carried out the order, but he reserved a good position for himself, just as the present day officials or cadres did for themselves. When the last person was deified, he was ready to go to his reserved position. But Tai-gong omitted one from the list. Just as he closed the list to go to his own position, one more person came running to him. He had no other position to offer and so gave the position he had reserved for himself to this last comer. As Tai-gong himself had nowhere to go, he declared that wherever he went, that deity would step down to offer the position to him. However, on the last day of the year, all deities would remain on their posts receiving incense and sacrifices and prayers from human beings. Nobody would make room for Tai-gong. He would wander aimlessly. Anybody who came across him would have bad fortune. So the sesame stalks were spread to warn Tai-gong not be there when people passed. And when going anywhere that had no sesame stalks, people would cough first before actually walking there. (The authentic religion in China was Daoism—meaning 'the way'. Dao is the underlying essence of the universe, which can neither be described in words nor conceived in thought. The goal of Daoism is to bring all elements of existence—Heaven, Earth, and Human—into harmony. To be in accordance with the Dao, the individual must empty him or herself of doctrines and knowledge, act with simplicity and humility, and above all seek Nature.)

On the door lintel, on the windows, on the horizontal bar that my father rigged up at the entrance of the yard, my parents glued colourful patterns of paper cuttings, which were bought from town. Door deities were glued to the doors. It was said that during the Tang Dynasty (618–907), the Emperor Tai-zong (enthroned 626–649) was sick. He was haunted by the ghosts of his brothers and by the rebels who were eliminated by him. He could not sleep and he suffered greatly. Two of his generals, Yu-chi Jing-de and Qin Shu-bao volunteered to guard his doors for him. The ghosts were afraid of the two of them and did not come to bother the emperor. The emperor was grateful and ordered the pictures of the two generals to be painted and glued to the doors instead. That was sufficient to prevent any ghosts coming to him again. Since then the pictures of these two generals had been copied and glued to the doors by the ordinary people as door deities to protect them. In later years when printers no longer produced the door deities, the peasants just glued the single Chinese character '*fu*' (meaning fortune) to the doors. Sometimes they simply put on the entrance doors 'long live Chairman Mao' and 'long live the Communist Party'. There had to be something on the entrance door, at least for decoration—or maybe the peasants thought Mao and the Communist Party more powerful than the door deities.

In the streets, arches woven from pine branches were erected. Rope lines were stretched from fence to fence across the street. Each line had two loopholes spaced at equal distance from each other and from the fences. The distance between two such lines was about twenty paces. Glass-enclosed lanterns would be hooked to the loopholes of the lines. When it was dark, two villagers, each carrying a very big gong, would announce the kindling of the flower sticks and the street lanterns by beating the gongs and shouting loudly 'time to light the lanterns', and 'time to light the flower sticks'. The gong was very big and it was carried with the help of a wooden T-bar. The T-end of the bar was propped against the tummy and the other end, with the hanging gong, was lifted by the left hand. The free right hand would strike at the hanging gong with a very big stick, which had a big rag knot at the end.

My parents and I would dip the flower sticks in oil, and plant them in a line from the window beside the door along the lane to the street. They were inserted in the step crevice and in the sand along the lane. When lit, it was like a very long and gigantic dragon of flower stick lights, jerking, swaying and rolling, as if the dragon were alive. The flower sticks and street lanterns were like stars, twinkling and winking. This was the first time in my childhood that I had seen such a sight.

Clad in a new padded blue jacket, which my mother had sewn for me for the Spring Festival, and which was the first new jacket I had ever had,

I joined my former playmates, who were also my present schoolmates. We wandered along the street to the opera stage. The stage was rigged up in a very big yard enclosed by high walls. It was the yard of the village council office, which was the former residence of a landlord. The stage had reed mat walls and a reed mat roof. It was partitioned into front and back stages also by reed mats. Two embroidered curtains hung over the entrances on each side of the stage partition for actors to come on and off the front stage. Two lanterns were hung on the right and left front corner posts. Now and then, the stagehand had to pump air into the lanterns to increase the intensity of the light. Our village opera team, martial arts team, and opera teams from neighbouring villages would perform during the Spring Festival. Our villagers and also those from neighbouring villages would come to enjoy the performance every evening.

New Year's Eve was entirely and solely for family members to sit together. It was called the night for family unity. My father would tell us stories; although he had no schooling, he had a good memory. If he had listened to a story once, long or short, he would be able to repeat it almost word for word afterwards. Granny also told us stories but hers were always the same old ones she had told many times before. One of my aunts, who lived with her husband not far from our house and who had no children, would come to join us and would not leave until the firecrackers announced the first breakfast of the New Year. She enjoyed the warm atmosphere of our family and she enjoyed, in particular, the presence of my brother and myself.

Before the evening deepened, some boys called to me from the lane. Placing some cooked peanuts and melon seeds in my pockets, I ran off to join them. My mother's words 'come back early' trailed behind. We played cards and before I realised, I had eaten all my peanuts. I suffered greatly afterwards and since then I have never been able to eat peanuts. Others also overate, which was a mistake called 'too much happiness brings sadness'.

I went back home about midnight. It was custom that nobody should sleep. It was called 'seeing the old year out and welcoming the New Year in'. When I was too sleepy, my mother allowed me to lie on the *kang*, but not in the usual position and without the quilt. I just lay there with all my clothes on. But I did not ask why I had to lie that way. When my mother woke me in the small hours I could hardly open my eyes. 'Go and light the firecrackers, it is time for breakfast!' she said to me. That was enough to expel my sleepiness immediately. I ran into the yard, tied a string of firecrackers to a pole and asked, 'Can I light the firecrackers now, Ma?'

'Yes, do it now,' she replied, scooping dumplings out of the cauldron into a pottery basin.

Xiao Bao was a busybody running around to help me. A symphony of firecracker explosions had already reached its climax. Ours joined in immediately. Xiao Bao jumped and clapped his hands and sang 'bang, bang!'

'Dumplings ready!' my mother called to us.

The first breakfast on the first day of the New Year had to be vegetarian. Why, my father did not tell me. It was followed generation after generation. Perhaps nobody had ever questioned the custom.

We went in but we had to kowtow before we could sit on the *kang* to eat. I knelt down on the floor and said, 'Granny, I am paying the New Year homage to you,' and kowtowed to her. Then I repeated this to my parents. All the time Xiao Bao mimicked me behind my back. (As I grew older, I was reluctant to kowtow, but my parents insisted that I did it to pay respect to the elders. I dared not openly resist their orders, so I resorted to tricks. I would stand in front of my Granny, continuously picking my ears. 'Kowtow and come onto the *kang* to have some dumplings,' my father would urge. But I pretended that I did not hear, picking my ears all the time. This resulted in my parents calling me 'the little deaf one'. 'Come onto the *kang* and eat,' Granny called. She never worried whether I kowtowed or not. Once she gave the word, my father would not insist. He was a pious son and he never once disobeyed my Granny.)

We were seated around the table on the *kang*. (In winter we placed the meal-table on the *kang* for our three meals.) Wheat flour vegetarian dumplings tasted great but, because I had eaten too many peanuts, I was not able to enjoy the dumplings. I ate just a little bit and the coin of good luck did not come to me. Nobody spoke about the coin. The secret was well kept by the one who had it.

After sunrise, I paid homage to my uncle Yong-jiang, my Da Ma, and my elder cousins. My brother Xiao Bao again kowtowed behind me. Then we started to do it to the other Li families. By then we had a bigger group, my two elder cousins, Quan and An, and my young cousin Xiang from the other room, Xiao Bao and myself. We five walked together to my uncle Song-lin's place in front of our house. Thereafter, two cousins, Chung and Shan, from that uncle's family joined us to go elsewhere. By the time we finished paying homage to all the Li families, our group was fairly big. Then we regrouped to play. When paying homage to the elders, we sometimes got a bit of money as New Year luck money to line our pockets.

The opera started after dusk. The two lanterns made the yard as brightly lit as broad daylight. On the stage, musicians were tuning the flute, the Chinese violin (*er hu*), and so on. On the back stage, actors were applying their make-up. Along the walls of the yard, peddlers displayed their goods on tables, on pushcarts, or in baskets. Apples, water chestnuts, sugar cane, candies, cooked ox offal, grilled peanuts, cooked sweet potatoes, persimmons, firecrackers, and plenty of small toys, were all well arranged to attract the opera audience. One toy called *bu-bu deng* was particularly attractive to children because it was only two hundred yuan (two cents) each. It was made of very thin glass and had a long stem where children blew air into it and its bottom vibrated, making the sound *bu-deng, bu-deng*. It was very fragile and very few children could make it last more than one hour. People from neighbouring villages, men and women, old and young, were already streaming into the yard. The opera was about to begin.

I could not just sit and enjoy myself in the yard where the opera was performed. I had to earn my school fee during this period. My father bought four hundred pieces of Manchurian candy for me to sell. He bought them at fifty yuan (half a present-day cent) a piece and I would sell them at one hundred yuan a piece. The candy was as thick, long and white as chalk. It became soft and sticky in the mouth. I had to dust icing on them to keep its original snow-white colour. I carried it in a basket of one hundred pieces at a time. I would go to the opera early so that I could sell all of the candy before the opera began.

I hawked to women with children. 'Manchurian candy, tasty and sweet! One hundred yuan for one piece.' This white candy was bigger than any other candy and would last longer. It was not too much, or extravagant for a woman to spend one hundred yuan for a piece of candy to please a child. The first basket of a hundred pieces was sold the first night. I still had time to watch the second half of the opera. I was happy. But the happiness was hard-earned. I was a child myself and I liked candy very much, but I could not eat them, for I needed the money for school. My mouth would water when I watched a child suck at the candy I sold. It was not easy to suppress a childish wish to taste something good. The second day my father went to town to get more stock for me.

Within three or four nights, two boys from our neighbours also began selling the Manchurian candies. Competition arose, not by cutting the price but by the pitch of the voice when hawking. But I adhered to my old policy, that was, to hawk near and around women with children. We three boys would now and then come across each other and compare our results. The quantity I sold was not much affected. By Lunar 15 January I had sold sixteen hundred pieces or in other words I had made a profit of eighty thousand yuan (eight new yuan). I no longer had any problems that year as far as school fees, buying books, notebooks, pencils, and any other things for the new term were concerned. This money would also provide my mother with oil, vinegar, salt, thread and needles.

On Lunar 15 January, the daytime celebration, which the villagers called 'to tread the street', took place. Three teams took part: the martial arts team from our village, the stilt team from the neighbouring village to our south-west, and the cymbal team from the neighbouring village to our east. Every team had its own musicians to accompany them. All team members had special costumes. The martial arts team were dressed like ancient warriors such as Wu Song (a character from the famous Chinese novel *Shui Hu Zhuan*), Emperor Zhao Kuang-yin (960–976) the first emperor of the Song Dynasty (960–1279), and other historical warriors. The stilt team was dressed in beautiful costumes to act like the fisherman, the foolish boy, the girl who raised silkworms, and other characters from *Shui Hu Zhuan*. The cymbal team all dressed in the same style—red head turban, blue jacket with black hems, wide sash at the waist whose tassel ends draped to the top of the feet, black trousers, and boots with double seams at the toe.

In the big front yards bordering the main street, each owner positioned a square table and a few benches. On top of the tables were cooked peanuts, cooked watermelon seeds, candy, a pot of tea and tea cups. This was the invitation for the teams to perform in the yard. When the first team left a yard, the second immediately arrived. And when the second left, the third would arrive. The teams attracted big crowds, mostly children and young men. The team and the crowd were too big for the street to contain and fences on both sides were pushed flat on the ground and crushed by the passing feet, hence people called the celebration 'to tread the street'.

There was a big yard bordering the end of our lane. One table, four benches, melon seeds, and candy were all presented in the yard, ready to receive the teams.

'Don't follow the teams, you might get hurt,' my father warned me. So I got an advantageous position to wait for the performers to come. Very soon, children poured into the yard, a sure sign that the teams were coming.

The first to appear were the musicians for the martial arts performers. Two strong young men carried a gigantic drum hanging from a thick round timber pole. A man dressed like a martial arts man beat the drum with two long tasselled drumsticks. Sometimes he beat the leather surface of the drum to make it boom and sometimes he beat the drum rim to make different noises. Flanking the drummer and the drum carriers were the musicians. Those musicians played instruments of various kinds: flutes, trumpets and very large cymbals. All the instruments were tuned according to the variations of the drum sound. Sometimes the music made you feel very excited, and then the music changed and made you feel tranquil and peaceful. Immediately after came Wu Song staging a combat with several fighters clad in black jackets. The wide, long, tasselled sashes round their waists dangled and swayed. After him was the sham fighting of a man with a spear versus a man with a sword mounted on a long handle. The spear was aimed at the throat and the sword was aimed at the nape of the neck. But they always missed the targets by just a hair width. My heart thumped violently, fearing that they might hurt each other from the slightest mistake. Then there was the performance of the rope spear. It swung around the performer's neck, entangled with his elbow and leg, darted away from him stretching the rope tight like a spearhead fixed to a long handle. His big, broad-rimmed hat never got in the way of the rope spear. Still to come were the fighters using a weapon called 'the three-section stick' that was made from three short sticks connected to short chains. It was the most difficult act to perform. Any carelessness and the sticks would either hit the performer himself or hit his 'opponents'. The 'monkey stick' performance drew much laughter. The performer, who displayed this style of martial arts aped the movements of a monkey very vividly. He scratched his neck, ran in circles with one hand holding the stick, prodded it vertically on the ground, jumped up and momentarily stayed on the stick with his legs holding it. His right hand shaded the eyes to look around in the way a monkey did. The performances were all done to the drumbeat, like gymnastic floor dancers to their music.

Martial arts people from a neighbouring village who learned the same thing from the same teacher joined in the performance. One of them also performed the rope spear. When the drumming and music were reaching a climax, he lost concentration and the spearhead hit his own cheek. He was taken away injured. His mates, who realised that they were not used to performing with the drum and music, immediately quit the performance after that accident.

As soon as the yard cleared, the stilt team arrived. The footrest of each stilt was over one metre above the ground. The whole team performed and proceeded towards the yard. The audience followed on both sides. Sand dust was stirred up and fences were flattened by the squeezing crowd and crushed by the tramping feet.

First the fisherman, with his right leg held up by his right hand over his shoulder, hopped on a single stilt into the yard. The fish on his fishing rod swayed up and down. In his wake 'the girl who raised silk worms' pranced into the yard with her two stilts forming a cross under the knees. A resilient reedy stick with a butterfly on its top vibrated rhythmically with her steps. The 'foolish boy' followed, crossed his legs, turned three hundred and sixty degrees, and mimicked foolish tricks to catch the butterfly. Next a white-bearded old man hobbled into the yard with mincing steps.

When all the stilt actors came into the yard, three square tables were put on top of each other. Several actors climbed onto the topmost table and jumped down with a somersault. It was an awe-inspiring acrobatic performance. My heart beat so violently that I wanted to close my eyes for fear of seeing an accident and to keep them open so not to miss the unique acrobatic performance.

The cymbal team came next with the huge clatter of sixty pairs of large cymbals striking all at the same time. Their hands were raised high into the air, their cymbals glistening brilliantly in the sun. Drums boomed. Trumpets blared. The combined sound was deafening but also nice and musical. As soon as all its team members entered the yard, they changed formation patterns continuously. Then they started to perform acrobatics. A score of performers climbed onto the topmost table of the three overlapped tables and the same numbers of performers bent backwards to ninety degrees with their arms holding their cymbals upward. The performers somersaulted backwards and fell with their cymbals striking the cymbals held by performers waiting down below. Applause broke, sudden and deafening.

Teams performed from one yard to another and the audience followed them from one yard to the next. The audience grew, like snowballs, bigger and bigger. No fence could stand upright and intact. But no owner complained. He enjoyed the memory of such a good time until the performance the following year. (This activity stopped in 1956 when the government rationed the grain supply for each person.)

When the 'street treading' finished and the last night of the opera came to an end, the first real celebration of the Spring Festival in the Paradise Palace, which I remember, concluded.

A New House Appears in the Village

Under the reign of the new government, the life of my uncle Yong-jiang's family underwent a quick change for the better. Orders for harnesses for horses, donkeys, mules and things connected with carts, as well as orders for whips came pouring in. He had to work from morning to night during the winter.

Bricks, timber and lime were gradually brought to his yard. He was planning to construct a new house. He did this not only because he had the money but also because his one room was not big enough for the family. He planned to make a three-roomed house with a lean-to as a storage room and kitchen. The construction site was the yard bordering the old house on the eastern side. The planned house was not on the line with the old house but was several metres back to the north, leaving the maximum space for the front yard.

The foundation of the house was of most importance, especially for the outer and partitioning walls. First, following the line drawn by the carpenter in charge of the construction, grooves for the walls were cleared. Crushed bricks, lime and burnt coal dust were piled to fill up the space between the lines. Then my uncle invited neighbours to pound the foundations. Foundation pounding was done manually and two devices were used—a smooth round stone block and a big stone roller. The stone block had a diameter of sixty centimetres, and about thirty centimetres in thickness, with two recesses arranged on opposite sides for hands to hold. It was about forty kilograms in weight. One by one the helping men used this to pound the foundation. One man raised the stone high above his head and threw it down onto the ground, four times on the same spot. The width of the foundation was just enough to be pounded four times abreast. The young men would compete to see who could pound deeper and who could pound more times.

The second device was rigged with a big stone roller used in the yard to grind wheat kernels off the ears. The frame was taken off and two thick round timber poles were secured to it with ropes. Four thinner sticks were secured on the top half of the stone, which helped to stabilise the stone. Eight people, four on each side, used this device for the pounding. This was used when the pounding stone block could no longer pound the soil deeper.

'Up!' they chorused and the eight people lifted the poles simultaneously and raised the device high above their heads. 'Pound!' they sang again and thrust the device down onto the foundation. The soil was driven harder. Again they did four times within the width and four times on the same spot. When doing this, one led the singing, and the others repeated:

'Lift up hu hai,
Thrust down hu hai!
Raise high ya me hu hai,
Thrust down heavily ya me hu hai.'

The leading person would change the wording all the time to direct the pounders to do the job without thinking about the weight. When they had pounded the entire foundation, another eight people would take over. When the stone roller could not make any further marks on the foundation, the foundation was considered solid enough for constructing the house.

Uncle Yong-jiang did not need to pay the pounders, he just treated them to meat dishes and alcohol as well as wheat flour *man tou* (steamed bread). This was the tradition. Any family that wished to construct a new house would do the same.

After the carpenter had directed the positioning of the corner posts, the bricklayers started to make the walls. Among them there were a couple of professionals. The others were all peasants, but there was never any worry about the job. The walls were made straight and to the required quality.

The positioning of the central beam of the roof was the most important part in constructing a house. The night before, the site would be kept under watch, either by my uncle Yong-jiang, my Da Ma, one of my cousins or my father, to make sure nobody would take the opportunity to bury a knife or a pair of scissors in the site. That, to the peasants, would bring about bad luck and would make the family fight or the family members sick.

My uncle Yong-jiang asked Ma to check his almanac for an auspicious date for the carpenter to fix the central beam. Firecrackers, incense, and alcohol should be ready to use to celebrate this event.

When the time for fixing the beam arrived, my cousin Xiang let off the firecrackers. That was the customary way to announce the commencement of laying the central beam. Then incense was kindled. My uncle prayed and kowtowed. At that moment, the carpenter, without a safety belt, walked along the beam to the middle of it to fix a picture of incantation. It was a picture of the Chinese 'Ba Gua'—eight diagrams from the *Book of Changes*, China's oldest book of philosophy, which represent the sky, earth, thunder, wind, water, fire, mountains and marsh land. The picture was glued underneath the beam. Lengthwise with the beam were secured two red lacquered chopsticks, one on each side of the picture. A tassel was draped from the chopsticks with a copper coin tied to it. The rooms had no ceiling and so the picture could be seen. When this was finished, my uncle offered alcohol to the carpenter.

When the rafters were in position and when thick mats made from reeds were spread over them, it became the work of several people to make the roof. Six to ten people mixed clay with chopped straw. I helped to tread in the mixture with my trousers rolled up above the knees.

Two ladders were placed against the eaves of the house. About ten to fifteen people, a gunnybag hood over their heads, carried the mixture of clay and straw up onto the roof, one ladder for going up and another for coming down. They trooped quickly, like ants. There were about five or six people on the roof to flatten the mixture evenly.

No job was delicate and nobody could have a very short break. Everybody was dripping sweat. When the mixture on the roof was about one-foot thick the work came to a stop. The top layer, a mixture of lime and chopped straw, was laid the following day. That was a job for just a few people. It had to be done very well, so the roof would not leak when it rained.

When the laying of the clay on the roof was finished, everybody clustered around tables in the yard to enjoy a good meal of meat and *man tou*—and alcohol, of course! After the meal, smokers fetched tobacco from a basket to enjoy a puff of a pipe. Cigarettes were still too expensive for the peasants, and had not entered the life of the villagers yet.

While the building was going on, I had to take part in the labour as soon as I returned from school. My job was to carry mortar for the bricklayers. This was done with a piece of cloth, 0.8 metre by 0.8 metre in size. The four ends of two ropes were respectively secured to the four corners of the cloth. I would lift the two ropes to carry the mortar. Though the load was heavy, I could swing the load forward and land it on the ground before I swang it to another spot. I therefore did not feel the weight of the load much. I would also help carry the bricks to the place where they were most needed.

Windows and doors were made and fixed by the carpenter. The carpenter and one or two bricklayers were the only people that my uncle had to pay on a day to day basis. All the other helpers were neighbours.

Thereafter, more and more new houses were built in the village.

Purchase of Grain from the Government Shop

The land belonging to the peasants of the Paradise Palace was, mainly if not entirely, sandy. The sandy soil was not good for growing grain but it was good for peanuts, watermelon, and sweet potatoes. Wheat and corn were grown after the watermelon harvest because that same piece of land could not be used for watermelon in the second year.

Now that the poor peasants had land and the mutual aid groups were active, life changed steadily for the better, though torrential rain in summer flooded some fields, some water would remain until the following spring.

The fair at the town five kilometres to our south was regularly held for the peasants to sell their produce, to buy grain or simply to barter their produce. My father often went to the fair to sell some peanuts and to purchase corn. It was very convenient for the villagers. It never entered the heads of the peasants that it was necessary for them to store excessive grain at home.

Sometime in 1952 or 1953, the sale and purchase of grain was no longer free—it went under government control. Each family was given a book on which were written the total number of people in the family, the name of the head of the household, and their address. When any family wanted grain, they had to take the book to the government shop in the nearby town to buy it.

Early one morning before sunrise, my mother instructed me to go to the town to buy forty catties of corn. The sun had not risen yet when I arrived at the shop. In front were two long queues stretching snake-like from the window. I took my position at the end of one queue.

The sun rose and climbed higher and higher towards forenoon. The sales of grain still had not begun. On the right side of the waiting queues were gigantic granaries walled with reed mats. The tops of some of them were already sealed with reed mats, while others were still open and foot-wide wooden boards were propped up to reach the tops of the reed mat granaries. Such arrangements were called *tian qiao*—the sky bridge. Workers carrying full gunnybags walked up the sky-bridge to tip grain into the granary. The bridge vibrated under their feet. There were no safety arrangements, though the height of the granary top was at least ten metres from the ground. The work was constant because the government shop had to replenish what it sold every day either through government supply or through purchase from villages within the perimeter of the local district government. Sometimes the granaries could not be replenished with grain. The shop would sell whatever the government supplied it from other places, such as peanut cakes, dried sweet potato chips, or sorghum.

Eventually, the queues started to move, but from my position looking forward, they never seemed to shorten, not even a bit, though the queues behind me extended further and further. The reason why I was not getting nearer to the purchasing window was because newcomers pushed into the queues due to having friends holding positions for them. That, I found out later, frequently happened in China whenever queuing was necessary.

Noon came and went and I was still very far from the window. My stomach complained. I checked the money my mother had given me—it was just enough to buy forty catties of corn. I had not even one cent spare to buy food to soothe my stomach. Also I could not leave the queue—if I did, I would not be able to get back to my original position.

My turn came after the sun was set. It was already very dark when I got out of the town. I was very hungry. The bag on my shoulder became heavier with each forward step. When I passed the village between the town and the Paradise Palace, it was already dark. As well as that, I seemed to be the only person on the highway.

I had to rest by the roadside every kilometre I covered. I became weak due to hunger. I got out a handful of corn from the bag and put it into my mouth to chew. The raw taste was not good but my stomach was eager to receive it. Supper was already long over when I got home.

'Why are you back so late?' my mother asked. 'You must have been playing in the town.'

'Nowadays, the queues have become longer and longer. He must have been waiting all the time for his turn,' my father explained. He always knew more about a situation. That saved my explanation—I was too hungry to attempt any explanation anyway. It was not difficult for him to understand, because the grain needs of the poor peasants were all similar.

Eventually, there was not enough grain for sale. Grain seemed to disappear overnight. Peanut cakes were sold instead. I cannot remember how this happened and the government never explained what caused the shortage, which lasted for quite a few years.

Peanut cakes were used to feed pigs. After the peanut oil was completely removed, the remnants, mixed with a bit of chopped gunnybag fibre, were pressed into cakes as hard as rock. My mother (and other peasants' wives) crushed them with the millstone into flour, sieved the short fibres out, and mixed in a little bit of corn flour if she happened to have it, to make bread.

Back home from school, the sight of the food immediately destroyed my hunger. In my pocket, I always had a piece of the peanut cake, ready to attempt a mouthful when I was hungry. Many other children did the same.

Alternatively, we could buy sorghum or corn. Whatever the district government could get from the other districts would be for sale as food for the peasants. Nobody could predict what would be for sale the next day.

Gradually, the food situation worsened. The government fixed the quantity of supply for each person. A figure was fixed for a man. The allowance for a woman was less than that for a man. Old people got even less and children lesser still. Sweet potatoes were counted as grain supply with four catties of sweet potatoes being equivalent to one catty of corn.

Food became a constant problem for the peasants. The food shortage could only be alleviated from the private small plots of each family. This explains why, later during the senior co-operative and People's Commune years between 1956 and 1968, the government reassured the peasants that their private plots would remain unchanged for at least sixty years. During the Great Cultural Revolution, the private plots were taken away due to the fact that the plot was regarded as 'the tail of capitalism'. After the Great Cultural Revolution, the private plots were given back to the peasants again.

The sale and purchase of grain was under government control for the purpose of shattering the hoarding of grain by the capitalists in large cities. The peasants, through tightening their belts, supported the needs of the country and kept the country stable during those difficult years.

chapter 6

THE RESTLESS YEARS

Rumours, such as that the Third World War was imminent, the Americans were ready to cross the Yalu River into China, Chiang Kai-shek was coming back from Taiwan, the world was approaching its end, and green-haired monsters were roaming the countryside, ran wild. News of murders constantly came to the ears of the peasants. The villagers lived in fear; normal life was threatened. To eliminate the fear of the peasants and to strengthen the newly established young republic, the government acted resolutely, relentlessly and unswervingly to suppress counter-revolutionaries.

Brutal Crimes and the Green-haired Monsters

In the spring of 1950, while the poor peasants were sowing their own newly acquired land, fear slipped into their lives. Stories of brutal killings came to the peasants' ears, one after another. Between our village and the town to our south there was a big pond choked with reeds. Now and then maimed or slain bodies were found there. Villagers shunned that place whenever possible. But the most serious case happened in the main town of our district—the centre of all the district government offices. There was a bank in the town, which was under the direct control of the district government. The bank had seven employees, and one security officer, who had been a guerrilla during the anti-Japanese war. He was very alert and did his job well.

An unemployed youth came to look for a part-time job in the bank. The manager had to discuss this with the security officer and both had to report to the town government for instructions. Because the young man could write and calculate well and he had no undesirable record, he was given a job.

All the employees slept in the bank dormitory. I don't know why they were requested to stay in the bank every night, but I think it was because the bank was under military control at the time. The young man was the only one allowed to stay home for the night.

The bank business went well. One day, the bank got more cash than usual and had it locked in the safe for the night. All the employees went to bed as usual. The security man toured the place and returned to his room for a rest. Unfortunately, he fell fast asleep. He was taken aback when he opened his eyes, for the day had already broken. The courtyard was very quiet, too quiet for him to feel comfortable. He hailed the employees in the other room to get up, but there was no response. He became suspicious and went over to check. The door was ajar, which was unusual. He went into the room and was shocked. All seven people were slain with their throats cut. Blood formed puddles on the floor.

The security man rang the district government to report the murders in the bank. Soldiers came immediately and the slain bodies were carried into the yard. The security man began to check the cuts for clues. Fresh blood was still bubbling out of the slit throat of an employee. He was still battling for breath. Just then the part-time employee, the young man, came in. He exclaimed in sheer surprise at what had occurred and helped to arrange the dead. He noticed the one employee still alive and taking advantage of the chaos in the yard, he left unnoticed. But the security man had noticed his departure. The security man felt suspicious but did not stop the young man. Just then the employee, from whose throat fresh blood gushed out and bubbled, opened his eyes and stammered the young man's name and died with three fingers stretched out. The security man immediately understood that the young man and two others were the murderers. The security man took some soldiers with him to arrest the young man. When they arrived, the young man was just leaving with a gunnybag full of cash. He surrendered and confessed the names of the two other culprits. One was a butcher and the other was a blacksmith who fixed horseshoes. The two were still working, 'innocently' as usual, when they were arrested. Not all murders were solved as quickly as that.

When spring came, all sorts of rumours were running amok: 'There will be forty-nine days of yellow wind, it will be heavily overcast. And the sun will not come out.' 'The world will perish! There will be a third world war. Very soon Chiang Kai-shek and his army will come back from Taiwan! Land and everything will be given back to the landlords and rich peasants again!'

Peasants, especially poor peasants, were on tenterhooks. They felt worried and wished the government would do something to alleviate their fears. But still more fears arose. The rumour of 'the green-haired monsters' spread quickly. The monsters were described as having green hair all over their body, were very tall, and could leap onto rooftops as easily as walking on the ground. The monsters, either singly or in numbers, entered villages after dark. They ate children and killed women. It was said that they were actually men in disguise with springs fixed to their feet. They could cover fifty paces in one stride and jump onto house-roofs without much exertion and effort. They killed children to make medicine, which would render anyone taking it unconscious. They also opened pregnant women's bellies to take the foetus in order to make medicine of a similar kind. People did not know whether such medicine could be made with human organs. They just felt scared. People did not know whether such crimes were committed by real monsters or human criminals; they were scared by the spreading of the killings.

Then the villagers heard that in one small village by the Yong Ding River, a pregnant woman was killed and her foetus was removed. Her breasts were cut off and placed on the openings of two thermos flasks, and her intestines were scattered on the floor. She was nailed spread-eagled on a wall. The murderer or murderers were still at large.

Peasants began to hurry home before sunset. After then, nobody dared to step out of their house. Doors remained bolted. We students had to attend evening classes at school, mainly to do homework, to review lessons, and to prepare for the new lessons the following day. At the end of the evening class, all the children from neighbouring houses would race home together in great fear. Younger students, who could not catch up with the older students, often wet their trousers from fear on the way home. Once when we started homeward after the evening class, the big boys broke into a run. I could not run as fast as them and I would not call them to slow down to wait for me. My vanity forbade that. But I was so scared that I trembled and my heart seemed on the verge of escaping from my mouth and without warning my trousers were wet. My vanity was injured and although nobody knew about it except my mother, I felt I had lost face. I hated the 'green-haired monster' and my hatred was deep and real.

The whole village soon organised itself for the possible arrival of the green-haired monster. Each family was requested to have in readiness either a gong, a basin, a bucket, cymbals, or anything that could make a loud noise. If a green-haired monster or a human being in disguise broke into a house, the family should beat the gong or whatever they had to signal the invasion. Hearing the noises, the adjacent neighbours should also do the same thing right away.

When the noises for help sounded, all the villagers—men and women, old and young—were to come to the site with weapons such as knives, mattocks, axes, spears, forks, swords, sticks, or hoes, as well as with lanterns already lit. No matter whether they were monsters or human criminals, they should be caught and punished.

Militiamen patrolled the village during the night, but not at any fixed time. They did this because they did not want the criminals to predict their patrolling time.

My father and his elder brother spread sesame stalks in our yard, from the front entrance right to the doorstep. Sticks with entangled vines of beans were placed against the front windowsill. The pile was about a metre in depth. This served as barbed wire barriers in battlefield, and was used by my father to prevent the monster or criminal from approaching the window.

My father had a pitchfork placed near his head against the *kang*. My mother had the kitchen knife under her pillow. I had my crescent axe, which was awfully sharp and used to cut firewood, against the *kang* within easy reach of my hand. I was quite able to use it effectively and was confident that neither a monster nor a human criminal could get the better of me.

Children were never left alone and were forbidden to go into the woods to collect firewood unless they went with companions. This was particularly so after school in the afternoon. Three or four of us always went into the field together, each with a sharp crescent axe. We secretly wished that we could meet the monster and collectively kill it. Thus we could be heroes talked about by the villagers for a long time, 'Look, they are the boys who killed the monster!' How proud we should be!

The village security officer did not believe in such nonsense as green-haired monsters. Betraying no interest in the rumours, he started searching for the rumour-mongers who invented and spread these stories. He used a method that was called 'groping for the melon along the vine'. He must have learnt this from the security people of the county government, for he was only an ordinary peasant and he could not be that clever. He chatted with neighbours and other villagers and finally solved the rumour. Two landlords, one a spy for the Kuomintang Party, and the other a spy for the Kuomintang Army, were the source of the rumours. Their collaborators were three members of Yi Guan Dao (a religious sect).

A mass conference was held in our school to expose them. A number of desks were put together in the main yard for the school principal and the village chairman to sit at. Five villagers clustered at a corner not far from the desks. Militiamen with rifles in their hands stood by the five villagers, a sign that those men were under detention. Outside the school compound, a few slogans were posted on the school walls and on the trunks of trees.

The village chairman made a speech. He told the villagers that in our village those five people spread the rumours about the 'green-haired monsters and the forty-nine days of yellow wind'. In other places, their kind had killed people and committed atrocious crimes. Their aim was to sabotage our production and our efforts in Korea. They were Kuomintang spies and acted under Kuomintang instructions. They wished to have the Kuomintang back and reduce the poor peasants to the suffering they had experienced before 1949! When he finished, the school principal led the slogan shouting:

'Down with Kuomintang spies!
'Down with Yi Guan Dao!
'Down with the saboteurs!
'Long live the Communist Party!
'Long live Chairman Mao!'

When the principal sat down, the Dian Chuan-shih and his fellow members were ordered to make confessions and to demonstrate how they had deceived the villagers. A big tray with sand (the planchette) was carried to the desks. The three Yi Guan Dao people came forward.

'I am Yi Guan Dao Dian Chuan-shih,' the man said. 'I am sorry to have deceived you. I spread rumours as instructed by the other two spies. We spread rumours so that you dared not stay in the fields. We were instructed to sabotage production and create fear among you.'

Slogans were shouted by the masses. Then a demonstration of the meaning of the words was given. One man held a wooden device, which was round with a thin stick fixed vertically to it. He stretched out his arms and held the device over the tray with sand. Another man was holding a long wooden handle with a piece of wooden board nailed to its free end. The board was about half a palm wide and about two hands long. He, the scribbler, used this to make the sand in the tray smooth and wipe out the 'words' written by the other man holding the round device.

The scribbler closed his eyes, started shaking slightly at first and then violently. At that moment, the Dian Chuan-shih asked, 'please let us know which deity will now talk to us.'

'I am Lao Mu!' (The mother deity.)

Articulating something that nobody could understand, the scribbler started writing 'celestial' words on the tray. When 'celestial' words were written, nobody could doubt his writing—nobody dared to doubt his writing. When painting a ghost, nobody ever questioned whether the ghost looked like that, because nobody had ever seen a ghost. Likewise, nobody had ever seen 'celestial' writings. Whatever he wrote on the tray would be regarded as 'celestial' writing.

'Yellow wind,' he read, apparently with great difficulty. 'Forty-nine days.'

The other man wiped the sand flat and the scribbler started again.

'Join me,' he continued to read, 'or you perish.'

At the finish the scribbler stood there, trembling again. He opened his eyes as if he had just come back from a trance.

'Do you know what happened?' the Dian Chuan-shih asked.

The scribbler shook his head. He looked very tired.

The whole procedure came to the end.

'Fellow villagers,' the village chairman spoke again. 'Now you have seen how they deceived you. From now on don't believe in any superstition. Don't believe in rumours and don't pass rumours on. Tell the village council when somebody passes rumours to you. These five men will be under your supervision. They have to behave themselves and work hard. If they spread a rumour again, we shall send them to the county jail.'

These five men were lucky—really lucky. If they were sent to the county, they might have been sentenced to death for what they had done. They were merely kept in the village and could live to their natural death.

Suppressing the Counter-revolutionaries

In February 1952, the Chinese central government proclaimed 'The Rules and Regulations of the Republic of China Regarding the Suppression of the Counter-revolutionaries'. This served as the law governing the movement. In the countryside, the peasants called it the 'Twenty-one Points' because it contained twenty-one regulations and rules. All twenty-one points were beautifully written on street walls, but not many villagers could read them from the beginning to the end, let alone fully understand them. Villagers learned them from the village students. Tapered funnel-shaped cardboard tubes were made to serve as loudspeakers by the students and they would broadcast the points in relays. The starting point was on the roof of a house at the centre of the village. A teacher would read slowly phrase after phrase and the student 'shouted' out the words after him. On rooftops, within easy hearing of the central broadcasting student, were students with similar 'loudspeakers'. They repeated loudly what the central student had broadcast.

Villagers were very keen to listen to these broadcasts. This method, which radiated in a similar pattern as water rings do when throwing a pebble into a pond, lasted for quite a few years until wired paper loudspeakers were attached to the windows of every house to receive a direct broadcast from the commune station.

The first arrest of a counter-revolutionary in our village was the man who was the village chairman before 1949. We children knew him, or at least knew his appearance. He was a robust man but below the average height of the villagers. He once came to our school to demonstrate the power of martial arts.

It was winter. He stood in front of the whole school, on the raised platform in the main courtyard. His upper body was bare. He first displayed his muscles like the present day body builders do, then he was given a few red bricks. He picked up one brick and hit his head with a sharp corner of it. I closed my eyes, thinking he might smash his skull and have his brains spill out. I opened my eyes at the applause of my classmates. His head was intact, without even a bruise. But the brick was in tiny pieces, leaving stains of red powder on his head. Then he picked up another brick and hit his arm, again with its sharp corner. The brick broke into small pieces. Then he hit his back and one more brick was broken into pieces. Then six bricks were piled together and he smashed them into pieces with one stroke of his right palm. Long after that demonstration, we boys still talked about it. That's how we knew him.

It was said that during the period of Japanese occupation, he did a lot of good deeds for the guerrillas, such as buying arms and medicines for them. He was the village chairman at the time and he could speak Japanese. He also helped the 'pygmy Japanese devils'. (In the village, when people referred to the Japanese invaders they called them 'the pygmy Japanese devils'.) When the Kuomintang took over, he worked for the Kuomintang during the day and for the guerrillas at night. Strictly speaking, what he did was collect tax grain during the day for the Kuomintang and for the guerrillas during the night. He was called the 'double-faced' village council man.

A rabbit will not eat the grass around its warren. Likewise this man did not do bad things in our village or in the neighbouring villages. Locally, his good deeds were praised. But, it was said, he committed atrocious crimes elsewhere, far away from his home village. As a whole his good deeds could not offset his crimes. And so, as a result, he was arrested.

Then we heard about his behaviour in jail. He was very rude to the prison guards and was harnessed with a heavy shackle and chain. He would still exercise in all weather and practice his martial arts. He ran and jumped as if he had no shackles and chain locked at his ankles. The prison guards fixed an extra shackle and chain to him but he persevered in his exercise and his practice of martial arts. Jailers shook their heads and could not do anything to him. When the time came for him to be shot, he made his conditions:

'I will sit on a chair. Don't shoot me from behind. Shoot me from the front with a pistol, not a rifle.'

It was said that the executioner wanted to see how hard the skull of his head was and he ground the bullet on the sole of his shoe. (It was said that if the bullet was done this way, it would explode after entering the body.) The bullet exploded and the prisoner's head was splintered. Hard as his head was, it could be penetrated by a bullet! This story was told by the man who went to collect his corpse for the family and was retold by many.

The second arrest of a counter-revolutionary was another martial arts man, who had two wives. It was said that this man got his second wife by force. She was married to a man about fifty kilometres away from our village. He saw the woman and was attracted to her beauty and so he killed her husband and brought her back.

In the town about five kilometres to the south of our village, criminals of various kinds were shot at the riverbank not far from the bridge connecting the town with the eastern bank. Such occurrences were not uncommon. In this period, the town government had sufficient power to sentence the criminals to death (during those days, the district government was the highest authority in my childish eyes as well as in the eyes of the local peasants).

One day during the school holidays, my friend told me that he was going to the execution site to watch the shooting. He asked me to go with him.

'My Ma will not allow me to go. I must collect firewood.'

'Well, I will go with other friends,' he said.

Curiosity normally prevailed over fear, at least in my case. And my fear of punishment with a broom handle by my mother became a secondary consideration. I went with him. Several other boys, all our schoolmates, also joined us.

We arrived at the execution site a bit too early. We occupied the very top of the bridge, leaning against it with our forearms resting on its rail. We could see the execution ground clearly. A row of twenty-eight pits was already dug along the river edge. The pits were for the criminals to fall into after being shot.

More and more people came. Soon the crowd grew to several thousand. When the sun was high and noon had nearly arrived, the moaning of trucks was heard. When the trucks came nearer, we saw the criminals. Their heads were lowered, because of the way they were tied by the ropes. Their hands were tied behind their backs and white boards were inserted between their arms and backs. The boards extended more than half a metre higher than their heads and tapered downward. On each board was written the name of the criminal carrying it. Their names were crossed out with red marker, an indication that the criminal was going to be executed. This was, perhaps, the same way it was done in China's ancient dynasties. It was similar to what we saw on the stage, or as shown in the operas or movies.

Trucks full of soldiers were following in the wake of the trucks carrying the criminals. There was a machine gun on the roof of the truck driver's cabin and each soldier had a rifle in his hand. The bayonets on the rifles glistened in the sun. All the trucks stopped on the edge of the execution ground. The criminals were marched to the pits and each one knelt before one. Behind each kneeling criminal was a soldier with a rifle. An officer was standing by the end of the line of the soldiers.

'Ready!' the officer raised his pistol in the air and ordered.

Each soldier levelled his gun and aimed at the back of each criminal's head. The pistol sounded and a volley of rifles followed immediately. All the criminals fell, head first, into the pits, their legs jerked convulsively. The soldiers then stirred them with their bayonets to see whether they were really dead before the ropes were untied and the shackles were taken off their legs.

Later, I heard people say that one of the criminals was not shot. He was placed with the executed to get a shock as a kind of punishment, which was called 'accompanying the criminals to be executed'. He, too, fell into the pit in front of him. He was pulled out of it and was set free. He started to run frenziedly homeward. It was said that his home was about two kilometres away from the execution site. He was a landlord who was accused of doing double duties before 1949. During the day he worked for the Japanese and later for the Kuomintang, and during the night he worked for the guerrillas. He did plenty for the guerrillas and for the people in his village and in the villages around. He did bad things too, but his good deeds were much greater than the bad things he had committed, so it was justifiable to set him free, yet without some kind of punishment, he might not learn a lesson. Hence he was brought to the execution ground with the criminals to be executed. He had no knowledge that he would be set free. His soul was scared out of his body and he fell into the pit like a dead person. After being set free, he ran all the way home, like a scared rabbit. He reached his gate and when he was on the point of stepping into his yard, he trod on a tiny piece of brick chip, tripped, and fell face downward to the ground. He never got up again. He was dead. Nevertheless, he died as a free man, not as a criminal. This meant a lot to the fate of his families in the years to come.

The scene at the execution site haunted my friends and me for a long time. We never approached that place again.

A Man in Custody

The Paradise Palace had two main streets, one running north to south and the other east to west, making a very big cross. The street running to the south from the centre of the cross was called South Street, and the others were called East Street, North Street and West Street. In the very middle of West Street was a temple called 'The Temple of Five Daoist Priests'. The temple was situated on the northern side of the street, facing south. It had just one room and one courtyard. The courtyard was enclosed by high walls, which connected the room's sidewalls and gate. It had a double-leaf gate, which had a porch. Its only room also had a double-leaf door. Inside the room was a raised platform against the north wall. The platform was about one metre high, on which sat clay statues of the five life-size Daoist priests. The sidewalls were decorated with vivid paintings telling historical stories from ancient dynasties, such as 'The three heroes combating Lu Bu', which was the story from the novel *The Three Kingdoms* by Luo Gang-zhong. The novel had more influence than the history book, *The Annuals of the Three Kingdoms* by Chen Shou, about the same states. There was 'Guan Yu killed six generals to cross five guarded passes', and 'Three visits to the straw hut', which, again, were from the same novel. There was 'Cheng Ying rescued the orphan', which was a story from *The Eastern Zhou and the Warlord States* (771–256 BC).

'The Temple of Five Daoist Priests' was the place for women to report death; thus the activity was called 'report to the temple'. When an elderly man or woman died, the daughters and daughters-in-law from the same family group, which were still within five generations, would walk towards the temple in a line crying out their grievances at losing the person. The crying was similar to singing, sad but soothing to the ears. Such a practice was to inform other people how pious they were towards the dead, not to show their own feelings. At least in most cases it was so. On each of their heads was a white cloth-band about one inch wide. Their shoe uppers were also covered with white cloth. (Male youngsters wore a white cap, white shoes and a white waistband when they were in mourning.) Once inside the temple, they started to slip pieces of punctured paper, which were called ghost money, along the surface of the walls. If the paper was caught and stayed against the wall, it meant the soul accepted the money. Then all such money would be burnt for the soul to use in the other world. The more ghost money the soul of the dead received, the quicker he could be sent back to this world to be born again in a good family. In the other world, the dead soul needed the money to bribe his way back to this world. On the return trip, those women still walked in a line and cried all the way home.

It was in this temple that the following story happened.

It was during one summer's day in 1952 when a man from a village near Yong Ding River was brought to this temple and was locked in.

Militiamen from the same village were guarding the gate with rifles in their hands. Soon militiamen from our village came to their assistance.

The man was of middle height and had a strong build. His head was shaved in typical peasant style. His features were not particularly memorable. His upper body was bare and well suntanned. His age could not be more than his mid-thirties. He was brought to the temple with his arms tied behind his back.

We students were keen to know why the man was locked in the temple and why he screamed and moaned during the night. Finally, from the son of a militiaman who guarded the gate of the temple we got the story.

It was said that the brother of the man was dead. He wanted to marry the widow of his brother but she rejected him, so he brutally raped and killed her. 'Of all vices, lewdness was chief.' The man committed the worst of the worst crimes. Not only the relatives of the murdered woman hated him but also his own relatives. All the peasants who heard about him hated him. He was considered inhuman and beastly, and so he was treated like a beast.

In the small hours of the night, people living near the temple often heard shrieks and screams from it. The villagers knew the militiamen from the same village of the criminal were punishing him. But nobody knew what kind of punishment was dealt to him.

A month or so later, when we were marching homeward from school along the street in a single file, we saw a jeep parked in front of the temple. We stopped to watch. The man was sandwiched out of the gate of the temple by two men in white police uniforms. His upper body was still bare. His hands were cuffed in front, and he walked with difficulty. His upper body, his face, everywhere, was covered with small round scabs. He looked like a man with a serious case of smallpox.

'What's that?' we whispered to each other.

'Every night the two militiamen from their village burned him with incense,' the son of the militia volunteered in a whisper. My skin became gooseflesh when I heard this. I suddenly understood why there were screams, shrieks and moans during the night.

'That served him right,' was the comment by the villagers.

Such a man was despised. No punishment was too great for him. However, was it right that the militiamen punished him instead of immediately handing him over to the county authority?

Re-catching an Escapee

In the winter of 1953, a notorious criminal, a murderer who was sentenced to death and who was waiting for execution, escaped from the county jail after he strangled a prison guard. He ran away with his leg shackles and chains still attached, which were later found discarded near the railway lines.

My cousin An, the second son of uncle Yong-jiang, was on night duty in the Xiang government office. Having received notice from the county government of the escapee, he put the carbine, which was the only weapon the Xiang government had, on his desk while he was reading. The carbine was American made and was called a 'Tom' carbine. It was already old but still fired bullets, which were very thick and dome-shaped. The first bullet could go 200 metres, the second bullet could travel 150 metres, and the third could go 100 metres. Thereafter, the bullets would just fall in front of the user's feet. It was this gun he put on his desk, at arm's reach so he could snatch it at the slightest suspicious noise.

Cousin An was only seventeen at the time. He was transferred to work in the Xiang government as its secretary because of his performance during the flood in that summer. It had rained for many days in succession and the water level of Yong Ding River was dangerously high. Men from all the surrounding villages were requested on the dyke to fight the raging water. My cousin was just a Year Four student and was asked to stop school to work on the dyke as the accountant and secretary. He did an excellent job and got a third class award of contributory good deeds. When the flood receded, he got the position in the Xiang government. It was a position envied by many young men of our own village and the neighbouring villages.

The Xiang government building was in the compound of the quadruple houses of a former landlord. It was like a castle. An had the gate locked and barred. It was cold and he had no mind to go to bed yet. He was reading at the desk. A stove was burning beside him to keep him warm. Suddenly, the noise of a broken tile on the high sidewall disturbed his reading.

'It must be some bad person trying to come into the yard,' he thought. He picked up his carbine, loaded it, and had it at the ready to fire. He went out to check. He looked at the wall and saw a man just popping his head above the wall. In the right hand of the man was a hand grenade. Instantly he pointed his gun towards the man and shouted, 'Don't move!'

The man saw An at the same instant. He released his hold of the wall and dropped to the ground outside the yard and ran away.

'He must be the criminal!' An realised and felt regretful that he had not shot him. He told the Xiang Zhang first thing in the morning. (Xiang Zhang was the first official of the Xiang government.)

'He is still in our district. We must act quickly lest he gets away. He has a hand grenade and it is a threat to the lives of the people,' the Xiang Zhang said to An. He sent for the security man of the village, instructing him to get the militiamen ready.

'Where might he hide himself?' he and the militiamen discussed. 'Definitely not in his own home. He is not a fool.' Then they decided the most probable place was the house of his relative, who had a big family. The father and son of that family were good people, so they would not help the criminal willingly. If the criminal was really in that house, the father and son could give the Xiang Zhang and his men valuable assistance.

They surrounded the house in the latter half of the following night.

'Don't act rashly. He might hurt the people in the house. He might hurt any one of us. We must surprise him.' Xiang Zhang was an experienced guerrilla. He instructed two militiamen to get onto the roof of the house and the others to be on either side of the gate. He would lead An, as well as two or three young militiamen, in a dash into the room to catch the criminal.

'Nobody should make any noise! Nobody should move without my signal,' he cautioned again and again.

Morning came. The son of the house came out to the toilet at the far corner of the yard, looking in all directions to see whether he could spot anything. He went into the toilet, and silently, Xiang Zhang got into the toilet, too, from the wall.

'Thank heaven!' The son of the house did not make any alarm. He whispered excitedly to the Xiang Zhang. 'We have been expecting somebody to come all the time,' he said.

'Tell me the details, quickly. Don't stay too long to arouse his suspicion,' Xiang Zhang cautioned.

'He has a hand grenade. He either keeps me or my father at his side. He never allows my father and I to come out together. He has the ring of the grenade string on his finger, ready to pull at any minute. He only sets it down beside him when he has his meal.'

'We shall catch him at breakfast time. You and your father pin him on the *kang* when he puts the hand grenade beside him. We shall rush in immediately.'

'But I have no opportunity to speak to my father.'

'I will wait for him here in the toilet. I will tell him myself.'

The son went back into the room. The criminal did not suspect anything because it always took the son some time in the toilet. A while later, the father came out and went into the toilet. He was not surprised at all to see Xiang Zhang there, and heard the instruction clearly.

Life in the yard went on normally. The mother, wife of the master of the house, opened the gate, collected firewood and cooked breakfast.

Finally, the son shouted 'Come!'—the signal agreed to between the father, son and the Xiang Zhang. It meant that they had pinned down the criminal.

The Xiang Zhang and the militiamen rushed into the room. Brave but lacking experience, my cousin dashed into the room but nearly fell on the burning stove. Xiang Zhang was the first on the *kang*. In a twinkling of an eye, he locked the handcuffs on the hands of the criminal.

The father and son still pressed the criminal down on the *kang* without releasing him. They had exerted even 'the suckling strength!' (When somebody was using great strength we would say he used the strength with which he suckled his mother's milk!) The criminal wriggled but could not get free from the father and son. Faced with the possible death of the family members, the two peasants, father and son, were too powerful for the criminal to fight off.

'You can let him free now,' Xiang Zhang said to them after he had cut the criminal's tendons from behind the heels of his feet.

'Let's see how you can escape this time!' Xiang Zhang said to him. He ordered the criminal to be taken away to the Xiang office, where he rang the county government to report his recapture. The escapee was taken back to the county jail. Before long, he was executed.

This story I heard directly from my cousin. It showed that the peasants were determined to fight the enemies when their freedom was challenged.

chapter 7

THE CO-OPERATIVES

The co-operatives came into being because of the needs of the peasants. In 1953, mutual aid groups were organised into co-operatives where tools, animals, fertiliser and labour were shared on a permanent basis. Co-operative members were compensated with a share of profits from the ensuing harvests according to their input of goods and labour. Although small private plots were permitted, most of the land was owned by the co-operative. The government encouraged the setting up of more and more co-operatives, which was a big step forward for the Chinese peasants—from individual to collective farming. In the process, the peasants discovered the way to permanently solve the land problem in China. If the peasants had been given more time to consolidate the junior co-operatives, their way of thinking would have gradually become set—firmly set. If the peasants had not been hurried into the People's Communes and if the government had not interfered with the peasants so wantonly, there might not have been the three years of national famine in the early sixties.

The Junior Co-operative (1953–1955)

The beginning of 1953 brought with it quite an important event in the life of the peasants of our village. It was the appearance of the junior co-operative and it had an important influence on our village.

When the Chinese Spring Festival of 1953 was over, Granny said to my father:

'Sixty years ago when I was a teenage girl, Yong Ding River breached its bank. Our village was flooded. Water in the street was a man's height deep. Water was everywhere. Our house and yard were the only dry places at that time. So many families came here! Everywhere there were cooking pots. There was no space even to put one foot forward. Children were not allowed to make remarks or to cry. Nobody was allowed to criticise anything.'

'What if somebody did say something?' I asked.

'A small girl asked "why is there no water here?" and she immediately received a slap on the face by her mother,' Granny said. And then she turned to tell my father, 'People say Nature repeats itself every sixty years.

Now it is exactly sixty years from the time Yong Ding River broke its bank to flood our village. The river may break its bank again this year. Get prepared for the worst.'

He believed what Granny said to him and when summer approached, he began preparations. He pulled the ladder onto the roof of our house. He secured our wooden chest to the ladder, and two pottery jars as well. He connected several ropes to make one long one and then he connected one end of the rope to the ladder and the other end to an elm tree behind our house.

'If water comes from Yong Ding River, get into the chest with your mother and brother. Store some food in the jars,' he told me. 'It is better to be prepared.'

Granny's prediction seemed to be accurate. Summer brought with it the arrival of torrential rains for quite a few days in succession. Yong Ding River, about fifteen kilometres away to the west of our village, was full to the brim of raging and racing currents. Its one-kilometre width seemed not quite wide enough to contain the water. Men in our village and the surrounding villages were all called to the site to build a dam by increasing the height of the riverbank. The work continued day and night, non-stop. The original bank was about twenty or thirty metres above ground. The river actually rose to a level much higher than the houses. My father told me that with every gust of wind, the water would spill over the dam. The eastern bank of the river was low and flat and its dam was increased every year to prevent the river from overflowing.

As I have explained, this river was said to be the type of river that had 'a copper head, an iron tail, and a bean curd middle section'. It had a copper head and an iron tail because those sections were mountains. The middle section flowed through the vast Hebei plain. The riverbed was wide and the water flowed slower. The soil carried by it from upstream areas settled to the bottom here, making the riverbed higher and higher. In summer, when it rained heavily for a few days in succession, the river tended to breach its east bank—the 'bean curd middle section'. All the villages in our region were situated around this 'bean curd middle section' and were therefore threatened by the river every year.

When my father came home from Yong Ding River, we heard that we had nearly said goodbye to him forever. He was instructed to deliver a letter to the headquarters of the authority directing the dam site about five kilometres from his unit. He was suffering night blindness at the time. He was walking along the road on the dam top where the clay was soft and sticky. The rain alternatively poured and drizzled. The river water splashed up the dam against his trousers. He arrived at the headquarters despite his poor eyesight. He returned to his unit in the morning and on the way back he saw his footprints along the water edge—had he stepped a little bit astray, he would have fallen into the river and been carried away.

The Paradise River, which cut our village in two and was normally only knee deep, became ferocious. At the elbow-turn about one kilometre to the north of our village, it overflowed across the surface of the highway into the fields on the other side. It invaded about one hundred metres of our village along the east-west street. The small timber bridge was swept away.

One night it was raining hard and it was dark.

'The dam has collapsed and the water is coming!' somebody shouted. The villagers, mostly women, children and the elderly people (because the men were protecting the dam of the Yong Ding River), were panic-stricken.

'Remember,' my mother told me, 'when we find water coming into our yard, climb up onto the roof immediately.'

It turned out to be a false alarm, but the Yong Ding River did cut through its dam. Fortunately, the floodwater did not pass our village. Had it not been for the setting up of the co-operatives, however, many families including our own would have had no harvest at all because of the rain.

When the junior co-operative was established in the village, it changed the way of thinking and the life of the peasants. It was set up despite disbelief, doubts, sneers and suspicions. Not many people noticed how it came to be. At the beginning of the year, during the Spring Festival, the deputy village chairman came to chat with my father. He was in his mid-thirties, tall, slim, with a rectangular face, and milky white skin rather than sun-tanned. Even a scarred upper eyelid could not prevent him from being called handsome. He was clad in an American army overcoat given to him from the government's relief to the villagers. He had a special skill in making beautiful and tough piggyback baskets. Like my father, he was a man of few words. He came to see my father almost every evening. The two of them sat at the square table and sipped homemade tea. It was made from either wild tea plants or date leaves. My father was not rich enough to buy tea from the town yet. They exchanged a few words and fell silent.

My mother did not enjoy their conversations. To her, it was frustrating to listen and talk to them. She just went about her own work. She would not forget to add more hot water to the teapot for them and she would give them some baked watermelon seeds (she collected the seeds with my help). She did not know the traditional etiquette towards a visitor or guest because she had never been taught. But, like all other villagers, she was hospitable. Hospitality was in the marrow of the bones of the peasants. My mother would offer such meagre hospitality as she could afford to give.

Sensing that something important was under discussion between the two of them, I hung around to overhear their conversation. My father looked at me but did not drive me away. My presence was tolerated but not my comments, which I understood. It was really frustrating to listen to them. They seemed to exchange ideas by silence rather than by words. But the advantage was that I had ample time to chew over their words.

'Your mutual aid group?' the chairman asked my father without completing the sentence.

'Better than alone,' my father replied.

Long silence.

I had worked in the mutual aid group and I could understand the two of them, even if my mother couldn't. I knew the deputy chairman was asking my father his opinion of the mutual aid group. My father told him the mutual aid group did better than an individual family alone. Individually, some families, like ours, would not be able to sow in season. He also said the harvest was better.

'If we have too much rain?' the deputy chairman asked again.

Silence.

'Hard,' my father replied after a few minutes silence. Then he filled in a few details.

'Hard to dig drainage ditches. Fields around yours may not have water. The owner might not allow you to dig through his field.'

Silence.

'People start selling land,' the deputy chairman broke the silence.

'I know.'

'Willingly?'

'No,' my father shook his head. 'Land is our life support.'

'Could he have avoided it?' the deputy chairman asked.

'No.'

'Why?'

'The man was sick,' my father said. 'He had so many children. His wife could not manage to get money.'

Long silence till the deputy chairman stood up for home.

I could not fully understand their conversation. But the heavy and oppressive atmosphere explained how serious the problem was. I felt my heart sink, afraid that some day we might need to sell our land.

During the next few days the conversation continued. Both agreed that an individual poor family could hardly survive natural disasters—that people should not rely on relief from the government because relief could help an emergency but not alleviate long-term poverty. They knew that people did not wish to sell their land and return to their poor life before 1949.

Then my cousin, Quan, another man of few words, joined them in the discussion. This cousin of mine was discharged from the County Guerilla Brigade a couple of years after he joined the army in 1948. He went into the army illiterate but when he returned he could read and write a little. He was tall and slim. He never opened his mouth unless he had fully weighed what he wanted to say. My uncle Yong-jiang, and particularly my father, respected his opinions.

'Uncle,' he said to my father, 'I heard that in some villages mutual aid groups have formed together to make larger ones.'

My father looked up at him, saying nothing.

'They put land, animals, seeds, and fertilisers together,' the deputy chairman added.

My father remained silent, thinking hard.

'How do they share the harvest?' he finally asked.

'Land, big animals and farm tools share fifty per cent of the total harvest, the labourers share the other fifty per cent of the total harvest. But of course this has to be discussed further so that everybody will think it is fair,' Quan said.

A very long silence followed.

'Good,' my father said. 'A group of honest and fair people is decisive.'

All three of them smiled. It seemed that the three of them shared the same understanding.

'Uncle,' my cousin said, 'you speak to our mutual aid group. They will listen to you. I will speak to the other groups.'

'I will talk to the other groups, too,' the deputy chairman said and then he cautioned, 'no more than thirty families.'

'Keep it secret until the meeting to set it up,' my cousin Quan added.

By then I came to understand that they wished to organise about thirty families together so that they could do better in natural disasters and that they could help each other. My father's group agreed to join willingly. Several other groups also joined willingly.

A meeting of all the members was held and a board was hung at the gate of one member's house, reading 'The first agricultural co-operative of the Paradise Palace'. A big bell was hung on a large branch of a date tree in the yard, the signal for members to set out to the field. At the meeting, the deputy chairman was elected as the co-operative chairman and my cousin Quan was elected as the deputy co-operative chairman. Also at the meeting two groups were elected: one to appraise the land, and another to appraise the big animals, the farm tools and the fertilisers. The rules and regulations were also declared. First, all members had to set out to the field to work at the bell in the morning, and no one could be late. If one wanted to be absent, he had to ask for leave. Secondly, there would be no quarrels. Disputes should be brought to the chairmen. Thirdly, nobody was to damage the property of the co-operative. Any deliberate damage had to be compensated in full. Other rules and regulations would be added, when necessary.

Somebody kindled firecrackers hanging down to the ground from a few long poles to celebrate. Smiles were on every face of the members. The atmosphere was like that of the Spring Festival. There were many onlookers and some of their comments were derogatory.

'Even brothers cannot stay together! How can so many families stay together?' some commented.

'The older generations never had such a thing,' others said. 'Who knows whether it will work or not?'

'Some will be too smart, some will be too lazy' a few sneered. 'Let's wait and see it get interesting.'

Nobody argued with them. Members of the co-operative went into action immediately. First, one group checked the fertilisers of each family, measuring the quantity and classifying it. All the fertiliser was moved to the yard where the co-operative office was. Winter was not over yet, but men were instructed to process the manure right away. The dung-heap made in this way was huge. The other group was checking the land, not only to decide the size of the plots, but also to decide what to grow for the year and to plan where the drainage ditch should be dug. They also decided the allocation of fertiliser to each field. For instance, first class fertiliser was sent to the fields where watermelon was to be grown.

Then the labourers were classified into the strong, the fit and the weak, with daily points fixed as per the classification. Women were also classified into three grades and points were fixed accordingly. Women who were not fit for working in the field, older children on holidays, and the elderly would all collect grass in the spring and summer to feed the animals. It was fixed how many kilograms for one point in spring and how many kilograms for one point in summer. Because the peasants were discussing what they did every day, it was not difficult for them to reach a fair standard.

Long before spring ploughing began, fertiliser was transported to the fields. Four or five horse carts were doing the job simultaneously. Singing, laughing, joking, the work was finished quickly. And then before the start of the spring ploughing and sowing, the chairmen obtained some transportation jobs for the horse carts because the co-operative needed cash in spring. Before the co-operative, such jobs were seldom obtained.

In the co-operative, everybody was a labourer—the chairmen and the team leaders were no exception. They all had to do the actual manual work in the field or elsewhere. No work equalled no points and no points equalled no share of grain. Their time spent at long evening meetings was without material compensation. They were truly 'the servants of the people'. My cousin, Quan, was the only person in our village who continued to behave like this, from the junior co-operative right until the end of the People's Commune.

Donkeys and weak and old mules were allocated for women to mill or grind their corn. Nobody was allowed to use good animals for such a job. This pleased the owners of the animals and the co-op members as well.

Work went fast in the co-op, quicker than when it was done by individual families. But every step was accompanied by derogatory comments from outsiders.

'They laugh now,' some said, 'but when it comes to getting their share, they will quarrel!'

'Who digs ditches in spring?' others would say. 'We don't have enough rain!'

'Why don't you join?' a man with an animal and cart asked a poor peasant.

'If they treat me with *man tou* and sesame oil daily,' he said, 'I may join!'

Both laughed.

Just then a young co-operative man was passing by and retorted, 'One day you might bring *man tou* and sesame oil to us to ask for permission to join!'

Sweet potato planting showed the advantage even more strikingly. Men trooped to carry water. Women, children and old men were sealing the seedlings in the pits on the ridges, which were made by ploughing for this purpose. Work went on so fast that before an individual family finished planting, seedlings in the field of the co-op were already alive! (In late winter, the co-op would construct a *kang*, on which they placed sweet potatoes vertically and tightly against each other and topped them with sand. They heated the *kang* with logs to keep it at a constant temperature and they covered the sweet potatoes with a thick straw mattress. When the young plant's shoots were about a foot long, it would be time to plant them in the field. Peasants would pull up the young shoots and bundle them to transport to the field for planting. Individual families had to buy the young shoots from the fair in the local town.)

Then the wheat harvest came. The co-op organised all the strong labourers to pull the wheat. Transporting wheat back to the yard, cutting the ears off with lever-knives, drying the ears, and winnowing, all were non-stop, like a battle for life.

'We cannot do it slowly as we did before as individuals,' Quan warned. 'We don't know when the rain comes. We must not let our wheat get mouldy!'

By the time the incessant drizzle came, all the wheat had been bagged and stored away in the storerooms. A storekeeper was nominated so that the wheat would not get mouldy. As soon as it cleared up, the wheat would be dried again in the sun.

I have used the expression 'pulling the wheat' several times. In our village, neither machines, such as combine harvesters, nor sickles, were used in wheat harvesting. People just pulled the wheat out of the ground—roots, stalks and all. Wheat pulling was a very hard job. The harvester had to bend his back, push the wheat stalks forward, grasp a big handful tightly and yank backwards with a quick jerk. Then he had to knock the sandy soil off the roots against his left or right foot. He had to bundle the roots neatly with wheat stalks. During harvesting, young men always competed for who was the best.

The most important cash crop in our village was watermelon, so the co-operative planted a very large piece of land with watermelons. A group of the most skilled men were assigned the job of caring for the watermelon field. A very big hut was set up in the middle of the border of the field. When the watermelons grew to the size of a football, they worked in the field, and ate and slept in the hut.

All the carts were used to transport big, ripe, beautiful watermelons to Beijing for sale instead of to the local town. When the first harvest of watermelon had nearly finished, the summer downpour came. Members of the co-operative were not as scared as before. They felt a bit confident, for their wheat harvest was good, their watermelon had already brought them good cash, their drainage ditches were ready, and not all their land was low. But the chairmen of the co-operative were men of prudence. They would not leave anything to chance. They organised two or three groups of young men to tour the field to help smooth the drainage, and to dig wherever necessary. Quan would get up in the night to check for himself when it rained too heavy.

Then, in 1953, the Yong Ding River was in a state of emergency. All the men were called to the site to protect the dam. My cousin, An, was chosen to be the accountant in the dam protection headquarters and he had to quit school. He had just finished his fourth year and turned sixteen. He had to be responsible for the feeding of over ten thousand people, the dispatch of pebbles, reeds, bagged clay or bagged sand to places in need, and to keep records of everything.

The co-operative at home was left to the women and elderly. Except for some land which was too low, or which was surrounded by land of non co-op families and therefore drainage ditches could not be made, all land was drained as quickly as possible. Outsiders begged to be allowed to utilise the ditches. Women were kind-hearted and gave permission.

As a result, except those co-op fields that were too low to drain and remained waterlogged, most of the co-op fields had some kind of harvest. The damage to non co-op families by waterlogging was more serious.

When the males of the co-operative came back from the Yong Ding River, they were pleased with the result. If they had not had the co-operative, it would have been disastrous. None of them was in a panic. They discussed going further and decided to level the fields when there was time and to plant some trees from the north-east to south-west to protect the topsoil. They decided to widen and deepen the drainage ditches and to buy one or two more horses.

The flood was very bad, but the co-operative members did not rely on relief from the government. They lived much better than they could have in a similar situation before the establishment of the co-operative. By the end of the year, more families applied to join. The deputy chairman suggested forming more co-operatives. It was better to have more smaller sized co-ops than to have all the families in one large co-operative. The smaller sized co-operatives were easier to manage.

The co-operative had won the respect of its members. If a family quarrelled, the co-operative chairman would be called to arbitrate. Members referred more and more to 'the co-operative'. Despite being something new to China, the co-operative was firmly established.

When reading Mao's article 'Who says that a hen feather cannot fly into the sky?' a few years later, I could feel the warmth of his heart in support of the co-operatives.

The Senior Co-operative (1955–1958)

By the end of 1955, all the co-operatives in our village were combined into one senior co-operative. Whether this was ordered by the Xiang government is unknown to me. Except for my cousin, Quan, who was the former deputy chairman of our co-operative, the executives of the senior co-operative no longer did any physical labour in the fields. It was the first time some people in the village had to be supported by the other villagers. Such cadres exempted from actual manual labour became the source of undesirable conflict in the countryside.

Under the senior co-operative, the whole village was divided into twelve teams, based on the former junior co-operatives. Ours became team number four. Land, taking into consideration its distance, fertility, convenience and size, was divided into twelve shares—one for each team.

Only two families remained outside the co-operative. One lived on the southern tip of the village, and was well-off. The father and son were carpenters and the daughter was married to a cadre who worked in Beijing. The family was nicknamed 'Taiwan' by the villagers, meaning the 'non-liberated' area. The other family lived by the junction of the streets. This family had only females—the mother was a widow with several daughters. They did not join for some unknown reason. This family was nicknamed 'South Korea'. At that time, in the minds of the villagers, Taiwan and South Korea were regarded as the most reactionary places. The families were given the nicknames because they were considered as bad as Taiwan and South Korea. Those two families were included in the People's Commune later through 'liberation' by the villagers, led by the cadres, of course.

Most of the land given to our team was higher. There was no longer any fear of waterlogging in the majority of fields, but there was the problem of water in spring. There was also the problem of protecting the topsoil, which tended to be carried away by the howling wintry wind.

There was not much difference between a team and a junior co-operative except that every few years the land would be swapped with other teams and each had to allocate some money for the senior co-operative, supporting those who were doing nothing except having meetings. The only income for the peasants, as always, was from the land. Therefore they took very good care of the land and tried their best to get more from it.

We children were not needed to work in the fields, nor did we get shares from the harvest. To me, my junior high school holidays were still spent in the same way as before. I still had to do my best to help the family. Though life was much better, there were still difficulties due to the waterlogging each year. My help was only solicited in some evenings when the grown-ups were having meetings or when they had something special to do, like in the following story...

My father was one of the two night watchmen for the sweet potato field. When the sweet potatoes were as big as cucumbers, the night watchmen had to stay in the field to guard against theft. Sometimes, when my father had to attend meetings in the evenings, I was sent to be a watchman there. Another boy from the neighbourhood would accompany me, on his father's behalf. Each of us had a very sharp spear, not for the thieves, but for the animals.

There was a hut for the watchmen to stay in, but there were also mosquitoes. We preferred to stay outside on the sand, talking at random about our future. The stars shone like gems in the sky and the mosquitoes sang beautifully after having fed upon us. There was a very slight breeze, which could only be felt by a sensitive person.

'I want to go into the army and then get a job,' the boy told me. During that period, a soldier, when retired from the army after a full term of a few years, was always given a job in a county town or in Beijing. For peasant boys, a good way to get away from the countryside was to join the army. Young men competed for entry, even using back door tactics, such as special favours or offering secret food to the recruitment soldiers.

'I wish I could continue schooling,' I told him.

'But Granny said it is hard for your family to support you.' He called my mother Granny.

'I know. Your goal is easier to realise,' I admitted.

'Do you like watermelon?' he asked.

'Of course I do,' I replied. 'But why do you ask?'

'Look,' he said, 'over there is our watermelon field. We are watchmen here and we have nothing to eat. We can only chat. There, the boys can eat watermelon.'

'We can do nothing about it.'

'Why not?' he questioned. 'Why can't we steal some?'

'I dare not.'

'I know that,' he said. 'You never did such things before. If I get some, nobody will ever suspect us, because of you.'

'It's too dangerous,' I warned him. 'They can see you before you get there.'

'No worries.' He was stripping off all his clothes. 'If I get caught, I will not involve you. Take care of my clothes and the sweet potatoes.' With that he left.

He came back to join me after about a full mealtime. He put on his clothes and lying on the sand he told me how he did it.

'I crawled into the field from the woods. They could not distinguish my body from the sand. I just ripped the melons from the vines and kicked them with my foot into the woods. I got four—two for you and two for me.'

'But we might be caught on the way home.'

'No way,' he said. 'When my father and Grandpa come, it will be after midnight. Nobody will be in the street.'

He was right. It was well after midnight when our fathers came to replace us. We left. He did not mention the melons to me at first. When we were quite some distance from the sweet potato hut, he pulled me into a peanut field. From under the plants, like a magician, he produced four big watermelons—two for him and two for me. I was very scared. The creaking of my basket seemed to be the melons crying for help. A cat ran past and it frightened me so that I had sweat trickling down my face. I would not dare to let my father know. He hated thieves and he surely would beat me with a big stick. I promised myself on the way home that I would never do such a thing again and that I should never again be drawn into something I thought was not right.

It rained during the small hours, rather heavily. In the morning, the watermelon watchmen checked the field and found four melons were missing. They could not find the footprints because of the rain.

'It must be the sweet potato watchers!' some said.

'Not possible,' others refuted. 'Shuang Xi would never do such a thing.'

'But the other boy has done this so many times!'

'We can do nothing now,' some said. 'We cannot prove it.'

My father asked me about it. What could I say? For the first and last time in my life, I lied to him. How I wish I hadn't!

Then one day, the grown-ups went to attend a wedding party. I was asked to be the watchman in the watermelon field. The field was quite big—about three hundred *mu* in total. I lay on the bed in the watchmen's hut, reading. I saw a boy was grazing the oxen and cows of our team in the other field some two hundred metres away. There was not another living soul around. I was hungry and the melon they left under the bed for me could not satisfy my hunger. The more melon I ate, the hungrier I felt afterwards. I lay there and closed my eyes—I was asleep before I realised it. When my father and others arrived with my lunch, my nephew (who was older than my father, but had to call him Great Uncle and me Uncle) joked with me. 'Uncle,' he said, 'even if you were carried away by the thief, you would not wake up! Even if the watermelons were all stolen you would not know.'

'It is not possible!' I said. 'I fell asleep just for a short moment!'

'Look, the thief has walked around the hut three times!' he pointed at the small footprints.

And it was true—the cow herder did steal the watermelons.

This was a lifelong lesson to me. I was never careless about my duty ever again.

chapter 8

FOOD

In 1958, Mao began the Great Leap Forward—an initiative to modernise China. With it came projects to build bridges, roads, canals, railways, mines, power stations and irrigation. These projects took the farmers and peasants off the land leaving many harvests to rot. By 1959, it was evident that a famine was approaching. Food, to the people, is god. The content of a peasant life is the toil of finding food to survive, and it became even more so now. My job was to obtain wild vegetables, tree leaves, leftover sweet potatoes and peanuts, to help my parents solve the food shortage. Food was the only word I could not forget even for a moment.

Cicadas and Worms

Food was very important to all of us, though what we ate varied greatly. In my childhood, my father could not afford to provide meat such as pork, mutton, or beef for our meal table. Even if he bought a small quantity of meat for special occasions, I would have long forgotten its taste before any such treat was possible again. My stomach very rarely digested animal meat. I had, like many other poor children, to look for a substitute in the form of insects or worms, which a person with a well-filled stomach would not look at.

The best substitute for meat, to me, was cicadas. Its marvellous musical chirping was not something I enjoyed much, because I did not think about it. I just wanted its meat and its shell—the meat satisfied my gluttonous mouth and the shell equipped my pocket with petty cash.

The best time to catch cicadas was early in the summer morning, when dew beads stayed like tear crystals on the blades of grass. The cicadas were yellowish white, soft winged and not long out of their shells at this time of day. They could only crawl and they were tender. When the sun was out, they would gradually change into a black colour and fly into the tall trees—their meat was no longer fit to eat and it was hard to catch them when they could fly fast with a long chirping, like a meteor flying over the night sky.

On early summer mornings, I would search around bushes for the newly shelled cicadas. Later when I was in primary school and when my brother Xiao Bao was able to follow me, we would, during the summer holidays, search for cicadas in the bushes and in the woods. I would collect the shells as well. We scanned the bushes quickly.

'Look, a cicada on that twig!' Xiao Bao would call to me when he could not reach it.

Sometimes three or four of them could be located in the same bush. The cicada shell would be perched dangerously on a leaf or on a twig concealed by leaves or simply on the trunk of a tree. In some cases, a cicada had just pulled its tail out of the shell, or it might still have its tail in the shell, trying to get out. Usually the cicada was crawling away from its shell, trying to conceal itself under the leaves till its wings were hard enough to carry it to a safer place.

The newly shelled cicada was white with a dash of yellow evenly spread over its whole body. It was soft to touch. Its big eyes bulged out from the left and right extremes of its head. Its filmy wings were thin and transparent, on which web-like veins could be clearly seen. Dew kept a cicada vulnerable, for it made the wings soft.

I used a resilient willow twig to tie the whitish cicadas together like a string of coins in ancient China, while the shells were carried in a small basket, for fear of breaking their legs. But morning was not the time to collect cicada shells—morning was the time to get the cicadas.

When Xiao Bao and I returned home, more often than not, my mother would have just finished cooking breakfast for the whole family. The cinder ashes would still be very hot, burning hot to be exact. I would throw the string of cicadas into the mouth of the cooking range and bury them with the hot ashes. Cicadas would elongate almost instantly in the heat, sometimes with a sizzling sound. They could not be left in the cinders for long, for they burnt easily which spoilt the taste.

The back part of a cicada, the tail, is empty. It is crisp but not fleshy. The forward part, the body, is full of lean meat, which tastes like beef. We would put the meat in between two halves of *bing tzi*, like sandwiches, dusted with a bit of salt and sprinkled with a few drops of sesame oil whenever my mother had it. Such a sandwich tasted grand. My brother and myself enjoyed them heartily. To us no other meat was as good because cicada meat was the only meat we were familiar with.

I sometimes caught cicadas for my Da Ma to feed her cat. It was done during the noon nap when, hiding in the foliage of tall trees, cicadas chirped away non-stop, making the grown-ups restless in their sleep and the hot air seem hotter. I made a device to catch cicadas hiding high on the trees and to get the shells down. The shape and trigger arrangement of the device was very much like a cross-bow. The stock was a long pole and the bow, being small, was made from bamboo. The arrow was short and its head had a tiny hook to prevent the cicada escaping. The tail of the arrow had a long piece of string attached to prevent it from being lost.

When I had located a cicada high in the tree, I aimed the arrow at the back of the cicada and kept the arrow's pointed head twenty centimetres away from it. I then steadied the pole with my left hand and pulled the string with my right hand. Sure enough the cicada would be caught. And when seeing a shell on a leaf of the tree, I would hook it off with the bow.

'Don't go into the woods during the noon nap,' my mother would caution me. 'There are kidnappers there.'

I never really believed that. I thought it was a tactic all parents used to keep children from roaming in the fields. But I was cautious. On the one hand I had bigger boys as company when seeking cicadas in a group, or, on the other hand I always avoided strangers.

Cicada shells were used by pharmacists for making Chinese herbal medicine. The pharmacist would buy the shells from us at one hundred yuan for ten (one cent of the new yuan, the *ren min bi*). During the noon naps, I usually went shell hunting with my cousin, Shan, who was six years older than me. Each noon, we would collect about fifty or more shells.

Before 1949, through collecting cicada shells, I had accumulated a big pile of Golden Paper Notes (*Jin Yuan Juan*—paper notes issued by the Kuomintang government). They were brand new and looked beautiful. I hid them under the reed mat of our *kang*. These paper notes became pieces of waste paper during the latter half of 1948 when our village was liberated. I cried quite a bit about it. I found out that it might not be a good thing to save money, even a small sum. My mother glued them all to the wall of our room as decoration. Whenever I looked at them I felt betrayed and failed by the government which issued those paper notes. I continued shell collecting after 1949, still getting a hundred yuan for ten shells, but the paper notes were different to the Golden Paper Notes. The currency changed again after 1953 to *ren min bi* at a hundred old yuan to one new cent.

Shell collecting provided me with pocket money, which was always borrowed by my mother to buy salt, oil or vinegar. Unfortunately my mother was never rich enough to pay me back.

When autumn was replaced by winter, the cicadas disappeared. By then a kind of white worm found in willow stumps became a good treat for Xiao Bao and myself. I never tried other kinds of worms and my father never told me of any other that was edible.

The worm was similar to a silkworm but was whiter, longer and thicker. It filled up the hole it ate out of the inside of a stump or root. It lay there very still. It was hard to imagine how it was possible for it to eat the wood within the stump. When my father split a willow stump for firewood in winter, two or three or more worms would be exposed. He would knock them out on to the cold icy ground. The worm would wriggle its head and tail a few times. It would be frozen hard like a stick if not picked up and eaten. I would immediately bake these worms in the hot ashes. Like cicadas, they became longer shortly after being buried in hot ashes. When cooked, willow worms turned golden and straight. I had to be very careful when eating them. The worm had no meat but an oily juice inside its hollow tubular body. The fluid was yellowish, similar to melted butter or margarine. If it dripped onto your clothing, it would leave oil stains. It tasted marvellous in a sandwich of *bing tzi*. They tasted better still when fried in oil, but my mother never had enough oil, and even if she had, she would not have allowed me to do that. A greater pity was that the worms were rarely available because my father could not find many willow stumps or roots to split for firewood.

Wild Vegetables and Elm Leaves

'Chaff and wild vegetables make up half a year's victuals.' This was the reality for the poor peasant family and was true, at least, to the poor peasants in our village until 1965 when they, for the first time in their lives, had sufficient rice and wheat flour for food. When I was old enough to work, which was at four years of age, it became a very important part of my life to collect wild vegetables or elm leaves, until I went to senior high school in Beijing in 1959.

The edible wild vegetables in our area were quite varied, but only two kinds played a major role in stuffing our stomachs. One of them was a plant, the roots of which we called 'sweet roots'. We ate these roots in the spring and the leaves were fed to the pigs. As spring began, Xiao Bao and I, with several other boys, would go digging for the roots with a rake—the 'small four teeth'.

We never had any problem finding them. We knew from the previous autumn places where the plants were abundant. Also we could not be mistaken about the roots—their colour, shape, and thickness were all familiar to us. The root was white, long, and easily broken by the rake. It was as thick as our thick noodles, and buried at a shallow depth in the soil. There was no shortage of such roots, and one dig of the rake would unearth many of them. Sand could be shaken off the roots easily, since sand was not inclined to stick to them. Root digging was not strenuous, and never hampered our childish discussions about dreams, games, or of where we could dig next.

When our baskets were full, we sat by the roadside playing 'getting into the horn'—a game where two players would move two pebbles or twigs to try and block his opponent from getting his piece in the corners of a drawn horn. If he was forced into the tip of the horn he lost the game.

Children never wanted to get home early, for there would be jobs waiting. Parents never considered that they should willingly allow more time for children to play. As a result, though I was an obedient boy, I would look at the sun and would not get home before noon or before sunset.

Whatever happened, I was not too late to give my mother enough time to wash the roots and cook them with corn flour. She spread the prepared roots on a tray to steam them—any food, when cooked with corn flour, was called *zheng gao*. Under the tray she cooked porridge simultaneously with the mixture of corn flour and roots, to kill two birds with one stone.

The roots tasted similar to sweet potatoes. They agreed with my palate and stomach but not with my bowels. It made my lower abdomen heavy and I had to visit the toilet frequently. It did the same to other people, too. Yet in spring it was the only food we could get to help us fill our stomachs. It gave us the strength to work. As long as the food gave more nutrition to the body than it could take off, it was considered 'good food'. Otherwise people would not dig such roots every spring.

A wild vegetable, called *jian zi gu*, was much more popular with poor peasants and only grew on alkaline land. It was leafy, wider than a finger, but much longer. It was very fleshy, wide in the middle section and tapered towards the tip. It was bright green in colour and would turn a darkish green as it ripened. We only ate the tender young leaves.

A special knife was used to cut the leaves from the plant. The blade of the knife was straight and very sharp; the other side (the back) was shaped like the back of a bow. The end had a handle bent vertical to the flat knife. The iron extension was then bent parallel to the flat knife and fixed with a wooden handle. The wooden handle would be about ten centimetres above the ground, thus making it possible to cut along the surface of the ground. This knife was widely used to cut Chinese leeks, grass, and to weed the vegetable garden.

When the leaves were carried home, my mother would select the tender ones and clip them off the stem with the nails of her thumb and forefinger. The other older leaves would be cooked for the pig. When describing the food peasants had before 1949, the sentence would always be 'eating the food of pigs and dogs'. Yes, whatever wild vegetable people could eat, the pigs could. But what the pigs could eat might not always be suitable for humans.

My mother would wash the leaves and then place them in boiling water in the cauldron. She soaked the leaves into the water and got them out quickly. Next she would chop them with the kitchen knife—sometimes she would ask me to do a big quantity of them. She would then finely grind a handful of baked peanuts and mix them with the minced leaves, which had already been squeezed of their juice. Chopped spring onion, salt, very hot oil, and homemade condiment sauce, were all added to the minced leaves. After being mixed well with chopsticks, the filling was ready. Next she prepared the corn flour dough. She scooped a handful of dough and pressed it flat between her hands. I ladled the mixture onto the dough in her hands. She moved her two hands, the way a potter made a porcelain base, to hold the mince, and I ladled more mixture in. She would close it up when no more mince mixture could be put in. This was called *cai tuan zi*, meaning a vegetable ball. The pastry was so thin that it had to be carried with two hands lest it would fall apart when being eaten. A bowl of thin corn meal porridge and one vegetable ball would be enough for the stomach. But one got hungry quickly.

The bellies of poor children protruded, big and round with a greenish vein bulging under the skin from top to bottom. My belly, though I was very thin, was also more prominent than any other part of my body, with a greenish vein from the recess of the breast to the lower part of the belly, a sure sign of malnutrition. The stomach was like a bottomless pit and seemed impossible to fill.

The flowers of the wild pear tree, which were used as a graft for big juicy pears, could also be used to make tasty and fragrant corn flour *zheng gao*. But the trees were few and far between and the flower quantity was too small and therefore could only be used as a specialty. The leaves of a tree called *xiang chun* were good for making a noodle salad and a tasty dish with eggs, but it was grown only in a courtyard because the leaves were hard to get and peasant's could keep a watch on this food source. Willow buds could be used as a dish for the table but only for a very short time in spring.

The only tree which could be relied upon for food was the elm tree, which was common in our area. The elm tree flower was called the 'elm coin'. In spring, elm flowers could be eaten raw as fruit and could be used to make tasty *zheng gao* or *wo tou* or *bing tzi*. If elm flowers were mixed with corn flour, salt and water, and were grilled in the cauldron, it was hard, crisp, and very tasty. There was a common story told about elm flowers:

'Once upon a time there was a poor peasant couple. They lived in a shabby house and they toiled day and night. They never had enough food after paying the officials, who were more ferocious than tigers. They had an elm tree in their yard. The elm tree spirit saw their difficulty and was sympathetic. The spirit entered their dreams one night and told them that in the deep of the night they could shake the elm tree to get some coins. He also told them they should shake off only a few coins each day, enough for them to buy food for a few days. When they woke they told each other about their dreams and they found out that they were exactly the same.

The next day they got up in the dead of night and shook the elm tree. Five or six coins fell onto the ground and jingled. They picked up them up and were very grateful and excited. The following day they bought corn flour and had pure corn flour *wo tou*. The man worked harder because he now had a full stomach.

By and by his wife became greedy. She wanted to shake off more money from the tree to buy luxuries. One night she got up secretly, without waking her husband. She kept on shaking the tree until no more money fell. The next day the tree died. The money she got turned into dried flowers.

The husband watered the tree and prayed for it to live again. His sincerity and earnestness moved the spirit. He paid a second visit to the man in his dream.

"Honest young man," the spirit said, "for your sake I allow the elm tree to live again. You will not be able to get money from the tree anymore. But when you have not enough food, you can eat the flowers and the leaves."

The following day, the elm tree became alive. Next spring, the tree had plenty of flowers, which clustered around the twigs just like coins strung together. In memory of the spirit, they called the flowers "flower coins".'

Elm tree leaves, when tender, were as good as the flowers used to make *zheng gao* or *wo tou*. Old and tough leaves could be used to feed pigs. In a natural calamity, even old and tough leaves could be used to stuff a human stomach. Elm tree leaves saved a lot of people during the difficult years.

During my primary school years, I often went to get elm flowers in spring or elm leaves in summer after school in the afternoons. If I got more than we could use for one or two meals, my mother would dry them in the sun, crush them into powder and store it away. Elm leaf collection was generally an easy matter, though sometimes it could be very difficult. One day when school was over in the afternoon, I went to get elm leaves. I could not find an elm tree from which I could strip the leaves. I walked from wood to wood and at last came across an elm tree suitable for my purpose. But the tree was terribly high and it curved not too far below its fork. To get from the curve to the fork would be like crossing a single timber bridge—difficult and dangerous. Some way below the curve there were branches on the same side as the curve of the tree.

I tied one end of a long rope to my waist and the other end to my piggyback basket. I climbed up the tree with some difficulty. Once I was astride a branch and had my basket secured below my feet I started to strip leaves into the basket. The leaves were untouched. They looked green and fresh. It did not take long for me to fill the basket. I was happy and became a bit careless. I lost my balance and fell from the tree. If it had not been for the branches below the curve of the tree, I would not be writing about myself now!

The elm skin of the root was also used by poor peasants. Elm root skins were chopped into tiny pieces, dried thoroughly in the sun and crushed into powder on the grinding roller stone. The powder was very, very fine, like potato starch, but of a pinkish colour. A mixture of corn flour and elm root skin powder could be used to make noodles and dumplings. These were called red noodles and red dumplings—food people had for special occasions like the Spring Festival, if they could not afford pure wheat flour.

Sweet Potato Collecting

Before 1949 I was not old enough to do much potato collecting, but after 1949 I spent my autumn vacations mainly, but not solely, potato collecting. I always took Xiao Bao with me, for I had to do the potato collecting and baby sitting at the same time. And when he was a bit older, he became my helper, and later still, a companion. My cousin Xiang, who was my uncle Yong-jiang's third son, sometimes joined us.

It was a bit easier when collecting in a field that had just been harvested, but a newly harvested field was not always available. We could not return home from the field with an empty basket. We then dug in the field, which had already been thoroughly combed by sweet potato pickers. It was a work thinly rewarded.

One late autumn day, it was cold and windy. Xiao Bao and I wandered from one sweet potato field to another—each field we combed at least two or three times. Then I thought about the sweet potato plot of my uncle Song-lin, whose house was in front of ours. No sweet potato picker had tried their luck in his plot because he was known as the cleanest harvester. It was also because the plot was so sandy and dry that sand just slipped through the teeth of the rake, so it was not possible to turn the soil up to look for the sweet potatoes. I told my brother we would try our luck there.

'Are you sure? I think we will just waste our time there!' he commented. He was already old enough to go to school. He had a good brain and was fond of using it. When choosing where to look for sweet potatoes, he always liked to have his opinion heard.

We had no luck with our rakes but then I hit upon an idea. I bared my feet and ploughed the sand with my feet, like a pig using its muzzle. When the soles of my feet felt a sweet potato butt I would use my hand to pull it out. It turned out to be a piece of sweet potato as thick as a hen egg and as long as a carrot. The method worked. Xiao Bao did the same.

'I got one!' he pulled one out and showed it to me proudly.

'One again,' he declared. His mirth made me happy, too.

'Look,' I showed one to him.

We laughed and ploughed the sand faster with our feet. We were so happy that we did not feel much of the slapping of our faces by the wind and sand. We worked fast and the result was good. Very soon our baskets were half full.

When we had combed the sweet potato plot twice, we sat in the lea of a thick willow bush munching the raw sweet potatoes to pacify our stomachs. It tasted sweet, for it was the sweet potato planted after wheat harvest. Sweet potato planted at that time was always very sweet.

The next day, Xiao Bao and I set out without any particular aim. Before we had any idea what to do, we came to two men ploughing a sweet potato field. I told him to follow one and I followed the other. Pieces of sweet potatoes were now and then seen in the upturned soil. It was easy work. By noon each of us had a full basket of sweet potatoes. We were very happy but such luck did not come to us every day.

Wheat Gleaning

Wheat gleaning was done during the wheat harvest holidays. I did the wheat gleaning each year during these holidays, but here I will just write about one particular occasion. It was 1952 or 1953, and when the wheat gleaning time arrived, Granny took me to a village about ten kilometres south of our village. It was situated in the wheat growing area. She took me to a house she knew and asked permission for us to stay. We were allowed to stay, not in their house, but in the hut sheltering the millstone. We were given a water bucket and a gourd ladle for our usage. We were forbidden to get water from their vat, because they were Hui people (Chinese Muslims). They suspected anything that touched our lips.

It was getting hotter every day. In the night the hut was full of mosquitoes. When I lay down on the board the owner placed as my bed, they hovered over me in hordes. Their droning kept me awake for a long time. They swooped down on my face, my hands, and wherever the body was not covered. I slapped my face with my palm—each strike would kill plenty of mosquitoes. I punished almost every part of my body to kill mosquitoes, but my eyelids would become heavier and heavier and finally even mosquito bites could not keep me awake.

In the morning, my face, hands, and body were terribly itchy. When I washed my face the water was coloured with blood. My shirt and trousers had bloodstains everywhere. As I had no spare trousers or shirt, I had to wear the blood-stained and sweat-soaked trousers and shirt until we returned home two weeks later. At home I could sit in the river, wash my trousers and shirt with river water and sand, and dry them by spreading them over a bush.

Wheat was harvested by pulling the plants out—the stalk and roots. The work would start in the small hours of the morning and stop about mid-morning, because in this period of the day wheat stalks were more resilient due to the morning dew. The ears would be cut off with a lever knife as soon as the wheat was transported to the yard.

Granny and I had to get up and set out when the sky was still starry. We waited by the edge of the field where wheat was being harvested. Lots of people were waiting, but to pick leftover wheat was different from picking sweet potatoes—any wheat dropped on the ground could be seen. To collect sweet potatoes depended on clever digging. To pick wheat depended solely on the quickness of the legs and hands. With wheat, where the bundles were piled was where most leftover wheat was found. When permission was given, I had to run quickly from one pile to another, not to pick up wheat stalks one by one but to stretch out my arms and scoop indiscriminately and put them under one arm and run to another site. A big armful could be collected in less than five minutes. Thereafter, I would scan the field to pick up individual ears.

Granny was not at all slow, though her feet were once bound ones. In her time, all girls had to have their feet bound. But after marriage, she had to work outdoors every day and gradually, though four toes of each foot were broken, her feet grew bigger, becoming 'half big feet', meaning feet between unbound and bound ones.

We quickly moved to another harvesting field and repeated the procedure. We had breakfast mid-morning while we were waiting for permission to start collecting wheat. There were plenty of mulberry trees around, whose branches were used to make pitchforks, which were in great demand in the countryside. As long as one did not break a branch, there was no interference from anybody if one picked mulberries to eat.

So I collected mulberries for us to eat with our bread.

We brought with us enough corn flour for three days. Then we would crush the wheat we had collected to make pancakes. We did not separate the flour from the chaff. We mixed them altogether to make pancakes. To do our cooking, we had brought with us a small wok with a handle. We used two bricks to serve as our stove. Our firewood was just the dry wheat stalks after we had beaten off the wheat kernels.

In the afternoon when it was hot and no more wheat harvesting was underway, we went to look for wheat ears in the fields where we had collected wheat in the morning.

At the end of my vacation and also the end of wheat harvesting, Granny said goodbye to the owners of the house and thanked them for their hospitality.

'Leave the water bucket and gourd ladle in the hut,' the landlady said to Granny. 'We must scrub them clean before we can use them again.'

The tone in which she spoke to us sounded as if we were beggars and the dirtiest people on earth. We were, because for fourteen days I had worn the same unwashed shirt and trousers, on which bloodstains overlapped sweat stains. But I sensed that our repulsiveness to her was not our physical appearance.

The result of the two weeks hard work was fifteen catties of wheat kernels, which was a big booty for the following Spring Festival.

That holiday I was nearly twelve years old.

Collecting Soybeans

Food and firewood were two things the peasants in our area had to do their utmost to obtain. So in autumn, in the late afternoons during weekdays, in the afternoons on Saturdays, and on Sundays, my mother would instruct me to collect firewood, but only if the collection of sweet potato and peanuts had finished.

In autumn, soy butts with roots were very good for digging up as firewood as they were easy to store and gave stronger flames than dry tree leaves or grass. I was always sent to dig soy butts with Xiao Bao, but I had to remind him every now and then not to tread on the butts, which were as sharp as daggers.

Soybean plants were cut manually with a long-handled sickle. The sickle was sharpened to a fine edge before going to the field to cut the soy plants.

The ripe soy pods and plants were resilient in the morning because of the dew. The harvester pushed the plants forward, grasped them tightly (the pods prick fiercely if not grasped tightly) and inserted the sickle blade into the lower part of the plants, as close to the ground as possible. He then yanked the sickle backward with a sudden jerk, so the plants came out. The butts left behind had very sharp edges pointing to the sky.

About mid-morning, the sun became hot, the dew disappeared, and so the soy plants and pods became dry. Over time, the sickle would become blunt. The harvesters had to yank the sickle with two or three jerks before the plants were cut off. The violent jerks shook some very dry pods open, spilling beans to the ground. Such beans were big and good. If not spoilt by dew or by moisture from the soil, they were ideal for collecting.

One day when I was soy butt digging, I pushed aside the leaves with my hands and saw some big, round soybeans lying scattered on the ground between the rows of butts. Soybeans were more valuable than soy butts, so I decided to collect the beans instead of digging up the butts. I tied both sleeves of my shirt up at the cuffs with grass to hold the beans collected. It was quite warm and to have my upper body naked would not give me a cold. Xiao Bao also shed his shirt and asked me to tie up his sleeves at the cuffs.

We began to collect soybeans immediately. It was easy work and we found it very interesting. We were very happy when we talked about the possibility of swapping tofu (soybean curd) with the beans we collected. (1 catty of soybeans could be exchanged for 7 catties of tofu. Only when the Spring Festival approached, did my parents make tofu themselves.) We enjoyed the bean curd salad very much, and the discussion made us eager to collect as many beans as possible. But gradually it became harder and harder to do. When we squatted down, not only did our legs became sore quickly, but if we were not careful enough, the butts would prick our arses. Bending our backs double for this work gave us backaches in a very short time. All I could do was kneel between the two rows of butts, and crawl forward like a baby while clearing the ground of beans within the reach of my arms. Xiao Bao copied me. He knelt in the lane next to me and crawled as I did. He used his nimble hands like a chicken uses its beak. When we were a bit tired we would sit up and compare our results. Then we would start again, eager to pick more and more beans. Our fingers became numb, our right arm muscles became sore from contracting and stretching thousands of times to pick up the beans, and our necks were also sore from the continuous strain. The head became numb, too. The motion of the hands and arms was mechanical and automatic.

Though cushioned by the layer of soy leaves under my knees, which I scooped there as I cleared them away so that I could see the beans, the knees of my trousers were soon wet from the moisture in the soil. My knees were slowly soaked and began to ache under the pressure of my body. Though my eyes were as sharp as those of any other boys, I still picked up beans I would throw away, wasting the time for picking up good ones. The tips of my right hand index finger and thumb ached, and the soil which was deposited under the nails, was black and difficult to clean afterwards.

By the time we went home for lunch, one of my tied sleeves was filled with beautiful beans. My brother also got quite a big quantity. He would not let me carry the beans for him. He insisted on doing it himself.

'Ma!' he called as soon as we entered the yard. He wanted to show her what a good deed he had done. She came out but did not see any butts in our basket.

'You are already about ten years old,' she snapped at me, 'but you only know playing.'

Her words were like a tub of icy cold water poured over my head. I swallowed the words, which were already on the tip of my tongue, to show how proud my brother and I were. She was like that. She never wanted to see me idling about, which I never was. She wanted results. So I kept silent.

'We did not play, Ma,' Xiao Bao said.

'You did not play? But where are your soy butts?'

'We collected soybeans,' I put in. 'Beans are better than butts.'

She was surprised. Only then did she realise that our upper bodies were bare. She took over the shirts, untied the sleeves to empty the beans into a basket. She took a handful of beans in her hands and examined them. A smile appeared on her face.

'Where did you get them?'

'From the eighty *mu* plot,' I replied. I no longer felt the happiness I had a moment ago.

'Good beans,' she said. 'You two can collect them every day. Have your lunch.' She added, 'collect more beans after the meal.'

She gave us a flour bag, and two empty tins, which were given to us during the re-organisation of the 49th army in our village. One full tin of beans was about one-and-a-half catties, but how many beans there were in one full tin, I did not know. Nobody in the family knew. My mother was just interested in how many tins of beans we got—that was her understanding of quantity. I got two tins that afternoon.

The following day, my cousin Xiang joined Xiao Bao and I. The third day two more cousins from my other uncle's family who lived in several houses in front of ours joined us. Very soon, our bean collecting team grew to about ten boys.

To save time, we stopped coming home for lunch. We each took our own lunch. We could play a bit in the fields and we had more time to collect the beans. We could also have a bit of time lying on our backs under the sun on dry sand to rest our tired and sore bodies. Each day, a quick picker like me could get about four tins of beans. A slower one could get three tins.

During those years, my mind was so simple that it contained only the thought of how to get wild vegetables, sweet potatoes, peanuts, and soybeans. My simple mind harboured only considerations of how to get a bit of money to solve my school fees and expenses. Each year my activities after school and during the holidays were exactly the same.

Stripping Grass Seeds

Peasants were always at the mercy of Nature. Until all the harvesting was finished, it was very hard to know whether the harvest would be good or bad, the weather being too fickle to be reliable. Peasants never dared to feel sure about a good harvest, because so many good crops had been damaged by continued heavy rains before harvesting in the past.

Stripping grass seed became my major job during the latter half of the summer holidays each year. If the harvest of that year was bad, grass seed could be used to make food such as *wo tou* or *bing tzi*. If the harvest was a good one, grass seed could be sold as pigs' feed. Whichever the use, it was a good backup for the year.

Eighteen days after Li Qiu (the arrival of autumn), all grass, even grass that had grown only about an inch long, would bear seed. A month after the arrival of autumn, I would start to strip grass seed. I could not start later than that because the new school term would be drawing near.

My equipment was simple—a piggyback basket, a flour bag, and strips of cloth rags. A loop of lace was sewn to the open side of the bag so that I could hang it from my neck. A small finger-thick young willow was bent into a ring and was also sewn to the opening of the bag so that it stayed open all the time, making it easy for me to put the seeds in. The cloth strips were used to protect my right hand index finger because it was chafed tens of thousands of times each day by the grass ears and stalks.

Again Xiao Bao was my follower and companion. He was already a hard 'worker', doing everything with me. If there was not much rain, we could only get grass seed from the woods or by the roadside. The seed from most types of grass is very tiny. Only the seed of the wild tares is bigger. Tare grass could grow anywhere—when the fields were waterlogged, it grew very quickly. When they grew in water their stalks were thicker, their leaves broader and fleshy. Peasants also used tare grass to feed their horses and pigs.

Our main target was to strip the seed from the tares. My targeting of the tares had the dual purpose of getting the seed and cutting the grass to make hay for money. The former was to meet my mother's requirement and the latter to solve my difficulty about fees and expenses.

Every day, the early morning was spent cutting grass. When the grass was laden with dew, it was so fresh that it was cut off with the least resistance to the sickle. The hay also had a greenish lustre, which attracted the buyers. Besides, by the time we went back home for lunch, the weight of grass could be greatly reduced by the drying sun, which affected the price we could ask for it. The more the grass weighed the more we would earn. The latter half of the morning was used for stripping grass seed.

First of all I wrapped cloth rag strips round my brother's forefinger to protect it. Then I would wrap up mine. We would wade in the water from one cluster of tares to another. Catching the ear with my left hand, I stripped it with my right hand. The friction of the ear against the finger cut through the cloth rags very quickly. Then I would rotate the undamaged side to the front. That was cut through very quickly again. I had to be very careful to remind Xiao Bao now and then and I had to check my own hand frequently. Careful as I was, my finger was cut the very first day. The raw flesh did not heal properly until I went back to school again.

By the time I got home at noon and in the evening, my finger ached, my legs were sore, and my stomach was empty. I had to carry at least fifty kilograms of grass on my back all the way home. Sweat trickled down my face profusely—this was both because of a hungry stomach and the scorching sun. The sand underfoot burned the soles of my bare feet a pinkish colour. To cover the one or two kilometres to get home, I had to take quite a few stops to rest my legs, which became weak from hunger. Xiao Bao suffered too. Like me, he never complained how he suffered because he knew complaints would not help.

Work in the afternoon was even more difficult than in the morning. The sun was scorching and the heat reflected from the water made breathing uncomfortable and crimsoned the face. My finger ached terribly when the grass ears passed through my hand and a shiver would pass through my body. I had to grit my teeth to continue stripping the grass seeds.

No matter how hard I tried, I could only strip half a bag in the morning and half a bag in the afternoon. To get just half a bag of seeds, I had to let hundreds of thousands of grass ears chafe against my fingers. It was simple work but a hard job. It needed no skill but it demanded willpower.

chapter 9

MY PRIMARY SCHOOL YEARS

Peasants did not expect much from their children's school education. 'It will be all right if my son or daughter can read and write his name. We do not need much lettering for tilling the land.' This was always on the lips of peasants. It was also always on the lips of my mother. In most cases, the end of primary school education was the beginning of being a peasant. My primary school years were between 1949 and 1955. During that time, Mao established the Young Pioneers, a program to teach young children about the Communist Party, the importance of respecting authority and the merits of doing good deeds. Members wore red scarves, elected classmates as team leaders, raised the national flag, inspected each other's dress and discipline, and participated in after-school activities such as chess, music or dancing. It was a time when following political ideals became a part of my life.

My Early Follies

Mischievous behaviour is contagious. In the early days, in every class studying the Chinese language, we would have an examination by Teacher Zhen. Mostly it was to write texts from memory on the slate with pencils. Older students, boys in particular, were seldom able to do it correctly. To avoid criticism from the teacher, they tried tricks.

Before the language class began, the older boys would sharpen their slate pencils very finely. When they were asked to write from memory a text on the slate, they wrote the words as small as they could and in places difficult for Teacher Zhen to read, such as along the slate's frame. When Teacher Zhen checked each one to give marks, it would take him a long time to identify each word. It would be difficult for any teacher with good eyesight to check their writing, let alone for Teacher Zhen, who was very short-sighted. He would stand by the window, put the slate at eye level to squint at the words. The students tried hard to choke back their laughter.

We younger students found it amusing and copied them. This was too much for Teacher Zhen.

'Students,' he addressed the whole class with sadness on his face. 'I am very sorry for you. Do you realise how precious this opportunity is to most of you? Many of you, especially the older ones here, may not be able to continue studying after Year Six. Don't you wish to learn as much as possible? Do you still want to be like your father and your father's father—not able to read, to write and to communicate in writing? You can trick me now but you will be tricked by the words later.'

Like a pebble thrown into a pond, Teacher Zhen's words sent ripples of shock waves in my mind. I felt ashamed to copy the mischievous tricks of the older boys. However, the boys had too much energy to stay quiet. During the free exercise class one afternoon, when I was in Year Two, some of my male classmates were practising 'walking on the surface of the walls and flying along the eaves'. They propped the principal's door against the wall and tried to run up the wall with the help of the door. The door was the principal's 'wind door', mounted in the position of today's security door. He had not the time to put it in place yet so it was left against the wall below the window. I became fascinated and joined them. We ran up the door to the wall and slipped back to the ground. Perspiration trickled down our faces, which were already rosy from exertion. When it came to my turn once again, I raced to the door with such might that one piece of the door board broke under my foot. I was not hurt but I was a bit scared. The other students ran away, so as not to be involved in the trouble.

I went to the principal. The principal was in his mid-fifties and very slim. His back bent a bit forward as if always ready to bow. His thin face had many lines and creases—not stern ones, however. When he smiled, he had more lines and creases on his face. His hair was cut in the style of the time, parting in the middle and oiled. He wore a blue Mao style jacket, which was then in fashion. The finger on his left hand were scorched and tainted yellow from cheap cigarettes. His eyes were very large, shining with a bright lustre and pouring kindness onto people he was speaking to.

'Principal,' I bowed to him in his office, 'I have made a mistake.'

'What mistake?' he smiled. 'Let me know what it is.' He pushed his chair back a bit and lit a cigarette.

'I broke your door.' I told him timidly.

'How?' he asked, his kind smile still there on his face. He was a bit surprised.

'I tried to learn "walking on the walls and flying along the eaves",' I told him. 'But my stamping was too heavy for the door.'

'Brave boy,' he said kindly, laughing at my silly attempts with mirth. He laughed so much that water welled into his eyes. Other teachers looked at him questioningly. 'It is not possible to walk on the walls and to fly along the eaves. It is the nonsense of rubbish writers!' he explained to me. 'Are you hurt?'

'No,' I replied.

'Good, don't worry about my door.' He patted me on the head. 'I can repair it. Don't do such a silly thing again in the future. It is too dangerous.'

'What's my punishment?' I asked. One of the disciplines and rules of the school was that if a student damaged school property, the student should be punished and compensate for the damage.

'For what?' he asked. 'The door is mine. It is not school property. I do not need you to pay. Go and play.' He tried to set my mind at ease by telling me that.

Happily I ran out of his office—happy, not because I received no punishment or penalty, but because I saw a kind of love in his face, his voice and his eyes. Fifty years have elapsed but I still miss him in my heart.

Each Week a New Task and a New Song

It was my second year in school. Every Monday morning before class, we lined up in the courtyard to raise the national flag, to be told about the task of the week and to learn a new song. The principal would call students at random to check whether they remembered the task and the song of the previous week. The flag-raising ceremony was very solemn, though not as elaborate as the one at Tiananmen Square today. Our school band would play the National Anthem while a student slowly hoisted the national flag. We all stood at attention, feeling very proud at heart.

The principal would then announce the name of that week and explain the task. For example, when the name was 'Tree Planting Week' it would mean the students would, led by the teacher in charge of our class, plant trees around our school sportsground. When the name was 'The Week of Patriotism', we would help to get donations to buy fighters for the volunteers in Korea. When it was a 'Week of Cleanliness', the teachers would, in the morning, stand by the school gate to check our necks, hands, nails and faces, to see if they were clean or not. And we had to kill flies and rats to fight the American 'Germ War'. It was said that during the Korean

War, American planes flew into China to drop flies, mosquitoes and rats carrying germs, in order to make the Chinese sick or dead. If a week was named a 'Week of Good Manners', the teachers would make sure our manners were good. All such tasks were new to me and to the other students and we eagerly did our best to fulfil them.

Each week our music teacher would teach us a new song. We were taught 'The Sky in the Liberated Area is a Clear Sky', 'The Great Production Movement', The National Anthem 'Hei La La', 'Drive my Gas Truck', 'A Man from Afar', and so forth.

One Monday morning, a boy from our class was picked to answer some questions.

'What's the name of last week?' the principal asked.

'Corn meal porridge.' he replied.

Thunderous laughter exploded.

'What song did we learn?'

'Feet bondage.' he answered. Actually he just remembered the similar sound and in a hurry he made up the reply.

Vociferous laughter broke out again.

'Students,' the principal spoke when the laughter died down. 'It sounds laughable. But it is a pity that you children at such a young age should always have food and work on your mind. He answered mistakenly and that was bad. But doesn't it remind us that it is not easy for many of you to study in school? Cherish this opportunity and study hard, students.'

Back in our classroom, the boy was criticised for not being attentive and for paying no attention to such activities. We were all warned to take a lesson from that.

On another Monday, a student was selected to direct our singing with the movements of his hands, as a conductor does in a concert. He was not tall enough and so was lifted onto a square table at the front corner of the platform. Our eyes followed the movements of his rising and falling hands and our voices rose and fell accordingly. He directed the singing eagerly and sincerely. But when he raised his right arm and his feet tiptoed to lift his body higher, his trousers suddenly slipped to his ankles just as the song was halfway through. The details of his body, everything that was given to him by Buddha, were exposed to the whole school and were seen by all, though his trousers were lifted up to his waist instantly by the teacher standing next to him. His trousers had no belt but elastic strings. We envied him for that, because we had to fold the waist of our trousers and tie them with a piece of cloth, which served as our belt. The song broke off to the embarrassment of the teacher and the student. (He had no underpants, though his family was a bit better off than most because his father was a carpenter. None of us boys had underpants at the time, because our parents could not afford them.)

Wave upon wave of thunderous and deafening laughter rolled on, and the teachers joined in. Such episodes did not happen every Monday, but the memory of those that did remained.

Winter Evening Classes

From Year Three, we started to have winter evening classes—two classes each evening during the weekdays. In the rural schools, class was over early in the afternoon so that the students could help their parents do farm work or to collect pig feed or firewood. Teaching hours would thus be affected and some texts could not be finished as planned, so in the winter evening classes, teachers had to utilise the time to make up what they had failed to pass on to the students during the day. Students returned to school in the evenings to take new lessons as well as to do the homework assigned by teachers. Teachers also made another use of the evening classes, to prepare the students for the end-of-term examinations.

Attending evening classes was regarded of equal importance to attending the day classes. Absence from evening classes had to be approved by teachers and no student could stay away from them. Unless sick, we seldom considered staying away from such evening classes, anyway.

When the teacher gave explanations, he wrote points on the blackboard, which we had to jot down. The teacher had a safety lantern hanging from the top corner of the blackboard—though not very bright, we could see what he wrote, but we could not write on our notebooks as the light was not strong enough. So we had to solve the problem ourselves.

I got an empty inkbottle, drilled a hole in the middle of the cap, rolled a piece of paper from my old notebooks and inserted it through the hole of the cap to serve as a wick. Then I filled the bottle with kerosene and thus my lamp was ready for use. The pity was that the flame had too much black smoke spinning upward from it and the kerosene gave off too many fumes. Most students had lamps similar to mine. The classroom would become filled with smoke and permeated with kerosene fumes. Our nostrils became black after the classes but we never worried about it.

A few of the older students made very nice looking lamps. A big boy used a small piece of wooden board, two wires, some sorghum stalk skins, and window paper, to make a 'safety lantern'. We envied his invention. Some of the older girls elaborated the idea by making different lampshades. But whatever was done, the smoke and the fumes could not be eliminated.

One night in 1953, six or seven of us boys, who lived close to each other, took a short cut through a big yard and some fields to get home. The chilly night sky was clear and high. A full moon illuminated so brightly that we could discern things clearly from afar. There was no wind. There was not even a stir of the chilly air.

When we approached a yard that was very big and was used to process peanuts and other crops, we stood frozen at the edge of it. Our hair stood straight on our heads. About fifty metres away seven or eight transparent figures as tall and as thick as grown-up humans were standing right in the middle of the yard, in a round circle under the bright moonlight. The contour of each of them was very clear. It was similar to looking through glass windows. You could see things clearly and you knew there was glass. We saw things clearly through those figures but we were sure we saw the figures. That night, my cousin An brought his big black dog with him for safety. The dog saw the figures, too, for it dashed towards them barking fiercely. As soon as the dog approached, the figures retreated, the circle became bigger and bigger and when the dog reached the spot, all the figures disappeared. The dog barked confusedly to and fro. What did we see? This has perplexed me for nearly fifty years and I still have not found a plausible explanation.

The Pioneers Shut Me Out

In 1953, the 'Pioneers' was set up in our school. During one Monday morning gathering, a teacher declared to the students that everybody could join the Pioneers and that whoever wanted to join should pay three thousand old yuan (thirty new cents) for a red scarf.

Our monitor started to list the names during class breaks. When I was approached I said I had no money to buy the red scarf and I had to ask my mother for the money and I could only say yes or no the following day. That night I asked my mother for the money, but she said no, not seeing the necessity for me to spend thirty cents for just a corner of red cloth. To my mother thirty cents was quite a considerable sum of money. It meant her hen had to lay eggs for half a month for her to earn that amount. So I needed time to persuade her and I told this to the monitor the next day.

Two weeks later, more than half of my classmates were given the scarves. They were taught how to tie the scarf around their necks. Various 'leaders' such as squad, team, and brigade leaders, were nominated. It was not difficult for a teacher to organise these, because they had experience in organising the students' scouts corps before 1949.

Then sometime later, on the left arm of the Pioneers, mainly on the girls, a small square-shaped badge with one, two or three signal-red stripes on a white background were attached. All of a sudden, a sense of superiority permeated the air through which they carried themselves. The Pioneers were soon exempted from bowing to the teachers or to anybody else to show their homage. They needed just to raise the right arm above the head with the forearm parallel to earth and the palm open towards the person or persons. That was the way the Pioneers paid respect. Soon all the Pioneers assumed an air of superiority towards other non-members.

The activities of the Pioneers grew more with each passing year. They became the main body of the flower stick dance team; they became the backbone of the waist-drum team; and they stayed at school until late afternoon. They were required to have white shirts and blue trousers for some special occasions. They started to have meetings without the rest of the class.

As a child, the sense of distinction and superiority also attracted me. I disliked being left out and I did not like to remain an outsider. I said to my mother one day, 'Ma, I must join the Pioneers. I will find the money myself. Look at the Pioneers, how proud they are!'

'What is the point of joining the Pioneers? Is it any use to satisfy your thirst or your hunger?' she scolded me.

However, I accumulated the money and approached the teacher to tell him that I wished to be a Pioneer.

'Next expansion of the membership is still some weeks away,' he told me. 'I will discuss with the Pioneer leaders whether you can join.' I was dismissed.

I had the feeling that I would not be allowed to join. I got this feeling not from his words but from something unsaid—something I had observed about that teacher.

He was a young man, not handsome but well dressed, in our eyes. His eyes always smiled when he looked at girls of good appearance in beautiful dresses. He did not like to look at us boys in shabby clothes. There was no love between him and us poor boys, and I sensed that I would not be accepted.

The waiting period began. The days grew into a week, the weeks grew into a month, and half a year went by. More boys and girls from our class were accepted into the Pioneers, but I was shut out. I was notified that I was backward in my thoughts and I needed to be tested further for membership. I did not say anything, but anger boiled within my breast. What was backward in my thinking? This was simply a stupid excuse to shut me out. Didn't I get better marks in examinations? Didn't I obey the teachers more respectfully? Did I lag behind in my thoughts? Of course not!

After this, I went home immediately after the last class of the day. Getting more grass, or firewood, or wild vegetables, was much better than wasting time in school. I did not look down upon any of the Pioneer members but I did not regard any of them as being better than me. I turned my eyes away from that organisation.

When I was in Year Five, except for a few boys too naughty to be accepted, I was the only outsider in our class. One day, the teacher in charge of our class called me to his office.

'You are up to the standards to join the Pioneers now,' he told me.

'Am I?' I asked. 'But I still don't have the money to buy the scarf!' Then I asked, 'What are the standards?'

The teacher felt a bit surprised. Still, he replied.

'Study hard, help other people, respect the teachers, love the motherland, love to work.'

'I met those standards from the very beginning. I was kept out because I could not get the money for the scarf,' I said to the teacher, with a bit of sarcasm but not without due respect.

'I wish you to reconsider it,' he said when I started to leave, at his dismissal, of course.

'Thanks.' I went back to our classroom.

My friend raised his eyes when he saw me coming into the classroom.
'What's it about?' he whispered to me.
'The teacher told me I can join the Pioneers.'
'Good.'
'But, I don't want to join,' I shook my head.

The teacher spoke to me several times after that. Stubbornly, I refused to join. I was rejected at the beginning simply because I could not afford to buy the red scarf and they labelled me as backward. It was a humiliation too much for me to swallow. No matter who came to speak to me, I would not join.

Looking back, I am of the opinion that it is very wrong to divide children in primary school by an organisation like the Pioneers. All children in primary school are honest, naïve, full of energy, and sometimes a bit naughty. To leave some children out of such an organisation will hurt their feelings and their self-respect. It will even affect their lives in the future. All children want to be good boys or girls. A father is to blame if his son has bad manners or bad habits. A teacher is to blame if his or her student does not study hard in school. Children should never be made to feel inferior as I was, by the Pioneers.

Guidance

Upon entering Year Four, we began to learn how to write compositions. The first step was narration. When a heading was given, for example, 'planting trees', we would sit there biting the end of our pencils, not knowing how to begin, or what to write about. When we did write something, we would not know why good or bad marks were given.

Up till now, we were very good at memorising the theme of a text, new words from each text, sentences made with the new words, and so on. Such tasks were written by the teacher on the blackboard and copied by us in our notebooks. We memorised them and we were examined on them. As long as we spent a bit of time over the notebooks and texts, it was not difficult to get full marks.

Now we had to write compositions and we were told to have a beginning, a climax and an ending. But the skills were not explained to us and no examples were given. The teacher never explained to us how to describe a thing, a person, a scene or a feeling. Perhaps the teacher himself did not know how to do a composition in the correct way?

Composition classes became classes of 'punishment' to most of us, except for a few girls. I bit my pencil tip so much that a groove was made around it. Most of the boys did the same. The word 'composition' was enough to frighten me. I thought I could never write a composition correctly.

During the second term, our language teacher changed. The new teacher was a young man from our village. He was the son of a landlord family who was always well groomed and looked sincere. His pronunciation was clear and his writing on the blackboard was very handsome. He wore a Mao style jacket, grey in colour and very well ironed. He never joked with the students, for fear of losing the power of authority. I never saw him smile.

The new teacher spent an hour each day reading a novel to the class. The name of the novel was *Stories of the New Heroic Sons and Daughters*. It was a story about a guerrilla team behind the Japanese line. It was a stirring story. When the teacher was reading, our mood changed in accordance with the development of the story. We became angry when we heard about the Japanese devils burning the houses; we were elated when he read how the guerrillas punished the traitors. The teacher would repeat some paragraphs when they described a scene or a guerrilla. When the quiet of the night was vividly described, he would ask us why it was written like that. We were so fascinated that we looked forward to the novel reading eagerly every day. Gradually, we became able to write about a thing, a person, and so on. We wrote about a thing, a person, and a certain kind of weather in our compositions. If he had summed it up and let us know the key points with which to make a good composition, we would have been able to write better still.

This encouraged me to start reading novels by myself. The first one was called *Advancing Towards Victory*, which was a story about the tug of war between the People's Liberation Army and the Kuomintang Army to control the city called 'Si Ping'. The next book I read was called *Life is Beautiful*. Through reading those two novels I learned more words and expressions and ways to express myself. Novel reading also gave me one bad habit—I became less careful about the accurate definition of a new word.

By the time we finished Year Four, our composition improved greatly and we became more confident in writing. If we had not had the guidance of our teacher, I don't imagine I would have passed the end-of-year examination in composition writing.

When we reached Year Five, and especially into Year Six, the contents of our language texts took a new turn. Articles about young students going to settle in the country villages crammed the pages of our textbook. There was more discussion about the pride of being the first generation of peasants with bookish knowledge. One of the texts was a letter by a famous writer to his daughter, a high school student. The writer's name was Zhao Shu-li, who worked in the liberated areas in the Taihang Mountains. He wrote quite a few novels during that period which reflected the struggle in the countryside. They had a great influence in the villages because he was very familiar with peasant life in rural areas. His daughter went to settle in a village as a peasant. In the letter he encouraged her to work hard and make a good contribution to the country. He told her that her knowledge could be used well in the countryside. He concluded that there was a bright future for her as one of the first generation of peasants with bookish knowledge.

During my schooling years, my mother had dinned into my ears that I should quit school to take part in co-operative labour to earn daily points to get more grain and money by the end of each year. Now that my primary school studies were nearing the end, she spoke to me almost daily:

'After graduation from primary school, you must join us in the co-operative. You've already learnt enough. Look at your cousin, An; he stopped at Year Four and he did quite well. He's now the secretary of our Xiang government. You have two more years' education, you can do better.' And sometimes she would complain how hard it was for her and my father to feed the whole family. Though at heart, I wished to go to junior high school and even further, I had to consider the situation of our family. Now that the government called on us to be new peasants with bookish knowledge, my determination to complete further schooling wavered. To me, whatever the government said was right because they had made it possible for me to go to school. I believed I should answer its call to show my gratitude.

When we had time together, my friends and I would discuss working in the village, being a peasant, and our future.

'I will not go to junior high school,' my friend next door said. 'If one wants to be a peasant, it will be better earlier rather than later.'

'I agree,' his cousin put in. 'We can buy more books about farming, we shall work more cleverly than our father's generation, and we can introduce new methods.'

'We can all read and write,' another one said. 'We will be co-operative chairman, deputy chairman, accountant and team leader. The co-operative will some day be under our control. By that time we will be able to make the land yield more harvest and make our life better by farming in our own way.'

I made up my mind to stay in the village. Such discussions became more frequent when the time drew nearer for us to do the entry exam for junior high school. We dreamed about the future of our village. We argued how to control the sand, how to level the land, how to get a good harvest in a drought, and how to avoid waterlogging. We promised one another not to let anybody know about our thinking—not even our parents.

The guidance of the texts had worked well. Without further thinking or reasoning, we decided to fail the exam, regardless of whether the papers were easy or not. The exam took place in the district centre, which was the town five kilometres to the south of our village. Two teachers, from other schools, were supervising the students during the exam. My friends were all there in the same room, sitting not too far from me. I was not nervous and nor were my friends, but the faces of the students around us looked awfully worried. I did not experience the tremor in my arm and fingers as I did in normal examinations in our own school. I was not surprised at my own coolness when I read silently through the papers before answering the questions. I took out my lunch and started eating while I was writing my composition and answering the questions.

Though the papers did not seem difficult and I judged it should be no problem for me to pass, I did not treat it seriously. My friends were doing the same. One of the supervising teachers looked at me, came over and stood by my desk for a few minutes, saying nothing, and walked to the platform, which was the advantageous point for him to see everybody clearly.

In the afternoon, after the examination finished, we went back home together, all in high spirits. I went to work in our team the following day to earn points. So did my friends. A month later, as expected, I did not get the enrolment notice for junior high school, as some other students did. I had failed.

I became a peasant myself.

chapter 10

PEASANT FOR A YEAR

Students who graduated from primary school, junior high school, and senior high school were twice encouraged by the Chinese central government to become the new generation of peasants. First, this happened during the beginning of 1955, and secondly during the Great Cultural Revolution. The first round was induced through personal choice; the second round was compulsory. With proper assistance and guidance, this could have had strategic importance—not only could it raise the cultural level of the countryside, but it could also alleviate the urban job situation. Most of the students who went to the countryside in 1955 settled down in the peasant villages and some of them became model peasants of the country. Most of the students who reluctantly went to the countryside during the Great Cultural Revolution on government orders returned to their respective cities. Here is my own experience of being a peasant between the winter of 1955 and the autumn of 1956.

Digging a Reservoir

Water was the biggest problem in our area. In spring, the Paradise River was dry right to the bottom and rain was as precious as sesame oil. In summer, consecutive downpours flooded the fields and made some of them waterlogged. Digging a reservoir, as suggested by the local Xiang government, the lowest level of the government in China, was the solution. It called five or six senior co-operatives together, telling them to dig a reservoir to solve the water problem. The senior co-operatives welcomed the idea.

It was the winter of 1955. All the male members of the senior co-operatives were gathered at the site where the reservoir was to be dug. I had returned to being a peasant and so was there with my father. 'Xiang Zhang', the local government chairman and the top authority in our area, was standing on a high point to address the masses. He was a man in his twenties, of slim build, tall, and clad in a very stylish blue overcoat. The flaps of his blue fur hat were tied on top. He articulated his speech loudly in the wind. His words were few. He said that a reservoir would be good for the surrounding senior co-operatives (each village was a senior co-operative). In spring, water could be pumped to irrigate the fields. In summer, the reservoir could store the rainwater for later use and thus the peasants would not fear either drought or waterlogging. 'When the reservoir is completed, you can grow rice like the people south of the Yangtze River. You will have fish, ducks, chicken, rice and wheat flour. You will live down or above stairs. You will have telephones and electricity; all such things can be had through your own hands.'

Even children could recite what he said. All the peasants felt excited by the idea of making this area as good as a country village in southern China. Though 'distant water cannot quench immediate thirst', they applauded him vociferously for painting such a picture for them.

The proposed reservoir was to be fifteen hundred metres long and forty metres wide. The depth was 'as deep as possible'. It was to be located in the middle of five or six villages, to the north-west of our village. The distance varied from two to three kilometres from each surrounding village.

Each village, or each senior co-operative, was assigned one section for digging as per the total number of the population of that village. Ours was the eastern end section, which was then subdivided into twelve sections for each team. Our team ruled that one cubic metre of earth dug out was worth ten points. By the end of the day, the team leader would measure the pit each person dug out.

We four teenagers, the former schoolmates, the failures at the examination and the ambitious new peasants, worked together. I was fourteen years old and the others fifteen. We wanted to show that we could do as much as the adults could. I was the weakest of the four but I did not wish to do less.

The earth was frozen at least half a metre deep and was as hard as rock. A shovel could only scrape the top shallow dry soil. We collected some firewood and lit a fire to melt the ice and make the earth soft. It worked but we could not get enough firewood to keep the fire burning. The digging was very slow, then somebody suggested using sledge-hammers and long steel picks, like workers at the quarry.

We worked in pairs. One held the pick and the other swung the sledge-hammer onto the pick. Gradually, we would cut one piece of frozen earth out. The size was about half a metre square and half a metre thick and its weight was no less than a hundred kilograms. To cut one piece out, we had to swing the hammer about two hundred strokes before we swapped the role of pick-holder and hammer-striker. Sweat trickled down our backs under our padded jackets. Sweat messed the hair on our foreheads. When it was your turn to hold the pick, the sweat, which wet the lining of our jackets, would become cold and very uncomfortable, touching the flesh. Then your hands, your face, and your feet would be freezing cold. I was always eager to swing the hammer, though it was a bit too heavy for me.

We carried away the pieces of frozen earth with ropes and a round timber pole. The ropes were tied to the pole and could be pushed a bit forward or pulled a bit back to adjust the weight on the pole. The ropes dangled with two large loops, which were put under the opposite ends of the frozen earth lump. Two of us would carry the pole on our right shoulders. My partner gave me two advantages—he allowed me to straighten up first and he placed the ropes a bit back towards him. The last to straighten up would have to raise much more of the weight. Even when the ropes were moved just one inch to his side my load would be greatly decreased.

The first day when we were just moving the earth on level ground, we could still manage well under the heavy load. Each step forward was an exertion, and our shoulder ached as if it were on fire. I wanted to walk fast when the load was on my shoulder and slowly when the load was dumped, but we could not. I had to grit my teeth each time I stooped to lift up the pole.

When a trumpet blared declaring the lunch break, I joined my father behind the lumps of frozen earth. He passed me a white cloth bag already on the dark side of grey from frequent use and infrequent washing. I fished out a *wo tou* made from sorghum flour and a salted turnip. The *wo tou* was as hard as rock and blackish-red like old curdled blood. Cracks on the *wo tou* were filled with sand dust, which was carried by the wind and crept into the bag. I could not chew well because when my teeth ground the sand dust the contact was unbearable. And I was very thirsty, which made chewing all the more difficult.

I went to look for water. There was a ditch not very far away. I cut a square hole through the ice, which was about two feet thick. The water was covered with a very thick layer of fleecy green growth. I brushed the growth aside and got a full cup of water. I washed the *wo tou* down with the water. My father drank just a few mouthfuls. He was as tenacious as a camel in the desert. He could always stand thirst to a degree that very few people could match. My mother gave us eight *wo tou* and we finished them all.

'How do you feel?' my father asked me. 'Can you manage?'

'My shoulder is on fire,' I told him, 'but I think I can manage.'

'Tomorrow will be worse,' he told me.

In the afternoon after the break, it was already worse. My shoulder ached badly at the touch of the pole. My legs moved with difficulty. The short winter day seemed not short at all. The sun was moving very, very slowly towards the western mountains. By the time the trumpet announced that we could leave for home, my legs were already too heavy for me to move. Each step was a test of will. And my stomach was so empty that my belly seemed to touch my spine!

'You are a brave boy!' a neighbour sneered at me, laughing. 'This is better than going to school!'

'Of course it is better,' somebody chimed in, 'otherwise why didn't Shuang Xi study harder?'

'Now Shuang Xi can have a full stomach for the next couple of days. He will have a *wo tou* on his shoulder to satisfy his hunger!' a robust young neighbour added, referring to a swollen lump I was going to have on my shoulder the following day.

I was too tired and hungry to retort. My father never argued with anybody, so it was not possible to expect him to fence off the sneers against me. I swallowed the humiliation, but that was not the worst of it, anyway, because they were also very tired and hungry though better off than me. They had not the energy to make more jokes about my friends and I. The worst humiliation was to come when spring sowing began.

My mother had our supper ready as soon as we entered the house. Though it was still the steamed sorghum *wo tou* and porridge of sorghum meal, they were steaming hot and much more attractive than the *wo tou* at lunch. I firmly believe that hunger is the best appetiser. 'When you are hungry, bran tastes as sweet as honey. When you already have a full stomach, even honey does not taste sweet.' The food was better than anything I had ever tasted.

After supper I went to my great uncle's. He had boiled water on the stove that I used to wash my face and feet and to clean my upper body with a wet towel. I felt better but was very sleepy.

'No more chat today,' my great uncle said to me.

My great uncle had to shake me awake in the morning. My right shoulder had a swollen lump as big as a hen's egg, which hurt terribly at the touch of my finger. That was the '*wo tou*' the young man referred to the previous day. My legs were aching and sore.

'After washing, refill the kettle and put it on the stove,' my great uncle told me. He was still in the quilt and would not get up without at least another two hours sleep.

I brushed my teeth with tooth powder, washed my face, placed the kettle over the stove as instructed, closed the door behind me, and went home for breakfast.

'What about your shoulder?' my mother asked.

'It hurts a bit, but it will be all right,' I replied.

We set out at the call of the trumpet. The sky was thickly clouded. A few snowflakes floated in the air. It felt soothing when some incidentally caressed my face. Everybody headed to the reservoir site, in silence.

As the trumpet signalled the start of the morning's work, snowflakes like goose down fell thickly to shroud everything in silver white. Snow fell on our heads and on our backs and gradually melted making the outside cloth of the padded jacket wet.

When we started to carry the frozen earth lumps, I put the shoulder pole on my right shoulder abruptly. If I had tested whether I could put the pole on my shoulder, I would not have had the bravery to put the pole there at all. But tears gushed out of my eyes no matter how hard I tried to hold them back. Very soon it became a dull ache and then numb, as did my brain. After two or three trips I sensed no more pain, but my legs and feet still felt the strain. With each step forward, the muscles bulged to give more strength.

By the time the bugle announced the break for lunch, there was no sign of the snow abating. At first, snowflakes crept into the collar and it felt soothing when they melted against the flesh. A short while later when the body heat dropped back to normal, it was agonising. My padded jacket was wet inside from my sweat and outside by melting snow. Now the outside formed ice and the inside became cold. I felt miserable.

My lunch was still the sand filled sorghum *wo tou*, a piece of salted turnip, and water collected from the ditch covered by fleecy green growth. They filled my stomach and made me feel a bit better, though they did not taste good. My shoulder hurt awfully. I thought it was raw, for it felt stuck to the jacket lining. I tried to shut it out of my mind. Why think about it, if one could do nothing about it?

The afternoon was much worse. The snow on the ground was trodden on and had melted making the ground muddy. My shoes were soaked through and my toes slipped in the sticky wetness inside. The soles of my shoes became thicker and thicker as they collected more and more sticky slimy mud and they were as heavy as lead. Each trip of carrying frozen earth became more difficult than the last and it became more dangerous and risky. The slightest slip of the feet and I would fall to the ground and the load might fall on top of me.

After supper, I scraped the mud off my soles and went to my great uncle's. The snow abated but did not stop completely. After I had washed myself, my great uncle asked me to creep into bed and he dried my shoes and jacket for me by the stove.

'Like some ginger and brown sugar soup?' he asked.

'I am not sick,' I said, 'just a bit tired.'

Still he made a bowl of soup for me. It was made from minced ginger, a pinch of brown sugar and boiling water. The soup helped to drive out the chills from the inside of my body. I turned to lie on my stomach to drink it, when he saw my bleeding, swelling, raw shoulder. He shook his head but said nothing. Either sympathy or encouragement would be useless. We both understood that and remained silent.

The following morning when I stepped out of my great uncle's, I was taken by surprise. The world around had become silver. I wanted to find an apt expression to describe the scenery and two lines of a famous poem from the Tang Dynasty came to my mind: *It seemed as if a spring wind had come suddenly overnight, and tens of thousands of pear trees were in full bloom.* The universe was all silvery. All the trees were white, exactly like pear trees in blossom. I forgot, for a moment, my aching shoulder. I seemed to be in a fairyland. 'The Paradise Palace!' Yes, there was no doubt about that. Why couldn't we make it a paradise with our own hands? My favourite song sprang to my mind:

'My home village,
The maples clatter in the wind.
My home village,
The river sings beneath the wild chrysanthemum.

Red fruits hide in the green foliage,
Birds fly under the white clouds.'

One day we would make our village like that, true to its name. I laughed at my aching shoulder. I laughed at my aching legs. A good life would not fall on me from the sky. Everything had to be exchanged for hard labour, otherwise, why was there a need for a new generation of peasants with bookish knowledge?

Immediately I felt fortified. I struggled with my body and with the heavy load day after day. We stopped working in pairs. Everybody carried two baskets with a shoulder pole. The load was not the least bit lighter but the swelling on my right shoulder was pressed flat and, instead, a layer of callous skin appeared like a patch.

The reservoir became deeper each day and the earth dug out was piled on both sides, like small hills. By then, we had reached a thick stratum of clay. It was like rubber, hard to insert the shovel into and also hard to get the shovel and clay out. One would be sweating to fill up a basket. With the shoulder pole and the baskets hanging from my right shoulder and the slippery muddy clay squelching underfoot, I struggled up the slope. Climbing up the hill-like slope tested my strength. The surface was slippery and quite steep. My toes seemed to dig the sole of my shoes into the ground to get a firm hold. I had to hold the two baskets with my hands to release some of the load off my shoulder. My calves stiffened and the muscles of my thigh hardened with each step up the slope. The load on my shoulder was over seventy kilograms!

Then we came to a depth where water oozed out to the ankle. Not many of us had rubber boots and those who had stood in the water to fill our baskets while we placed them on a ridge left for us to walk on. The server had to take turns because it was too cold to stand in the water for too long. Water kept dripping from our baskets onto the slope and froze into ice in no time, making it even more difficult for us to climb up the slope.

The Xiang Zhang, always clad in his blue overcoat, came to visit the site twice a week. He would tour and check the site like an important leader from the central government, acting stylish and condescending. The Qui Zhang (the Qui was the government above Xiang. The Qui Zhang was the top boss of the Qui government) frequented the site, too. He was an old man in his late fifties. He had a black padded Mao style jacket, which was washed almost grey. His jacket seemed to be always covered with a light sandy dust. He was of average height, his face was broad, tanned and creased. He was a guerrilla in our area and he knew most of the villagers. He would come on a bike, accompanied by a young man as his communicator and errand runner.

The Qui Zhang made no speeches to the people at the site. He would sit with a group of peasants, share a pipe of tobacco with them, and listen to their suggestions and complaints. Then he would move to another cluster of peasants. He suggested each senior co-operative build a fire and boil water for the peasants at the site to warm them up a bit during the breaks. Everybody was pleased.

Progress was good and he checked with the peasants whether the work would be finished before the Spring Festival. One time, when the Xiang Zhang was also touring the site, the chairmen of the senior co-operatives were called together for a meeting. During the lunch break, the Xiang Zhang made a speech, requesting the peasants work harder and finish the job before New Year's Day, so that everybody could celebrate the Spring Festival without worrying about the reservoir. The work went faster, for everybody wished to have New Year at home, not at the site of the reservoir.

Except for the pump site the reservoir had reached the required depth about two weeks before the arrival of the New Year. The pump site had to be deeper, but when the digging reached the sandy stratus, water gushed out. The water was belly-deep. The pump site was not as deep as required and nobody was willing to jump into the water to solve the problem. It looked as if the work might not be finished before New Year's Day.

The Qui Zhang came to the site again. He heard and saw the problem and went to the pump site, flanked by peasants. The Xiang Zhang also came. He kept on rubbing his hands and knitted his eyebrows.

'How much deeper is needed?' the Qui Zhang asked.

'About half a metre,' somebody replied, 'but the sand will collapse if you dig it.'

There was a fairly strong wind. The maximum temperature would not have been higher than minus ten degrees centigrade. The Qui Zhang discussed with the older peasants how to stop the sand. The discussion was very short but a means was found.

'Go to the shop to get some *er guo tou* alcohol.' He gave some money, his own money, to the communicator. 'And get some *man tou*.'

'Build up several big fires,' he ordered a senior co-operative chairman.

'Young men,' he shouted around, 'come with me!' He took off his shoes and socks. He stripped off his trousers except his underpants.

'What are you doing?' somebody asked.

'Working on the pump site!' With that he walked towards the site. He was sick, frail and old.

Some thirty or so young men, from the five or six senior co-operatives, took off their shoes, socks and trousers and jumped into the belly-deep water with him. The other peasants were moved to tears. Willow wands and pikes were handed to them. A group of young men immediately drove the pikes in and wove the wands between them. After about twenty minutes, the Qui Zhang was pulled out of the water and more young men jumped into the water to replace the first group. The first group clustered around the Qui Zhang at the fire, sharing a few gulps of alcohol to drive away the chill.

'Qui Zhang, you are not young. You should not jump into the icy water. You just need to give us the order,' the young men around him reproached him, lovingly.

'Why? Just because I am the Qui Zhang? I am the man who has to lead you to do the job!' he said.

More young men volunteered to go into the water. Within two hours, the work was finished. All the peasants came to the Qui Zhang. Almost everybody was moved to tears. Unfortunately the Xiang Zhang was not in sight. He had left while the Qui Zhang was in the water with the young men at the pump site. To me, the Xiang Zhang's behaviour and attitude was the first indication that some cadres treated their position simply as a career, not really caring about the life of the peasants. This was the beginning of the Communists drifting away from the people.

The reservoir was completed well before the Spring Festival. A mass meeting was held at the site to celebrate. The Xiang Zhang made a speech at the meeting, but everyone was looking for the Qui Zhang. He could not be found. He did not come!

Unfortunately, the reservoir was too small. In spring, it could only supply water to the nearby fields. In summer it could not store much water from the fields. What's more, the site was too high for the surrounding fields to drain water into it. In spring, our team members stared at the irrigation ditches but not even one drop of water came from the reservoir because our fields were too far from it. In summer, when we needed to drain the water quickly, the reservoir could not accept even one drop because the location of our fields was lower than the reservoir itself!

'We toiled for nothing!' the peasants sighed. But nobody cursed the idea. The water problem had to be solved. Did the peasants forgive the failed trial? Perhaps!

No Points Today

None of us four so-called 'new peasants' were happy with the situation, yet it was hard, even impossible, to refute or retaliate. We lived in a village where everyone was related in one way or the other. The community was like a clan. Uncles, cousins, and nephews were the people we worked with. Any uncle could silence us if we made any complaints. If we answered back, we would be regarded as disrespectful to our elders or not setting a good example for the young. If we embarrassed the team leader too much, he might just give us a thrashing and we could do nothing to him. I felt exasperated. Resentment smouldered in my breast, ready to erupt.

One day, the four of us new peasants were instructed to weed a field about two kilometres from our village near the Paradise River. We were instructed to '*hao* the plants', not to hoe them. The tools we used were special, called in Chinese *hao shao zi*. The tool had a steel head, like a hoe but not flat. The edges curved slightly towards the user. It was about one and half palms in width, and about the same in length. The free end was sharply edged and could be sharpened anytime. The top end had an eye in which a handle was fixed. The handle was about two feet in length and as thick as an egg.

Each of us was given two of these tools, one for each hand. When weeding, I was doubled over straddling the row of plants with legs astride, alternatively cutting weeds off and clearing a thin layer of topsoil from near the roots. The two hands just cut weeds and scooped soil at an angle, away from the row of plants. I had to go backwards to proceed along the line of plants, buttocks first. Everybody did it the same way, because that was how the work was done.

My back became sore before long and blood surged to my head. Now and then I had to straighten up to ease the strain on my back. Everybody did the same. Older peasants never straightened up before they got to the end of the field.

It was hot. Sweat dripped onto the soil continuously. Our pants and shirts became wet and stuck to our bodies even before we had worked from the roadside to the other end near the bank of the river.

The plants were between rows of peach trees because the field was an orchard of white peaches. The peaches were already as big as a fist, not ripe, but already good for eating and very tempting. My throat was dry—everybody's was—as if it were on fire. I looked at the peaches and saliva drooled from the corners of my mouth.

'Why not have a few peaches to kill our thirst?' one boy suggested.

'The team will punish us if we do,' I cautioned him.

'Punish us? Who cares about that?' the third said. He then quoted the saying, 'The bold die from overeating but the timid die from starvation.'

'I would rather have the peaches first and have the punishment later,' the fourth commented vehemently.

Throwing down our tools at the end of the field near the bank, each of us picked three or four of the big white peaches. We sat in the water of the river, which was knee-deep, and enjoyed the peaches happily. They were still hard and crisp but already sweet with a dash of sourness. I knew it was not right to eat the peaches, which belonged to the co-op—we all knew it was not right—but we did not care. We wanted to avenge the cadres who gave each of us only five points for our daily work, which was half of what the grown-ups received.

We hoed faster than ever after eating the peaches, right to the other end and, when we got back to the end near the river again, we again threw down the tools and ate more peaches while enjoying the cool in the water. We had never been so happy since we started our life as the bookish peasants earning our daily points.

Evening came. We went to the team office to have our points registered.

'There will be no points for Shuang Xi and the other three boys!' the team leader declared. 'Every team member must be wondering why I decided not to give them any points!' He stopped for a few minutes to make the atmosphere more oppressive.

'The reason is very simple,' he continued when he heard no questions. 'Firstly, it took them a whole day to finish the job while they should have finished it in just half a day. Secondly, they ate peaches without permission. Each of them consumed at least twenty!'

Angry murmurs broke out.

'Twenty peaches are worth much more than the seven points they each can get!'

'Yes,' the team leader emphasised, 'each of them gets seven points for a day's work! Since they each ate so many peaches I therefore decided not to give them any points.'

'The punishment is too light,' somebody said loudly.

'Yes,' the team leader agreed. 'But this is their first offence. If they do it again, the punishment will be severe!'

We never did it again because we were no longer ordered to do the job in that field. A watchman was posted in the orchard from the following day. It was impossible for anyone to have the peaches from the orchard. That was the only time the four of us tried to vent our resentment and we vented it in an improper way. That was the only punishment I ever received and the punishment was fair. Even my ever-present protector, my mother, was not able to open her mouth to protest this time.

Planting Sweet Potato

The spring of 1956 came. Unlike the winter, which had been physically hard for everybody at the reservoir site, spring was desperately hard for me both physically and mentally. Not even a single day passed without humiliating remarks being thrown in the face of us four who wanted to be a new generation of peasants.

'The skunks!' a man was saying when he saw us four boys approaching during the sowing of peanuts. 'No damn good at studying, so they didn't get into junior high school.'

'To junior high school?' another man joined in. 'If any of them can get into junior high school, I will drink a big bowl of snot.'

'I will make a bet,' another said. 'I will treat them with good food in the restaurant in the town if any of them can get into high school this year.'

'High school? You must be joking,' still another said. 'Face to the sand and back to the sun, that's their future.'

Spring sowing, though pressing, was not physically hard. To make fun of us became their daily entertainment. While bodily tiredness was easy to overcome, mental humiliation was hard to forget. I found the road to becoming a new type of peasant was not a smooth one.

The wheat harvest finished. Our team decided to plant about fifteen acres of sweet potatoes. All the team members, both men and women, were present for the job. The men and us boys carried water while the women planted the vines.

Water had to be fetched from a well a little more than a kilometre away, but the distance from the far end of the field would be over one and half kilometres. The well had been dug for the purpose of planting the sweet potatoes. It was in the riverbed.

The field was sandy, the sand about ankle deep. It was like a desert, though it was good land if water was available. I had to be, when carrying water, barefooted. The shoes I wore had shallow uppers and an oval opening for the feet to get in and out. Sand got into the shoes within a few steps over the sandy surface, so I could not wear them to work on that sandy field—no water carrier could. To walk over a one kilometre sandy field with empty buckets was not very difficult, though the hot sand baked the feet. Coming back with two buckets of water, together about fifty kilograms in weight, was not an easy thing. After working at the reservoir, the weight of fifty kilograms of water was nothing to worry about. The difficulty was the sand. I put one step forward and my feet would slip back one third of a step—at least I felt my feet slipped back that much. Normally, the up and down motion of the shoulder would make the shoulder pole vibrate rhythmically making the weight on the shoulder seem a bit lighter, giving the person carrying the load a short spell of rest. Walking over the sand, I could not achieve that vibration in my shoulder pole, so the load became 'dead' weight. There were also thorny plants in the sand. Old thorns from the previous year were the same colour as the sand and could not be avoided. The thorns pricked the soles of the feet frequently and I could not always put the buckets down to get them off. I had to get them off with one leg supporting the load, like a rooster standing on one leg. This was frustrating.

The sky was clear blue, with not a single cloud in sight. Leaves hung lifelessly from the twigs and branches. Neither the trees nor the grass stirred. Upward air movement from the sand looked like evaporation above a steamer. The air felt like the air in an oven, hot and dry. Sweat poured out from every pore of the body, dripping over eyebrows, invading the eyes. I had to wipe my eyes every now and then with the back of my hand.

I had thrown my straw hat to my mother. My head was a 'steamer' head, which is what my mother called it due to the fact that in summer my hair was constantly soaked by sweat and my head sent 'steam' into the air. A hat would make it difficult to release the heat from my head and stopped the sweat from trickling freely down my face. I also stripped off my shirt and threw it to my mother, not because I did not want it to get soaked by sweat but because I felt my body too hot to wear it.

With the length of bucket, bucket handle, and chain hook, it was too long for me to lift the buckets off the ground with the shoulder pole. I had to wind the hook and chains around the ends of the shoulder pole, one clockwise and one anti-clockwise. Even thus arranged, the bottom of the buckets sometimes knocked against the ground and water was spilt. By the time I got to the planting spot, the buckets were only half full.

'Yu Yan (Jade Eye), what are you doing?' somebody sneered. 'Do you call this water carrying?'

'What do you mean? Yu Yan is not a name for a man like you to use!' my mother retorted. She was one generation his senior and so it was justified for her to use that tone.

'You get ten points and he gets seven. What's wrong with it if he has just half buckets of water left? You should not criticise him for that!'

But once out of my mother's hearing, they ridiculed me as before.

'You walk just like a Yang Ge dance!'

'What's better, this or study?'

'Don't say that, Yu Yan is no good for study.'

'Doomed to beg from the soil!'

'Yu Yan, if you can get into high school this year, I will treat you in the town restaurant,' one of my uncles said.

'Yu Yan, if you can get into high school this year, I will drink a bowl of snot!' my immediate neighbour said. He lived just on the other side of the lane on our right. He and my father belonged to the same mutual aid group in the early fifties.

I felt angry with myself and with them. I was angry because if I had been a bit older and stronger, I would not have suffered such ridicules. I was angry with them because they could not understand that in ridiculing me they were actually ridiculing themselves. At worst, I would be just a copy of them in a few years time. Why should a peasant look down upon a peasant-to-be?

I could no longer feel the burning sensation of sand under my feet. I no longer cared about the pricks of the thorns. I no longer worried about the blinding heat. All physical miseries, I could bear. But now my heart was bleeding. This was too much for me to bear.

'Does your back hurt?' my mother asked me in the evening over supper.

'No,' I replied. 'But I want to go for the examination for junior high school this year.'

My father stopped my mother's protest.

'You can do it,' my father said. My dream of being one of the new peasants having bookish knowledge came to an end.

Getting Away

I checked with our former teacher from the primary school about the exam. His name was Wu and he had been assigned to our school in 1955 from Beijing. It was said that he was the son of a big capitalist. He severed his relationship with his family (a way of self-protection) and came to our school. He never left our school or our village. All my brothers and sister were his students, as were the many youngsters of my generation and generations after me. He shared the hardships and the good days with the villagers. In the mid-eighties, he finally retired and lived in the village.

Teacher Wu told me that I could resit the entry examination for junior high school. I told my friends and our names were included. He told me that I could go to him if I had difficulties in reviewing my old texts. He gave me a few topics for compositions and asked me to give my finished compositions to him for suggestions. I still had to go to work in the fields, to earn the points and to endure the sharp tongues. I came to fully understand the expression 'the tongue can crush a man to death!' However, now that I had decided to go for further schooling, the ridicule no longer disturbed me.

Only the long noon, if I sacrificed the nap, could be used for reviewing my texts. The room could not be used, for the families were having their noon nap. The ground under the shade of a tree was good but there were plenty of ants. Finally I decided to do it on the house roof. The elm tree behind the house gave quite a big patch of shade. The roof was hot from the heat of the sun the whole morning yet there was always a breeze. I decided I would read under the shade.

My limbs were tired and my eyelids heavy. I had to get down from the roof a number of times to fetch water from the well to soak my head to get rid of my drowsiness. My brain was slow and the lines of words danced before my eyes. I had to rub my eyes to keep them wide open.

Every day I had to fight to stay awake, a battle harder than carrying the frozen earth at the reservoir. My brain simply refused to work effectively. If I could not find a way out and if I continued like this, I would fail. There was no hope if I went on like this.

'Give, if one wants to receive.' If I wanted to be quick and alert when I reviewed my books, I had to get some sleep first. I planned to have a short nap at noon. I would lie near the western edge of the shade. I fell asleep instantly. But very soon the shade moved eastward and I was exposed to the sun. Then the heat would wake me up. This short sleep was not enough but it was sufficient for my brain to work faster and more efficiently.

Every week or ten days my friend Liang and I would drill each other in mathematics or the definitions of words and phrases, or making sentences. We exchanged our compositions for suggestions. When we were satisfied with our preparation, we went to the teacher to be examined. We asked the teacher to comment on our compositions.

'Quite good.' The teacher was surprised and pleased. 'Much better than I expected.' We were pleased by his comments.

'In another two weeks I will take the students to the town for the examination,' he told us. 'Don't be late in the morning for the start.'

We were punctual. I carried the same kind of food I did a year ago and so did my friend. We covered the same five kilometres to the town over the same road. We were allotted the same classroom. What was more, we had the same supervising teachers who distributed the papers as the previous year. One teacher seemed to remember me because I noticed a flicker in his eyes when he handed me the papers. But I was not the same. This time, I wanted success and I meant to get it.

The first two hours were for the mathematics papers. I read them carefully, and checked all the factors before starting my calculations. I finished the papers in less than one hour. I suppressed my impulse to be the first to hand in the papers. I calmed myself down and re-examined every question. I checked and rechecked my answers three times. I felt confident and assured. I moved slowly to the supervising teacher. Simultaneously, my friend Liang rose from the other lane and advanced towards the teacher.

Outside, students were comparing the answers with each other. We found a quiet corner to have our lunch. Our own teacher came.

'All right?'

We bolted up to him and replied, 'We feel sure about it!'

'Try hard in the language examination!' he said as he left.

The supervising teacher walked past us. He looked at me and gave me a nod, which made me elated. He was telling me by the nod that my answers were good.

When the papers of the language examination were in my hands, I calculated them quickly. The composition alone was forty per cent, so I had to use the first hour to finish the composition. If I could get thirty or more marks for the composition, the whole thing would be easy!

The topic was one I had already practiced. It was 'My Career Selection'. I finished it well within time. I checked each stroke of the words, punctuation, and so on, before I started the other half of the paper. My handwriting was poor, yet I wrote each stroke carefully. My paper was very neat and clean. I did not hesitate even once. After a double check, I handed in my papers. Again, my friend Liang came out almost simultaneously. We found our teacher to ask whether we could go back home.

'When the enrolment notice comes to school,' he said, 'I will let you know.'

Both of us were confident that we were successful. As soon as I got home, Granny told me her expectation about the examination.

'You will be successful,' she said seriously. 'I have asked the kitchen god.'

To Granny's generation, the kitchen god knew everything and could help in every situation. She would ask the kitchen god whenever she wanted to know the outcome of something. This time she wanted to know the result of my examination and so she asked the kitchen god. The method was simple. Granny would first burn incense and then choose six chopsticks where she would place them at right angles on top of each other on the windowsill. Then she would press hard on all the ends and, when she was sure they would not slip off one another, pray.

'Kitchen god, if my grandson will be successful, please turn inward. If my grandson is going to fail, please turn outward.' Next she would watch how the chopsticks would move.

The fingers were not able to control and decide the movement of the chopstick—they could only turn inward or outward. So there was only one answer to her, either success or failure. She believed the result of the chopsticks.

Most old peasants believed in the answers given by the kitchen god. This time I also believed the answer.

Twenty days after the exam, a student delivered a letter to our house. Only Granny was at home. She put it on the windowsill before the kitchen god. When I came back, she pressed her palms against each other and reverently placed them in front of her breast and prayed. Then she took the letter and handed to me. I cut the letter open with scissors, pulled out a piece of paper and started to read. It turned out to be the notice of enrolment.

'What did I say?' Granny said. 'I told you that you would be successful. The kitchen god knew it in advance.'

'Go to our neighbour and let him drink a bowl of snot,' my mother said when she returned from the field.

Just then he appeared on the other side of the fence.

'I heard Shuang Xi was enrolled by the junior high school. Yes?' he asked.

'Of course,' my mother replied. 'But what about your pledge to drink a bowl of snot if he succeeds?'

'That was a joke,' he laughed. 'If nobody had ridiculed him, would he have made up his mind to get away? Would he have succeeded in his examination?'

My mother was silenced. His remark alleviated the humiliation I had felt.

I quit the work at the co-operative the following day. I had to raise the money to pay for the expenses to start my high school education. I went to cut grass to dry for hay. My brother Xiao Bao, when he had time, helped me. The weight of seventy to eighty kilograms of grass on my back seemed no weight at all. I walked home like a whirlwind. Within twenty days, I had cut more than three thousand kilograms of grass, which were dried under the sun into seven hundred and fifty kilograms of hay. My father sold the hay at the town fair, and got altogether fifteen yuan, enough to pay my school fee for the first term, to get me new winter clothing and to buy books and pens. There was still a bit of money remaining, which, of course, found its way into my mother's pocket to help her buy oil, vinegar, and other things for the family.

My life as a peasant ended...and it ended forever.

chapter 11

MY JUNIOR HIGH SCHOOL YEARS

My junior high school years were between 1956 and 1959. Except for the classrooms, nothing was ready when I began at the new junior high school constructed in 1956. My parents could not give me any real financial support for food, books, pencils and other equipment I needed to study. In addition to constructing and beautifying our school and environment, I had to support my own study. However, the school offered me a life I can never forget.

Junior High School

It was the autumn of 1956. The opening of the junior high school year approached at last. My friend Liang, the other 'new peasant with bookish knowledge' for a year, and I went to school together. (One of the other two 'new' peasants went to Beijing as a worker and the other joined the army.) The school was in the county town about two kilometres north of the Royal Horse Well village. Though the town was just seven-and-a-half kilometres from the Paradise Palace, I had not been to this town before. Neither had Liang. The town became the county centre only from the latter half of 1955. The county government hurried the construction of the new junior high school for the Year One students of 1956—the only students of the school. Another junior high school had been constructed several years earlier in the former county centre town about twenty kilometres away from our village, which is the school I would have attended if I had succeeded in 1955.

When we crossed the Beijing–Tianjin railway line on our way to see our new school, we saw a poster on a tree trunk that read 'Huangcun Junior High School to the north'. We were elated, for we were wondering in which the direction the school was. Happily we marched northward. We came across four or five more posters before we got to an east-west street crossing the highway. I called it a street, though there were no more than three or four houses along it. A road sign pointed west to the county government. On the other side of the highway the road sign pointed east to the Huangcun Junior High School.

We turned right, following the road sign, to go along the 'street', which was merely a road marked by one shallow ditch on each side. We came to a 'gate', which faced north and was just two square columns made of grey bricks. On one column was a majestic vertically hung board with a white paint base and on it the name of the school with black Chinese characters—'Huangcun Junior High School'.

There were no fences to mark its perimeters. There was no road from the gate to the school domain. There were only six independent single-storey buildings of grey brick, widely spaced but symmetrically arranged. Everywhere was knee-deep grass, debris of broken brick, bits of timber, and dried mortar. The only other structures were two reed-mat enclosures, which, we knew from our own experience, were the male and female toilets.

To the east, knee-deep wild grass extended more than one hundred metres to the bank of a tiny creak. To the north, it was wilderness as far as the eyes could see. To the south, houses could be seen about one kilometre away. To the west, the wilderness extended to the highway broken by a lonely neighbour with a single small house.

Green, pink, and red banners were planted in two rows from the gate columns southward to a two-house group, about a hundred metres away from the other four houses. We waded through the grass between the lane marked out by the banners to one of the two houses marked 'enrolment office'. On the wall by the door was a notice saying that the ceremony to mark the school opening was to be held at nine o'clock the following morning in front of the building. We had no watches or clocks and we had to get up very early to make sure we would not be late for it after walking seven-and-a-half kilometres.

The next morning, the ceremony began punctually at nine o'clock in front of the office building. A desk in front of the building served as the rostrum for the principal. We students sat on the grass. The principal spoke at the meeting. He said that the conditions at the time were not very good but that would be changed with our own hands. He said that the most important thing was that we should try to be students of 'the three merits'—good in health, good in study, and good in conduct. He also said that whatever examples we, the first batch of students of the school, demonstrated would be followed by students in the years to come. The principal encouraged us not to let down our parents, who had to overcome great difficulties to support our study in school. He requested us not to let down the new government, who had to do so much from scratch and yet had overcome difficulties to allot the finance to set up this school for the needs of more students from peasants' families. He wished us not to let down the teachers, who would pass knowledge onto us. Then he told us to construct our school with our own hands while studying hard and to alleviate our parents' burden through self-support in our studies.

The principal was a man of average height, thickly built, not very handsome but radiating confidence. His words were not flowery but weighty enough to evoke confidence in our hearts, particularly in my heart. Such a confidence I had never experienced before. I had no end of energy and I would do my best to help make the best environment for the school, the place where not only myself, but also many others like me, would acquire more knowledge. I would try my very best to be a student of 'the three merits'. Though I was not quite sure yet what I would do in the future, a yearning for a bright future, for a new life, and for making myself useful to society, had taken root in my heart.

Legging it to and from School

Students who lived outside the radius of seven-and-a-half kilometres could stay in nearby peasants' houses, which the school arranged through negotiations with the owners. I lived just within the radius and so I had to live at home as did all the other six boys and three girls from our village. We lived scattered throughout the Paradise Palace so it was hard for us all to start for school together in the morning.

I had no watch and our family had no clock. It was hard to know what time to get up in the morning to be punctual for the first class at eight o'clock. My solution was to start early, which became a life-long habit.

Mornings in autumn presented no problem whatsoever. It was not hard for a teenager to cover seven-and-a-half kilometres in two hours. It was just a morning's physical exercise.

I would take a short cut along a sandy country road. Once out of the village, I would put my shoes in my school bag and walk several kilometres barefoot, for fear that when they were worn out my mother might not have the time or might not have money to make new shoes for me. The sky looked higher, much higher, and bluer in the autumn days. The air was cool and refreshing. 'Hong Dian', a bird whose breast turned red as it matured, sang beautifully in the trees. Peanuts and sweet potatoes in the fields ripened, ready to be harvested. The sand was soft and comfortable underfoot.

Happily I would hum the songs I had learnt from primary school, where besides our music classes, we learnt one song each week, or I would review my lessons by heart and, when I could not recollect something, I would open my book to check before resuming my review again.

In the afternoon, after class, I would carefully but hurriedly finish my homework and then work for an hour to move debris or grass, or join others to dig a moat around the perimeters of our school or to construct our school road. Like all my classmates and schoolmates, I did the work happily.

After an hour's work, we seven boys from our village would head for home along the highway. I forget how the girls covered the seven and half kilometres to and from the school everyday, I just remember they never did it together with us boys. Very soon we boys all became friends. Sometimes we discussed mathematics or geometry or competed for who could run the fastest. Thus the homeward journey was not felt much.

Winter came and the laughter gradually died from our lips. I had to start early in the morning, so early that it was pitch dark when I set out with my friend Liang who was a close neighbour. It was terribly cold, even if there were no wind or snow. Our breath belched out like steam from a train and formed ice on our brows. My ears felt the cold under the flap of my cap and I had to warm them with my hands. Over a period of five or six days there would be a gale force wind from Siberia, which was called the 'cold current'. The temperature would drop abruptly. I had to bend my upper body to press forward. The wind carried sand with it that whipped my face relentlessly. The wind would break the protection of my padded jacket through the collar. Though I had tied the flaps of my cap down by knotting the string under my chin, my cheeks and ears still felt the severe cold of minus fifteen to twenty degrees.

Now and then it would snow heavily. Snow whirled against the face and crunched under my feet. Snow got into my shoes and melted. Sometimes my toes felt so cold that I feared they might be frozen! My padded jacket was thick but the cotton inside was old. My bare upper body was clad just in this padded jacket. Though my mother tried her very best to make my jacket fit me well, wind would easily creep in from the waist and from the collar. I felt awfully cold.

The homeward journey was better than the journey to school on windy days. The howling wind pushed us from behind, compelling us to go faster and faster. But if it snowed, the homeward journey was very bad. The road was wet and muddy. My shoes would get soaked before long. My feet, which were cracked at the heels, hurt badly with each step forward. The energy provided by a lunch of two pieces of sweet potato or by two pieces of corn *wo tou*, had long been burnt out. My stomach was always empty and complaining. Soaked shoes, cracked feet, and an empty stomach were what I carried along the muddy highway. I had to walk fast, for when the mud became frozen hard, it hurt my feet more.

One evening, the wind roared and the ambient temperature became terribly low. We had just passed the railway when a truck came from behind and slowed down to cross the railway lines.

'This is the sand transportation truck,' a boy said. 'Let's get a lift.'

Everybody acted simultaneously, and so did I without thinking whether it was right to do so or whether it was dangerous to catch a running truck. My left hand caught hold of the truck's tailboard. Instantly my whole body was yanked and I was flying like a kite. I contracted my belly and landed myself on the truck inside the surrounding boards—the stoppers. Everyone was in at the same time. We huddled against the foldable tailboard. Nobody spoke, for fear of attracting the attention of the driver. It was cold and our backs were to the wind. We felt much better and more comfortable. When the truck arrived at the sand dunes about one kilometre from our village, we jumped out to get away as soon as the truck stopped. The driver came down from the cabin and stopped us.

'Boys,' he said, 'it is very dangerous to catch a speeding truck. If one of you was hurt or died, I would be jailed.' Then he added, 'I have a family and I have children. I don't want to be jailed. Next time when you see a truck coming, raise your arm to give a signal for a lift. I will let other drivers know.'

From then on, our journey home became a bit easier. However, it was really rather frustrating to walk fifteen kilometres on winter days, leaving home before sunrise and arriving at home long after sunset. Together with students from the neighbouring villages, we wrote an application to the school authority to let us stay and board at the school. Approval was finally given but it was already the start of the next winter.

Beautifying Our Environment

Before the space in front of our classroom was cleared up, it was very dangerous to step out and play during the breaks between classes. One might step on a nail or something sharp in the grass. Our first priority was, therefore, to clear this ground. We had to do the clearing of the ground by ourselves because the school would not employ workers to do it for us. However, most of us were from peasant families so just a word from the teacher was enough for us to act promptly. We looked for debris and pulled the grass during the breaks between classes the first day. But the grass was tough and hard to pull out. The following day, seemingly by special agreement, we all carried tools with us.

The space between our classroom and the office building was fairly large, about a hundred metres in length and fifty metres in width. Yet, through 'nibbling' bit by bit during our breaks and through concentrated 'massive attacks' in the afternoons, the space became smooth and clean within a couple of weeks. Then we could all stand in a big circle to play volleyball.

The school road from the gate to the office building became the next target. Firstly, two rows of bricks were buried on both sides to make the edges of the road. Then we dumped waste mortar, crushed brick, coal residue from the furnace boiler, and lime on the road and pounded them hard. Later, when spring came, we planted poplars all along the road just a bit outside the brick edges.

We were then asked to dig a moat to mark the boundaries of our school and to keep away trespassers. The moat started from the gate. Each class was allotted a section a day. To me it was an easy job because I was already used to digging the reservoir in the winter of 1955. The earth that was dug up was placed on the inside edge of the moat to make a ridge serving as a wall. We extended the moat westward to our neighbour and eastward fifty or sixty metres leaving a wasteland of about sixty metres or so to the bank of the small creek.

During the early years of the Qing Dynasty, a warlord could just jump onto horseback and gallop along until the horse collapsed. The land encircled was his. Similarly, at least I thought it was so, whatever we could encircle with our moat, that land would belong to our school. For a long time I felt confused as to why we were not instructed to extend our moat to the bank of the creek. The only explanation was that the ambition of our principal was not boundless. He was satisfied that the land we encircled was already big enough for the junior high school, and for setting up a senior high school and a teacher's college.

Poplars were planted on the ridge as well as along the outer edge of the moat. Meanwhile, basketball frames and nets were ready for rigging up. All these jobs were done with enthusiasm. The large sportsground for sports such as soccer was completed with equal eagerness. Though the school had two more buildings constructed, the buildings were still few and far between.

However, no flowers were planted. This, perhaps, was not on the principal's agenda as yet, for he had to consider the teachers' quarters, the students' dormitories, and more classrooms for students of the coming years. Moreover, he had to have more teachers. I doubt that he could have predicted that some years later having flowers would be regarded as a lack of revolutionary spirit. By the time we were in Year Two, our environment was already a world different from what it had been when we had entered the school. However, for me personally, school life was not easy. I had to support myself, with the teacher's help. I never minded the hard life I lived and I am not ashamed to describe in detail some of the work I did.

Fire and Electricity

At the start of the second year, we were allowed to live and board at school. The dormitories for the boys were not yet ready and we had to stay in a peasant house about one to one-and-a-half kilometres away. It was better to walk that distance than to cover seven-and-a-half kilometres each morning and evening.

We stayed there for a few months and there was one episode to mention. All together we had ten boys sleeping in two rooms on two *kangs*. It was winter and particularly cold. Except for two or three boys, none of us had a mattress. We had but one quilt each. Sleeping on the *kang* without warming it was just like sleeping on the ground. I wrapped myself tightly in the quilt and put my trousers and jacket on top of it. Still the coldness of the *kang* penetrated the quilt gradually, making my limbs and back ache. I huddled in the quilt and almost every night had cramps in my legs. Every morning we joked that we had been *tuan zhang* the whole night. This is the term for a regimental commander, and has the same pronunication as the term for huddling, so the expression was borrowed to mean we huddled.

The monitor and the branch secretary of the youth league of our class were among us. The monitor was from our village and the secretary from a neighbouring village. They were also from peasant families and were, without exception, night long *tuan zhang*. The two suggested we should carry some firewood from school to warm up our *kang*. 'If the sky falls the tallest persons would support it'. If the school authority found out we were taking the wood, they would claim responsibility. And of course we all agreed. Each day two boys in turn would carry firewood from the school. There were no worries about being found out because the school was under construction. Broken timber and timber waste was everywhere at the site.

One night the *kang* was too hot to sleep on for those near the cooking range because too much timber had been burnt in the cooking range. I slept well because I was at the other end of the *kang*, far from the cooking range. Somebody shook me violently to wake me. The rooms were full of smoke and there was the smell of burnt rubber. The branch secretary of the youth league was cramming ashes into a crevice of the windowsill where flames had come up and burnt the bottom frame of the window. An area the size of one-third of a fist was already burnt away from the frame. A student had put his new sports shoes on the windowsill for fear that somebody might tread on them during the night. One of the soles of his shoes had a hole as big as a quail egg burnt through it. Smoke came from the burnt window frame and from the sole of his shoe.

We opened the window to let in the cold air to chase out the smoke. The monitor opened the door to check for water in the vat in the yard. Thick ice had formed on the water surface inside the vat and he dared not knock the ice hard for fear of waking the host of the house. We had to make sure that the flames were thoroughly put out, but we had no water.

'Let's pee on it,' said the boy whose shoe was burnt.

Immediately one 'hose' after another poured 'water' into the burning crevice and the fire was completely put out.

The next evening, new window paper was brought to change the old one and to cover up the burnt frame. From that day onwards, we never dared to burn that much wood again. The lesson was twofold. Firstly, fire should always be handled with care. Secondly, moderation was best in everything, even in as simple a matter as warming up the *kang*.

When I was allowed to stay and board in the school, my lack of money was still a concern. Students would bring food from home, which was then combined and distributed among the students. At first we brought corn flour to school, but the quality brought by each student was different. It was hard for the school to have a uniform standard with regard to food brought to the school, so it introduced a food allowance. The payment was five yuan for a month's board including food—an amount I had to raise, as my parents could not afford it. It was not a big burden to pay just one or two months, but when it had to be paid every month, it became a very big burden.

By this time the teacher in charge of our class had changed. She was a new graduate from Tong Xian Teachers' College and her family name was Zhu. She was just twenty-two years old and she cared very much for her students and tried hard to help. In one way or another, she secured work from our neighbour, the Electricity Distribution Bureau, for us poor students to do during the evenings. It was a simple job but heavy to do. The remuneration was excellent. Three of my classmates and I were given the job. It was to construct foundations for electricity poles. We were to dig pits, each being one metre squared, and we were required to fill every one with pebbles. The pay was one yuan and twenty cents per pit completed.

The first day when we arrived at the site in the evening, everyone immediately started to dig. Each one wanted to do more to perhaps, get more money. That was a display of selfishness that was inherited from the practical mind of the peasant. It seemed to me a foolish way to do the job. I took a quick look and made a suggestion to them.

'Don't be in such a hurry,' I told them. 'If we do it like this, nobody will finish a hole today. And everyone wants to do the pit near the pebbles. Who wants to do the one far away from the pebbles? If you wish to do it quickly, listen to me and let's do it in two groups.'

All three of them agreed. I suggested the digging of two pits by each group. I then allocated the pits and pebble heaps for each of them. I suggested two dig one pit first and then one person fill it with pebbles while the other dug the second pit. The digging of the second and the filling of the first finished almost simultaneously. The two could fill the second pit together. Within a number of hours, we had completed two pits per group and happily returned to school. The whole job took us ten days to finish. Each one had enough money for two months board.

Then the teacher paid a visit to the families of poor students to check whether he or she really needed help. She saw with her own eyes the conditions of my home and had a talk with my parents. She visited some other families. Finally she decided to get me more jobs so that I could continue to study.

'If you quit study because your parents cannot give you much help,' she said to me, 'it would be a pity because you are a good student. Now I understand why you always get full marks for every subject, I will try my best to get you more jobs to do. But don't lag behind in your study.'

I promised and I kept my word.

Pulling the Big Rake

Winter came again, the second winter for me in junior high school and the first winter boarding at school. It was too cold and the teacher could not get another job for me, so I turned my attention to the big rake my father used to get leaves and dried grass for the cooking range. I could get dried grass and sell it to the cart drivers. My father could use the small rake to collect leaves and grass as fire material. He could find a way to do it anyway.

The rake was very big. It had one metre long steel prongs spread out like a fan with a space of two inches between each. Underneath the prongs was a flat tray of thin branches from trees. It had a very long detachable pole, which served both as a pulling shaft when getting grass and as the shoulder pole to carry the grass collected. The pole was fixed to the rake with another short piece of timber to form a clip. Another piece of timber about two feet long had a hole, into which the pole, like a nut and bolt, was secured. This was hooked to my shoulder so that the rake could be pulled along. Every now and then I would get the dry grass up onto the tray with a hook which had a long handle.

Near our school was plenty of wasteland. In winter, the grass died and became thoroughly dry. When I pulled the rake along, it picked up the grass easily. I could only do this on Sundays, and as long as it was not snowing or there was no snow covering the land, I would gather grass with the big rake.

Wind was very frequent. It struck the face, cutting it like a knife. I would start at nine-thirty in the morning and work till about four in the afternoon. Even then it was still very cold. I would usually hide my hands under my armpits to keep them warm. I tried to pull the rake in big oval circles so as to make shorter trips against the wind. The load of the rake became heavier with each step forward. When the tray under the prongs was nearly fully packed, the load became so heavy that I had to strain my neck and upper body forward, each of the muscles of the legs contracting strenuously to move forward like an ox pulling a heavy slow coach. My back sweated inside my padded jacket and my face had to stand the cold wind.

I did not waste time by just raking. I had my textbook with me. While I pulled the rake I was reading and while I read I was pulling the rake. The two did not interfere with each other.

I sorted the grass from the mud cakes, which were picked up by the rake without discrimination. I would make two very tight bundles in order to carry them to the place where the drivers and horses rested. It was about one-and-a-half kilometres away but the journey seemed many times further than that. With a heavy load on the shoulder, the stomach empty, and the legs sore, I struggled to get there with the stamina acquired during my one year of peasant working life. I was always the only grass seller and it never took me long to wait before I could sell it. Some driver would buy one kilogram for one cent. Normally I would get seventy to eighty cents per day. With money in my pocket, I would buy two pieces of *wo tou* from the restaurant, where the drivers dined, and munch them on my way back to school.

During the weekdays I would, as almost every girl or boy from the poor families did, stitch shoe soles for the army, a job also obtained for us by our teacher. The requirements were very strict—eighty stitches within an area of one square inch and the soles had to be very hard and solid. Eighty cents was the payment for completing one pair of soles. I could make one pair each week.

Winter thus went by, hard but without much worry about my board. Thanks to the help of the teacher, I could concentrate on my studies happily.

Making Chinese Herbal Medicine

When spring was replaced by summer, the teacher found a comparatively stable part-time job for me. I was to manufacture Chinese herbal medicine two hours a day in the afternoon, twice a week. I call it Chinese herbal medicine because the expression was also used in China to distinguish it from Western medicine.

It was a small one-man factory about two-and-a-half kilometres from our school. It had only two rooms. The outer room, the manufacturing place, had the blinds drawn and the door shut to prevent outsiders from prying into the secret of making medicine. In the middle of the room was a stove which burnt coal all day. The fire was kept in such a way that it gave a stable temperature. On the stove was a melting pot filled with liquid wax. Hanging around the stove were tiny soldering irons beaten from wires that were as thick as incense sticks. Near the stove were two stools. By each stool was a table, on which was placed a tray to hold finished products and another to hold the empty wax shells. A basin with plenty of wooden balls in it and another basin with herbal pellets to be processed were beside the trays. A pile of wax paper, which was neatly stacked and already cut to the required size, and three or four anchor-like devices, was also placed on the table within reach. The wooden balls were all the same size, each a little bit smaller than a golf ball. The door connecting the inner room and the outer room had a curtain whose colour could not be identified from long use. It looked as if it were a piece of oilcloth sheeting. I was not allowed to set foot into the inner room, because it was the place the boss prepared the herbs—a secret he did not want other people to know.

The room had a strong smell of blended herbs but it was not unpleasant. Having no ventilation and thus no circulation of air, the room was like the inside of an oven. As soon as I stepped into it, sweat would pour out from every pore of my body.

'Take off your shirt and trousers,' the boss said to me, 'just leave your underpants on.'

Then he added, 'You may take every piece of your clothing off if you like, even your underpants. Nobody will come into the room.'

The boss was an old man in his late fifties or early sixties. He was so thin that I could count his ribs when we were making the medicine pellets. His hair was the Buddhist monk style but from the length of his hair I could see he did not go to the barbers to shave his head. His face had so many wrinkles that it seemed to be a piece of creased parchment. His eyes were mild, kind and penetrating. His back was hunched from the constant stooping of his body over his work. He never wasted his breath in uttering an unnecessary word.

It was agreed that I would work for him for two hours on Wednesday and Saturday afternoons. He would not let me work one minute less, nor demanded me to work one minute more. Once I had my clothes off, he would set the alarm clock to ring exactly at the expiration of the two hours. It was a fair deal.

The job was simple for me, but it required care, nimbleness and patience. It consisted of six steps—pelleting, dipping, cutting, sealing, stamping, and packing.

Pelleting meant I had to make the herbal dough into small lumps, which were as big as a glass bead, in my palm, one at a time, and shape them into a round ball with the grinding movement of my palms. When all the small lumps were round balls, I would wrap each one with a piece of wax paper. These were called the pills or the pellets.

Dipping meant I had to dip wooden balls into the wax melting pot to make wax balls. Each time, I had to put about thirty wooden balls firmly on the tips of the hooks of an anchor, which was a cluster of wire hooks with their handles bundled and tied together. The balls were soft and stayed firmly on the hooks with just a little bit pressure of the hand. I would then hold the anchor handle, dip the hooks and balls into the melted wax, take them out and dip them into the liquid wax again and again. In both dipping and taking out the hooks and balls, the timing had to be correct. If the dipping and taking out were a bit too fast, the layer of wax on the balls would be too thin. But if they were a bit too slow, the wax layer on the balls would be too thick. If it was too thin, the fourth step (the sealing) was difficult or impossible. If too thick, it was hard to cut the balls out without breaking the wax shells and it would increase the cost by using too much wax. So silently I counted the seconds for the wooden balls to stay inside the liquid wax. After adjusting the dipping time in the first couple of days, the wax shells I produced were smooth and their thickness was just what I needed.

Cutting meant slicing open the wax balls to get the inner wooden balls out. I held a wax ball with my left thumb and middle finger, neither too tight nor to loose. If too tight, it would be hard to make the ball rotate between the two fingers. If too loose, the ball would fall out of my fingers when I cut it with a knife. The trail of the cutting should be a line exactly in the middle with about two millimetres of wax not cut. The two ends had to face each other without the slightest deviation. Then I opened the wax shell to empty the wooden ball, very much like opening a clam to get out the flesh. When a wax ball was cut and the wooden ball tipped out, I would immediately put a pill, which was wrapped in wax paper, into the shell and close it up. If I closed the shells up too late the thin connection might break and separate the two halves. Then it would be hard for me to seal them together.

Sealing meant sticking the two halves of the wax shells together to make an integral ball. I had five soldering irons placed with the iron tips in the flames. The tip was red and I had to use it gingerly. Again with my left thumb and middle finger I had to hold the wax ball, with a medicine pill inside, not too tight and not too loose. If too tight, the two halves would cave in. If too loose, the two halves might not exactly fit. The trouble was the burning iron. My right hand had to be very firm and steady. I had to use the exact pressure on the shells. If I touched the wax shells with the iron too lightly, they would not be sealed firmly together. If I pressed the iron a bit too hard, the wax might be punctured and the whole procedure had to be repeated. The thickness of the shells achieved in the second step (the dipping) could decide a success or a failure of this step. When the sealing was finished, the seam was thin and smooth.

Stamping meant to put the patent stamp of the manufacturer on the surface of each wax ball. The stamp was small, rectangular and made of wood. It had three Chinese characters on it. I pressed it into the inkpad and then stamped the shell. The words and the rectangular contour surrounding the characters had to be very clear. Here the same problem arose. If I pressed the stamp too lightly, the words would be not clear. If I pressed too hard, the wax shell would cave in under the pressure. If the ball broke at this stage, it was very frustrating.

Packing meant to put the finished wax ball into a satin box. The outer surface of the box was a darkish red satin and the inside surface was lined with satin of an ivory colour. I just needed to put the wax ball, with the red Chinese characters facing upwards, into the box. The boss himself would make the final check before he sealed the satin box with his trademark.

The boss was doing the same work beside me, but his hands were no longer steady. When he cut the wax shells, in one out of five the cut line was not matching and he would throw it into the wax pot again. When he sealed the shells, his hand trembled very slightly and would damage the shells with the jerking motion of his burning iron. Again, he would throw the holed shells into the wax pot. The same would happen again when he stamped the shells. As a result, my productivity was about three or four times higher than that of the boss.

'Advancing age spares nobody!' he sighed.

When the alarm rang, my boss would stand up and get a basin of cold water for me. I would rub my upper body and my legs clean with my towel before I put on my trousers and shirt. The boss would finish counting the finished products and press into my hand the correct money, one yuan and fifty cents (one cent for each finished medicine ball). My best rate was completing seventy-five finished wax-ball-clad medicine pills in one hour. In other words, I could finish the whole process of making one wax ball filled with medicine in forty-eight seconds. No matter how I tried, I could not increase the speed. I had to be happy to produce one hundred and fifty pieces within two hours.

When I left for school it was about five o'clock in the afternoon. The bright daylight was blinding and I could only see properly after a few minutes of adjusting my eyes. I was a bit light-headed and dizzy due to the lack of fresh air in the factory and too much sweating. After walking about one kilometre on the way back to school I would feel normal again. Feeling my pocket lined with one yuan and fifty cents, I would be pleased and happy, for that would enable me to continue my study without worrying about my board.

Every Wednesday and Saturday afternoon when at the factory, I would immediately concentrate on my job. The boss and I did not speak once I sat down on the stool. As far as I was concerned, I could not waste even one minute, for I was doing piecework and got paid according to how many balls I made. Bonus payment was a word I had never heard of yet. In the dictionary of my boss, I am sure, the expression of 'bonus payment' could not be found. As far as he was concerned, he did not like me wasting time either, for he was getting old and he could not produce as many medicine balls as he used to. He had to fulfil his contracted quantity. My time was therefore of the same importance to me as to him.

A month or so later, the boss spoke to me when I finished my two hours' work.

'Li,' he said, 'you have nimble hands and if you worked eight hours a day, you could earn more than a professor. After graduating from junior high school, why not come to work for me?'

I looked at him, feeling a bit surprised.

'I inherited the formula of the medicine from my father, and my father from his father. And I can trace quite a few generations of my family making the same medicine. Nobody else makes it and nobody has this recipe. If you agree to work for me, I will pass the recipe on to you. One day you will make big money.'

He went into his inner room and got two cups and a teapot, all not very clean, at least not to my eyes. He brewed some tea, poured one cup for me, and another one for himself.

'Look, I am alone. I have no wife, no son, and no daughter. You are the only one I like immensely. I am getting old. My hands are shaky and I can no longer do the work as quickly as before,' he sighed sadly. 'Age does not spare anybody! If you do not join me, my recipe will be carried to the coffin.'

He sipped at his tea and continued.

'Look, I have plenty of money but I don't show it. If you inherit this business, you will be rich soon.' Then he added, 'You have had schooling. You can read and write. I have watched you and I know you are clever. In your hands the business can flourish some day in the future. Think about joining me, seriously.'

I did not make any reply. He was not expecting a reply that day and he did not mention this again until I said goodbye to him because he knew my junior high schooling could not be finished within a couple of months. He did not wish to push me hard. He wanted to give me ample time to think it over.

When finally I had to prepare myself for the last end of term examination, I told him that I would not come back to work any longer.

'Decided?' he asked.

'Your business is a good one,' I said, 'and yours is the only medicine of this kind available in the shops throughout the country. There is no other producer of it. I know you are offering me a good career, but I wish to continue my study if I can get into senior high school.'

'Though the future is undecided,' he said, 'there is a house of gold in the books, there is plenty of grain in the books, and there are beautiful girls in the books. It is good to continue schooling as long as you study hard. But my profession is the most stable and has a great potential. It is a pity that you cannot join me.' He sighed. 'If you fail to get into senior high school, come to me. You are always welcome to join me.'

We enjoyed his tea from his not very clean cups, in silence. Then he continued. 'Your family has a hard time, otherwise you would not be doing a part-time job to support yourself. It would be wise for you to discuss my offer with your parents. It would be even wiser to discuss this with your teacher. You have no experience in life yet. You cannot understand how important this offer will be to you. At least this can help your family have a better life in a short time. Do give my offer serious consideration.'

I promised him that I would. Then he invited me to have a look at his inner room. I thanked him and refused.

'If I join you later, I will have plenty of time to see it. If I don't join you but continue my study, I don't want to have something on my mind I can never mention to anybody.'

When I thanked him and started to go, a mixture of sadness, loneliness, expectation, and helplessness flowed from his eyes fervently. I turned my head abruptly and left. Had I stayed there one minute longer, I would have decided to join him for sure.

I never mentioned this to my parents. My parents, my mother in particular, were very practical. The advantage of joining the old man would be apparent to them. Had I mentioned this to them, they would surely have forced me to join the old man. I did not mention it to my teacher either. She would have been against my taking that career because I was a good student in her eyes and I could have a better future.

This decision robbed me of many nights' sleep. Immediate material gain was a great attraction, but my inclination for further education and of seeing the outside world was a stronger attraction. Getting further schooling was a big challenge to me, particularly as far as financial support was concerned. Yet after months of long struggle, I decided to take the difficult road, to continue my study.

Digging a Well for Our Vegetable Garden

Our school was just in its early stage of development, and had a lot to improve. Yet the school always had the students in mind and tried hard to help them.

We had no dining room or dining hall, but we had the largest dining place—the open ground in front of the teachers' office. Two rows of bricks, spaced two metres apart, were buried in the ground with the surface of the bricks level with the ground. The surface of the bricks had serial numbers written on them. These were our 'tables'. Around each brick 'table' were about ten students, all squatted on the ground to have their three meals. This was our dining hall till I left the school. Sitting on benches around a table in a hall to have our meals never entered our heads. Only when it rained or snowed were we allowed to go back to eat in our respective classrooms.

In the morning, our corn meal porridge was in a tin bucket, our *wo tou* in a basket, and our diced salted turnips in a bowl. The table head would deal out the porridge with a ladle, each portion fair and equal. Then he would give everyone a piece of *wo tou* and we all fished salted turnips from the same bowl with our chopsticks.

Lunch was a little bit different from breakfast. Instead of a bowl of porridge, we were given an additional *wo tou*. The rest was the same, turnips and one *wo tou*.

Supper was similar to breakfast. The porridge was good and filling, anyway.

We Chinese would say that breakfast should be good in quality, lunch should fill the stomach, and supper should be less in quantity. But this did not apply to us poor students. Five yuan a one month for one person was just enough for that. The chief steward tried hard to provide variety by giving us some steamed sweet potatoes at lunch or supper. He could only do that much. He had no more money to spend. Though the principal requested him time and again to improve the meals for the students, just as the saying 'a capable daughter-in-law cannot cook without edible material', he could not do this without money.

Our three meals were taken under the eyes of the principal and the teachers. During each meal, either the principal or the education manager or one of the teachers would tour our 'tables', asking:

'How do you like your meals? Any suggestions?'

'Very good, nothing to complain about,' we would answer in high voices to show we were happy with our meals.

To us the food was what we had at home. To me the food was better than what I had at home. We never thought about variety or about anything better. To us students, if the quantity and quality remained unchanged, we would be quite satisfied. We knew the chief steward had done his very best. Nobody else could do better.

But each time when the principal watched us having our meals, his round face would become longer. His eyes betrayed a kind of sadness, worry and helplessness. Something was troubling him. At first I could not understand why he was like that. I know we did not make mistakes and we did not behave badly. So why was he like that?

One day our teacher came to the classroom, looking very excited.

'Students, the principal is very worried about your health. When he saw you drinking your porridge hastily, biting at your *wo tou* in big mouthfuls and chewing heartily, picking up the salted turnips with your chopsticks and savouring them contentedly, he was very worried about your health. He not only requires you to study hard, but also wants you to be healthy. You are growing and you need more nutrition. It will not do just to have *wo tou*, corn porridge and salted turnips for the day, for the week, and for the year. The principal wishes you to be able to have staple food of better quality. He wishes you to be able to have stir-fry dishes of different vegetables, and some dishes of meat. But your parents cannot afford to pay more. The school has no money to help you improve your meals. The principal requires you all to use your brains to find a way.'

Those words made our hearts warm. Never before had we heard such hearty emotional words from anyone. We were so moved that girls wept audibly and boys were trying hard to hold back tears in their eyes. The principal, and our teacher, loved us more than our parents, in a different way. In his eyes, we were the future of the country. In his eyes, some of us might do great things in the future. In his eyes, we were his sons and daughters and more than that. But it was 'easier said than done'.

'Three shoe repairers are as good as Zhu Geliang,' said the author of *The Three Kingdoms*. Zhu Geliang, a character from the book, was a strategist who helped Liu Bei establish the kingdom of Shu. The Chinese considered him wise and clever, so the principal instructed us to find solutions like Zhu Geliang.

Most students came from peasant families. We were familiar with the land. To us the land could give anything and everything. Our school had a vast stretch of land, which was not utilised for construction or for the sportsgrounds. We turned our attention to this land.

'Make a vegetable garden,' we chorused. The principal was pleased with the idea. His knitted brows smoothed out. He decided to cultivate a vegetable garden.

It was already nearly the summer holidays. During this time, in addition to the students helping in the construction of the houses, a well could be dug and vegetables grown for use in the following term. The land within the southern end of the school domain could serve this purpose well. That land was about one acre in size, and a bit more fertile than the rest. About fifteen students were chosen to finish the job during the summer holidays.

It was a big thing to dig the well. First it required skill, especially in the construction of the brick wall lining of the well, and solving the collapsing of the mud wall as the well went deeper. Fortunately, there were a few students who had such experience. They were group leaders of the three groups doing the digging. The well pit grew deeper and deeper. A meeting was held on the second day to prepare for an emergency. Bricks, pikes, and wands were collected, ready for use.

I was one of the three students rotating the windlass rigged up for lifting mud from the well and for lowering the diggers in and lifting them out. The sun was scorching my back and the winding taxed my strength. Sweat dripped from my face down into the well.

The second day about mid-morning, the well was about three metres deep and water oozed out. The air from the well was very cool.

'Lift me out, please.' one student shouted at us winders. We did so. He was shivering and his teeth chattered. A short while later, the other two in the well were also lifted out. They shivered and their teeth chattered also. Their lips were blue from cold. By now there was not enough room for five students to work down below.

The teacher in charge of our class was present at the site. She immediately went back to her office and came back with some money.

'Go get a few bottles of alcohol,' she ordered a student. Then she went to the kitchen asking for a basin of stir-fry vegetables. The principal heard about this and offered a few yuan for buying more alcohol. When digging a well, it was the custom for alcohol to be used to drive out the chills from the body.

It was about noon, the sun shone brightly in the pure blue sky. The few trees nearby stood lifeless, not even stirring one leaf. The air was hot. The scorching rays of the sun on my back hurt so bad that I thought a fire was burning me. We three windlass winders were all perspiring heavily. Then it was my turn to be lowered down to do the digging. The water was icy cold, so much so that the cold seemed to quickly penetrate into the marrow of the bone. I gritted my teeth but they chattered violently and I could not hold my teeth against each other. In less than twenty minutes, I was lifted up. I was offered a cup of alcohol and I gulped it down. It burned all the way down my throat. I still felt cold and the shivering became controllable.

The outside and inside of the well seemed to be two different temperature zones—the Equator and the Antarctic. It was decided that each group would stay in the well for fifteen minutes. Five groups were doing the job in turn. The teacher was checking her watch every few minutes. When the fifteen minutes ended, she would order, 'Lift them out!' with her hand making a lifting gesture. With, 'lower the other group down!' her hand made a lowering gesture. She looked like an out and out army commander.

As soon as a group was out, they huddled around the basin to gulp down a cup of alcohol. After a short period of running around, their lips would gradually return to normal.

When the teeth stopped chattering, the hands stopped trembling and the body stopped shivering, it was time to go down to relieve the other group. As the brick wall lining of the well came up higher and higher, the water also grew higher and higher until it reached half way up the well shaft. The brick wall finally reached the surface of the ground. We were so happy that we shouted and jumped. To mark this success, a few strings of firecrackers were bought and fired. We had quite a few 'bottoms-up', not of wine or of alcohol but of water. Alcohol was only given to us for driving out the chills. It was an exception, because students were forbidden to drink alcohol. Neither the teacher nor the principal would give us alcohol as a treat. Water was always used as wine or alcohol, even in ancient times. Smiles were on everybody's face.

Irrigation ditches were made. Late beans were sowed. Plots for Chinese cabbage and turnips were prepared. Six students were asked to remain at school to maintain the garden. Six or more, including me, remained to help in the construction of the houses.

The vegetables grew well and stir-fry dishes appeared on our table the following term. The chief steward sold extra vegetables to surrounding companies. He stored up a bit of wheat flour for the sake of giving us a treat during the New Year. He also put aside a bit of money for buying meat for the same occasion.

Bailing Water out of a Pond for Fish

Lunar October the first drew near. The principal wished that the students could have better National Day meals. Again, he tried to solve this with the students. One student suggested that he knew a pond that contained fish, which did not belong to anybody. The fish could be eaten for the National Day celebration. He suggested that the school organise students to bail the water out of the pond into an empty ditch from which the water was originally bailed from it. The principal and the student went to investigate. There was no problem to hold and contain the water that was bailed out. So it was decided to get the fish on the Sunday prior to October the first.

The whole school was mobilised. Teachers and students were eagerly looking forward to the day. Buckets, baskets, ropes, shovels and basins were all brought to school by the students who lived nearby. The school cart was also used to transport food and drinks for the students.

The Sunday morning came. The sun showed a smiling face. It was a bit windy but quite mild. Apart from the cooks, a few teachers, and those students who were sick, we all set out to the pond after breakfast. We were in two single files, class by class, like marching soldiers. The banner of our school fluttered in the wind. Classes sang on the way.

We arrived at the place but it was not a pond, but a wide, deep ditch. There was already a dam across the ditch. It was apparent that water had been bailed into the ditch from the other side of the dam, definitely for getting fish, though not recently. My brother and I had bailed water for fish when there was waterlogging, so I knew about this. But if the student living nearby said there was fish here, there should be fish.

The headquarters were set up under a big tree, in the lea of a slope. The chief steward positioned the cart there, too. In the cart was a huge rectangular basket covered with a padded quilt. Lunch was inside that basket. Beside it was a big cylindrical aluminium container, which contained hot tea. There was also a very big aluminium basin, also covered with a padded quilt, which held the dishes. Bowls and chopsticks were stacked in two big willow baskets. The chief steward, with a cigarette between his lips, sat beside the cart with a big smile on his face.

Girls from each class, with metal teapots and bowls in their hands, were ready to serve tea to their classmates. The boys from our class, which was class number four, were allotted to work one-fourth of the dam at the side near the headquarters. I suggested that we start in two groups. One group was to patch and increase the height of the dam, while the other was to rig up the buckets. Only my friend, Liang, who was my close neighbour, and I were experienced in doing this. So we two were the only members of the second group.

Liang began with one bucket and me with another. The ropes had to be tied in such a way that unless you untied them they would become tighter when you started to bail the water out. Two long loops, one on each side of the bucket, were made as handles for the bailers. When we had all the buckets rigged up, the dam was already patched and increased as required.

Liang and I, holding the loop firmly in our hands, took up positions on the dam and demonstrated how to bail out the water with the device. Representatives from the other three classes were all present. We swung the bucket backward to the water, lowered the ropes at the opening side of the bucket by a dipping motion of the forward hand, lifted the opening side of the bucket up and lowered the rope by the other hand. The bucket would be full of water. This had to be done almost simultaneously. Then we swung the bucket forward to throw water to the other side of the dam. After the demonstration I explained the key points.

'Lower and lift the ropes just a little bit. Keep the ropes taut. Never slacken them. Lift the bucket with the help of the back, not just with the arms.'

'Understand?' our school principal asked the representatives when I had finished my explanation.

Ten pairs of male students bailed out the water simultaneously. The buckets flew rhythmically. The water in the pond dwindled quickly. Young male teachers also tried their hands, clumsily at first but by-and-by they could also do it skilfully.

At noon, the bailers had lunch in shifts. 'Resting the persons, not resting the horses!' was the saying we followed. In other words, the bailers could rest, but the buckets had to keep working. Teachers and bailing students, their clothing smeared with mud from the pond and splashed with water, sat in a circle to enjoy a special picnic meal of steamed wheat flour bread, salted turnips, and a small piece of soybean curd cake. Everybody ate while they laughed and laughed. Girls were busy offering tea to the teachers and bailers. The pocket of the chief steward must have been drained substantially, but he laughed with us. Even the principal, unlike his normal self, laughed and joked with the students.

By mid-afternoon, the pond had no more water left. Fish, such as big carp, bream and eels, were all struggling for breath in the mud. Male students, even some male teachers, bared their feet and got into the pond to collect the fish. Fish that wriggled in our hands and escaped were caught again. Loud shouts and laughter mingled.

The march back to school was high spirited, like a victorious army coming back from battle. Back at school steaming hot food welcomed us. The cooks beamed upon us and waved at us which reminded me of the scene when we offered green lentil soup to the People's Liberation Army heading south in early 1949.

Though our booty was not big, merely a bit more than four hundred kilograms of fish, the whole school was in triumphant happiness. Relations between the teachers and students had changed—the change could be felt. In class, we were teachers and students, but out of class we seemed to be members of the same family. After this, the students studied harder. No longer was it necessary for the teachers to spur us on.

chapter 12

THE YOUTH LEAGUE AND THE THIEF

School is the place to train the future professionals needed in the construction of a country. It is also the place to train communist followers through the Youth League. Mao established the Youth League to promote the study of communism and to sustain the ideals of the Communist Party for generations to come. The Youth League was expanded every term with new members. However, when attracting more students to follow the communist cause, there can be exceptions, and the thief caught from our class was one.

The Free Speech by Volunteers
In our school there was a general branch of the Youth League, the head of which was the secretary who had to be a member of the Communist Party. The secretary was a young teacher who taught us politics. Unlike the principal and the education manager, he had a solemn face, and his protruding teeth added more to this solemnity. He never smiled, or at least, I never saw him smile.

Each class had a branch of the Youth League. Under each branch was a secretary and a deputy secretary, as well as groups that again had a leader. The group leader's responsibility, in theory, was to attract the prime of the youth into the Youth League. The Youth League was regarded as the helping hand of the Communist Party and each member had to choose one or two students as his or her friends to whom they would offer help so that they could meet the standards of the Youth League and become members. This activity was called 'one helping one and the two becoming red'.

In our class, the academic performance of some of the Youth League members was not good. One or two did not behave, in the eyes of my friends and I, in the way demanded by the Youth League. At the time, I could not understand that it did not matter to be academically good or not. It did matter that the Youth League had to grow continuously, because it was merely part of the country's ruling machine. I could not understand that students joined it as a way to attain a better position in life.

At first I had never turned my eyes to the Youth League. I was not conscious of its existence. My spare time was spent in solving my financial demands. My mind was on my study. During the first one-and-a-half years, I had not even considered joining the Youth League. Similarly, the Youth League branch of our class had never turned its eyes to me. It was not conscious of my existence. It had never included me in the category of activists. As a result, I had nobody giving me the 'one helping one and the two becoming red'.

One afternoon, all the students in our class were called to form four lines to attend the ceremony of the 'Youth League Augmentation Conference'. About six or seven students would be accepted as members of the Youth League at that conference. We were taken there to be politically educated and to learn from them.

The site of the conference was the theatre of the county. It had been recently constructed and, at the time, was the best building in the county town. It had the biggest hall I had ever seen. At one end was a stage, which I called the platform. Expensive, dark red velvet curtains draped from the high ceiling. A desk covered with white cloth, on which sat a megaphone, was placed in the middle of the stage front. Near the right and left wings of the stage were rows of desks, which were also covered with white cloth. On the curtain at the back of the stage was a huge picture of Chairman Mao and beside it was a red flag.

Overhead on the front of the stage were the words in large writing 'Youth League Augmentation Conference'. On the walls were slogans such as 'Long live the Communist Party!' 'Long live Chairman Mao!' 'Study hard, be a docile tool of the Communist Party!' 'Study hard, be a successor of Communism!' and so on.

The whole atmosphere in the hall was solemn, formal, and a bit oppressive—the faces on the stage showed it. The faces of my schoolmates in the audience showed it. A girl, who was the deputy secretary of the Youth League general branch, came forward to the megaphone, tapped it with her finger and announced the agenda of the conference.

'Now,' she declared, 'speech by the secretary of the Youth League!'

The secretary came to the megaphone to make the speech. He emphasised that the Youth League was an assistant of the Communist Party. He said that Youth League members were the models of the youth, the elite of the youth. He announced that those who were already members should discipline themselves harder and those who were not members should learn from those who were accepted that day. He said that all the students who wished to be progressive—who were willing to discipline themselves in accordance with the criteria of the Youth League, who were determined to carry out the duties and obligations of the Youth League, and who made formal applications—could be accepted into the Youth League.

As he finished his half-hour speech, the deputy secretary announced the start of the oath-taking ceremony. Six or seven students were lined up in front of the red flag. The girl said, 'Raise your right fist and pledge after me.'

All those students under the red flag raised their right fists.

'I pledge that I am loyal to the Communist Party, loyal to the cause of Communism. I am always ready to devote my life to the cause of Communism. I accept the rules and regulations of the Youth League and let it guide my actions and performance. I accept the supervision of the organisation of the Youth League. I will be a League member up to the required standard.'

Then the deputy secretary solemnly pinned a Youth League badge to their breasts, in the position above the breast pocket on the left front of their jacket or dress. Their faces, crimsoned to a rosy colour, were a mixture of excitement and pride.

'Next, representatives of the activists wishing to be Youth League members make speeches.'

One by one they jumped onto the stage to speak at the call of the girl, the deputy secretary.

The room became warmer and warmer. Sweat appeared on my forehead. Excitement was in the air. Everyone's stare was nailed to the stage.

'Next, free speech by volunteers,' the girl declared. She looked at her paper. 'The speaker is...'

The ceremony moved me greatly. It flooded my mind with a sublime thinking I had never entertained. It seemed to be a rushing current to draw me in. An urge in my breast pushed me to bare my heart of the determination I had to become a member of the Youth League some day in the future. My head was full of the lofty ideas I was nurturing. I forgot the environment. Abruptly I stood up, hastened forward a few steps, pressed the stage edge with both hands, curved my knees and jumped onto the stage. Quietness gripped the hall, so still that even a pin falling onto the ground could be heard. On the stage, the deputy secretary of the Youth

League, her right arm half raised with a piece of paper in her hand, was at a loss of what to do. The secretary, his big eyes surprised, sat motionlessly at his seat. Below the stage, my teacher and the branch Youth League secretary were gazing at me with obvious concern. My classmates were pouring encouragement to me from their eyes.

Blood rushed to my head. Shyness disappeared. With steady steps I approached the desk, tested the megaphone with the middle finger of my right hand, and started to speak.

'Dear principal, dear Youth League secretary, dear teachers and dear schoolmates, I wish to express my determination here. I want to join the Youth League. I will act and behave in accordance with the rules and regulations of the Youth League. If it were not for the Party, it would not be possible for me to study in junior high school. If it were not for the school authority, it would be impossible for me to continue my study. I wish to be an assistant to the Party some day in the future. I pledge to you that the next admittance here under the red flag will include me. Thanks.'

I jumped off the stage and returned to my seat.

Silence, then deafening applause exploded from the audience. A second later, the people on the stage joined in.

When the applause died down, the girl came to the megaphone to announce the first volunteer speaker. As soon as the first one finished she would announce the name of the second volunteer speaker from the list in her hands, until four or five students had finished the 'free speeches' by reading from one or a few pages of paper written in advance.

On the way back to school, my teacher said to me, 'Come to my office for a minute.'

So, instead of going back to my classroom, I followed her to the teacher's office.

'Why didn't you let me know you wanted to speak on the rostrum?' she asked.

'I didn't know I wanted to speak. I was so moved that I thought I should make a speech to show my determination.'

'You scared me to death,' she exclaimed. 'Without reading your speech paper first, who knows what you were going to say!'

I was astounded, confused, and bewildered.

'Wasn't it a free speech by volunteers?' I asked.

'Yes, but the volunteers were chosen by the Youth League and their speech papers had been checked in advance,' she explained. 'Also, those who spoke as volunteers on the stage were the candidates to be next accepted.'

'So they were not volunteers making free speeches?' I faltered.

'This is necessary. The organiser should know exactly what each speaker wants to say so as not to spoil the atmosphere of the meeting.'

'I just thought I could volunteer to make a free speech and yet I did not know the speakers were pre-fixed.' I said. Intuitively I realised that I was too simple and naïve in such matters.

'Forget about it,' she told me. 'You have never spoken in front of people. I could not imagine how you dared to speak in front of the whole school.'

'Did I say anything improper?' I asked.

'No, not at all.' The teacher said. 'You made a very good speech. But you must keep your word.'

'I will,' I said. 'I will write an application immediately.'

'Do you know how to write it?'

'Not exactly,' I said, 'but I will try my best.'

'Bring it to me before you hand it in,' the teacher told me.

I handed her my application the following day. She told me it was all right and I handed it in to the secretary of the Youth League branch in our class.

A week later, a member of the Youth League was having a very serious talk with me.

'Why aren't you a Pioneer?' he asked me.

I explained that I had no money to buy the red scarf at first but when I had earned enough money I was no longer accepted.

'We shall check whether that is true. Now tell me why you want to join the Youth League.'

'Why? To contribute to the cause of Communism.'

'For any other purpose?'

'Like what?' I asked.

No reply was given.

'Who do you wish to be your introducers?'

'That is up to the Youth League.'

'Do you know the rules and regulations of the Youth League?'

'Yes.'

'Do you have the booklet?'

'No.'

'I will lend you one.' And the conversation came to an end.

I felt choked by mixed feelings, which I found very hard to explain. As I understood it, the Youth League was an organisation made up of the best youth. But when looking around, some members were not as good as normal students either in study or in behaviour. The one who had the conversation with me, for instance, was below average in class. He was not as active as other students in the construction of the school, yet when he conducted the conversation, he seemed to be the standard of the Youth League.

Two weeks later, one of the introducers nominated for me arranged to have a talk.

'Our branch had a discussion about your application. We all agreed that you are one of the activists. But you have not reached the standard yet. You must overcome your shortcomings and you must subject yourself to the tests of the Youth League. To compare your performance with the criteria, we wish to point out your shortcomings. Firstly, you leave school too early every day. You seldom join the activities of the class. Secondly, you are a bit conceited. Lastly, you do not help others enough in their studies.'

What could I say? What should I say?

Before the application I thought I was good, very good. After the application, I was regarded as 'no good'. Before the application, I was praised for whatever small 'good deeds' I did. After the application, I was requested to do more and more and more. In handing in the application I was handing over my freedom. In handing in the application, I was trying to remould myself into a 'product of a machine, without my own will, without my own liking, without my own decision, and without my own identification'.

I later told my teacher about the conversation between my introducer and myself.

'Don't worry,' she told me. 'Just do your best.'

'I can do that. But I have to earn money to support myself and you know that best of all,' I said to the teacher.

'If you have such shortcomings, correct them. If you don't have them, guard against them in the future. But remember you must be tolerant of others' opinions.'

I promised that I would. For the sake of my future, I had to be always tolerant of the opinions of others.

I was admitted into the Youth League at the end of 1958 or early 1959, though I did not know myself how the three points of my shortcomings were overcome. My friends congratulated me. I was determined to study well and contribute to the Party that had done so much for my family.

The Thief

In the novel *The Journey to the West*, when Monkey and his comrades and teacher came to the heartland of Buddhist paradise, the host who sheltered them was robbed shortly after they departed from the house. Whenever I read that chapter I would ask myself how it was possible that robbery could happen in paradise. When everybody in our class was trying hard to study well and to progress politically, a thief turned out to be one of my classmates. My classmates and I felt it hard to understand the reason. Then I recollected what happened in the Buddhist paradise and I said to myself that if a thief could exist in paradise then a thief could exist in our class. (*The Journey to the West* is a very famous classic novel. The hero of the book is a monkey who was born from a piece of rock. The monkey found a cave curtained by waterfalls in a mountain full of fruit trees. He made it the home of monkeys. He went to look for a teacher and he became very powerful. He borrowed weapons from the East Sea Dragon King. He fought the celestial generals and armies. He was buried under the 'Wu Xing Mountain' when he was defeated and caught. Monk Tang, who was sent by the Emperor of Tang to fetch Buddhist Doctrines, got him out of the mountains. The monkey became the student of the monk. He escorted the monk, his teacher, to the West Paradise. On his way there, he overcame eighty-one difficulties. In the end the monkey became the Buddha who fought and won.)

I was once told this story about a thief:

'In a certain northern Chinese village, there was a family that was so poor that it literally had nothing other than the four walls of a house. One winter night the husband and wife were sleeping. Their door was not locked. A thief came, tried the door and got into the room. The husband heard the noise and turned on his stomach to have a look. He saw the thief groping in the room. The thief could not find anything except a few catties of corn kernels in a pottery jar.

"Poor devil!" the thief cursed. He spread his jacket on the floor and went over to get the jar containing the corn kernels. Meanwhile the man, who was the owner of the house, pulled the thief's jacket into his quilt.

The thief tipped the corn kernels onto "his jacket". He then started to gather its edges in order to take the corn away.

"Where's my jacket?" he said to himself. "I did spread it here."

The wife of the house was awaked by the noise.

"My old man," she said, "I heard some strange noise in the room. Get up and see whether there's a thief in our room."

"There's no thief," the husband replied. "We have nothing for a thief to steal."

"Who said there's no thief?" the thief himself asked. "If there's no thief, who took my jacket?'"

The story of the thief in my class happened one late autumn morning. The air was chilly and very fresh. As usual, we were brushing our teeth and washing our face in front of our dormitory.

'Look,' somebody exclaimed. 'What happened to the steps of the General Service Department?'

We all ran over to have a look. A big hole was underneath the threshold where bricks had been dug out. The hole was smooth owing to the friction of somebody's passage. This was reported to the head of the Service Department, a man in his late fifties who was tall and slim. He came and with anxiety on his face, took out his key to open the door.

'Don't open the door,' said the principal, who also came to inspect the theft. 'We must report this to the County Public Security Bureau.'

A jeep came within twenty minutes. Two public security men got out and hastened to the spot. They asked the students to stand off from the site, so as not to damage any possible clues. One was circling slowly around the place, jotting down something now and then. The other was talking to students for details. Then the two of them squatted down at the hole, examined it and took notes.

The bell called us to our respective classrooms for morning classes. During the breaks, we craned our heads in that direction to see what was happening.

At lunchtime, when we squatted in a circle around our brick 'tables' in front of the teachers' office building, the principal told us briefly what had happened. He said that the office of the General Service Department had been broken into. The drawer holding the students' meal money was prised open. About one thousand six hundred yuan was stolen. Anxious sounds broke out in murmurs. The principal calmed us down by declaring that the school would advance the money for the month.

At the end of lunch, Youth League secretaries and monitors were called to the principal's office. Details were given to them. In daily life, if something important happened, it was the usual practice to call the secretaries of the Youth League branches and the monitors of the classes.

By the evening when we lay in bed, twenty or thirty boys side-by-side, like sardines, I got the story from the Youth League secretary of our class. He was my friend. We had our heads under his quilt before he whispered to me the details, but cautioned me not to disclose them to anybody else.

The thief, according to the public security men, was a professional. He first got rid of a few bricks from under the threshold, which was not a difficult job. He then dug a hole into the room underneath the threshold timber. The hole was just big enough for him, head first, to creep into the room. The drawer was yanked open with one jerk of a screwdriver or something like a wire rod. The thief left by the back window. He placed one foot on the bed, the bed of the Head of the Department who was not there for the night, and one foot on the windowsill and got out. His footprints were big and clear, but the security men said the thief was not big. From the prints the security men saw that the thief had a pair of bigger shoes over his own. The points of stress betrayed that. The security men summed up:

The thief was a professional.

The thief was about 1.7 metres high.

The thief was a young man.

The thief knew the Head of the Service Department would not stay in the room that night and that the money would be put in that drawer.

The thief was from the school.

The last point made the whole school uneasy, for every student was a suspect. That was the reason why the principal did not tell all those points to the whole school and that was the reason why my friend warned me again and again not to pass the information on to anybody else. Days passed. Teachers and students no longer mentioned the incident. It was, at least it seemed, forgotten.

One afternoon, a couple of months later, the monitor of our class pulled me aside and asked me to find a way to keep the whole class in the classroom for half an hour. (I was the representative in charge of study.) I went to the algebra teacher to get a few questions and copied them on the blackboard. I advised the class that except for the monitor and secretary of the Youth League, who were going for a meeting, everybody should finish the answers within forty-five minutes.

To some, the questions were difficult but to others, they were quite easy. Within twenty minutes, five or six students had already finished the answers. I told them to recheck them and not to hand their papers in until the end of the individual study class.

Very soon the monitor and secretary of the Youth League returned, and started to answer the questions. A while later I said the papers could be handed in. When there were no others around, the Youth League secretary told me the story.

'Student Luo Xin from our class aroused suspicion. His family is not well off but in the past month he has changed a great deal. He went to the town restaurant to dine, which other students could not afford to do. He began smoking cigarettes. He bought razors, face cream, new shoes, and new clothes. A rough calculation was made and we found that he spent more than sixty yuan within a short period of time. The question is where did he get the money?

'We reported this to the principal. He told us not to mention it to anybody. Luo Xin was very alert. I once lay on his pillow and felt something hard and very uncomfortable in it. I asked him what it was and he told me he put newspapers in it instead of millet husks.

'The men from the Public Security Bureau decided to make a check. In order not to arouse suspicion they came disguised as teachers from another school undergoing training at our school. The principal, the monitor and myself were present at the scene when they investigated the belongings of Luo Xin.

'The pillow was opened but there were only old newspapers. Then the quilt was opened and several hundred yuan were hidden in its cotton wadding.

'We are not good at sewing. That's why we asked you to keep our classmates in the classroom. After a while Luo Xin will be taken away.'

A jeep came and headed towards our dormitory. Luo Xin was led to the jeep, without handcuffs. He looked very calm and undisturbed—not at all afraid. The students watched while he was taken away. There had to be some explanation of the events and so we were all called back to our respective classrooms.

The date for an open trial was fixed. All the students from our class, class number four, were invited to be present for the sake of criticising Luo Xin and of being educated.

Luo Xin was led into the room where we were all seated. He had no handcuffs. He was directed to a chair to sit down. The trial commenced immediately, without any delay.

'Name?' the judge, or who I thought was a judge, asked.

'Luo Xin.'

'Age?'

'Sixteen.'

'Profession?'

'Student.'

'Address?'

'New Village.'

'Did you break into the office of the school's General Service Department?'

'Yes.'

'Did you take the money?'

'Yes.'

'How much?'

'About sixteen hundred yuan.'

'Where did you hide it?'

'About seven hundred in my quilt, five hundred in my house. The rest is already spent.' I could not understand why he did not hide all his stolen money in his house, which was over five kilometres away from our school. If he had done so, it would be more difficult for the public security men to find it.

'Did you realise that the money was the one-month meal money for the students?'

'Yes.'

'What prompted you to steal it?'

'When I went to pay for my month board, I saw the Department Head put money in the drawer, and I discovered that he was regularly out of his office a couple of days a month. I checked the bricks and found that it was not hard to pull them away. So I decided to do it when the time came.'

'How did you steal the money?'

'I found the Department Head put the money in the drawer again and that he would not be in the office during the night. I pulled the bricks away from under the threshold and made a hole with a screwdriver. I crept into the room, head first. I used the screwdriver to force the drawer lock open. I did not expect it to be so easy. Five-yuan notes, one-yuan notes, and fifty-cent notes, were all bundled and neatly stacked in the drawer. I scooped them all into my school bag. Then I put on the shoes belonging to the Department Head, stepped onto his bed with one foot, placed the other foot on the windowsill, opened the window and jumped out. I went out of the school, discarded the shoes and returned to the dormitory, unnoticed.'

'Did you think of what would happen to you if you were caught?'

'No.'

'Have you stolen anything in the past?'

'Once.'

'What did you steal?'

'The people of the co-operative were weeding in the field. They left their clothing by the roadside. I bundled their clothes and took them.'

'Have you ever been sorry for what you did?'

'Yes.'

The judge turned to the audience, the teachers and students. 'Does anybody want to say something?'

A few did, mainly to criticise Luo for his lack of self-criticism and for becoming a victim of bourgeois thinking.

The judge then spoke about the necessity of digging out the roots of selfishness and encouraged us to be good students of the 'three merits'.

Luo was sentenced to three years in the teenage disciplinary centre, where teenagers under eighteen, who broke the law, were subject to disciplinary education.

chapter 13

COMMUNISM

The Great Leap Forward, launched in 1958, was a five-year plan to develop agriculture and industry. Mao believed that industry could only prosper if the work force was well fed, while agricultural workers needed industry to produce the tools needed for modernisation. To allow for this, he reformed the peasants into a series of communes.

The average size of a commune was about 5000 families. People in a commune gave up their ownership of tools, animals etc so that everything was owned by the commune. People now worked for the commune and not for themselves—their life as an individual was controlled by the commune. The commune provided all that was needed—common dining rooms so that women were liberated from their cooking range, schools and nurseries for children, and health care for the elderly. It was now easy for adults to work and not have to worry about their families.

The population in a commune was sub-divided. Twenty families formed a work team and twelve work teams formed a brigade. Each sub-division was given specific work to do. Party members oversaw the work of a commune to ensure that decisions followed the correct party line. Peasants, ahead of the workers in the cities, began a life of 'communism'.

The People's Commune

It was 1958 when it became evident that a senior co-operative could not solve the water problem—the spring drought and the summer flood. The senior co-ops were therefore joined together to form an even bigger one, which was called the People's Commune. It was a government organisation that replaced the Xiang government and an organisation of production—the role of lower level government and the role of production were now merged into one. The People's Commune had the authority to instigate the law and the right to deploy labourers. Under the People's Commune, the senior co-ops were called 'the production brigades'.

I first heard of the People's Commune, not in our village, but at our junior high school. One day the whole school was lined up to attend a meeting of 10,000 people to mark the establishment of the People's

Commune. At the mass meeting, I didn't catch the speaker properly and at the time the commune leaders were not able to talk much about the commune, due to the fact that they had not been taught what to say yet. I suspected that it was more important to mark the beginning of the People's Commune than to really make people understand what the speaker was talking about. However, the celebration remained vivid to me.

My friends and I watched neither the stilt dancers, the martial arts teams, the donkey dances, the lion dances, nor the donkey cart dances. We just watched the three wrestlers from Beijing—one was a teacher about fifty years of age, and the other two were students. One young student, about twenty-two years of age or so, was strongly built. The other was about thirty years old and tall and slim.

'I am from Beijing,' the youngest of the three spoke. 'I heard that this district is known for its good wrestlers. I wish that some really good ones would come forward to show me how good they are.' He walked around the circle several times but nobody answered. He continued, 'Nobody dares to come forward? The reputation is unfounded, then?'

'Let me have a play with you.' said the man aged about fifty. 'I am not a good wrestler but if I lose, some really good wrestlers will come forward.' He bared his upper body, and his ribs were clearly seen through his skin. He picked up the wrestler's waistcoat.

'Do you know that once you have this waistcoat on, you cannot claim against anybody if you die in the ring!' the young man said to him. The ring was just the trails the wrestlers drew on the ground with a stick, but its function was similar to that of boxers.

'Don't worry, if I die I am not dying young, anyway,' he said. He put on the waistcoat.

The two circled with dancing steps, then the young man turned back and the two met in the middle of the ground. Their hands pushed and pulled a few times and the young man was thrown into the air. He covered his head with his two forearms and fell to the ground with a thud. They circled again and met in the middle of the ground. Their hands pushed and pulled a few more times and the young man was thrown into the air again.

The other young man came forward and started wrestling the old man. It was just the same wrestling as with the first young man, and the second young man was thrown into the air twice.

'Young men,' the old man said, 'in this area never say you are the best wrestler. I am just a mediocre wrestler. There are many good ones.' He then changed into his padded jacket.

'Thanks for not hurting my students.' The teacher came forward to speak to the old man.

'I just played with them,' the old man said. 'I just want to let them know there is always a better wrestler behind.'

The People's Commune became the main subject in our political classes. The Education Manager was our lecturer—the best lecturer I have ever met in my eight years of schooling. He told us the advantages of the People's Commune. 'Firstly it is big and secondly it is publicly owned,' he said. Under the People's Commune, it became possible to have large-scale co-operation, such as in building reservoirs, highways and so on. When a special booklet called *Answers to certain questions about the People's Commune* was published, the Education Manager began to teach us it. He could recite the whole book without referring to it during the class. The term 'People's Commune' took root in our brain. However, we learnt more about the commune during the weekends.

The two families in the Paradise Palace, 'Taiwan' and 'South Korea', who were considered outsiders to the senior co-op, were now 'liberated' and included in the People's Commune. The day they were 'liberated' is still vivid in my mind. The brigade leaders were at the head of the procession, while the students from the primary school followed. Behind the students were the villagers. I happened to be at home and was following them to have a look. When the crowd arrived at the gate of 'Taiwan', it stopped. The father and son of the family, each with a sharp axe in hand, were guarding the gate. They refused to let anybody through. The crowd began shouting slogans.

'We do not wish to join!' the father and son shouted back.

Militiamen were called to disarm them. They were tied up and sent to the 'county', where leaders would decide what to do with them. I did not know when they came back to the village, I just knew that the family became commune members after that.

The People's Commune came as fast as lightning and as momentous as an all-engulfing flood. The cadres of the commune, suddenly empowered with the authorisation to direct such a large number of peasants, ordered them to dig reservoirs, dredge rivers, widen roads or do any work they considered urgent, without concern for the day-to-day farm work in the fields. The peasants, who were now called 'the commune members', were in a 'New World', like Alice in Wonderland.

Nineteen fifty-eight was a year, which, according to the elderly, could only occur once every sixty years—the land would give an exceptional harvest. Prior to the setting up of the People's Commune, all the land was sowed and with or without fertilisers, all the crops grew well—exceptionally well. The villagers were happy at the possibility of a bumper harvest.

Like soldiers in the army, the young and strong male commune members followed the orders of the commune to dredge rivers or to dig reservoirs in other parts of the district. They worked and worked without returning home for days, weeks and even months. The crops, though having approached harvest time, were left in the field. Women and old men, besides caring for the animals and children, had to do the harvesting alone without effective organisation and direction. Most of the main crops—sweet potatoes and peanuts—could not be harvested.

My mother and my Da Ma tried like mad to dig up more and more sweet potatoes. They tried to cook them, and dry them in the sun. They worked without a break during the day—but they could not do much. Watching the good crops in the fields abandoned, they cried. Still they worked harder.

When the male members finally returned to the village, it was too late. Most of the crops had rotted in the fields.

When the 'wind of Communism' abated, most of the grain had been consumed and most of the crops had rotted in the fields. Each commune had to pay a tax, which was many times higher than the normal tax, because of the commune cadres having made boastful reports about the production of every *mu* of land. Therefore, the commune members started to suffer—this being the prelude to the serious national famine of the early sixties.

Perhaps the government realised the absurdities committed in the countryside. Consequently, a document was issued to lay down the rules of a commune. It explicitly stated that a commune had three levels of ownership but had the brigade as the foundation. The brigades were actually former senior co-operatives. In the case of the Paradise Palace, the former senior co-op was now called the production brigade. The production teams were renumbered, but the numbers of families in a team remained unchanged.

Right after the 'wind of Communism' my father was transferred to a village where my mother's elder sister lived. It was about fifteen kilometres from our village. The commune set up a workshop to weave carpet in that village and my father became a carpet weaver again. He returned home every two weeks for a one-day visit.

My father had not touched a woollen yarn for about twenty-seven years—after his apprenticeship had been terminated—but he was still able to weave carpet. Yet, he still finished less than one square foot per day. My father returned to the brigade when the carpet factory was closed shortly after the three years' famine.

However, most of the villagers remained in the village, toiling on their land. They woke up from their transient joy during 'communism' to less interference from the commune. They realised that they should pay more attention to their land, to their crops, and to the deployment of the labourers. They began exerting themselves to solve their own problems.

The major problems facing the brigade of the Paradise Palace were water shortages in spring during which 'rain was more expensive than oil' and the 'manger' lands that were like a basin—low in the middle and high on all sides. There was little rain in the spring but too much in summer. In spring, they had to beg the heavens for rain to sow the land, while in summer, the middle of most of their land was waterlogged. They decided to tackle these problems.

Firstly they transformed the Paradise River through lining its bottom and banks with cement slates, but the situation remained unchanged. In spring, when water was mostly needed for irrigation, there was not even a drop available. In summer when water was drained from the field, it was so full that water in the fields could hardly be led into it. Then, in winter, the men went to dig a canal. With the promise that water would be released for irrigating their fields in spring, they did the canal willingly and with high expectations. But when spring came, no water came to their river, let alone to their irrigation ditches.

Finally the brigade realised that it could only rely on itself to get water. Young men were organised to learn how to drill deep wells from people living more than fifty kilometres away. When they returned to the village, well drilling commenced at the start of winter.

Drilling rigs made from timber were erected, to at least thirty metres in height. On the very top was a big wheel with a diameter more than three metres wide. It looked like two gigantic bike-wheels linked together with timber boards to provide a walkway. The inner distance between the two was about a metre, giving people enough room to move freely. The spoke battens prevented people from falling out of the wheel. Looking up at the wheel from the ground, it resembled an electric cable wheel, but it had people inside to rotate it. A few young men were walking in the cage to lift up the drill or to help the up and down movement of it.

The lifting up and thrusting down of the drill was achieved with a long band made of bamboo strips connected into a long one. The young men in the caged wheel would walk in one direction to wind the bamboo band around the big wheel which then lifted the drill up from the drilled hole. They walked the other direction to have the band lowered down. When the drill reached the bottom, they would walk a few steps to lift up the drill and a few steps in the opposite direction to lower the drill down again, while a few young men on the ground sent the drill further down with a big thrust.

The young men persisted for several winters—including the three winters during the national famine—to have ten wells drilled. The depth of each well was about one hundred and ten metres. The volume of water from each well could irrigate about one hundred *mu* (a bit more than sixteen acres). Then, in 1964, these *mu* were turned into rice paddies.

Side by side with well-drilling, the males of the brigade began levelling the land. To achieve good productivity, the production teams constructed a pushcart for each male labourer. Bit by bit and winter after winter, they levelled their land. They did not slow down the work even during the famine years. They tightened their belts and gritted their teeth to fight their hunger, but they never gave up the levelling of their land. When ten wells were ready in 1964, their land was ready for growing rice.

In 1965, for the first time in the life of the peasants in the Paradise Palace, they had enough production from their own fields. For the first time they stopped buying grain from the government. For the first time the villagers could have rice for nine months and wheat flour for three months of the year, pure, without wild vegetables. For the first time the brigade sold half a million catties of rice to the government. For the first time they ambitiously announced that they would sell one million catties of rice to the government the following year.

Simultaneously, the villagers started to rearrange trees in order to prevent the topsoil from being blown away by the wintry wind as well as to preserve water. All the trees surrounding the 'manger land' were dug out. New trees were planted, which were called the wind screen woods. From the north-east to the south-west and from the north-west to the south-east, ten trees stood abreast, like long laces, all planted to surround their fields, cutting them into one hundred *mu* square patches. The wind, which swept up the topsoil in winter, was largely stopped.

Thereafter, the brigade employed professionals to drill five more wells to expand five hundred *mu* rice paddies. Four more wells were also drilled in the village to provide the villagers with running water directly to their cooking ranges in the peasants' houses. Irrigation systems were put underground and drainage systems were all improved. To give the devil his due, I wish to say that without the above-mentioned back-breaking work, the peasants would not have been able to have their present-day luxuries after they were forced to do individual farming in the mid-eighties.

Meanwhile, through the experience gained from 1958 and especially from the three years' national famine, the peasants paid more attention to the 'private plot' allotted to them by the commune. In 1958, peasants were allowed to cultivate wasteland and as a result private plots were increased. After the establishment of the People's Commune, these private plots were taken away. During the national famine, the People's Commune returned the private plots to the peasants and promised the land would not be taken away from them for sixty years, but of course, they were at the onset of the Great Cultural Revolution. The so-called revolutionaries who issued the order declared that taking away the private plot was to cut off 'the tail of capitalism'. At that time, only such a small plot for each family was private. That is why the private plot was called 'the tail of capitalism.' Shortly after the Great Cultural Revolution, the private plots were once again returned to the peasants.

The 'private plot' was given according to the standard of $\frac{1}{30}$ acre per head. The total given to a family depended on the number of people in the family. Thereafter, a newly born baby would not be given a share and the share of a dead person would not be taken away. The private plot for the peasant's own use was usually a small piece of land not far away from the peasant's home. It was convenient for the peasant to look after it after a day's work collectively in the field. The peasant could spend only his spare time on his private plot.

This small piece of land became invaluable. Once when I went back home from school in Beijing, my father told me what he did on his private plot and what he had achieved. In spring he grew watermelon in the whole plot which was one *mu* of land. As the watermelon plants grew, he planted sweet potatoes around each one and in between the rows of the watermelon plants. Among the sweet potatoes, he grew corn. And around each corn he grew string beans. When the first harvest of watermelon from a vine was sold, he pulled the vine up so that the sweet potato could grow. When the time for planting Chinese cabbage was due, he cleared half the plot of sweet potatoes. On the ridges of the cabbage plots he grew turnips. That year, watermelon sales earned forty yuan for my father. Corn provided ears to grill for the kids. String beans furnished the family with stir-fry dishes throughout summer. Sweet potatoes gave a harvest of more than one thousand kilograms to alleviate the food shortage of the family. Chinese cabbage harvested was also about one thousand kilos—enough to feed the family as the winter vegetable. Two hundred kilograms of turnips were also reaped, partly for making salted vegetables and partly for sale. Lastly, the sweet potato vines and leaves contributed largely to a pig's feed.

The brigade started to diversify their business. Firstly more pigsties were built and young men were assigned to look after hundreds of pigs. Then a motel was built bordering the highway, just opposite the bridge of the Paradise River. A foundry was set up and this was followed by a glass instrument workshop.

The life of the peasants in the Paradise Palace changed quickly and for the better. However, corruption began spreading among the brigade cadres—they feasted on excuses of all kinds. Six thousand kilograms of rice disappeared from the storerooms of the production team that my family worked for. Team members started fighting the cadres, but without success. Then, suddenly, the People's Commune was discarded and the peasants were told to go into private farming again. When China opened its doors to the West in 1969 and adopted a market economy, the People's Commune was officially discarded and the peasants were told to go back into private farming again. The People's Commune had been part of the Chinese peasants' life for over two decades. It came into being by encouragement and was discarded by government decision.

Strangely, the peasants, now free to run their own land, missed the collective farming in the brigade. I asked Xiao Bao why, and he just smiled and told me, 'We used tractors to plough and sow our land and we used combines to do the harvesting. Now each family has only unconnected small patches of land. How can we still use the machines? Shall we buy horses, mules and donkeys? Shall we buy ploughs and other primitive farm tools?'

Strangely, even though the peasants suffered greatly during the national famine, and even though they were not happy with some of the cadres, they did not blame the commune for their sufferings. They still missed the communes. In their mind, 'Mao's policy is good! The commune is good! It is the commune cadres who carry out the policies mistakenly!'

The peasants in our village had their reasons not to blame the People's Commune. In our village, through the commune, the villagers finally turned the land into rice paddies and for the first time since liberation, they became self-sufficient. In their mind, this could not have been achieved without the commune.

The Wind of Communism

The 'wind of Communism' came to our village shortly after the People's Commune was established. It came in the form of a 'common dining hall'. The peasants thought that they had entered Communism. Each family handed over edible materials, such as flour, pigs, chickens, vegetables and cooking oil to the dining hall. Every day *man tou* and cooked pork meat were served at lunch and supper for the peasants to eat as much as they could. In the peasants' words, every day was New Year's Day.

As if in a trance, nobody worried about tomorrow. Nobody checked the storerooms of the production teams. They thought Communism could offer them no end of good food and good life.

I cannot remember when it exactly happened in 1958, except that it was a Saturday. I came home from school. It was already lunchtime, but my mother had no intention of cooking. I was hungry and very surprised that my mother was not as interested in cooking lunch as before.

'Xiao Bao,' my mother picked up a basket and spoke to my second brother, 'let's go fetch our lunch.'

My father, who had not yet been called to be a carpet weaver by the People's Commune, explained to me, 'We are now in Communism. We do not need to cook any more. We just fetch our three meals from the common dining room.'

'How do you like it? How does everybody like it?' I asked.

'Very much,' my father said. 'No need to worry about firewood, no need to worry about cooking. We fetch meals at the bell. We go to work in the field at the bell. It is good—really good.'

Very soon, my mother and brother came back with *man tou* and stir-fry dishes and porridge to serve as soup. We sat on the *kang* around the table to eat, happily.

'How do they control the quantity?' I asked my mother.

'We can fetch as much food as we need,' my mother said. 'There is no limit to what quantity each person can eat.'

'How do you like the common dining hall?' I asked mother.

'A great deal,' she said. 'In the past, I had to get up early to cook breakfast. Coming back from the field, I had to cook lunch and supper and do the washing. I never had enough time for a good break. I could never get away from milling round the cooking range. Now, I don't worry about salt, oil, vinegar, soy sauce or firewood. I only need to spend the time to fetch the food and dishes. I just need to work hard. It is really good.'

My Da Ma had handed all her edibles to the common dining hall, such as salted vegetables, cabbage, corn flour, wheat flour—everything. So did every other village family! When I talked to her, she said, 'The common dining hall is good. We now just need to work hard, eat good meals at a fixed time, and sleep well at night. We are having Spring Festival every day now.'

'More than that,' she added, 'the brigade will construct a centre for the aged villagers. There is no longer any worry whether a son is filial or not. The brigade will care for the old. Whoever has had such a worry-free life before?'

The villagers gave everything that was edible to the common dining room, eating happily without restraint, and without thinking about tomorrow. They were told that they had entered 'Communism'. Two or three months later, the government called it the 'wind of Communism'.

Both the People's Commune and 'the wind of Communism' greatly influenced the life of the peasants. The commune lasted over two decades. The 'wind of Communism'—the free eating in the common dining room—lasted about two or three months.

I talked to a few other neighbours and the opinion was almost the same. It was not a surprise. For years and years the peasants' first and foremost worry was about their life when they got old. They relied on their son or sons, but some of them ill-treated their parents. Unlike workers in the factories, the peasants had no pensions when they got old. If a peasant had no son, old age was something dreadful. Now the brigade aged care centre would support them. That was even better than having a pension and living alone, so of course the peasants loved it.

For thousands of years, women in China's rural areas were bound to the cooking range, even if they worked as hard with their husbands in the field. The duties and responsibilities of women were the heaviest—working in the fields, cooking as soon as they got home, waiting at the table for the elders and the husband, washing, making clothes, grinding corn for flour, caring for the children, and so forth. Now that they did not have to worry about cooking, their burden was very much lightened. Of course women loved the common dining room.

Then, after no less than two months, the 'wind of Communism' disappeared. It came and went like lightning. But its blinding brilliance had left its mark.

When the national famine was almost over, I told my Da Ma that the 'wind of Communism' was to blame for it. She said to me, 'That few months of Communism was good. I had already been in Communism. I will have nothing to regret when I die. I enjoyed a life for a few months that we never dared to dream about. That's enough!'

The 'wind of Communism' was one of the major factors that caused the national famine. The unrestricted rations given to the peasants in the common dining halls led to most of the food being consumed. The peasants suffered in the early sixties. Most of them fortunately survived by eating tree leaves, grass roots, and whatever they could get. But some, if not all, argued that the national famine could not prove that the 'common dining hall' was wrong, nor could it prove that the aged care centre was wrong.

chapter 14

ACTIVITIES IN THE GREAT LEAP FORWARD

Four major events took place in China between 1957 and 1958—the beginning of the Great Leap Forward. Firstly, in 1957, the movement opposing rightists emerged after non-Communists helped the Communists rectify their style of work. The movement to oppose the rightists', though an important event in China, left a small impression on me due to the fact that, like all junior high school students, I was not personally involved. Then, in 1958, the People's Commune came into existence and the 'agricultural satellites' were boastfully launched, and the whole nation was mobilised to make steel in a big way. I was involved in steel making. I was instructed to learn and to teach how to make steel. Since 1958, though the Communist Party committed many serious mistakes in that year, the mentality of the Chinese people changed. Spiritually, the Chinese stood up. 'A roar from the working class will make the earth vibrate three times!' was one of the well-known slogans of the time and it would demonstrate the Chinese spirit both during and after the Great Leap Forward years.

Launching 'Satellites' in Agriculture

'Agricultural Satellite' was an expression created in 1958, which meant the highest records of harvest for all crops. A new per *mu* (⅙ acre) harvest was called a 'satellite'. Compelled or encouraged by governments at various levels, higher and higher per *mu* yields were reported, and so one 'satellite' after another was launched. Launching 'satellites' in agriculture became an historical record of how the cadres in China told lies, but when it first came to the land of China, the junior high school students, did not realise this.

On the outside of the west wall of our classroom, facing the main school road from the entrance, was a blackboard. News extracted from the official newspaper, *Ren Min Ri Bao* (*People's Daily*), was always written beautifully on that blackboard. Now news from the agricultural front was very encouraging. The education manager, who wrote with a beautiful hand, recorded the news on the blackboard personally. He wrote only in the morning at first, but then began to change the news several times a day: 'Good news: Wheat production from the third team of the East Breeze Co-op totals 250 kilograms per *mu*.'

That was very good news. In our village, if 100 kilograms per *mu* could be harvested it would be a good harvest as far as wheat was concerned.

The following day still better news came onto the blackboard: 'Good news: Wheat production from the second team of the Red Gate Co-op totals 1000 kilograms per *mu*.' In the afternoon of the same day, the extract from the *People's Daily* was that wheat production from the fifth team of the Da Hua Co-op totalled 3200 kilograms per *mu*. The production rose, like a 'satellite', to 7200 kilograms per *mu*. Teachers and students were cheered by such good news and were expecting better still. Nobody doubted whether it was possible to produce that much wheat.

One day, the whole school was called to a meeting in the county theatre, which was nearly fully packed when we arrived. As soon as we were seated, a cadre from the county government came forward to the megaphone and began a short introductory speech. He announced that the meeting was held for the purpose of welcoming a troupe of model peasants and to listen to their reports on their agricultural production. The troupe came from Hebei Province. They had about five or six people in all. A man, just a bit below average height, robustly built, round-faced, well sun-tanned, in a newly made blue Mao-style jacket, looking more like a cadre in a high position than a peasant, came to the megaphone to make the speech. He was eloquent, theatrical, and emotional, or at least in my eyes, better than some professional actors or actresses as far as eloquence was concerned. He told the audience how in his village he created 50,000 kilograms of rice per *mu*. A noticeable hush fell over the audience. Then thunderous applause arose, wave upon wave, for at least five minutes. He spoke for about one hour, winning applause at frequent intervals. Sometimes the whole audience stood up to applaud him. The atmosphere was exciting and emotional. The slogan shouting was deafening, threatening to damage the eardrums.

At the end, the cadre from the county government called on the cadres of all levels to learn from the troupe and to lead the peasants to produce more grain, which for our commune meant sweet potatoes, corn, peanuts and soybeans. He called upon the peasants to let new 'agricultural satellites' fly high in the sky. After this, boasts, exaggeration, fabrication, even lies, gradually began to come from the lips of the cadres from various levels in the rural areas, and in the industries as well.

Back at school we had discussions in political classes. Opinions about the per *mu* production were always one-sided. Opposing opinions would not be tolerated. This was a Chinese tradition for thousands of years that opposing opinions were never allowed. Everybody had to state an opinion. I tried to delay this to the last moment, but even the last moment would come. I had to speak. I started to work at the age of four. I was working with my father for quite a long time. Like all peasants, we wished one day to produce more. In my heart I knew it was not possible for our village to produce 7200 kilos wheat per *mu*, but I could not tell whether it was possible elsewhere. I had never tasted rice, never planted rice, nor ever seen a rice paddy. It was not possible for me to know whether it was possible that 50,000 kilograms of rice could be produced per *mu*. But I had to speak.

One's speech was the demonstration of one's political attitude and my political attitude would decide whether I could be a Youth League member. As long as one showed his political attitude as the great majority did, his attitude was good.

In my speech, I said I was very excited that our peasants had such advanced knowledge in agriculture in that they could produce 50,000 kilograms of rice per *mu* and 7200 kilograms of wheat per *mu*. I wished that my home village could do the same. Then there would be no need to eat elm tree leaves or wild vegetables. *Bing tzi* or *wo tou* could be replaced by wheat flour bread. More land could be reserved for the construction of factories and very soon our country would be the richest in the world.

Actually, my classmates all came from peasant families, and all should have known it was not possible to have such high yields per *mu*, but they all hailed the 'satellites'. Only a few years later I came to realise that one should always repeat what the newspaper published or what the Party said. One should not speak the truth. One should not be like the child who pointed out that the emperor had no clothes on.

Steel Making

The autumn of 1958 arrived, bringing great happenings in the country. One day I was called to the education manager's office. Teacher Seng, who was in charge of class three, and her student Ko, were already there.

The look on their faces signalled to me that we would be discussing something important.

'I wish to advise you,' the manager spoke as I sat down on an empty chair, 'that the four of us will represent our school to go to Gao Bei Dian Steel Mill to learn steel making. Train tickets have been bought. We shall start early tomorrow morning.' Then he added, 'You must memorise everything you are taught. You will teach other students when you come back.'

I harboured the thought of being trusted as I fell into a sound sleep. A light touch on my head awoke me. It was still dark. I opened my eyes and saw a man bending towards me. He whispered in my ear, 'Time to set out. Be quick.' It was the education manager who had come to wake me. I recognised him clearly when he tiptoed out of our dormitory.

It was a chilly morning and the breeze was a bit severe on my face, but the stars winked in the sky, welcoming us early risers. I hurried to the manager's office, where the other three were already waiting for me. We set out immediately.

The railway station was at the Royal Horse Well about two kilometres to the south of our school. We walked as fast as we could. The two females, Teacher Seng and her student Ko, walked no slower than we did. The morning chill soon disappeared. We arrived too early for our train, so we went to the waiting room that was quite roomy. At this time of the morning it was solely for the four 'steel-making students-to-be'.

'Have you ever travelled in a train?' the manager asked me.

'Like a girl sitting in a sedan chair—the first time,' I replied. The manager laughed at my reply and so did the two females. I borrowed this witty *xie hou yu* from the peasants. The peasants used simple and obvious things to make a witty remark. In the past a girl would never sit in a sedan chair until she was taken to her bridegroom. So to say 'like a girl sitting a sedan chair', meant to do something for the first time. The stress is 'first time'. Another example is, 'a mouse getting into the bellows—being blown from both sides', which means that no matter what you do, you get criticised or blamed. *Xie hou yu* is witty, interesting and colourful. We had plenty *xie hou yu* sayings.

'When we change trains at Feng Tai, I will buy oil cakes or oil strips for our breakfast,' the manager said.

'Li never ate in front of a teacher,' Teacher Seng said to the manager but she eyed me teasingly. 'Let's see what he does this time.'

'I'll make sure he does eat in front of us,' the manager said. Then he abruptly changed the topic. 'Li, what do you think of this trip?'

'A privilege and a burden. It is not a simple thing to make real steel. It is even more difficult to teach others to make steel. I feel honoured to be chosen as a representative but I feel the burden is too heavy. Anyway I think it will be a good trip.' Then I added. 'I am very excited about seeing more of our country. Later I can have more material for composition writing.'

When waiting for a train, it never seems to come. When seeing somebody off, the train seems to arrive too soon. But the rambling talk, without any intention, as far as I was concerned, helped us forget the length of time we were waiting.

The train slowly clanged into the station, puffing out plenty of steam like an angry ox before darting at its victim. I was the first on the platform to see the coming train, but I was the last of the four to embark, wishing to see more.

We arrived at Feng Tai within thirty minutes. The connecting train was due in thirty minutes time. So the manager asked me to go with him to buy the oil cakes or strips. (Oil cake is a piece of dough flattened and fried in boiling oil. An oil strip is a piece of dough made into a long strip before being fried in boiling oil.) It was still early but we got the oil cakes and some *shao bing* of typical Beijing-style with sesame seeds dusted on the surface, for each of us.

Feng Tai station was a huge junction. The side rails and shunts looked like a labyrinth, or, to describe it with the language of our villagers, they looked like a spider web. An overhead bridge provided access to different waiting platforms covered with awnings. It would have been impossible for me to get onto the correct train without the manager as our guide. My world so far included only the district town five kilometres to our south and our junior high school to the north. Now I was in a place outside my world. I had to follow the manager step by step. I seemed to be 'a frog in a well'. Once the frog got onto the ground from the well he found the sky was too big for him. Now that I came outside my world, it became too large and too fascinating for me to comprehend and to cope with.

I was given a window seat opposite the manager. The train sped forward, much quicker than galloping horses. The trees, houses and fields all dashed swiftly past me, like a huge scroll being unfolded and folded.

The eastern sky was gradually paling into pink, when the train flew past the twin towers of a county town.

'Li, look at the twin towers,' the manager drew to my attention. 'Do you know the place? Did you know Zhang Fei was born here?'

'No, I didn't.' I had to admit my ignorance.

'Have you ever read the story of *The Three Kingdoms*?' (A novel about the three states of Wi, Shu and Wu from the end of East Han Dynasty.)

'Yes, I have.'

'Do you know how Liu Bei, Guan Yu and Zhang Fei became sworn brothers?'

'No.' I shook my head and the manager started to tell the story:

'This place is called Zhuo Zhou. Zhang Fei lived here about two thousand years ago. He was a butcher who sold meat in the town. When evening fell he would put all his meat into a basket, tie a piece of rope to the basket and lower the meat into a well. He covered the well opening with a huge rock and on it he wrote, "He who is able to remove the rock can have the meat free of charge."

One day Guan Yu came to the town with some bags of green lentils to sell. He heard about Zhang Fei and his well. He wished to strike up an acquaintance with Zhang Fei, but he had no opportunity, so he pushed the rock aside and got the meat out. He announced to the onlookers that his name was Guan Yu and he took the meat away. The following morning he went to the fair to sell his green lentils.

Zhang Fei came to the well for his meat and found that it was gone. He inquired around and was told that Guan Yu took his meat away and that he was selling green lentils at the fair. Zhang Fei felt surprised that somebody else could move the rock and he wished to become acquainted with Guan Yu, but he had to find some excuse for doing it.

Zhang Fei went to the fair and found Guan Yu without any difficulty because Guan Yu had a red face and a beautiful long beard and moustache. Guan Yu recognised Zhang Fei immediately because he had heard him to have round eyes and a head like that of a leopard.

Zhang Fei came to Guan Yu. He scooped a handful of green lentils into his hand, squeezed them into powder and exclaimed, "Your lentils are damp and mouldy."

"My green lentils are completely dry," Guan Yu retorted.

"No," Zhang Fei said. "If your green lentils are dry, how can they be crushed into powder by my squeezing them?" He thrust his palm with the powder under Guan Yu's nose.

A quarrel broke out and soon the two men were in a fierce fight. The onlookers could not stop or separate them because they were too powerful for them.

It happened that Liu Bei was selling straw sandals at the fair. He saw the crowd and went over to see what the fuss was about. He elbowed through the crowd and said, "Why does not anyone separate them?" He approached them, grabbed each by one arm and drew them apart without any difficulty. This is called "the dragon separating the two tigers". Actually, Guan Yu appreciated Zhang Fei's martial arts and vice versa. When they saw Liu Bei, they immediately recognised that he was unusual and both wanted to make acquaintance with him. That's why the two were so easily separated. The three men, Liu Bei, Guan Yu and Zhang Fei went to a restaurant together. After a few drinks they found they liked each other so much they agreed to be sworn brothers. Liu Bei later became the emperor of Shu and was called the "dragon". Guan Yu and Zhang Fei became two of his five bravest generals and were called "tiger" generals. It was the custom for the Chinese to call an emperor a "dragon" and a general a "tiger".'

'A good invention,' Teacher Seng commented derogatively when the manager finished.

But I was fascinated, not only by the story itself, but by the manager's skill of narration—his style and his eloquence. I did not worry whether what he said could not be found in the novel. I did not mind whether it was his invention. Fictitious stories were all invented. If everything was true, it was the work of historians. Even historians would not tell the whole truth, otherwise we would not have so many mysteries in history.

We finally arrived at our destination at noon. The manager took us directly to the steel mill, where a cadre was waiting to show us around. This, I thought, meant there were plenty of visitors. In order not to interfere with their normal work and production, they had a few cadres available to deal with any visitors. We could see that some groups of people were already learning how to make steel.

The cadre showed us a huge furnace, which he said was modern. We were just in time to watch the workers opening the door to let out the molten steel. We could not make that kind of furnace back at the district town, of course, so the cadre took us to the primitive furnaces, which were numerous and close to each other that I compared them to a forest. Some of the primitive furnaces were also releasing molten steel. Here the cadre explained to us in minute detail how to build such a furnace—the materials used in its construction, the size of its inner chamber and the door. He then explained what timber was used for generating heat, how to feed in iron and charcoal and in what proportions, how to decide when the molten iron had turned to steel, and how to check the temperature from the colour of the flames. He stressed that the key was the temperature. He gave us a small piece of glass to look into the furnaces and then told us to keep it as a souvenir.

I took my notes quickly, as did the other three. Mine were almost word for word. I was afraid of missing a single point. By checking the notes, I had to be able to make a similar furnace and I could tell my friends exactly the same details. The cadre answered our questions. He told us the height of the furnace, the inner dimensions, the dimensions of the door, the kind of bricks for the furnace body and for the door, the place to use an electric blower or bellows, and the way to make the tunnel for the fan. When we had no more questions to ask, the cadre excused himself and went away to guide more newcomers. Visitors kept on entering and leaving the mill. I saw many of them but did not realise it was a nationwide movement then.

We watched the workers feeding the furnaces with iron and charcoal. On the point of letting out the molten steel we asked them to let us look at the colour of the flame in the furnace. Then we asked what the steel was used for. 'Making sickles, shovels, hoes and kitchen cleave knives,' a worker told us. 'Such low-grade steel is necessary to meet the needs of the peasants, anyway.'

We then examined what tools would be needed. We also checked how to make the receptacle for the molten steel and we watched how the workers opened the doors. Before we left the mill, we asked about the safety measures and the risks.

As we left with satisfaction, the sun was already setting. My stomach was complaining continuously. The manager led us through the main street, located a restaurant not far from the train station and we entered.

'Time to satisfy our comrade, Belly,' he joked. He ordered stir-fry chilli chicken, szechuan-style stewed soybean curd, Gong Bao diced pork, and a river fish. Steaming hot *man tou* was ordered as our main food. We were seated around a square table, each person on one side, just like card players, with students between teachers and teachers between students.

'Li,' Teacher Seng teased me, 'this time you must eat before your teachers. You cannot get away.' I blushed but remained silent. I shunned the teachers because I was never taught table manners and was afraid of being laughed at by them. I decided to watch before I ate, a tactic I used repeatedly in the years to come.

This was the first time I had ever entered a restaurant. The way to order food and dishes, the way we were served, and the way customers talked or shouted, were all new to me. While eating, a bit uneasy under the eyes of my teachers, I was all eyes and ears to the people around me. Before I realised it, we had finished the meal, a treat to me, and we were in the waiting room of the railway station.

We arrived at Feng Tai at eleven o'clock at night. There would be no train until four o'clock in the morning. We were the only occupants of the waiting room, so it was under our 'monopoly'. There was a huge stove in the room, which emitted little heat from its fire. In need of warmth, we stood around it until our legs were sore. We discussed the steel making and compared our notes but we could only do it for so long.

The manager had expected the delay and brought a chessboard with him. He and I played to kill time while the other two talked. We were players at the same level, much lower than the professionals but much better than the rookies. On the chessboard, there is no distinction between teacher and student—they are only 'opponents'. We 'battled life and death' for four or five games before we 'ceased fire'.

The females were huddling together, dozing. The manager lay on the bench on his right side, ready to doze off his waiting hours. I, too, lay on the bench, reading the *Selected Poems of the Tang Dynasty*. My eyes were soon fatigued due to the dim light. I closed my eyes to sleep but it would not come. It was too cold. I tossed and turned but I felt colder and colder. Finally I gave up and got up to mill around the boiler-shaped stove.

The arms of the clock in the waiting room seemed to be standing still. They moved forward like a rickety, tottering old man with hesitant steps. I walked around the stove while the cold intensified. Gradually, the other three joined me around the stove. Now and then, each one would rub his or her hands or stamp his or her feet to get warmer.

The train came punctually and thirty minutes later we were on the way back to school. The chill was too much for us to strike up a conversation. We walked briskly, our bodies shuddering and our teeth chattering.

I had become a 'qualified' steel maker! A steel-making teacher! I could not believe it myself. I shook my head and crept into my quilt. Instantly I was asleep.

The following day, a meeting of all the teachers and students was held to discuss a general mobilisation for making a great deal of steel. The importance of this movement and the target of the school were all dealt with in detail. 'To catch up with old Britain within fifteen years' was very encouraging to us young enthusiastic and patriotic students.

Lively discussions were carried on in our class immediately after the meeting. It was decided that all the male students would be at the work site to construct and operate the furnaces and that the female students would be responsible for providing water and food to the work site and collecting firewood and iron for the furnaces.

The students had to find something to fan the flames. There was no electric blower available for our use. I thought about my mother's cooking bellow, which was not in use due to the peasants having their meals in a common dining hall to enjoy the 'life of Communism'. I decided to fetch it that very night. My friend and neighbour, Zhang, volunteered to keep me company, the night being very dark.

We walked the seven-and-a-half kilometres like a whirlwind. Very soon our backs were covered in sweat and it trickled down our faces. We were discussing how to make the first steel in high spirits and I explained how to make a furnace with the view of being the first person to start one.

We made the journey back to school in a hurry. We bared our upper bodies to keep cool and, to save time, we alleviated our bladders by peeing while we walked. Everybody was in a deep sleep when we arrived at our dormitory, the bellow being left in our classroom. The school had no bathing facilities, so we just crept into bed to sleep. (A bath could only be had in the common bathing pool in town. It had three pools—one lukewarm, one warm and one hot. The entrance fee was twenty-five cents per head. Once inside, a person would be allocated a bed to lie on, towels to dry themselves after stepping out of a pool, and a locker for their belongings. Such a bathing pool was a luxury to the students but too expensive for them to frequent.)

We had to be very careful not to wake the others. We had one row of double bunks against the south wall and another against the north wall. The access between the two rows of bunks was just enough for two people to pass each other. The double bunks were wall-to-wall, firmly secured, timber boards and each student occupied a space about eighty centimetres wide. We lay with our heads towards the alley because we believed the air near the walls was less fresh.

After the afternoon classes the following day, we headed for the steel site, which was at the Royal Horse Well, just south of the railway lines and by the Beijing–Kaifeng Highway. As we neared the site we found it looked as busy as a beehive. Cadres and workers from various companies and factories were already busy constructing the furnaces. Some were already in shape and electric blowers were being used to increase the temperature of the fire.

I was a bit disappointed, not being able to make the first steel because of my late arrival and of having no electric blower, but the ambitious males from our class still wanted a try. The furnace was soon erected according to the dimensions, the shape and the arrangements we had learned from the steel mill. Materials, such as firebricks for the door and wire rods for the gratings, were available. The education manager and the two females were also directing the other classes to make furnaces. The progress of their furnace was no slower than that of ours. The manager cast a look at our furnace, smiled and nodded approvingly at me.

Meanwhile, four groups were sent to collect firewood and iron from the depot. The four furnaces of our school looked more professional than those constructed by the cadres and workers. It seemed that they had not visited a steel mill.

Firewood and iron were fed into the furnace. Fire was kindled with the help of kerosene. The three strongest boys from our class were assigned to work at the bellows. They worked in turns, twenty minutes a shift. The manager had handed me some goggles to look at the flames. The glass pieces from the steel mill were no use. I had a very long steel bar to probe the inside of the furnace. I looked like a steelworker. Five boys from our class, goggles over the eyes, were standing beside me, also learning.

The bellows breathed faster and faster and the flames turned whiter. I stirred the molten iron to make it mix thoroughly with the charcoal. The molten iron boiled. I called the manager over to check whether it was already molten steel but we could not be sure. We called over the only steelworker from a real steel mill to decide for us. He looked into the furnace and ordered, 'Increase the wind volume! It's nearly right.'

The bellows screeched and creaked. The wooden board tongues at the two air inlets of the bellows clattered merrily. The temperature the steelworker recommended was reached. The outlet door was opened and molten steel flowed out along the groove into a trough to form an ingot. This was the first steel and it came from our furnace!

We applauded, jumped and shouted so madly that we looked like a crowd of fools. People from other furnaces came over to see. We all felt very proud.

'The first steel is produced!' the loudspeaker at the site blared. 'This came from the furnace of the students from the junior high school! Comrades, cadres and workers, let's learn from the students! Let's exert ourselves to make more and more steel! Let's contribute to the cause of 'catching up with old Britain within fifteen years!' Then came the song, 'Catching up with old Britain within fifteen years'.

'Catching up with old Britain within fifteen years, Hai, unanimously we sing the song of victory!'

An electric blower was instantly brought to our furnace, perhaps, as an award to the students who made the first steel at the site. The new cycle of steel making started again, with more zest. The boys at the bellows were relieved.

We four, the education manager, Teacher Seng, the female student Ko and myself were called to the second, the third and the fourth furnaces of our school to check whether the steel was ready. My vanity ballooned and I imagined myself as a real steelworker.

Three more ingots were formed. The supervisor came over to check and nodded his endorsement. Though they were low-grade, they were still real steel ingots!

In addition to the loud speaker, a huge blackboard was placed at the site, recording the achievements of each furnace. The number of kilograms were written on it and the highest quantity became the main criteria. Our furnace soon lagged behind, as well as the other three furnaces. We worked non-stop, but the quantity would not grow as fast as the furnaces of the cadres and the workers. I was urged by my classmates to learn from the others. I toured among the furnaces and what I found out shocked me. The cadres were using a steel band ring. Molten steel and residues were all put inside the ring when they became solid but still soft. They beat the residue and steel together as one ingot with a huge hammer—that was why their quantity soared so fast. The quality of the steel, however, was poor.

The following day we went to the site as soon as the last class ended in the afternoon. Supper would follow later, carried to us by the girls. Materials, such as charcoal, firewood (date wood), pig iron scraps and cauldron scraps were already piled beside our furnaces. This was from the junkyard of the scrap collecting company, which was just on the other side of the highway. They were real scraps, not, as some people have written nowadays, grabbed from peasant houses.

There were rumours of crushing cauldrons to get scrap metal. I checked with my family who said that the idea had been suggested because since the villagers were already in the 'wind of Communism', cauldrons were no longer of any use. They should be crushed to contribute to the movement of steel making, but the villagers refused. They argued that the cauldron was worth more than a handful of steel made from its scrap and that the cauldron would be used now and then. Therefore in our region, real scrap metal was used in steel making.

We had no target set for us and we still followed the procedures we had learned. The steel we made was the real stuff, though the quality was just suitable for making sickles, and other farm tools for the peasants.

The cadres still followed their own method. They still broke record after record. To them, I guess, the performance in steel-making might mean promotion. To us students, steel making was to contribute to the target of the country, and it was also part of our study.

In about one week's time, materials became scarce. We students returned to school, no longer needed at the site. For us, steel making ended.

Chapter 15

TRADITIONS, SUPERSTITIONS AND FOLLIES

The traditional wedding and funeral ceremonies, which had been regarded as the most sacred by the Chinese people since ancient times, were, in the early fifties, regarded as feudal and superstitious by the Communist Party and could no longer be seen in the life of the people in our district. These ceremonies, in my opinion, should have been kept as a part of the peasants' culture. Many superstitious beliefs, stories and practices were held by the peasants in my village. I also witnessed some strange events while growing up. The greatest folly of all, though, was the elimination of pests. Peasants had no scientific knowledge about the relationship between agricultural production and sparrows, which they regarded as pests. They were mobilised by the government to eliminate the sparrows and many other pests and animals found in the countryside. When people realised this was all foolish, it was already too late.

To Sit in the Sedan Chair

Starting from the proclamation of the marriage law in 1950, young couples were encouraged by the government to get married in the new style. The bridegroom, with red satin ribbons stretching from the shoulders to the waist crossing at the breast and with a big red satin flower pinned to the cross which was formed by the ribbons, would ride on horseback to fetch the bride. The horse, of course, was also decorated. In some cases, the bridegroom would ride a bicycle to fetch the bride. A bicycle, a new one in particular, was a demonstration of economic status of a peasant in the countryside as not many families could afford to buy one at the time. Then the bridegroom and the bride carried a framed picture of Chairman Mao to get married. Later, some people got married by having a journey to national scenery spots, in the same way as tourists visited them.

During the mid-fifties, a bride carried in a sedan chair was very rarely seen. It had become a thing of the past.

My cousin An fell in love while working as a secretary in the Xiang government. The girl was in the same class as me at the Paradise Palace primary school. She was the monitor, to be exact. She embroidered two pillowcases for An and my Da Ma accidentally saw them. She asked me whether I knew who embroidered them. The work was familiar to me because in our art class I had seen her embroidered works.

'She is the daughter of Tian, living on North Street,' I told her.

'I know the girl. She and An are of the same age. She is a good girl. Her family is not related to our Li families. They can get married. Don't let An or the girl know that I found out they love each other. They may feel embarrassed,' she cautioned me.

When the two families discussed the marriage, the girl insisted on being carried to my cousin's house in a sedan chair, arguing that this was the only opportunity in life to sit in a sedan chair. Cadres working in the Xiang government were not allowed to use a sedan chair to carry the bride—it was regarded as feudal and backward. But the girl insisted. So my uncle decided to order a sedan chair and the sedan carriers to get my cousin married.

The wedding not only involved the sedan chair and the four carriers, but a small musical procession as well. The sedan chair started from the bridegroom's house with my cousin Xiang in it, which was called 'to escort the sedan chair'. Leading it were two lantern bearers, each holding a lantern with a red cloth casing over a folding wooden frame. Those two bearers were always close relatives. In this case it was my young cousin, Chung, who was the first son of my uncle Song-lin living in the house in front of ours, and myself. We walked ahead of the musicians. Behind the musicians were the four bearers carrying the sedan chair. The sedan chair was sandwiched between and followed by the rest of the procession, who were relatives to welcome the bride.

The musical instruments included several kinds of trumpets, cymbals, a tiny gong, and a rectangular frame with many gongs as big as a fist dangling from it. They played classical pieces, which had been played for generation after generation.

When the sedan chair and the procession arrived at the bride's house, the gate was closed, so the relatives of the bridegroom threw coins to the children and the music played continuously. The relatives of the bride would not open the gate until they judged that all neighbours were aware of the wedding and the onlookers had enjoyed the music long enough. Then the sedan chair was allowed into the yard. The bride would cry, expressing to her mother her reluctance to leave home. The bride's mother and aunties would utter endearing words to flatter, induce, and urge the bride to get into the sedan chair. As soon as the bride was inside, the relatives of the bridegroom would order the bearers to lift it on their shoulders and return to the bridegroom's home. When the sedan chair and procession got back to the gate of the bridegroom's house the same thing happened before the gate was opened for the sedan chair to enter the yard. The sedan chair was placed at the steps.

The two lantern carriers raced into the bridegroom's room before the bride. New quilts with flowery patterns were placed in neat piles on the *kang*. On top of the quilt was a new basin placed upside down. We took the basin off and grabbed the money underneath. When we left the room the bride was ushered into the middle room, where the bridegroom and the bride kowtowed to Heaven and Earth, to the parents, and to each other. Then the bride was ushered into the room specially prepared for her and the bridegroom. That room was called 'the marriage chamber', or the 'nuptial chamber'.

Meanwhile, relatives and friends were sitting around many tables, enjoying the wedding banquet of eight plates and eight bowls full of meat and vegetables with *man tou* as the staple. A big bowl full of strong alcohol was passed from one person to another, until most of them were drunk and the bridegroom had to pour alcohol from one table to another. He was sometimes forced to drink with the guests.

When the bridegroom and the bride were finally alone in the new room it was already dark. By then the girl's relatives would come to present a mattress, which was to prove the virginity of the girl. The mattress was presented to the mother-in-law first thing in the morning by the daughter-in-law. One of the bridegroom's aunties, who had both sons and daughters, would make the bed for them. It was said that by doing this, they would have sons and daughters too. At the corners of their quilts, there were dates, nuts and peanuts. The Chinese pronunciation of these three together meant to have children quickly and to have sons and daughters alternately.

During the night lots of young men would hide under the window to listen to the newly married couples' conversation. If they were not careful, the eavesdroppers would mimic what they said to each other as fun for many years to come.

After the marriage, An was dismissed from his position. The Xiang government would not employ a person with feudal and backward thinking.

Funerals

In northern Chinese villages, two kinds of funeral ceremonies were performed—the grand formal funeral and the simple one.

I saw a few grand formal funerals in the Paradise Palace, but the last one I remember in particular. Around 1952 or 1953, the young wife of our immediate neighbour committed suicide by taking arsenic. Her parents and brothers lived in the Paradise Palace, not very far from her husband's house. They wanted to know why she committed suicide, but the husband's family was not able to give a plausible explanation.

'Middle' people, who were respected by both families and villagers as arbitrators, were invited to settle the matter. (The government, whether it was the Xiang or a higher level, would not interfere unless one of the families went to it for help. As the saying goes 'if the civilian does not report, the officials will not interfere'.) The agreement was that the best funeral should be arranged for the dead. The wife's family had to see the intended procedures of the services first, and if satisfied, they would not complain to the government. Both sides agreed.

The husband's family arranged the funeral as follows:

Horses and men were to be made from paper and sorghum stalks.

Monks and Taoist priests were to chant scripture for forty-nine days.

A thick cedar coffin was to be made for her body.

The husband was to wear hemp and mourning clothes, as a dutiful and filial son should.

The best hearse had to be arranged.

Entire bolts of black or blue cloth, donated by friends and relatives, were to drape the whole place—the front fence, the front wall and gate, the canopy specially rigged up in the yard to shield the coffin, and the front windows of the main and wing houses. This was a sign of mourning.

Wreaths were not used to mourn the dead in our district at that time. Lines were drawn on which were fixed miniatures of human figures. Each figure carried a candle on the right palm. When it was dark, the candles were all lit and the figures moved round and round. There was no electricity then. I could not imagine how they, the monks and Taoist priests, made the figures move.

Monks and Taoist priests were clad differently. The priests were in grey robes while the monks were in something a little bit brighter. They were all chanting scriptures. I could not understand a word and could not tell whether they sounded differently to each other. I always suspected that they were not real monks and Taoist priests. I thought they were peasants clad in such clothing, earning good meals for the seven weeks. (The Chinese saying goes, 'he who prefers showing off in front of people becomes an actor; he who is lazy becomes a monk; he who likes eating becomes a musician for weddings and funerals'.)

Many skilled peasants were making figures of oxen, horses, donkeys, pigs, sheep, golden girls and boys, carts, and so on. The Chinese believed that if those things were burnt for the dead, they would then own them and be rich in the other world. They would then have the means of bribing officials governing the world of the dead to let them come back to the human world as soon as possible.

A coffin was placed in the middle of the yard, which was covered with an awning rigged up for the occasion. The coffin was painted with shiny black lacquer. The front of the coffin had a golden Chinese ideogram 'Dian', meaning to mourn or to pay the dead respect. The husband was kneeling beside the coffin to greet the mourners.

When the funeral was near, the best *guan zhao* was rented—a decoration respecting the dead and showing the wealth of the family. *Guan* means the coffin and *zhao* means the covering. The very top of the covering was a beautifully decorated wooden device. It looked like a circular tower but with patterns carved from wood symmetrically attached to it. Below it were oriental square-shaped pavilion-like frame works. The roof and the sides were all covered with needle embroidered satin fabrics. Such a coffin covering would be placed over the coffin.

The coffin was placed on a platform formed with round poles, the ends of which would be used by sixteen pairs of strong peasants to carry the coffin and the covering. The whole thing was so heavy that there would be thirty-two pairs of the bearers to work in turns. When they changed shift, the whole device would not be put down and the hearse would not be halted. Everything would be smoothly done, while moving forward.

Once the bearers were ready to raise the whole thing onto their shoulders at the signal of a leader, the husband would crush a piece of tile (normally done by the eldest son). He stood up to hold a jar against his breast, and carried against his right shoulder a dragon-like paper streamer rigged with sorghum stalks (again, a dutiful son would normally do this). The wife's family had two sons but they demanded this to shame the husband.

When the hearse started to move, the husband had to kneel down to thank the bearers every fifty metres until the hearse reached the tomb field (there was no cemetery for the dead villagers). By and by the husband could not stand up himself. He had to be pulled to his feet by helping hands beside him.

The simple funeral, which was done by most of the poor peasants, was more common in the village. When Granny died in 1956 at the age of eighty, she was placed on a wooden bed in the middle room shared by our two families, my uncle's and my father's. She would remain there for three days and nights before she was put into a coffin. It was quite necessary for the dead to lie for three days without being sealed into the coffin—in some cases the dead might not be really dead and might come back.

Between her lips and teeth was a small red packet. Why this was put there I had no idea and I never asked my father. She was dressed in special clothes for the dead. Her eyes were closed. She lay there so peacefully that I thought she was sleeping. I could not accept that she was dead. When I felt her face and her hands, they were cold, but not icy cold. Every day I would hold her hand for some time, because she loved me very much.

That was the first time I stayed by the dead and felt no fear. But her daughters-in-law were scared whenever they passed through the middle room. They asked me why I had no fear. I said Granny loved me and I loved her and she would not scare me if her soul still remained with her. I said that they were afraid of her because they never loved her. It was said that during these three days the soul of the dead was beside their own body, and the bodies of the others around, to keep watch. It was the presence of the soul, which made those who never loved her or did not love her enough, feel scared.

On the evening of the third day, Granny was moved into the yard to be placed in her coffin. Her face was covered with a square cushion. It was said that when a dead person was moved, a last breath would escape from the mouth. That breath was poisonous. Whoever caught that breath would become sick. That was the reason that the face was covered with the cushion. When she was placed in the coffin, somebody shouted, 'Look out!' and the cushion was thrown into the air. The shouting was for people around to get away from the cushion. If the cushion hit anybody, he would have bad luck for the rest of his life. At the first hammer knock of the carpenter, everybody in the two families knelt around the coffin and cried. My family all did this except my cousin An, and myself.

'Kneel down and cry,' my father ordered me. 'Your granny loved you so much.'

'I loved her when she was alive,' I replied. 'Why not save the crying but love her more before her death.'

Such a thing should not be said. Lots of daughters-in-law dislike their mothers-in-law and these words would enrage them. In my case my mother, my Da Ma, and uncle Yong-jiang were all displeased. My father stood up to give me a lesson but I was quicker than a rabbit and disappeared from the scene.

The funeral was on the following day. The rigging for carrying the coffin was for four pairs of bearers. The coffin was light and the coffin covering was a simple one. Around noon, a table was placed near the gate. One man sat there to write the names of the visitors who came to pay their respects, as well as the sum of money they contributed, which was put under each name. After that, people would go to sit at a table to eat.

The food prepared for the guests was a mixture of meat, Chinese cabbage, fried soybean curd, and vermicelli noodles. There was *man tou* but no rice. Almost all the members of the neighbouring families came.

When the coffin was lifted up, my father and his brother played the role of the dutiful sons. Our tomb's field was just outside the village and she was buried beside my grandpa, who was already dead when I started to remember things. The dragon-like streamers were placed in front of the tomb mound. This was the only simple funeral I witnessed.

During the Great Cultural Revolution, all tomb mounds were levelled to grow rice. All the people who died during or after the Cultural Revolution were cremated. To encourage this, each cremation was compensated with sixty yuan by the brigade—the top authority of the village that directed the farming activities and administration of the village.

Nowadays, people can bury the dead underground, but the depth of the pit can be no more than one and half metres and no tomb mound is allowed. The regulation of the depth of the pit is so no land is wasted. The coffin now used is made of cement. This is the regulation in our village, anyway.

The Toilet and Manure

'Disgusting', 'deplorable', 'dreadful' and 'uncivilised'—such were the adjectives used by tourists when they talked about Chinese toilets away from the hotels in which they stayed. Once I heard a European lady telling her friends to have neither tea, nor coffee, nor to have liquid food of any kind before sightseeing, and to order a taxi to come back to the hotel if necessity arose. But what would a tourist say if he or she, from urgent necessity, saw or used a toilet in the peasant village? Faint? Very likely!

In a very, very cold winter evening, we were unshelling peanuts to get the kernels for seeds. To keep my brother, Xiao Bao, and me awake, my parents were giving us riddles to solve while we unshelled the peanuts. Granny asked us, 'Tell me, which part of our body fears no cold?'

'The face,' Xiao Bao prompted.

'No,' she shook her head.

'The hands,' I replied.

'No,' again she shook her head.

'The nose,' Xiao Bao shouted triumphantly.

'No,' she shook her head for the third time.

My mother and father smiled but gave us no hints, not to deprive Granny of the triumph of telling us the answer herself.

'Granny,' my brother and I chorused, 'tell us the answer, please.'

'The buttocks!' she told us, laughing.

We were silent at first. Then we laughed boisterously.

True! Very true! In the toilet, icy winds came and the chills bit. The snow might also be very deep. But one had to expose one's buttocks for convenience, with no hesitation.

A peasant toilet was, nine times out of ten, located at the far corner of the courtyard, away from any window and the gate. It was more often than not sandwiched between a pigsty and the courtyard corner walls or fences, allowing its structure to form the privacy-providing enclosure. The corner walls or fences were high enough for the toilet. The pigsty side needed to be increased in height. Only the front wall needed to be constructed. Such an arrangement also meant that the pigs could mix the house or yard sweepings with the manure in their trotting around. In very few homes in our area, but in all homes in the middle of Hebei Province, a permanent chute was arranged from the bottom of the toilet pit slanting into the pigsty.

Few families could afford to roof the toilet. Some families could afford brick-walled toilets, but most families made the toilets with fences of sorghum stalks or corn stalks or tree branches. Fences, if damaged, were easy to repair.

In the very middle of the enclosure, a pit was dug as the toilet, which, in most cases, was lined with bricks. Two wooden boards were placed over the pit, leaving a gap between them for the users to squat over like riding a horse. Both ends of the boards were secured so that they could not move.

If a chute was arranged to lead directly into the pigsty, it would make a user uncomfortable and nervous to use the toilet, because the muzzle of a pig would enter the chute, its nostrils would expand and contract expectantly, continuously, and noisily. Of course the pig could not reach high enough to bite at the buttocks or to snatch anything off the user!

It was always hard to get used to riding the toilet pit with the ever-present loyal muzzle of the pig. Once when I was staring at the large eyes of the pig, which were staring up at me, I was trying to imagine what the pig would say if it could think and speak like human beings do. I shunned using a toilet with a chute from the pit into a pigsty ever since.

The shabby condition of a peasant toilet was not the most repulsive thing to a Western tourist. What was really repulsive to him or her was the irritating and sickening stench, and the sight of the wriggling long-tailed maggots. After a heavy rain, maggots crawled everywhere around your feet and your own droppings splashed dirty water onto the buttocks. But above all, the burden on the legs and the knees might be too much for a tourist.

A peasant family, especially when a son was married, usually had two toilets—one for the males and one for the females of the house. If the yard of a house bordered the main street, the male toilet would have its entrance on the street side in order to attract passers-by to use it for convenience. The female toilet was private, for women folks of the house only.

The stench from the pigsty, the toilet, and the dung heap, permeated the courtyard of a peasant home. However, due to the importance of manure to a peasant family, this was not noticed or minded by the peasants. Except during the co-op and the People's Commune years, a dung heap would always be present in a peasant courtyard.

A peasant would by all means try hard to increase his dung heap. Night soil (the waste from the potty, which was used indoors during severe winter nights), floor sweepings and the rotten stalks of sorghum or corn were all thrown into the pigsty to blend with the manure already inside the pigsty.

The *kang* would also be dismantled every few years so that the burnt mud bricks could be used as fertiliser. These mud bricks, very much tarred by the cooking fires and smoke, were crushed into tiny pieces, heaped and sealed with a layer of clay made by the mud brick powder and water. Some days later, the heap was re-processed for usage. Fertiliser of this kind was good for watermelon growing, making the fruit rich in colour and sweet to taste.

In a peasant family, the grown-ups always had a piggyback basket on their backs when going to the field or anywhere. Any animal droppings they came across would be collected into the basket with a hand fork. On winter days, the master of the house and the older children would get up long before sunrise to collect manure along the main roads, be it windy or snowy. Some would tour round the outer edge of the village to look for dogs' dung and human manure.

My own experience of collecting manure in a wintry snowy early morning was when I was just ten years old. It was pitch dark when my father woke me. I sat up, groped for my padded jacket and trousers spread over my quilt, put them on and slipped off the *kang*. I got into the yard behind my father. A gust of wind whipped snow against my face. I felt so cold and wished I could withdraw into the haven of the room to stay away from the snow and cold. I went side by side with my father to the highway, where he turned north against the wind and I headed south with the wind.

The snow in the wheel grooves was already hard from the grinding wheels of the passing carts. New snow crunched under my feet with each forward step. The whirling snow, driven by the howling wind from Siberia, crept into the gap between my collar and my neck and between my jacket and trousers at the waist. Though my ears were covered and protected by the flaps of my hat, they still felt the biting cold. But my nose, without the protection of a mouth-piece, suffered the most. Every now and then, I would cup my hands over my mouth to warm up my nose with my breath.

It was dark and I was alone. I could not see far because of the falling snow. I was afraid and feared I would be late for school. Fear or no fear,

I had to go ahead to look for manure along the road. Pushed by the wind, it was not difficult to cover a few kilometres. But the return journey against the wind was a test of will. The load on my back was already quite heavy. Moisture formed on my back under the padded jacket. Wind and snow slapped my face and ice formed quickly on my brows and eyelashes. The snow was so heavy that I could not see a cart coming until it was close, but I had time to make way for it to pass. We had almost no trucks on the highway at the time, so there was not any risk of being crushed by one. The snow frequently got into my shoes, thawed, and made my feet wet. My feet became terribly cold. I prayed not to have my toes frozen off my feet. My hands, unprotected by gloves, were always in the opposite sleeve cuff to keep warm. But new, fresh bleeding cracks would be added to my hands during the few moments of exposure to the wind and snow when I collected manure with the fork.

Back at home a bowl of hot corn porridge and a piece of *wo tou* was waiting for me. That helped me to warm up quickly. I rarely complained, just as my parents seldom praised me. Picking manure on a severe winter's day was just part of the peasant family's life.

Early in the summer of 1953, many carts, drawn by horses, mules, oxen or asses, were transporting pebbles and reeds to the Yong Ding River. Each cart stopped by the well, which was at the end of our lane, for the animals to have a drink. I ran home to get a basket and a fork. It was easy to collect manure from such animals. My basket was filled up from the droppings of the animals from three or four carts. When the last cart left late in the evening, I had already collected a considerable heap of manure. Not only had I won the rare praise from my parents, but also from the neighbours.

Those peasants whose yard bordered the main street competed to attract passers-by to use their toilet, in order to get more manure into their yard. Such toilets were better walled or fenced. Some even had a roof to shelter the user from the sun, the rain or the snow. They looked much cleaner than the domestic ones.

Unless in very urgent cases, a peasant never used a toilet other than his own. He would din into the ears of his children time and time again to use their own toilets. If a peasant was out in the fields, he would always manage to relieve his bowels in his own field, even if he had to run for quite some distance to get into his own field. This led to the Chinese saying, 'never let the fertile water flow into a neighbour's field'.

The pigsty and the toilets were cleared regularly and all the manure was piled into a heap. The peasant processed his heap of manure very industriously. The processing was called the 'fumbling' or 'heap shifting' and the better this was done, the more manure there would be for the crops.

My father processed his dung heap with a long handled wooden shovel. Everybody used one to process his dung heap. My father would use a rake to pull a bit of dung to the ground and then press and ground it with the wooden shovel until no lumps remained. Then he would shovel the processed manure aside and start a new cycle. When the processing was completed, the heap looked neat and compact, like a work of art.

A big dung heap, such as that of the co-operative and production team, was also utilised by peasant wives to ferment their *jiang* (a condiment sauce which was as thick as ketchup). My mother would put any leftover *wo tou* aside, and when she had enough, she would cook some soybeans and peanuts. She crushed the dried *wo tou* and cooked soybeans and peanuts, mixed them together and let them go mouldy. She would then crush them again with the millstone into flour, mixed them with salt and water and put them into a jar. She would then seal the jar with a piece of flat stone slab, over which she tied a piece of grease-paper. She would put a big bowl upside down, making the bowl rest on the shoulder of the jar, to provide a good seal. Lastly she would mix some clay and cover the bowl completely to provide an extra seal. Then, after marking the jar so as not to get confused with the jars of the neighbours, she would bury it in the dung heap. The jar was dug out after twenty-one days, ready for use during the Spring Festival. My mother would give it a thorough cleaning with water, then she removed the clay, took off the bowl, untied the grease-paper, and removed the stone slate to check the *jiang* inside. The *jiang* looked a darkish coffee colour and emitted a pleasant aroma. Such *jiang* was much better than those sold in the market. It is a pity that, today, nobody makes the *jiang* any longer, not even my mother.

The Lightning and the Elephant

It happened one late summer afternoon in 1952 or 1953. Dark clouds suddenly covered the whole sky. Thunder boomed, low and menacing and there was a heavy downpour. I was sitting on the door threshold, watching the falling rain. One by one, three two-inch long fish fell down to the yard from the sky. I was surprised and fascinated.

'It's raining fish,' I shouted and ran into the yard to catch them. I put them into a basin full of rainwater, which I collected from the water cascade from the eaves of the house. My mother, father and Da Ma all came out to see the fish. Each one tried hard to offer an explanation about why the fish came from the sky, but none was plausible. My mother did not forget to scold me for being drenched in the rain.

Just then, a blinding flash of lightning split the sky. A moment later, a thunderbolt cracked so loud and lasted so long and rolled so far, I was very scared.

'The thunderbolt is chasing a devil,' Granny commented.

'Snakes, hedgehogs, foxes, scorpions and spiders can all become monsters or devils after many, many years of hiding and exercising for being immortal,' Granny said again. The old generation of peasants believed in that.

Just before dusk, the rain stopped and the sky cleared. We heard some shouting in the street and I ran out to check. People, mostly men and boys, were running towards the exit of the village. I joined them. Many people were standing around an elm tree about thirty metres from the village entrance, by the roadside. From the very top to the very bottom, the bark of the tree was skinned and lying on the ground in three hundred and sixty degrees, like the spokes of a bicycle. But the bark on the branches, big or small, was untouched. The tree trunk was not burnt by the lightning at all.

From the elm tree, in the north-east direction, about fifty metres away, was a forest filled with several rows of poplar trees extending fifty metres from its southern to its northern tip. All along its length, the bark was stripped at mid level with the markings facing one another. The stripped bark on each tree was about two feet long. There was no sign of knife cutting.

'The thunderbolt was chasing a monster,' the villagers said. 'The claws of the Thunder Deity yanked the barks off while trying to catch the monster.' That was the explanation for the incident. (The villagers believed the Thunder Deity had claws.) No more interest was shown and there were no more questions, and to this day it still remains a mystery to me.

I recollect a case of a pig giving birth to an 'elephant'.

'A pig can give birth to an elephant,' the peasants often said, but none of them had ever seen an elephant born from a pig.

This incident occurred in the early fifties.

We students were playing during the break between classes. We suddenly heard excited shouting coming from a pigsty near the street, about fifty metres away. We dashed towards the spot. I squeezed through the crowd to have a look. A sow was giving birth to piglets—six or eight were already born, all fighting to suckle their mother. Among the piglets was a strange animal, which the sow had also given birth to. It was bigger than the piglets and it had no black hair—its skin seemed to be naked. Its colour was between soil and grey. It had a very long nose, which could curl up like rope coil. It bumped into the other piglets in order for them to make way for it.

'A monster!' students shouted. 'The sow gave birth to a monster!'

The son of the owner came out. He snatched the thing up and threw it hard on the ground. With a thud and a short cry, it died.

In the late fifties when I had my schooling in Beijing, I had the opportunity to visit the zoo and saw elephants there. The 'monster' looked exactly like an elephant. In our area, peasants always said a sow could give birth to an elephant.

Can a sow give birth to an elephant?

Was it an elephant?

Was it a deformed piglet?

What was it? I'll never know.

The Roaming Magician

It was one afternoon during our winter holidays in 1953. A magician and his son came to our village to perform a show to earn money. They carried with them a wooden chest and a pile of steamer-like trunks containing their tools and belongings. The magician stopped in the middle of a big yard not far from our house. He beat a gong to attract the peasants. When onlookers arrived, he drew a circle about two metres in diameter as his stage. The boy beat the gong and walked around the circle, saying, 'We rely on our parents at home but on friends when we are abroad. Please help us with some money after the performance. If you don't have money, just give us warm applause!' While the magician performed his tricks, some coins were thrown into the gong, which the boy held.

The audience encircled the magician and his son on all sides. Except for the chest and the trunks, they had nothing else. They were strangers to the village and it was not possible for the two of them to rig up anything there and then.

The magician and his son carried the chest to the middle of the circle. The magician asked his son to huddle into the chest, which he then covered up. He then walked around the circle and beat his gong. When he opened the chest, his son was not in it. He dismantled the chest and the boy was not there. He opened each tier of his trunk and the boy was still not there. We looked for him among the audience and the boy could not be located. The magician had the chest rigged up again, walked around the circle and beat his gong. When he opened the chest, the boy was huddling inside.

The magician then asked for volunteers from the audience. A boy, who was my classmate, came forward. The magician asked him and his own son to huddle inside the chest. The chest was now very full. It was not possible to put anything else into it. The magician lowered the chest cover and locked it up. He beat the gong around the circle and spoke to divert the attention of the audience. He came to the chest and opened it. The two boys were gone. He dismantled the chest and the boys could not be seen. He opened the trunks tier by tier and the boys were not there. Everybody looked around to check they were not in the crowd. We hailed the name of my classmate and we got no answer.

The magician put the chest back into shape again. He had the lid covered and started to circle while he beat the gong. He went to the chest, opened the lid and the two boys were huddling inside. They stepped out of it.

'Have you heard us calling you?' we asked my schoolmate.

He shook his head.

'Where have you been to?' we asked.

'I don't know,' he said. 'We walked among lots of people in a street. I saw some very big red lanterns there.'

'You must be joking!' we shouted.

'No,' he said.

'What did you do in the chest?'

'The boy asked me to close my eyes,' he said. 'When he told me to open my eyes, we were in the street.'

'How did you come back?'

'He pulled me to a corner and asked me to close my eyes,' he replied. 'When I opened my eyes, we were here, in the chest.'

We did not believe what he said and we questioned him many times later but the answer was always the same.

With the help of modern facilities, a magician can do a lot on the stage. But here in a yard, with people around him on all sides and with a distance of only about one metre between him and the audience, it was not possible for the magician to play a trick to hide the boys away. I could not believe that the magician had magic power. I believed he played tricks. But what kind of tricks could he play under the eyes of the audience so near to him?

Misers

The Chinese peasant community had many misers, which was mainly because of the hard life led in the countryside. It became a habit for a peasant to save from the mouth, to work all day without rest, to collect anything they came across, and to release their bowels under urgent necessity in their own field if they could manage it. This was built into their character. However, some peasants behaved to the extreme and were nicknamed 'misers'. The first miser I want to talk about was one who was reluctant to part with his silver dollar, the coin used in the old society. The wife herself told this story about the thing her miser husband requested her to do in order to get back that silver dollar.

'I have had a secret in my heart for many years,' the seventy-year-old wife said. 'If I don't tell, nobody will know about it and I will take it with me to the other world.'

This happened when four old women, including the old wife, played cards together.

The other three looked up in surprise. 'What's it about?'

'About my dead husband.'

'Your husband?'

'Yes,' she replied. 'Many years ago, when I was still young, he employed a young man to help him work his fields.'

'We still remember that,' the other three said. 'You were married for just a few years then.'

'Yes,' she replied. 'We had no child yet.'

She continued after getting a card.

'The payment was one silver dollar for a whole year. We had to provide food and accommodation.' She paused a bit before she continued. 'The young man slept in our east wing house. My husband and I slept in the main house.'

She was interrupted to lay out a card to get a new one.

'It was the last day of the year and the young man was paid the money, the one silver dollar. It was hard for my husband to part with his one silver dollar. During the evening when we went to bed, he urged me to go and sleep with that young man to get that dollar back. I was reluctant to do it. I felt ashamed. 'What's the matter?' he asked me. 'You are not a virgin now. If you and I don't speak about it, who knows about it?' I still refused. He flared up and kicked me with his foot. 'Go and sleep with him to get the dollar back. Don't stay too long.' What could I do? Money was more important to him than my chastity. To him sex was not something sacred, anyway. As long as he got his money, he did not mind whoever it was to use me. So I had to go over to the other room and sell myself to the young man for one silver dollar. The young man willingly paid me the dollar and used me like mad. After we finished, I lay beside him to rest myself and comfort him a bit. Do you know what happened?'

'What?' they asked.

'My husband was cursing, "Stinking woman. Already finished the business and still lingering!" And I had to run back to my husband. He got the silver dollar from me, turned over on his back and slept.'

'You must be joking,' they commented.

'It is true,' she said. 'I was let down and if I do not speak about it, my soul will regret it!' She sighed and then added, 'The young man was useless. He failed to make me pregnant and my husband did not have the green cap on his head for the villagers to despise him until the end of his life!' Such was said with bitter venom. (To have a green cap meant that one's wife had affairs with other men. The husband was also called a 'turtle'.)

The second story was about a different type of a miser.

A man had a pregnant wife and a daughter. He was so miserly that his wife knelt in front of their kitchen god daily to pray, 'Dear kitchen god, let me die this time when I give birth to the baby in my belly. I don't want to live with this man any longer.' Three days after her labour, she was forced to get up to make flour with the millstone. She became sick and died a day or two later.

The husband went to his elder brother to see what to do about the baby.

'Employ a woman to suckle him,' his brother urged. 'I will share half the cost.'

'What about the other half cost?' He felt dissatisfied with his brother for not paying the full cost for him so he left. He put the baby in a basket and went hawking noodles, which were in another basket. When the baby cried, he would put a little bit of paste into his mouth with his finger. The baby lived for about half a month before he died.

The man sent his daughter to live with the mother's sister and never worried about her again.

A few years went by. On one clear autumn day, he was beating dates off a tree with a stick.

'What are you doing? Why knock the dates off? The dates are still green, not ripe yet,' his neighbours asked.

'My daughter is coming to see me tomorrow! I have to hide them away, otherwise she will eat them,' the man replied.

His neighbours shook their heads and remained silent.

Another few more years elapsed. Chinese people, the northern Chinese in particular, were in the midst of the great calamities caused by men and Nature. The daughter-in-law of the man's brother came to borrow some grain from him. Very reluctantly, he gave her a dustbin of grain, about five kilograms or so, and made her promise time and again to pay him back later.

All the villagers suffered during the national famine in the early sixties in China. Nowhere could they get grain or anything to tide them over the calamity. One day the man was having mouldy sorghum flour *wo tou* for lunch when a crowd headed by cadres of the village came to his house.

'Dismantle his inner wall and get the grain!' a cadre ordered.

A few men went into his room and started to dismantle his wall. There was a great cry of happiness. 'My! So much wheat!' they shouted. But how the cadres discovered the secret, nobody knew.

'You cannot do this to me!' the man shouted. But nobody heeded him.

'You are a bad rich peasant needing serious transformation,' a cadre said.

'The villagers are starving but you store wheat and watch people die. Now I declare we will confiscate your wheat.'

'My wheat!' he sat on the steps, crying.

Bag after bag of his wheat, which was hidden between the double walls of his house, was carried away. The total was about ten thousand kilograms. The villagers had broad smiles on their faces, for it was now possible for them to get through the calamity.

'My wheat,' he cried on his doorsteps for a whole day. But nobody sympathised with him, not even his own relatives.

Elimination of the 'Four Pests'

The 'four pests' were mosquitoes, flies, rats and sparrows. During the Korean War, it was said that the Americans were spreading diseases through mosquitoes, flies and rats. It became the duty of students to fight the American Germ War. Each student was given a target of eliminating a certain numbers of flies and rats each day. Each fly killed was put into a matchbox. When going to school the following day, the box was handed to the monitor to check the total. When a rat was caught, it was not necessary to hand in the whole rat, just to cut off the tip of its tail as proof.

It was easy to kill flies because there were so many of them. All we had to do was to make a flyswatter with cardboard and a stick. By cutting the cardboard into a handy size, punching it with many holes, making a split at one end of the stick to insert the cardboard and tying up the split to keep it securely fixed to the stick, the flyswatter was ready for use. But it was not easy to kill rats. We students had to push our fathers to catch the rats for us. At least I asked my father to do it for me.

The countryside was not short of rats. They holed the walls of the houses and they fought in the rooms in the night. Rat existence was already part of peasant life. When I was very small, Granny would say to me, 'The little rat climbs up the lamp-stand to steal the oil, but it is not willing to get down from the lamp-stand. When a cat appears, the rat immediately jumps down from the stand to escape.' Grannies or mothers always told this tale to their children. As rats were always present in a peasant house, it was not difficult for my father to catch the needed numbers of rats for me to reach my target.

In addition, we students tried to catch the rats ourselves. I learned from the older students how to make a 'brick cat'. It was made from two whole bricks. The wide surface of the brick was hollowed, leaving a rim of two centimetres on all sides and the bottom a similar thickness. The two pieces of brick were hollowed exactly, matching each other. One end of the rim was carved a semi-circular hole. When putting the two bricks together, one on top of the other, a complete hole was formed. In the top brick was cut a slit, behind the hole and behind the rim. The slit was a bit wider than the hole. The slit allowed a piece of wooden board to freely fall or be lifted up. This timber piece was the stopper, stopping a caught rat from escaping. In the very middle of the top brick, a small round hole was made for the purpose of securing a vertical stick. A stick was arranged with its middle secured to the vertical stick on the middle of the brick, with a piece of string. The front end of this horizontal stick, with a short string, held the stopper. The other end of the stick had a piece of string with a loop at the lower end. The bait stick was in this loop. Thus when the bait stick was put into the string loop, the stopper was up in the front slit, leaving free the entrance for the rat to come in.

The brick cat was placed near a rat hole. In the morning, when the brick cat had its entrance closed, I used a bag to cover up the hole, lifted up the stopper to open the entrance, and the rat was caught when it ran into the bag. I had to ask my father to help me.

'Before going out of a hole, a rat will put up its front legs to tell the luck of the day. The rat will guess which side of its hole has danger,' my father told me. 'Aha! The danger is at the right side of the hole!' the rat tells itself. But when the rat puts its front legs down, it forgets what it guessed. And so the rat can be caught.' Each time after a rat had been caught, the brick cat had to be thoroughly washed, not to leave any trace of its smell.

The elimination of mosquitoes had no set quota. We did it collectively. The teacher would lead us in getting rid of grass or filling in puddles with earth. We had the shovels and we had the strength.

Then in 1958, there was the movement of the 'elimination of the four pests'. Some people in high positions decided that sparrows had to be killed because they consumed too much grain. Sparrows also caused damage to a good harvest because they pecked the ears of wheat to spill the grain on the ground. I do not remember how this happened or what governmental level made the decision. I just remember that all people—workers, peasants, cadres and students—were all mobilised in the elimination of the sparrows. On the rooftops were people. In every field were people. In the woods were people. There was no place that was without people looking for sparrows. If China was short of anything at the time, it was not short of people.

Everybody had a flag or something that could make a great noise. The militia used fowling pieces. Firecrackers were used everywhere. All the noises started simultaneously so the sparrows were scared to leave the woods or houses. They flew here and there but there were no places for them to rest. They flew from village to village. They flew from wood to wood. Human shoutings, gongs, guns, and firecrackers made them fly non-stop. Nobody was chasing the sparrows with sticks or clubs. People just kept the sparrows flying. Finally, they were too fatigued to fly any longer and they crashed to the ground, dead.

Rabbits were also scared and ran around madly. They ran and ran and ran. Finally, they were no longer able to run, fell down and were picked up by those nearby to become a dish for the night. Jokingly, the lucky person would say, 'Dear rabbit, please don't blame me. You are my evening dish.' The death of the rabbits was what we Chinese described as 'the fish in the pond were victimised when the city gate was on fire'. (People have to use the water from the pond to extinguish the fire and therefore the fish in the pond become victims.)

The sparrows, though not entirely eliminated, dwindled drastically. On the rooftops, in the trees and in the fields, sparrows were rarely seen for some years after. Years later, this was proved to be a mistake. Some scientists showed that sparrows were not pests, in that they helped people to get a better harvest because they fed on pests, namely caterpillars.

Elimination of Dogs

The elimination of dogs occurred between 1954 and 1955.

What crimes did the dogs commit? I had no idea.

All the dog owners in the villages were ordered to have their dogs killed. If any owner failed to eliminate his dog before a certain date set by the cadres, the owner would face a severe penalty. Who made the order? Why was such an order made? I don't know.

Under the big elm tree at the eastern border of my uncle's yard, a huge cauldron was rigged up, which was kept boiling all the time. The cauldron was propped here because my uncle was the one designated to make good use of the skins.

Beside the cauldron were several date trees, which became the skinning scaffolding. When a dog was pulled to the place, some people would hang it to a branch of the date tree. Dogs were not killed with knives because it was said that they should not bleed. If the blood was drained, the meat would be as tough as wood. The butchers would start skinning and my uncle would get the skin treated at once. The intestines were thrown aside and the carcass was thrown into the cauldron.

Dog owners, more often than not, did not have the heart to kill their own dogs. They would just put a rope around the dog's neck and lead it to the place for extermination. Dogs seemed to understand their owners' situation. They seemed to understand that their doom had arrived. They followed at the owner's heel, head lowered, tail not wagging, despondent and sad. Once getting the dog to the place, the owner handed over the rope and would quickly run away home. The dog would not look up, would not bark at its owner; it would not even make a stir.

The close neighbour to our west had a dog. At the start of the dog killing, the dog would not approach her, and it would not touch the food given to it. It whined several times and then disappeared.

The last day that owners should kill their dogs arrived. Our neighbour was requested to hand in her dog. Our neighbour, a widow, explained that the dog had run away and she could not find it, but nobody would listen to her. Either she handed in the dog or she would face a heavy penalty. The widow cried. That very afternoon, the dog returned to her. The dog did not bark, it did not rub against her, and it did not wag its tail. It just looked into her eyes, begging to be spared. The widow was in tears. She had not the heart to part with the dog. The dog knelt in front of her and lowered its head.

The dog eliminators came. The dog bent its front legs in front of its owner, without making a stir as one dog eliminator put a noose around its neck. It did not bark or resist. It was led away to its end. The widow wept and talked about the dog's behaviour many times, for many years.

Many people were helping to cook the carcasses. It was a rare opportunity to have plenty of meat. Meat was something not many peasants could afford. Except the owners, not many people wanted to miss the opportunity. So there were many helpers and there were many people providing firewood.

My mother was also helping at the site, because it was near our yard.

'Go and crush some garlic and eat the leg,' my mother said to me, thrusting a hind leg into my hands.

Meat, whatever meat, was welcome. I had no particular preference. None of the villagers had. Meat was better than wild vegetables. When meat was available I was happy. Meat was seldom available for my consumption. So the cooked dog leg was welcome to me. I made a mixture of garlic, salt, and condiment sauce. I began attacking the leg hungrily, hurriedly and heartily.

'Ma, where will I put the bone?' I asked. My mouth was still covered with oily stains.

'Throw it to the foot of the south wall. We shall exchange it for matches later,' my mother replied. 'Go and clean your mouth. It still has the stains of what you ate.'

In olden times, when describing a country after war, the words were, 'White bones of human beings were scattered in the wild. No roosters crowing could be heard within five hundred kilometres.' Now it could be said, 'No dog's barking could be heard within five hundred kilometres'.

chapter 16

THE PREPARATORY COURSE OF THE PEKING FOREIGN TRADE INSTITUTE

The authority of the junior high school forbade students to apply for any high school in Beijing. It demanded that everybody continue his or her study in its own senior high school, which had just opened. It would be hard for me to continue my studies there, because my parents could not give me the financial support I needed. Teacher Zhu said that I would definitely get study aid in any high school in Beijing and suggested I send an application to a school I liked. I told her I liked the Preparatory Course of the Peking Foreign Trade Institute and she secretly recommended me to them. This changed my life, enabling me to get away from the countryside forever. After a few years at the Preparatory Course, Mao introduced the Socialist Education Movement. This work-study program sent students to the countryside and factories to participate in manual labour and classes were scheduled around the work schedule of the communes and factories. It was part of the Party's campaign to remove any bourgeois ideals from professional workers and intellectuals. Mao's propaganda accused them of being more concerned with having 'expertise' than being 'red'.

Going to Senior High School

When I graduated from junior high school, the students who got full marks in all their subjects for three years could be directly recommended to a senior high school without an entry examination. I was recommended to the Preparatory Course of the Peking Foreign Trade Institute, and in 1959, I was accepted. The Preparatory Course of the Peking Foreign Trade Institute, which was simplified by us students as the Preparatory Course, was a special senior high school established by the Ministry of Foreign Trade in 1958. It gave students intensive language training for three years and then passed them on to the Peking Foreign Trade Institute for a further five years of training in language and other subjects. The Peking

Foreign Trade Institute would then hand highly qualified students to the Ministry of Foreign Trade or to corporations under it as employees. I chose this particular high school for three reasons: I should be able to get study aid once I was accepted, I could go directly to university if I gained top marks for three years, and I would have the opportunity to work overseas. However, before I received notice of this enrolment, I had to do the entry examination into a senior high school. One day, I was having an afternoon nap, being tired from studying, when somebody pulled my ear. I opened my eyes and found my teacher was standing over my head.

'Get up immediately,' she ordered, grinning. 'Come to my office.'

I washed my face quickly and ran to her office where she was waiting for me. She raised an envelope and smiled.

'Guess what is this?'

My heart thumped violently.

'My enrolment notice?' I hesitated.

'Congratulations!' she said. 'But how will you go to Beijing? Quilt, mattress, clothing?'

Possible solutions flashed through my mind. The only thing I could do was to cut grass for hay, but that might not earn me enough money. My parents could not offer any help; life for them was too hard already. What else could I do? I had not the reply ready when my teacher spoke again.

'I've got a job for you,' she told me. 'Go to the Road Maintenance Bureau tomorrow morning at eight o'clock to report yourself. You and some of their people will cut trees along the highway. Your payment is one yuan and twenty cents a day. The job is for thirty days only.'

I was too pleased to know what to say. I simply stared at her with wide-open eyes.

'Don't stare at me like that,' she said. 'After breakfast, buy your lunch from school and carry it to your work site. Don't say anything about it. Other students are still preparing for the examination. Don't disturb their concentration.'

I promised her I wouldn't. The news was too good for me. The happiness was so great that I was too clumsy to find adjectives to describe it. The help from the teacher was so great that I was awfully moved. Had it not been for her, I would not have been accepted so easily. Even if I had been accepted, it would still be a big problem for me to attend the school, because it would have been difficult to get the money for the initial necessities.

The following day I went to the Bureau where I was introduced to two young men who were my colleagues and teachers in cutting the trees. I was given a very big and very sharp crescent-shaped axe and a piece of stone for sharpening it. We set out immediately after our introduction. We began from the south side of the railway line. One man marked the trees to be cut with a piece of chalk.

The weight of my axe was quite light. When I commenced on the first tree, one of the two men was supervising me. Firstly I made a full swing of the axe and it bit horizontally into the trunk about half a foot above the ground. The second cut was a slanted one reaching the first slit. A big piece of wood was cut out. I could cut deep because the force I used would be all concentrated on the axe head.

'Neat and smart,' the man said. 'You can do it better than me. I don't think you need me telling you how to do the job. Be careful when the tree falls. I am going to do some cutting now.' He left.

At noon, we sat on the sand by the roadside to eat our lunch.

The sky was very clear and it was very hot, being in the peak of summer. There was a breeze but it was too light to cool us down. We all had taken our shirts off while we worked and were covered with sweat. There was not much conversation, with everyone being unfamiliar with one another. We just ate our lunch in silence.

We had a two-hour break after lunch. The two of them lay down in the shade of a large tree and slept. It was too hot for me to walk the two kilometres back to school. I was also a bit too tired to do that. So I found a shady spot nearby and slept. The sand was soft and soothing. Almost instantly I was sound asleep.

When I was awoken, I went to the stream to wash off the sand from my body and I felt energetic again.

'You worked too fast,' one man said to me when I came back from the stream. 'You will be worn out if you continue to work like this. Do it moderately and you will be stronger by the time the thirty days finish.'

I could feel the necessity to slow down a bit. It would not only be good for me but also good for them. So I agreed.

We all sharpened our axes, each with his sharpening stone.

'If you can catch up with us,' one of them said again, 'cut as many trees as we do. If not, you can cut one or two trees less.'

Again I agreed (actually, it was hard for them to catch up with me).

When we approached the end of the day, all three of us were tired out. My shoulder joints ached so much that it seemed like a fire burning. I asked the other two, and they were not much better than I was because they had never done such a job before. As we said goodbye, they asked me to come directly to the site the next day. For the third time, I agreed.

Within a week we became friends. Both of them were from the county town. After primary school, they had not wanted to go to junior high school. 'We are not made to get more education. Books make our heads ache. We were friends at school and together we applied to work for the bureau and we were employed.' The taller one told me. Then he added, 'My name is Ma and his is Wong. What's yours?'

'Li,' I replied. I had not much to tell. I told them that my parents could not afford to pay for my education and I had to earn the money myself. Then I suggested that two of us cut trees and one cut the branches, swapping every hour or so. They agreed. We did as much as the other days but each one felt a bit less tired.

When we reached the northern tip of the Paradise Palace, my thirty days' employment ended. I went to the office of the Road Maintenance Bureau, and was given thirty-six brand new one yuan notes. I had never seen that much money. I went back to school and showed the notes to my teacher.

She smiled.

'Good boy,' she said. 'Let me keep it for the night, you may lose them. Tomorrow give the money to your mother to have the things you need prepared.'

'I will come back to say goodbye to you before I go to Beijing.' I told her.

I kept my promise.

My Beloved School

The Peking Foreign Trade Institute was situated at Che Dao Gou (The Cart Rut), which is where I stayed between 1959 and 1960 as a Year One student at the Preparatory Course. The Cart Rut was about five kilometres from Beijing Zoo, the start of the bus route to the Preparatory Course. From the Zoo to Huangzhuang (the name of a suburban village to the west of the Preparatory Course) was a narrow asphalt road lined on both sides with Huai trees (*Sophora japonica* or the scholar tree), which were thick and leafy from late spring to mid-autumn. In spring, when the Huai trees were in full bloom, the white flowers emitted such a strong fragrance, that people walking along the road would feel full of strength. In the early morning when the air was less polluted by the passing buses and trucks, the fragrance would make one feel they were in a fairyland. Bees were drawn to the trees and bee farmers would bring hundreds of beehives, which were boxes painted white, to this road and place them along the roadside, just in front of our school. From morning till night the bees were busying themselves among the flowers, bringing their booty to the beehives and coming out to work again, never stopping. They made us understand the full meaning of the English saying 'as busy as a bee'.

The Preparatory Course was just on the south side of the road. It had, at the time when I started there, merely four buildings: the classroom building, the teachers' building, the girl's dormitory building and the dining hall.

The teacher's building, which had three storeys, was the nearest to the road, blocking any noises from reaching the classroom building. The girls' dormitory building was about a hundred metres to the south-west of the teachers' building. It was a four-storey building and unlike the teacher's building, its outside was clad with white cement and bits of crushed stones and it had a flat roof, not gabled. The classroom building was four storeys high with floors that looked like marble which we called *shui mo shi*, meaning the floor was made from cement and tiny bits of white rocks which was covered with water first before being ground smoothly. The classroom building's main entrance was magnificent—it had steps up to the raised ground floor and faced north. In the centre point of the triangle formed by the teachers' building, the girls' dormitory and the classroom building was the dining hall, which served also as a recreation hall and general meeting hall. The dormitory for the male students of class three, to which I belonged, was the back part of our classroom on the second floor. Double bunks were placed in such a way that the sides faced the front of the classroom. We had some advantages. During the breaks between classes we could sit on the beds for a while.

The ground between the teachers' building and the classroom building was paved as well as decorated with flowers in the beds. (Later, around the classroom building, plenty of fruit trees were grown. The place was ideal for students to learn and to live for a few years.) On the southern side of the girls' dormitory were two large sportsgrounds. The smaller one was used in winter to provide ice for skating. The larger one had two parts—the northern part was lined with many pairs of basketball facilities and the southern part was a soccer ground and field for track sports. Bordering the eastern edge of the sportsground was a pine grove. In summer it was a good place for wandering among the trees, reading English texts aloud. The cool breeze could always freshen up the head and sharpen the memory.

Outside the school boundary and about a hundred metres to the south, there was a stream flowing from the west to the east. It was about ten metres in width and, except after heavy rain, had clear water about waist deep. In summer, we always swam in this stream after class in the afternoons. An elderly lady who taught us English and who was from Switzerland would lie leisurely afloat on the surface of the water for a long time without stirring her limbs.

Willows on both the northern and southern banks of the stream swayed their long twigs beautifully like the best dancers to please the students reading under them. Peach trees (ones that could bloom but not bear fruit), lined the stream on both banks alternatively with the willows. In the water, fish and shrimp, though very few and far between, would swim quickly to avoid the swimmers.

Some old teachers, sitting on folding stools, would rig imported fishing rods on the bank to enjoy a moment of relaxation. They were, I always thought, sitting there to adjust their ambitions rather than concentrating on earnest fishing. Fishing, to intellectuals all through Chinese history, was the way to demonstrate that authority had not yet appreciated the *fisherman's* knowledge, ability and ideas. At least it was so in the feudal dynasties in China. In the State of Zhou, King Wen wanted to have a military adviser. One night he saw a flying bear in his dream. He asked his subjects what was the meaning of the dream and was told he was to get a good adviser soon. One day, King Wen had a walk along the River Wei and he met an old man sitting on the bank, fishing. He chatted with the man and realised that he was the adviser he was looking for. King Wen asked the old man to climb onto his cart and he pulled it himself without the help of his guards, to show his respect for the old man. When he was too tired and stopped the cart, the old man asked, 'How many steps have you pulled?' 'Eight hundred and eight steps.' King Wen replied. 'All right, I will protect your regime for eight hundred and eight years' the old man said. With his help the Zhou Empire was established in the 11th Century BC.

The Empire lasted over eight hundred years until 256BC. The name of this adviser was Jiang Shang. Since then, fishing became the way for an intellectual to get known to rulers. Fishing can be also interpreted as fishing for position.

The Preparatory Course swapped school sites with the Institute the following year—1960. We moved to the Qian Ma Chang (Front Horse Barn), which was situated not far from the 'Drum and Bell Towers'. From Di-an Men Street, students could go to the school by two bus routes. We stayed there until 1962.

It was said that our school was the mansion of Li Hong Zhang, who was the Prime Minister in the late period of Empress Ci Xi (1835–1908) of the Qing Dynasty (1644–1911). I believed it was. Looking from outside the red lacquered gate, which had a low portico, it was not imposing at all. But once you had stepped inside the gate, it demonstrated the grandeur, authority, privilege, wealth and comfort of all that the original owner enjoyed.

There were so many houses and courtyards inside, that during the two years I studied there, there were many places that I never saw. I just remembered that at one time some of my classmates and I had our dormitory in a secluded and independent two-room house in a high-walled courtyard in the eastern part of the domain. At another time we had our dormitory in a similar two-room house with a courtyard in the western side of the domain. There were houses behind houses and yards behind yards.

Date trees, which bore the typical long, pointed, crisp, and sweet Peking dates, were present in almost every courtyard. The thickness of the trees showed that they had been there for many decades, probably hundreds of years. After the summer vacation approached, the dates would be ready for eating. During our basketball classes, at the beginning of the term after the summer holidays, whenever the teacher turned his head, the ball would fly to the branches of the date tree on the edge of the playground and bring down dates like hailstones. The dates were red, crisp and sweet. We would snatch them from the ground and put them into our hungry mouths. We responded to the snarls of the teacher with a sheepish smile.

Once during the summer holidays, a friend of mine from Qing Hua University came to stay in our dormitory, leaving for home the following day by train. My friend, Jiang, from my class, asked me whether we should give him something to eat during his long, lonely journey home. It was already very late at night and we could not go to Di-an Men Street to buy anything, and even if it were not late, we could not buy anything without a grain coupon. There were not many things available in the shops because we were in the midst of the national famine. So we turned our attention to the dates.

The date tree was in front of our dormitory but against the back wall of the building in which the Party Secretary of the school worked during the day and slept during the night. He was a very tall man from Yenan (the centre of the Chinese Communists during the anti-Japanese War). He was once part of the 359 Brigade, which was famous during the Great Production Movement. He was a very kind man and he was very alert. Of all the trees, the one against the wall of the Party Secretary's building gave the best dates.

We decided to try that tree for dates. Jiang and I, for the sake of carrying dates, put on jackets with many pockets. I told him to be careful not to make any noise and we climbed up the roof from the tree. We lay on the slope under the branches. Then Jiang broke a tile and the creaking of the door of the house told us the Party Secretary was coming out to check what was going on. We lay there very still and after a while he went back into his room. It was very dark and we could not distinguish the dates from the leaves. I closed my eyes to think of a way to get the dates. Then I realised that the dates were heavier than the leaves and if we jerked a twig slightly, the swaying movement of the dates and leaves would distinguish them. I told this to Jiang. Without difficulty we climbed down the tree with our booty to please our friend.

The next day, when the Party Secretary saw my friend from Qing Hua and I, he spoke softly to me with his forefinger probing my head. 'Naughty boy, you were up on my roof for the dates last night.' Then he added, 'Dates are not that important, but it was so dark that if you slipped and got hurt, what would you do? Don't do such a thing again in the future.' My friend and I grimaced. It was not difficult for him to know who did it, because we were the only students staying in the yard at the time.

There was one rare Chinese herbal tree called 'the fruit of King Wen', which was said to be the only one in Beijing. It was well protected and well cared for. One day a student snapped off one fruit from the tree, and opened it to see what was inside. The teacher who taught classic Chinese was walking past him at the time and reported it to the grade coordinator. A meeting of all the students was called to explain the incident. It was stressed that school property should not be damaged. The action was a breach of school discipline. The tree was rare and the fruit was valuable—the only fruit of its kind in Beijing. It was round and green and as big as a duck egg. The punishment was 'a major breach of discipline'. If a student made three major breaches of school discipline, he would be expelled from the school. It was a great pity that I never heard the use of the fruit.

There was also one rare variety of peony not very far from our classroom, which was said that even the top leaders of the country came to visit. I looked at the flower once but have forgotten whether it was purple, black or green. There was also a very large persimmon tree in front of the dormitory of some boys from our class. It bore so much fruit that when they ripened, each of the two hundred and twenty students was given one kilogram for free and the school shop had plenty for sale to the students at a low price. There were two white cherry pear trees, which bore such beautiful and attractive fruit that they made one's mouth water. The Chinese name for the fruit is *hai tang*, meaning 'looking like a pear but just as big as the largest cherry'. One student was tempted by them one night, but he forgot the hornet's nest in one of the trees. He was attacked so savagely by the hornets that he could only open his eyes to tiny slits the following day.

There were cherry trees behind our classroom, which we found by accident when we were studying for the mid-term examination. We filled up one large enamelled mug with the fruit, washed them clean and ate them. Some girls from our class saw us eating them.

'Where did you buy the cherries from?' they asked.

'From the Drum Tower Street,' we joked.

Off they hurried. We stopped eating from the mug when there was only half the cherries left. When the girls found nothing there, we would have a 'hard time'. The half mug of cherries could be used to pacify them.

'Tell us the exact shop where you bought them,' the girls demanded sternly when they returned.

'We bought them from here,' one boy pushed the cherry mug to them.

They sat down to enjoy them. But when they finished they still pressed for a reply until they were told the secret. The result was that very soon there was not a single cherry left on the tree—even some of the branches were broken.

Besides the trees mentioned above, there were walnut trees, peach trees, and other fruit trees in the school courtyards. There were also flowers of a special variety. When we got up in the morning during spring, their fragrance immediately entered our dormitory as soon as we opened the door. The courtyard air was permeated with their very strong fragrance. We were very surprised and checked why. We realised that the fragrance came from a few orchids—just three or four long stems with dark purplish-blue petals on top. They withered during the day. New flowers would come out the following day perfuming our dormitory and our courtyard. Only green leaves remained and flourished in the summer.

Amid this environment lived the students from the Preparatory Course, overseas students from Yemen and the cadres from the Ministry of Foreign Trade attending the training courses.

My English Study

In Chinese history, officials or emperors always called written languages from countries outside China 'tadpole writings'. Intellectuals who could read such writings were held in great respect. The 'tadpole' language was what I had to learn to read, write and speak. This itself was a privilege, but privilege in some cases can mean difficulty. English, a 'tadpole' language, meant difficulty to me. However, I had overcome many difficulties since I was very small and so I made up my mind to tackle this new difficulty again.

The textbook we used was printed by our own school, not the standard textbook sold in the bookshops. Each text included words, sentences, international pronunciation symbols, grammar, questions, and so on. The first text I remember is below.

Text: I am a student.
New words: I, am, a, student.
Pronunciation: [iː] [ei] [ai]
Pictures: showing correct positions of the tongue, the teeth and the lips.

In our English class our teacher, Han Guo-tai, would hang a large picture on the blackboard to show the position for each sound. The picture showed whether the tongue should be between the teeth, or against the upper teeth roots, or against the palate, and so on.

Every day we had two classes of English in the morning, each forty-five minutes long. Besides new text, new words, new sentences and new pronunciation, the teacher would demand that we practise English pronunciation in pairs. When one student was pronouncing, the other would watch the positioning of his or her tongue, lips, teeth, and the opening of the mouth. Any slightest deviation from the standard position would be immediately pointed out for correction.

Before breakfast and after supper, we had individual study for reviewing old texts and preparing for new texts, as well as doing our homework. But most of my classmates would spend the time reading English aloud.

In comparison with my classmates, I was very much disadvantaged in studying English. Whatever Teacher Han taught in class was what I could learn and nothing more. But many of my classmates were already able to read and even recite the whole book. While I was practicing the few letters I learned in class, my classmates were already able to write the whole twenty-six letters of the alphabet beautifully. My classmates had more time to work on other subjects but I had to squeeze as much time as possible for English.

Language learning, I reasoned with myself, consisted of skill learning and knowledge learning. Spoken English depended on practise because, in my opinion, it was a skill that could only be mastered by endless studying. As long as I could overcome my shyness to speak in front of other people, there should be no problem. A baby learnt to speak through hundreds of thousands of repetitions of a word or a sentence. In the same way, I could acquire the ability to speak through repeated practice. To memorise as many English words and expressions as possible, to know and utilise the grammar well and to write excellent compositions in English could be regarded as acquiring knowledge. With this understanding I allotted my spare time accordingly. I also tried my very best to talk to the teacher for extra practice. Because everything Teacher Han taught in class was new to me, I had to hang my eyes on his lips and be all ears to what he said. One day, through persistence and perseverance, I could be a top student in English.

To practise my handwriting and to memorise the new words, expressions and phrases, I used my pen. I could not afford to buy more paper for this purpose so I had to find another way. The exercise books of mathematics, algebra and geometry were all covered with pencil writing. First I would use the back of each page of the old exercise books by writing with a pencil. The second time I would write with red ink and then with blue ink. This was especially necessary in the second year when the 'Great Leap Forward' type of teaching was introduced. This style of teaching was called 'large unit' teaching because every text plus a list of new words, explanations and grammar had to be learnt every week. The whole unit was finished within one week. One or two weeks were all right, but when it was done week after week, it became a challenge—a real challenge. Unless each lesson was mastered well, it would be very hard to make progress later.

On Saturdays and Sundays I had to stay at school, because I did not have enough money to pay for the fare to go back home to see my parents. This was an advantage. I would write from memory all the texts learned, and check my memory as well as my spelling. Then I would cover up the English word list and just look at the Chinese equivalent to check whether I could remember the English words correctly and vice versa. At first this consumed much of my time but gradually, it became easier to do. Dictation or recitation no longer worried me. Surprise examinations were no longer something I feared.

Still I felt my vocabulary was not improving as quickly as I wished. I borrowed *Tales of Shakespeare* to read as 'snacks'. But this 'snack' was not easy to chew. There were about fifty new words in the first page alone! I had to look for the definitions annexed to the book and in the dictionary. More often than not, when I started to connect the words together to get the meaning of the sentence, I found that many Chinese equivalents I had jotted down were not the ones I needed. I had to look for them in the dictionary again. To understand a sentence was like conquering an enemy stronghold. I persevered, progressing as slowly as 'ants biting at a bone'.

'Don't bite off more than you can chew,' Teacher Han cautioned me when he saw me reading the book. He picked it up, turned a few pages and sat down on the opposite side of my desk. He chose a few sentences from the book randomly for me to explain and translate into Chinese. He then dictated a few new words from the book. At last he asked me to take out my textbook from the drawer of my desk, dictated a few words and requested me to recite a few paragraphs from different texts. He was satisfied and told me to come to him whenever I had problems in reading the stories.

'Tell me,' Teacher Han said to me, 'how have you managed to memorise so many new words and recite so many texts?'

'I believe that "a slow bird should fly first". I am not clever and I am a slow bird. I had to "fly first". I feel language learning is not just to memorise quickly. Language learning is mainly repetition. Unless I can remember them properly through repeated practice, all that I have learned might be forgotten some day. I don't want to rely on my memory alone, I want to rely on hard work.'

'Now I know why you always get full marks in the examinations,' Teacher Han nodded approvingly.

My memory was not bad, though I was not able to remember a word just by glancing at it once. I could recite a long text or article by reading it two or three times. But I found out that whatever I could memorise quickly I would also forget quickly unless I tried to refresh my memory several times to remember it properly.

My strong point was giving the proper length of time to everything. If I wasted a bit of time through playing, rambling talks, movie watching or labouring, I would find time to make up for what I lost for my English or other subjects. That was my secret in English study.

To save time, whenever I looked for a word in the dictionary, I would check the root of the word, check the spelling of all its forms such as the verb, noun, adjective and adverb. I would read all the example sentences about their usage, trying hard to learn the 'live' word, not the 'dead' word. In any case, any progress I made in English was a result of my teacher's guidance and help. My teachers live in my mind—they are unforgettable.

Red and Expert

Between 1961 and 1962, the ideological thinking of being 'red' and 'expert' was introduced to our school. Students were invited to debate this ideology. It was said that Marshal Chen Yi, the Deputy Premier and the Minister of Foreign Affairs at the time, had commented in his speech to the students of the Institute on the performance of interpreters at the Geneva Conference. He said that a good interpreter enabled the host and guests to exchange ideas freely and pleasantly while a bad interpreter, like cutting meat with a dull knife, made both the host and guests suffer. So he instructed any institutes teaching foreign languages to give five full years' education to students, thus prolonging our stay in the Institute for one more year.

In classes of politics and in specially arranged meetings in class, we students discussed 'red' and 'expert'. 'Red', as was explained, meant to love your country, the Communist Party and the socialist system. 'Expert' meant to be well qualified technically and professionally. Pilots and jet fighters were used as examples to expound the idea. 'Red' meant the pilot loved his country, the Communist Party, and the socialist system. 'Expert' meant the pilot mastered the skill of operating the jet fighter and could fight an air battle well. If the pilot was 'red' but not an 'expert', he could be shot down by an enemy fighter in the first air battle or he might crash to the ground before take off or he would crash when he landed. If he was an 'expert' but 'white', he might fly the fighter to the enemy. So, neither 'red' without being an 'expert' nor 'expert' and 'white' was needed by Communism.

The profession of interpreters was also used as an example. If one was 'red' but not an 'expert' in his profession, one could not be a good interpreter in making trading deals with foreign businesspeople or on the diplomatic front. Whereas if one was 'expert' enough but not 'red', he might pass information to the capitalists or he might betray the country and defect to the enemy.

'Expert' was a tool, which could be used either by socialism or by capitalism. 'Red' was in the thinking—only when one was 'red', could he or she contribute to the country willingly. However, due to the imminent entry examination for the Institute, the discussion did not last long. To be 'red' and 'expert' was not an easy label to acquire, but to be labelled as 'white' and 'expert' was not hard. If one was an excellent student but not on good terms with some of his or her classmates, it was not difficult for one to be seen as 'white' and 'expert'.

In *The Journey to the West* by Wu Cheng-en, Monkey, all the way to the Western Heaven, did his very best to defeat or capture monsters, devils or demons of various kinds. He tried his utmost to protect, rescue, and save his teacher and his mates. He nearly lost his life a few times yet he never thought of quitting.

Monkey, in my opinion, was an out and out 'red' and 'expert'. However, when the Pig reported on him to the teacher, the teacher would punish Monkey by reading the tightening curse. A gold band on Monkey's head would become so tight that he would hold his head crying painfully, doing somersaults, rolling on the ground and begging for mercy from his teacher. The Pig, whenever the opportunity arose, would urge to 'part company and divide the luggage' to return to Gao Lao Zhuan (the village where he was married to a girl). Also whenever the Pig was asked to catch a monster, he would find a place to hide and sleep, he would complain, or he himself would be captured by the monster he was asked to catch. The Pig, therefore, was not 'red' and 'expert', and yet the teacher never punished him. The result? Because of the exertion of Monkey, all of them arrived at the Western Heaven. The teacher, because he was wise, became a Buddha. Monkey, because he fought the monsters and demons so arduously, became a Buddha. The Pig became a Buddha, too, because, although he could not fight the monsters well, and he always advocated the group to part hands, he had done the hard work of carrying the luggage all the way to the Western Heaven.

In real life it was the same. People as able as Monkey would not be promoted because their manager needed them to solve problems and to do the work. It was also because the manager immediately above him would not want to promote him, seeing him as a potential threat. Furthermore, such a person would always have a 'golden band around his head'—whenever necessary his manager would speak to him privately and in his 'interests' about the opinions of the colleagues, which served as Monkey's golden band.

The manager, representing Monkey's teacher, did not need to be able. As long as he was accepted by the various managers above him, and as long as he was considered not a threat to them, he could some day become a Buddha—to be promoted. There were many Pigs in life back then. Because they preferred to speak behind other people's backs, their managers needed them as 'eyes', 'ears', and as the 'gold band to Monkeys'. It was a pity that I came to understanding this too late because for many years I worked hard and contributed unselfishly and I had never thought about it.

The 'red' and 'expert' ideology was the beginning of Mao's concern about the colour of the country, and the beginning of a string of events in China. Firstly, Mao wanted students to be 'red' and 'expert' and to guarantee this he demanded they live, eat and labour for one year with peasants or workers, after university. Then Mao discovered that in the countryside, some cadres wanted to operate in the capitalist way. He therefore sent students to the countryside and factories to take part in the 'socialist education movement' in order to purge the cadres who feasted on public funds, raped girls, stole the property of the production brigade or who had advocated private farming. He believed this would enable students to become real revolutionaries. Consequently, Mao found that there were two lines in the party—the proletarian line and the capitalist line. He started the Great Cultural Revolution to defeat his opponents.

chapter 17

MY BELOVED TEACHERS

The word 'teacher' is sacred and teachers are worthy of love, praise and respect. Teachers, unlike anybody else, are willing to give their knowledge unreservedly to their students and to expect wholeheartedly, but without jealousy, that their students will make progress. Teachers are the real pioneers that help the world progress.

The Flame

The coordinator, Liu Ji-wen, was a female teacher in her early thirties. She was of average height and her hair, like the other girls or young women, was cut short to her neck, or sometimes even a bit shorter still. Her eyes were 'phoenix eyes'—brilliant, clear and candid. Her face was nearly square-shaped with all her features satisfactorily positioned. She wore a blue jacket similar to that of the female students, only better fitting. She wore long trousers, always matching the jacket. She was seldom seen wearing a skirt, at least I could not remember ever seeing her in a skirt. Her leather shoes, by the standard of the time, were fashionable. Her legs seemed made of springs. She whirled here, there and everywhere tirelessly.

She was, according to herself, brought up in Yenan. I remember she once talked about the difficulties she had at the time. She said she had just one suit. All girls, like her, had just one suit. The girls would go to the Yen River together in the evening under the cover of the night sky and with two of them keeping watch, bathe in the river and wash their clothes.

Liu Ji-wen graduated from the Peking Foreign Trade Institute in 1958 and was employed by the Institute as a coordinator for our grade. She appeared in the classrooms, the dormitories—wherever the students were. Her voice could be heard when she was still a very long distance away. Laughter, clear and metallic like a golden bell, came with her presence.

She had a family to support but she was not as tight-fisted as some other people were. When a student of hers was sick, she would visit with fruit, if she could get it. It was a pity that during the Great Cultural Revolution, when she brought bananas and oranges to a sick student in hospital, that student, when out of the hospital, put a poster up accusing her of poisoning him with bourgeois fruit. I never could tell the difference between fruit belonging to communism or capitalism. For the first time in her life, she was too flabbergasted to utter a word. She could only shed tears of confusion and bewilderment.

She would be at the ready when a student needed help. I myself was one of the examples. It happened during my second year. The school was listing the names of students who wanted to buy an English–Chinese dictionary. I was the only one who could not afford it. I had tried many times to save money, but I would not have been able to scrape up enough to buy it. I had only thirteen yuan and fifty cents, the total of my monthly study aid. Twelve yuan and fifty cents had to be paid for my board and I had only one yuan left. Even if I did not buy any daily necessities such as tooth powder, soap and a towel, and did not have a hair cut, it would take half a year for me to get the money—and by then the dictionaries would not be available.

How I needed a dictionary! Trying to broaden my knowledge of English through reading more, the dictionary would be like a walking stick to help me get over one stumbling block after another. Without a dictionary, I would be handicapped in reading outside my textbook. I felt so sad that I could not sleep that night. When the dictionaries were delivered to the school, everybody's face broadened with big smiles. I became agitated when I saw the coffee-coloured cover of the dictionaries in the hands of my friends. I went to the library to read and to calm myself down. Very soon my friend, Jiang, came to look for me and told me that Teacher Liu was waiting for me in her office.

'Close your eyes. Here's something for you,' she said to me, smiling, when I stepped into her office.

'What is it?' My mind worked quickly but I could not find an answer.

She put something like a book into my hands.

'The dictionary!' I exclaimed and opened my eyes. I was so excited that my hands trembled a bit. I could not find another word to say. I wanted to cry, to laugh, to shout, and to thank her. I was in tears.

'Open the fly page and look,' she urged me.

'A gift to student Li Chun-ying,' was written with her handwriting. I pressed the dictionary to my heart, which was filled with warmer emotions than I had ever experienced before. It was a mixture of feelings

I was not able to describe at the time. (Sadly, the dictionary was lost when my family moved from China to Australia.)

'Study hard and make good progress,' Teacher Liu encouraged me. I nodded. It was a nod of determination from the very bottom of my heart.

Winter was already halfway through. Though poor, I was a boy who sometimes was so careless that my padded jacket was torn in places and the elbows had holes. One Sunday Teacher Liu came to our dormitory with thread and needles, and pieces of cloth. She instructed me to read my books with my quilt over my shoulders to serve as a blanket. She was mending my jacket for me. It was a big surprise that she was able to sew with a needle and thread, because girls who went to school rarely knew how to sew. She sat on a chair and began. It took her some time to get the thread into the needle eye. She then secured patches in place with long stitches. Her way of pressing the thimble over the needle seemed awkward. She now and then pricked her fingers. She sewed carefully and attentively. She cut the thread, like my mother, with her teeth when she finished stitching a patch.

When she finally passed the jacket to me, I was so moved that I dared not look into her face for fear that I might not be able to hold back my tears of thankfulness. The patching was well placed and secured but the seams were not straight—they were zigzag to be exact. Some stitches were too big and some stitches were too short. Some stitches were too loose and some were too tight. Clearly, even if this was not the first time that she handled a needle and thread, she seldom used them. Yet each stitch was a display of motherly care. Each stitch was a display of a great heart; a display of a flame warming people around her. Her needlework could not be compared to that of my mother, yet to me, it was the best needlework in the world. To use our Chinese phrase this was 'putting on the jacket over my body, I felt warm at heart'.

In the latter half of Year Two or the first part of Year Three, I received a letter from one of my female schoolmates from my junior high school. There was a big picture of the girl who wrote to me. In the letter she expressed her love for me. I had, so far, never had a girl casting her eyes at me, with what could be called affection. I had never had a letter from anybody, let alone from a girl. The letter made my head full of a feeling I had never experienced before and I found it hard to describe. The word 'love' hit me like a thunderbolt, bouncing non-stop in my heart.

When I went back to see my parents, my father told me that a middle person had talked to him. If I agreed to marry the girl I could go to live in their village or I could dismantle a three-room house of theirs to reconstruct in our village. My parents were a bit in favour of this but did not make any commitment.

This was the first love letter I ever received and the first decision I had to make about 'love'. I was at a loss of what to do. I handed the letter to Teacher Liu for advice.

'Return the letter and the picture to your schoolmate,' Teacher Liu told me. 'It's too early for you to turn your attention to a girl. Study hard and you may start to look for a girl after Year Three in the university.'

After a while she spoke to me again.

'This girl is not good for you. Your standard will change after your graduation from the university,' she said. 'Don't let such things divert your attention from your study.'

I took her advice and was glad of it.

Teacher Liu was a magnet attracting students around her. She was a friend to whom the students could tell their difficulties. She was a mother, from whom the students received care and love. She was a source of energy and to her, the students looked for encouragement.

In 1961 we went to work in Wang Jun-tan, a village about thirty kilometres from our school, in the eastern suburbs of Beijing. We were in the midst of the most severe famine. Our hungry stomachs were hard to fill. At the work site when we were hungry and fatigued, her voice and laughter made us all cheer up, forgetting our sorry plight. When students examined the *wo tou* mixed with wild vegetables, her appearance would make any hesitation in eating disappear and everybody ate like a hungry wolf.

The whole three years she was our coordinator, I never saw her in low spirits or angry. She was always just like a flame, emitting warmth to everyone—comforting and enlightening. The flame is still burning.

The Smiling Buddha

My English teacher, during my three years at the Preparatory Course, was Teacher Han Guo-tai. He was a man in his mid-sixties, of average height, but a bit over average weight. His hair, already thinned out drastically on top of his head, was entirely grey, combed upward and backward, and well groomed. His face was square. His brows were grey and long, which belonged to the type of brows indicating Buddha had given him a long life. His eyes always seemed like slits because of his constant smile, which gave him the honour of being called the 'smiling Buddha'. The grey moustache on his upper lip was always well trimmed.

Teacher Han had more patience than severity in our English classes. Hanging up a big picture to illustrate the position of our lip, tongue and the shape of our mouth, he would drill our pronunciation again and again. He would check each student to see whether the tongue was in the correct position or the lips were shaped as required. He dictated to us in every class. He corrected our handwriting minutely. He asked us to write the letters like an officer drilling the soldiers to turn left and right and to march forward or to stop instantly on command. He never flared up and even when he criticised somebody his voice would not be raised. His words were kind but could cut deeper than the severest words from others. During our individual study classes he constantly toured our classroom, even in our pre-breakfast reading. Book in hand, the students would read aloud while walking in the courtyard. Unexpectedly he would appear at your side to correct a pronunciation or an intonation.

One evening when we had individual study, he came into our classroom, his hands behind his back, and checked what each student was doing. My desk mate and I had finished our homework and we were reading *The Tales of Shakespeare*. The girl, Wee, in front of us was reading English while knitting. Teacher Han came round to us, turned a few pages of my storybook, gave it back to me and smiled encouragingly. He then stood behind the girl, watching. He remained there for quite a long while.

'Wee, now I understand why you cannot get good marks in the examinations.' He spoke to her as she raised her head with a start. 'I have been here for more than ten minutes and have only heard you repeatedly reading "I am a student" many, many times. Your mind is not on your English text. Your mind is on your knitting. You are a really good and fast knitter! You probably can get a better life through knitting than through English study!' Wee blushed, thrust her knitting away, and wept. She concentrated on her English for quite a few weeks thereafter, improved greatly, but returned to her old self again.

The tallest male student in our class was called up to recite a text during our English class. He faltered a few sentences and then stopped, not being able to recite the whole text.

'Xung, standing up you are a skyscraper! But in your English study you are not half as good as the youngest of the class. I don't think you can do well in other subjects either. Your mind is elsewhere. If I were you, I would look for a crack in the ground to creep into!' Xung was in tears. His mind was really somewhere else. One day he came back to the dormitory, very drunk. Only days later did we learn that his girlfriend had left him. He did not make any improvement in his studies. Teacher Han was disappointed and conceded that he could not do anything about Xung.

Yao was another student in our class whom Teacher Han criticised. In the end of term examination, Yao got fifteen marks for six subjects. Five marks were the full points for each subject. He got five marks in physical education and two marks in English, Chinese, mathematics, history, and political education. That meant he failed in all those subjects. Teacher Han spoke to him in front of the class.

'Yao, you are really great, getting fifteen marks for six subjects! You got full points in physical education only. This tells me why you are so good at riding your bike—transporting passengers on it on your way home. You made good money doing that, right? But study is not important to you. You have strong limbs but no brain!' Like the other two, Yao was in tears. He cried repentantly. But he made no effort to improve. He quit school sometime in the third year.

To all the other students in the class, Teacher Han never used a harsh word. His face was always beaming, like that of a Buddha. He was not jealous that students spent a lot of time on other subjects, but he always showed his appreciation when he saw students reviewing English lessons.

Teacher Han was exasperated by me once. It was a mid-term examination in English and the marks would count towards the entry into the Institute. I needed to go to the toilet immediately lest I would wet my trousers. I hurried through the last few answers, handed in the papers and dashed out of the classroom. Teacher Han chased out after me but could not stop me. When he saw me rushing into the toilet, he waited outside, puffing his moustache, indignantly.

'Come over here,' he ordered me and caught my right ear when I approached him.

'Come back to the classroom,' he said. His hand was rather heavy and it hurt. He pulled me into the classroom, to the platform, thrust my paper to me, released my ear, and spoke angrily.

'Go back to your seat and check the papers. If you needed to go to the toilet, why didn't you ask for permission?' then he addressed the whole class.

'Anybody else wants to go to the toilet? If you do, put up your hand!'

I went back to my seat, finished a minor question at the bottom of the last page. It was to write out the parts of speech of a few verbs. I read through my paper and felt satisfied. I sat there for another few minutes, handed in the paper in the wake of my friend, Jiang. Teacher Han did not say anything this time. He beamed at us and allowed us to leave the classroom.

One Sunday morning Teacher Han invited me to visit his house. I went with one of my friends. We were let into his study where tea was ready for each of us. Nobody else from the family was there. The study was carpeted. There were a number of bookshelves, which were heavily laden with books, a few armchairs, and one desk for Teacher Han to read and work at in his spare time. There was a tea table around which we sat to drink the tea offered to us.

On the wall facing the door was a life-size picture of his father sitting in an armchair. His father had a Qing Dynasty hat for officials on his head. From the very top to the middle of the hat was a large pearl. The hat top was red, indicating a senior position, but the bushy tail of it could not be seen. He was attired in official costume—an embroidered jacket over a long robe with a big patterned square at the breast, sleeves with horse hoof cuffs, his lap covered by the lower part of the robe. He wore very thick-soled boots. His face was in every way the origin of his son's. His eyes, unlike Teacher Han, had a cold, stern stare.

'He was an official,' Teacher Han told us.

Teacher Han told us he had been teaching English for about forty years. He started as a tutor to the two sons of a rich family. The two men later turned out to be high diplomats. He told us that English was the most useful international language, particularly if we wished to do foreign trade. He encouraged us to continue studying English after getting into the Institute.

'To master one language is better than knowing a little of many languages,' he told us.

Time flew and we reached the end of term examination for enrolment into the Institute. A few days after the examinations finished, Teacher Han saw me reading English in the courtyard.

'Li,' he called me to him. 'You have achieved full marks in all subjects. What course are you going to choose?'

'I haven't decided yet,' I replied.

'Put "English" in the columns as your first, second, and third preference. Don't hesitate.' He advised me. 'When you get into university, give me a report in English on whatever you read every month,' he instructed me, without any room for argument.

I promised. By the end of the first term at the Institute, Teacher Han wrote to me saying he was satisfied with my progress in English and my report was no longer necessary. A few years later, I went back to see him. He was no longer there. He had already gone to the other world. I felt so sad and missed him. I could still see his smiles and his persistence to push the students forward in studying English.

Dedication

Teacher Wu Bi-wei was another English teacher working at the Institute. Stepping out of our classroom after the English examination at the end of the first term of the second year, I saw Teacher Wu standing in the courtyard. He beckoned me to come over to him.

'Come to my house at eight o'clock in the morning every Sunday,' he said to me. 'I will help you to improve your pronunciation, intonation and fluency.' He told me the address and went into his classroom to supervise his students. I was excited. Teacher Wu was a linguistic expert. He could speak quite a few Chinese dialects. He specialised in English pronunciation, intonation and fluency. Now that he offered to help me, I was too moved to say words of gratitude to him before he went back to his class.

Teacher Wu, unlike Teacher Han, was quite slim. His face was thin but not sallow. His large glasses highlighted an air of austerity. His hair was not as grey as that of Teacher Han, nor as well groomed. His palms, like those of Teacher Han, were already damaged by the chalk sticks he had been holding for many years; having very little flesh colour. He seldom smiled but never was angry. It was said that he was quite hopeless in daily practical matters—he never remembered to carry cash when he left his house. His wife, to save him from any possible trouble, would put a bit of money in every pocket of his jacket. No matter which pocket he dipped into he would be able to get coins for his bus fare or for something he needed. Yet he seldom had the need, because he was, most of the time, either in school or in his house.

We were in the midst of the three-year long famine. Each time we arrived at his house for our tutoring (two of my classmates joined me to be coached by Teacher Wu), he would take us by bus, for which he paid the fares, to Bei Hai Park through the rear gate. Sitting around a square table in the open, outside a tea tavern in the park, he would order a pot of jasmine tea with four cups.

'Sorry,' he would apologise to us. 'I have no coupons to offer you any food, I can only give you a cup of tea.'

One by one, we would read our English text in turn for him to correct us. Teacher Wu would interrupt my reading now and then to tell me the correct pronunciation of a certain word, or to show me the correct liaison of the silent consonant of one word with the beginning vowel of another. He was so strict that he would not let me go on unless he judged it correct. A couple of months later, he was very much pleased when he listened to my reading. To him I had made progress. I was not able to tell certain subtle changes I had made, myself.

In winter, we were, more often than not, the only customers in the open. I would hold the teacup in my hands, not for the purpose of enjoying the tea but for getting the meagre warmth from the cup of hot tea. He would only dismiss us at lunchtime.

One summer Sunday morning, it was raining cats and dogs. I could not be sure whether Teacher Wu was expecting us in such weather. Yet from my understanding of the Chinese elderly intellectuals, I felt I should go to Teacher Wu's as usual. At worst, I would just get wet in the rain and walk the two kilometres to and from his house without being coached. I decided to go. My two classmates were hesitating. I persuaded them by saying that Teacher Wu demanded us to be there every Sunday and he did not say except rainy days. I said we had promised and we had to keep our promise. Any promise should be kept, and any action should have a result. Both agreed to go. With the legs of our trousers rolled up above our knees, clad in plastic raincoats and 'no front, no heel' plastic sandals, we set out in the rain. Our raincoats were flapping against our legs, hampering our progress. Sheets of water, driven by the wind, slapped our faces and flowed down to wet our T-shirts. The wide street was like a river. Water, ankle deep, raced along the roadside, too much and too fast for the drainage system to suck in completely.

As soon as we entered the lane to Teacher Wu's, we saw that fifty metres or so away, he was standing under the portico of the gate with an umbrella. We quickened our steps into a run. I was choked with emotion. When we reached the gate, he looked at his watch. It was eight o'clock sharp. A smile, the only one I ever saw, spread over his face, followed by an expression of relief, satisfaction and happiness. It was so transient that only a sensitive and observing person could detect it. We could not go to Bei Hai Park in this weather, so he invited us into his study. It was covered with red carpet. We stopped at the doorway to wipe our feet against our trousers.

'Enter, no need to wipe your feet,' he ordered.

His wife, a beautiful lady of the same age as Teacher Wu, was in a well tailored Manchu-style robe and had a beautiful hairdo, not seen in public places. This was because having a hairdo and robe of such a kind would be regarded as 'bourgeois'. She came into the study with a tray, on which was a teapot, a few cups and several biscuits on a saucer. She was shorter than Teacher Wu but better shaped in her figure. Her face looked at least ten years younger than her age. Had we not known her having ten daughters, we would have thought she was too young for our teacher. Her hair was dark and bountiful.

'Shih Nian,' the three of us stood up instantly and bowed. ('Shih' meaning teacher and 'Nian' meaning mother. This was the customary term with which students addressed the wife of the teacher. In China, once a man became a teacher, the students would respect him as a father all his life. That was why the teacher's wife was called 'Nian'.)

'Sit, sit,' she beamed upon us. 'Your teacher was waiting for you at the gate for at least half an hour. He got up very early, impatient with the rain. All the time he talked to himself. "Will my students come? The rain is too heavy for them, but they will keep their promise. They will be here." "The rain is too heavy. They will not come," I told him. "I bet they will come!" he said positively. He could not sit quiet for a minute. He was no longer his usual self. Look how happy he is now!' She placed the teapot and teacups on a square table against the wall facing the door, smiled at us and tiptoed out of the study.

Teacher Wu was indeed very happy and he seemed not to be in a hurry to start. I had time to look around his study. On the wall was a huge picture, which, I thought, was by a famous painter. On either side of the picture was a big scroll of calligraphy by a famous calligrapher. There was a desk by the window and there were two bookshelves laden with English books, not far from the desk. Except the square table and the chairs there was no other furniture or decoration in the study.

Teacher Wu was very talkative that day. He was as active and lively as teenagers were when they were excited. He corrected our pronunciation eagerly and happily. Till the very minute when we left he was in high spirits.

The rain had long stopped but we did not notice it. Walking back to school along the street, we three talked a lot about him. He gained nothing in teaching us and sacrificed his Sunday mornings. What a broad mind he must have! From that day onward, we were always punctual, be there rain, snow or wind. Every Sunday morning Teacher Wu would take us to Bei Hai Park to the same tea table. Sunday mornings were spent like this right up until we entered the Peking Foreign Trade Institute.

In 1976 when I passed through Beijing on my way to Pakistan, I had the opportunity to visit The University of Economy and Trade, the new name of the Peking Foreign Trade Institute. I went to see Teacher Liu. Fortunately I saw Teacher Wu, too. He was already seventy-eight years of age. The teachers all called him Wu Lao (Lao means old) to show their respect. I told him I was Li Chun-ying. He nodded and told me he still remembered me, but from the expression on his face, I thought he had taken me for anyone he once taught. Teacher Wu was no longer teaching classes. He was no longer requested to be at the school every day. But he still came to the university punctually in the morning. He still toured the classrooms and corrected the pronunciation of the students. When we shook hands, again I was choked with emotion. His palm felt like the bark of an old pine tree. The dry cracked skin pricked my hand, but I did not wish to release the hold. The palm alone can tell us so much! His eyesight was very bad. His movements were already very slow, but to me he was still the same active Teacher Wu of 1959 to 1962. His life was spent in school. His heart was given to his students. Pronunciation, intonation, and fluency were the full contents of his life. He had dedicated his life to educating the young. He would, I was convinced, leave behind him a great heart, a great spirit, and a great model for generation after generation of teachers to learn from and to imitate.

The Adviser

Teacher Wang Ru-yang was in charge of our class. He was above average height, about one hundred and eighty centimetres. His hair was black and bountiful, though he was already in his fifties. His face was angular and stern. His eyebrows were thick and black. His eyes were large, full of lustre, pouring out wisdom but also betraying that his health was not really good by the dash of yellow in the white of his eye. His nose was like a falcon beak, rather European in appearance. His cheekbones were a bit high and his mouth very masculine. His fingers were long and his nails well trimmed.

Teacher Wang taught us geography, both domestic and international. He had four classes a week, two at a time. All his classes were arranged in the afternoons. It made no difference whether the classes were in the morning or in the afternoon, in winter, but it was rather difficult to lecture during summer afternoons. In summer it was compulsory for students to have afternoon naps. When we were attending his classes, we were still sleepy, yawning and languid.

Teacher Wang, the adviser, never criticised our lack of attention or demanded our full alertness. He never flared up with any student. He would arouse our interest in his own ways.

'Do you know why cattle from Xinjiang had no tails when they arrived at Shanghai?' he asked, very solemn, when he found all the students were half-asleep at the beginning of the class.

Nobody had ever heard that cattle from Xinjiang had no tails. All eyes were widely opened and all stares were fixed on his lips. All were eager to listen to him tell why.

'You know, it takes a whole week for the cattle train to arrive at Shanghai. The cattle supplier failed to provide enough hay for the cattle. As a result, the cattle munched each other's tails to satisfy their hunger.'

We all laughed heartily, though none of us believed the story. We were all fully awake now and alert to his lecture on the relation between a factory and its source of material supply. He used the joke metaphorically to explain the principles governing the disposition of factories and the source of the material supply. Even if our notes were incomplete, we did not get bad marks in the examination. Once we recollected his jokes, we would be able to recollect his entire lecture.

Once he was lecturing about Tibet. The students were not yet fully attentive to his lesson.

'When going to an area of minorities, be careful about their traditions, customs and habits,' he started. 'Take Tibet for instance. There is one tradition you must remember. When you are in Tibet to organise commodities for export, the people there will regard you as their special guest. If you have to pass the night there, the host will give you the highest honour. Do you know what it is?' he asked.

Nobody replied.

'Let me tell you. The host will request that his daughter keep you company for the night.'

Laughter and giggles broke out.

'Don't laugh,' he said. 'It is true! But the host will tie a red string with a special knot of his own to separate you and the daughter. In the morning, the host will check the string. If the string is intact and the knot untouched, you will be regarded as the most important and honourable guest of the house, but if the string is broken or if the knot is untied, you will have great trouble.'

'We can sleep on the floor,' somebody shouted out the solution.

'What if the girl purposely broke the string or untied the knot?' the teacher asked.

No one could reply. He continued his lecture till the two classes finished.

'What shall we do if we really have business in Tibet?' someone asked him after class.

'You will have to work that out for yourself!' Teacher Wang smiled and headed to his office.

Teacher Wang believed it was up to the teacher to attract the students' attention. He never took a book or notes to class. What he carried was only one or two pieces of chalk. All texts seemed already imprinted in his brain. He could, if necessary, repeat a whole text word for word. His eloquence made you think that he was talking about something written by himself. Only the red veins in the white of his eyes would betray his work during the night in preparation for his lectures.

Only once did I not review what he taught about a certain country in Africa. He gave us a surprise examination, which would not be recorded. I could not give the full answers to the questions and I thought I would get two marks. To my surprise, he gave me the full five marks. I went to see him.

'Teacher,' I said to him. 'You must be mistaken. You gave me five marks.'

'Yes I know I gave you five marks. This is what I lend to you. You will get fair full marks in the future, right?'

'Right,' I answered. I felt so ashamed of myself. I made sure that I had all my subjects well prepared so that I could receive full marks without the slightest blush. To me those five marks were more jarring to my conscience than receiving only two marks would have been!

Teacher Wang was a model teacher in Beijing. His salary was not low but nevertheless not quite sufficient to support his big family. He was a filial son, a considerate husband, and a loving father. Everyone in his family was well cared for by him.

More than thirty-five years have elapsed since I said goodbye to him. His smiles are still vivid in my mind's eye. His clear and inspiring voice is still sounding in my ears. I still miss him—indeed, I do.

chapter 18

PHYSICAL LABOUR

Mao wanted students to be patriotic, as well as technically and professionally adept. To achieve this he demanded they live, eat and participate in manual labour with peasants or workers. Consequently, regular physical labour each year formed part of the education we received from the senior high school. Through physical labour, it was expected that the students would develop the sentiments of the peasants and workers. Through physical labour, it was also expected that students would be fortified to guard against the influence of bourgeois ideas. Physical labour was considered the most effective means to make sure that our generation would not go astray from the socialist road and the country would not change 'colour'. We just took physical labour as a natural part of our school life.

Planting Sweet Potatoes

In the spring of 1960, our whole class went to a production team in the Incense Hill (Xiang Shan) to help with the planting of sweet potatoes and the spring sowing. We lived in a primary school, the students of which were on spring vacation to help spring sowing. Wheat stalks were spread along the back wall as well as the wall under the window. On top of the wheat stalks were reed mattresses—these were the beds for us boys in one classroom. There was a similar bedroom for girls in another classroom.

Our school cooks provided three meals a day for us. The warm water for washing our face had to be prepared by ourselves. Every morning, my friend, Zao, and I would get up two hours before our classmates to get water into the big cauldron and boil it with firewood, ready for us to drink or to mix with cold water to wash our faces. We did this because we were cadres of our class.

The field for our class to plant sweet potatoes was on the slope of a hill. Water had to be fetched from the well at the foot of the hill. We had to carry the water with buckets attached to shoulder poles. This was the job for all the male students as carrying water was the hardest work. The girls were securely covering the sweet potato vines into positions already watered.

Many of my male classmates complained about their bruised shoulders, but they were urged to finish the job. Two weeks later, when we had finished, we had all become stronger but our stomachs were 'bottomless'. Even the appetite of the girls greatly increased after the sweet potato planting. This turned out not to be a good thing when we entered Year Two.

In the first half of 1960, food for students was not yet a problem. After paying eight yuan and fifty cents for the monthly board, we could eat as much as we liked—no limit was set for each meal. This year, in my opinion, was not only vital for us to get healthy but it was also vital for us to get through the three-year famine when our stomachs constantly complained.

During the planting, there were always activities in the evenings after supper. These activities ranged from watching a movie to group discussions and lectures by old peasants on their poor life before Liberation and the change of life after Liberation. To make a good impression on the villagers, our class would set out in line.

One evening we went in line again to listen to a peasant speech in the village where the brigade was situated, about one-and-a-half kilometres from the village where we had our accommodation. The girls were giggling and walked like a flock of sheep. I had the procession stopped and demanded that they pay attention to the impression made on the peasants by our class. Some girls started crying. Our adviser, Wang, told me not to be too hard on them.

'Discipline and freedom,' there had to be one choice, and I told Teacher Wang so. 'If you think everyone should have freedom, then there's no need to walk in line. If you think we should have discipline, the girls should walk orderly in line.'

Teacher Wang did not make any decision and we proceeded to the speech of the peasant. On the way back to the school where we slept, it was so dark that there was no necessity for walking in line. I told my classmates not to scatter too widely for safety's sake. The girls forgave me for my strictness, being aware of my efforts to take care of them. Still I wished to find a compromise. Everybody was tired after the day's hard work. It would be unfair not to let anybody have a pleasant evening, discipline or not. I suggested that we could set out in small groups for such activities, like the peasants did when they went to a neighbouring village to watch a movie. We were in a hilly area. It would not be safe for anybody to walk alone, girls in particular. Everyone was happy about this. Actually only two groups were formed—the girls' group and the boys' group. Probably the girls thought it was better not to be too far away from the boys. If the need arose, the boys could help instantly. As a result, the girls' group stayed just a few paces apart from the boys' group. We boys became good friends and preferred staying together.

Compromise or flexibility was always the best choice in times of trouble. Such a compromise or flexibility might not be easy to find, but it surely could be found if one thought hard about it. A step forward, one might fall into an abyss. One step backward, there was safety. One step forward, two countries might engage in war. One step backward, there would be peace. Compromise was needed in everything.

Digging the Soil

It was the autumn of 1961 when we were instructed to take part in physical labour in a village called Wong Jun-tan, about twenty-five kilometres from Beijing, in its eastern suburbs. It was about thirty-five kilometres from our school.

The whole grade, about two hundred and twenty students in all, had to take part. Since we were just in the three years of famine, we were requested to get to Wong Jun-tan on foot in order to save costs and for exercise. Each student was given a quarter of a kilogram food coupon every day by the school as an extra to their own allowance from the very beginning to the end of soil digging in the village.

Four students were to set out ahead of the others, as a vanguard to join the cooks who would get there by truck with their utensils. The four would also be responsible to arrange with the village cadres to billet the students. Each room secured had to be marked clearly for which class and whether it was for girls or for boys and for how many. The four vanguard members of the school would also be responsible for getting warm water ready for all the students and teachers upon their arrival, both for drinking and washing. I was one of these vanguards because I was able to teach the other three how to fetch water from a well. The two cooks were introduced to us before our departure.

'Bring more food with you before departure,' the older cook told us. 'Come to the kitchen when you are ready to set out. We shall have food and water ready for you.' The cook was below average height, his complexion a darkish coffee-colour and he had pock-marks on his face.

His tone was very high when he spoke. He was just the type of man described by the saying, 'The dwarf-wife has the loudest voice'. (The general opinion being that short women tend to speak loudly.)

Preparation meant we had to bundle up our quilt, mattress, pillow, clothes, wash basin, towel, tooth powder or paste, toothbrush, soap, as well as our English textbook, like a soldier making his bedding roll. The total load of a bundle, excluding food and water, was about fifteen to twenty kilograms. We carried our bundles in the way a soldier carried his gear.

Before we left, we went to the kitchen and each of us, as promised, was given four *man tou*, some salted turnips, one egg which was special, and a bottle of water. The water bottle could be discarded when we finished the water. We set out at about seven o'clock after breakfast. The other three, much taller than me, started with long strides in high spirits.

'Friends, don't walk so fast,' I told them. 'If we go like this we shall be exhausted before we even get out of the city.'

'You take the lead and control our speed,' the three of them chorused.

The streets of Beijing were already busy. Bicycles flowed past us like racing water in a river after torrential rain. Most of the buses, each of which had a very huge gas-bag on top, like a turtle carrying its hard shell, moaned loudly past. Other buses, with a furnace boiler secured to the rear, which had timber or coal as fuel, smoked noisily as they passed. The petrol shortage was obvious, which deepened our hatred for the 'Soviet big brother'—Russia—who, the Chinese felt, had betrayed them by calling back their technical specialists (who had come to China to help in the Great Leap Forward), and by pressing China to pay various debts, which in part, caused the three-year famine.

'Nothing is light to carry for a long distance.' This Chinese saying proved to be true very soon. Before we were out of Beijing, one by one we began putting our hands underneath the cords hanging from our shoulders to alleviate the pain and the pressure of the bundle. The jokes and chats became less frequent, and finally, died out completely. The bedding roll became heavier on the back with each step forward. However, nobody wanted to be the first to suggest a rest—vanity forbade that. I also kept my mouth shut, for after a rest, the remaining journey would be more difficult. We should have rests but not too soon. None of us had a watch so we could only estimate the time by looking at the sun. I thought we had already walked about four hours. We might be about half way to the destination.

'The man is iron and the food is steel, he is hungry if he misses a meal.' How about having a break and having our lunch,' I suggested, quoting the peasant saying to lighten the spirits of everybody. All agreed instantly. We threw our bedding rolls under a big willow tree by the roadside and we threw our tired bodies on the ground. We attacked our *man tou* and water like hungry wolves. We then examined each other's shoulders to see whether anybody was really hurt.

Before resuming our 'long march', we secured our towels and clothing around the shoulder cords of the bundle to serve as padding. Our tired bodies were reluctant to move on but our determination told us we had to set out as quickly as possible. Our shoulders were burning with pain. We continued, despite the pain, in high spirits, our stomachs full and our legs stronger. We sang in chorus with our not very beautiful voices. We asked our way at a roadside tea inn and we branched off the highway as directed. When we passed through a village, my friends urged me to get some water and to ask how far we were from our destination.

We had a drink of cold water from the well and learned from the villagers that we were only about three or four kilometres from Wong Jun-tan. Like a refuelled engine, we resumed our way in still higher spirits. We arrived at the village within an hour and were directed by the villagers to the place where our two cooks had set up the school kitchen. Hot food was already awaiting us.

'You need to be strong,' the cooks said, 'so that the preparations are ready by the time all the students arrive. One of you is to organise the rooms and the other three have to fetch water from the well about fifty metres from our kitchen.' I was one of the water carriers, for I was the only one with the skill to get water from a well.

Three shoulder poles and three pairs of water buckets were borrowed. The well was very deep. The chain and hook and the shoulder pole were not long enough to reach the water. I had to borrow a piece of rope to connect the upper chain and hook of the shoulder pole so to increase the length of the device. It became difficult to swing it uniformly so that the bucket would fall open-end first into the water. A slight mistake and the bucket would come off the hook and sink to the bottom. (We did not use a long rope, because it was easy to lift the bucket out of the well with the pole.)

For the first day, a half-day to be accurate, I suggested that I get the water out of the well and the other two carry the buckets to the kitchen. They would have to learn how to get water from the well later. They agreed. I promised to teach them the next day when we had a bit of time to spare.

When the water vats and the cauldron were filled up with water, we were instructed to help the cooks make porridge and to boil water. When the porridge, *wo tou*, boiled water, cold water and accommodation arrangements were complete, the first group of students appeared not far from the village. They looked like defeated soldiers. We ran over to help. We carried their bedding rolls and helped them to find the rooms assigned to them. Eventually all the students arrived. Very soon they all came to the kitchen to get water to wash off the dust and sweat. All of them did this in the yard in front of the kitchen.

'Don't pour water in the yard,' the older cook shouted to the students. 'It will make the ground muddy!' The adviser to each class was reminded of this so as to warn the students.

Each class sent their representatives to fetch food from the kitchen. Fatigued as the students were, they were still very lively and supper was finished happily. Then a meeting, attended by the monitor and Youth League Secretary from each class and their respective adviser as well as the grade coordinator, was held with the production brigade leaders to assign jobs for each class. When the production brigade leaders finished, the cooks spoke. 'Three quarters of a kilo per head is not enough. Wild vegetables should be collected to mix up with the corn flour. Also, because water carrying is hard work and requires skill, we want Li and the other two to be the kitchen assistants.'

I was the monitor of class three, and I should have been with the students of our class, but everybody agreed that I should be in the kitchen as an assistant. It was also decided that the three assistants would sleep on the same *kang* as the two cooks.

The younger cook was strongly built, square-faced, and a bit above average height. He was from Shangdong Province and, like other people from there, he was straightforward, honest and considerate.

'Once we lie on the *kang*,' he told us, 'you three don't join our chat. Sleep as quickly as possible. Within five seconds our other cook will be sound asleep and he snores like thunder. I will try my best to keep him awake until you are asleep.'

Actually we did not need his warning, for before he finished talking, we were fast asleep. Though I was a light sleeper and was always very alert in my sleep, I had to be awaken by the cooks in the morning, because I was so tired by the walking from school to the village and by the water carrying after our arrival at the site—so were my two mates. It was still dark and we had to be quick to fetch enough water for cooking and for washing, all of which should be done before the students got up.

After breakfast, the students were assigned to pick wild vegetables and to dig the land set out by their respective jobs. We three water carriers did ours. First, I demonstrated to my mates how to get water up from the well. I placed my feet apart, stood firm on the stone slab around the opening of the well, and explained how to make the bucket, the pole, and the rope move as one. Then I told them only when the bucket bottom was pointing upward could they lower down the whole thing to get a bucket full of water. I told them that we could not afford to have the bucket off the hook. It would take too much time for us to get the bucket up again. To get enough water for our schoolmates to wash themselves, we would need more than two hours work.

Water for lunch was not a hard job. We could snatch an hour-long nap in the morning when the students were in the fields. As I was the monitor of our class and should spend some time with them in the field, I would join them.

The task for our class was to dig up the roots of reeds. The reed plot was muddy clay and the digging was exhausting. From my experience at working at the reservoir, I showed my classmates how to do the digging. Thereafter, work went on a bit more smoothly.

Each afternoon when the water carrying was finished, I would join my classmates for about one hour before coming back for supper with them. One day my friend, Jiang, whispered to me, 'Li, we are very hungry. All us boys are hungry! *Wo tou* with wild vegetables fills our stomachs but does not last long. We are hungry all the time. Can you do something?'

What could I do? I was not a magician. I could not make them food out of nothing. I knew that they were hungry. I suddenly recollected that when we went back for supper we would walk past a turnip plot. This was a special kind of turnip—crisp and sweet—which was used as fruit in winter.

'On our way back to the village, watch my right foot!' I told him. 'But only this time!' We were working without any remuneration. The peasants, as I understood, would not make a hue and cry even if they found one or two turnips missing, because they knew we were very hungry.

We were passing the turnip plot. It was already dark but not yet pitch black. I pressed one turnip sideways with my foot and walked along. I did this three times and stopped. Supper over, five or six boys came to the river not far behind the kitchen. They washed the three turnips clean and halved them with the knife I gave them and started to gulp them down.

'We can only do this once. If more turnips are missing, the peasants will complain and we shall be in trouble.' I told them.

'Drinking alcohol with a big bowl and eating a big lump of meat,' was the customary expression of the good life in Chinese classic novels. Only when one's stomach seemed bottomless could one fully understand why people dreamed of that.

'The food we have here cannot sustain us for long,' Jiang commented. 'After two hours work, we are so hungry that it is hard for us to lift the shovels.'

'I don't want you or me or anybody to get into trouble,' I insisted. 'I will try to save a piece of *wo tou* and if there's any left over after supper, I can steal or ask for some more.'

'Save from your mouth?' my friends chorused. 'You have the biggest stomach. That's why your allowance is thirty-seven catties and ours is just thirty catties a month. You work harder here than any of us. Can we watch you work with an empty stomach?'

'A pavilion by the waterside gets the moon first.' I quoted (meaning that a person gets benefit first from what he is doing.) 'Don't forget I am working in the kitchen and I will not go hungry!'

Whether our arguments were overheard by the cooks or not, the following day we had two *wo tou* left over after supper. I asked the cooks and was given them without difficulty. My friends were very happy to soothe their stomachs a little. However, they understood that help could be offered when they were really in need and not to relieve their hungry stomachs daily. The cooks did not have leftovers every day. Only on a couple of days was there one, or some pieces, which, it seemed, were saved from their own mouths. The faces of the cooks seemed most unsympathetic, but their hearts were very tender and loving.

Two weeks later we went back to school by truck. We had all become thinner but stronger. Our stomachs seemed much bigger. A complaining stomach sharpens the brain for study, in any case.

Working on the Farm of the Institute

It was the summer of 1962. The end-of-term examination had finished and I had achieved full marks for every subject. Notice was given to me that I was enrolled in class number one, number one faculty of English at the Peking Foreign Trade Institute. Most of my classmates were also admitted directly into the Institute.

'Chun-ying,' the coordinator came to tell me, 'the Institute has more than one hundred hectares of land in Wen Nan-wa. The land was given to the Institute to cultivate in order to alleviate the grain situation of the students. The land was called the base of grain of the Institute. Corn and sorghum have been sowed and are growing well, but they need weeding badly. You are appointed as the team leader to head forty students to go there to do the job. Your friend, Chao, from your class will go with you. Your deputy is from class two.' Then she added, 'The list of names will be given to you before departure.'

Chao and I took T-shirts, towels, toothbrushes, toothpastes and basins with us, and nothing else. We forgot the Chinese saying 'taking clothes with you even if it is hot; taking food with you even if you have had your meal already' and we nearly suffered because of it. We set out with the drivers of two trucks. The weather was fine and the morning sun made us drink frequent gulps of water from our water bottles. The first hundred and twenty kilometres from Beijing to Tianjin was a nice drive along the highway, which was lined with willow trees. The breeze created by the speedy truck was pleasant. We sang song after song, again soldier style.

Our first break was at the Western Railway Station of Tianjin. We jumped down from the trucks to stretch our limbs. Ice sticks (ice blocks) hawkers, all small boys, came to pester us immediately.

'Ice sticks!' they shouted around us.

We could not see any ice sticks. In Beijing the hawkers would push a cart, but here, no such cart was in sight.

'Where are your ice sticks?' Chao asked a boy.

'Here!' The boy shifted his bag from his side to his tummy, opened it and took out an ice stick. His bag was very much soiled. His hands and face were smeared with stains I could not recognise. All the hawker boys were similarly equipped and similar looking.

'Give me one!' Chao said to the boy.

'Ten cents,' the boy told him, fishing one ice stick out of the bag.

'Double price!' Chao exclaimed but paid him. 'It's getting soft,' he complained.

I looked at the boy and at the bag, which was definitely below health standards. Chao did not care. Nobody cared. If the ice sticks were of such bad health standard in Tianjin, sanitary conditions would surely be worse once we were out in the countryside. My throat was also burning with thirst. I called for one, too. Everybody bought an ice stick before we were called onto the trucks to continue our journey. Unfortunately, nobody thought of refilling our water bottles and very soon we suffered from thirst. Tianjin ice sticks became our topic for a long time during our journey until we badly needed to buy water to quench our thirst.

We drove along unpaved roads. The trucks bumped and shook forward like a ship battling the waves of the ocean, rolling and pitching forward. I felt my bones being shaken loose. Everybody complained. The water had long been finished—not one drop of water could be poured from anybody's water bottle. Our throats were terribly dry and our lips began to crack. The drivers, sharp-eyed like eagles, pulled alongside a shabby inn by the roadside. The cloud of dust which followed in the wake of the trucks now engulfed us.

'Do you sell tea here?' the drivers asked when the innkeeper came out of the inn.

'Tea?' the innkeeper, a shabbily clad man in his late twenties or early thirties, spoke to the drivers in sheer surprise. The inn was merely a two-room house made from reed mattresses with the outer surface plastered with a mixture of mud and chopped wheat stalks. There was an awning in front of its one-leaf door. The awning looked rickety. The tree branches he put on top of it to create shade were already dried and the shade underneath was insufficient to keep the user from the scorching sun.

'Yes, tea. Do you sell it?' the drivers asked again.

'Tea? I have heard the name but have never tasted it,' the innkeeper replied honestly and with a broad smile. 'I cannot even afford to sell cold water!'

The drivers had seen much of the world and thought the man was pressing for a better price. They squatted together with the innkeeper, offered him a cigarette and chatted with him. The innkeeper took the cigarette, looked at it, but did not wish to smoke it right away. He wedged it in the groove between his right ear and his head.

'We can pay you a bit more,' the drivers persisted.

'I know you are good men,' the innkeeper said to them. He stood up, walked into his room and came out with two big water jugs. 'Look, I do not have even one drop of water in the jugs.'

'Not even cold water?'

He hesitated. Then he said, 'I can sell a bit to you but I don't know whether you dare to drink it.'

'Dare to drink? We dare to drink anything!'

'Come with me to the well to see whether we can get enough for you,' the innkeeper acquiesced. He fetched two metal kettles from his room and said, 'Twenty cents per kettle of water.'

We all followed him to the well, which was merely a shallow pit dug in the lowest part of a riverbed. A small quantity of water was in it, on the surface of which mosquito-larvae were jumping and swimming actively. The water itself was brown.

'This is the water. It is just enough to keep my family and the inn going.' The innkeeper asked, without much interest. 'Want it?'

The water was repulsive to look at. What if we got parasites after drinking it? We hesitated.

'Do you know any place on the way to Wen-nan Wa that sells water?' the drivers asked.

'There is no place selling water, as far as I know,' the innkeeper replied. 'Don't hesitate. I am not keen to sell.'

Not a single cloud could be seen in the blue sky. The sun seemed to be shedding fire. The only water in the 'well' could be evaporated any minute. Our throats were 'on fire'. Hunger could be resisted but not thirst. Finally the manager of the school's General Service Department decided to buy two kettles of water. He himself was also thirsty.

The innkeeper did his best not to disturb the bottom silt. He skimmed the surface very carefully with a ladle. The two kettles were hardly full and no more water remained in the 'well'. Water could only ooze out during the night to provide the family with water for cooking the next morning. The water in the kettles looked as brown as mud.

Reluctance and fear could not match thirst. Bit by bit, everyone drank some, and in no time the water was finished.

We drove on. I felt very uneasy about my stomach and yet, thank god, nobody was sick because of the water. The road became more ragged, the sun became hotter and hotter and no trees could be seen on either side of the road, as far as the eyes could see. In the surrounding fields, luxurious plants soothed the eyes with their greenery, but we could not make out what plants they were. Wherever a cluster of trees could be seen there would be a village concealed underneath. The road cut every village right through the middle and strung them together like fruits coated with sugar and strung on sticks (called *tang hu-lu*), which were sold in winter in Beijing. The villages were far from each other and each was constructed on a very high dome of clay covered with trees. The clay domes were all man-made, each about thirty metres high or so. The road was up a slope of about thirty degrees or more into the village, it flattened out at the top for some sixty metres and then sloped down again thirty degrees on the other side.

Each village had about twenty houses. All were constructed on the top of the mound, which were only covered with trees. Trees were also grown around the houses, which explained why they were so well camouflaged and could not be seen from a distance. By the gate of every house were wooden boats upside down on the ground and covered with clay plasters to prevent them from being damaged by the scorching sun.

'Are you wondering why the villages are so high above the ground and why there are boats in front of each house?' the manager of our General Service Department asked us, breaking the silence.

'Why?' we responded.

'People in this area say, "If we have a harvest, we have too much grain to store. If we have a flood, we shall not come back home within ten years,"' he said. 'When there is a flood, the villages become tiny islands. The water surrounding the villages is like a vast sea. Boats become the only means of transport.'

We reached our destination at sunset. It was the Farm Administration Centre of the Peking Foreign Trade Institute. The Centre was in the very middle of a village. The Centre had a row of newly built red brick flat-roofed houses of about six to eight rooms, three of which were already occupied by those who were 'permanent dwellers' (long-term care-takers) at the Centre. A shed, which was not walled, served as the kitchen. Two huge cauldrons were rigged underneath the shed for cooking porridge and *man tou*. Two brand new tractors were lying by the gate of the big yard, which had high walls on all sides. A water cart, which was a normal cart with a huge metal barrel and well secured on it, was resting by the side of the kitchen. No dining table or chairs could be seen anywhere. The Centre was the most sturdy building of the village.

The rooms of the Centre were not enough to accommodate so many students. Some had to stay with the villagers. Chao and I were assigned to live in a room in the house of the Production Brigade Leader. He had five rooms, which were separated by the kitchen into east and west quarters. We were given the east quarters. A very long *kang* stretched from the kitchen wall right to the eastern sidewall of the house. The *kang* was covered with wheat kernels piled about a foot in thickness. The Brigade Leader cleared part of it for the two of us to sleep on.

'The *kang* is a bit too warm during the night,' he told us. 'I have to dry the wheat thoroughly.'

We had no idea how warm it would be. We thought if it became too hot, we could sleep on the roof.

We had a very nice supper that day and went to the house of the Brigade Leader. We checked where the toilet was and how the door was opened before we went to bed. The night turned out to be very cold and we had no quilt. From experience of summer nights in Beijing, we thought it was not necessary for us to bring our quilts with us. Thank goodness the *kang* was warm—really warm. Since the Brigade Leader kept it warm, we did not suffer from the cold, but if we had taken our quilts with us, the *kang* would have been too hot for us to sleep on.

The floor of our room was filled with gunnybags full of wheat. When going to the toilet during the night, we had to be very careful to zigzag around the bags. Clearly the Production Brigade had a good harvest of wheat and the Brigade Leader had not enough places to store the wheat allotted to him by the Brigade. This just proved our manager of the General Service Department was right when he told us 'if there is a good harvest in Wen-nan Wa, there is not enough space for storing the grain'. His family was small, just his wife, a son and himself. We seldom saw his family members. When we left for the Centre in the morning, he and his family were still asleep in bed. When we came back to the house in the evening, it was already very dark and he and his family were in bed. The village had no electricity, no radio and no recreational activities, so the villagers went to bed early.

Breakfast was excellent. The *man tou* was puffy, soft and resilient. The rice porridge was starchy and sticky and slippery and it seemed to slip down the throat by itself. No single rice grain could be detected in the porridge. We could eat as much as we liked—there was no limit. Food at the Administration Centre was free to us. Nothing could be better than this! The work could be hard but as long as we had enough food, we should grow well.

A room full of farming tools was opened for us. Each of us was asked to take a sickle and a hoe. The hoe was a must but why we were asked to take a sickle we could not understand. The manager of our General Service Department took us to the field belonging to our Institute. It was a very big stretch of land, on which corn and sorghum grew wild. Only then did I realise why we were asked to take a sickle each. Without cutting the stalks off, it would be too much for the hoe.

The soil was very soft under our feet. It felt as if we were walking on a manure heap. I wondered why the Institute wasted so much manure to make the plants grow wild. Then I realised that they did not apply any fertiliser to the fields at all. The dung heap effect came from the decaying leaves and plants. Fertiliser of any kind was not needed. The branches of the corn and the sorghum were much thicker than even the main stems of corn and sorghum grown in our fields in the village of Paradise Palace.

After the manager's instructions, we started to work immediately. We divided ourselves into three groups: the first consisted of two people responsible for clearing away some wild jute plants surrounding our field, digging two pits to bury our water containers, and tying the tops of the jute plants together to make a cover for the cleared space. The second and third groups were of equal numbers. The second group was responsible for cutting away all the unneeded stalks of sorghum and corn, leaving a space of eighty centimetres between one sorghum plant and the next. The third group was to use the hoe to weed and loosen the soil.

The sorghum and corn grew like bamboo shoots in the spring rain. Each day the work became more difficult than the previous one. We had to press on faster. There was not a single tree around as far as the eye could see. A straw hat seemed not enough to protect our heads. We cut grass to make our own 'hats', a grass ring with plenty of stalks and leaves spreading out to provide the shade. The sky was as blue as we could imagine and there was no breeze to cool us down. By mid-morning, the temperature would be above thirty-five to thirty-eight degrees centigrade. Sweat flowed down our faces and dripped onto the soil. Only then did I recall the Chinese poem:

'Among the plants under the noon sun we are weeding,
Down to the soil under the plants our sweat is dripping.
We know that the food in the plate we are eating,
Each and every grain is the result of hardworking.'

The temperature rose to forty degrees before noon. The sun scorched our backs, piercing our thin T-shirts like a burning iron. Evaporation from the soil steamed onto our faces, it was both stifling and choking. Our faces looked like red cloth.

We ran to the water container every now and then for a drink, for we felt if we did not drink enough water, we might be mummified by the sun and the heat. The water we drank was the best water we could find within a diameter of twenty kilometres. The water was a bit salty. Water from other wells was saline, like brine. Water in the containers dwindled very fast.

We had two breaks each day apart from lunch, one mid-morning and another mid-afternoon. We had cut off the jute plants to clear four or five spaces, about four or five square metres each, for the purpose of taking our breaks. The broad leaves of the jute tops were connected to give us shade from the sun. We longed for the breaks and at the same time we were afraid of them. We longed for them because the scorching sun hurt our backs, but once we stopped working we would feel the full force of the heat. Except under the awnings we made, we had nowhere else to get away from the sun. Under the awning, there was not a stir of air. The sun seemed to be piercing through the broad leaves to chase us. It was hot and enclosed. We could only use a jute leaf as a fan to get some air to cool us down, yet this exertion drew more sweat out of us. The breaks truly meant agony.

The broad, leafy, wild jute was everywhere. It surrounded our land like thick, impenetrable walls. It blocked any possible wind from reaching us. Unless one used a sickle to cut his way through, it was not possible for a person to enter the jute field at all. To me, wild jute, thick and tall, meant wealth. My uncle treated wild jute like treasure. He would immerse them in water until the outer skin decayed and then peeled off the pure white jute bark. He dried them and used them to make strong ropes. Here, if harvested, hundreds and thousands of tons of jute could be made. It meant a lot of money. It would mean much more income than clearing a small plot to grow wheat or sorghum or corn. I could not understand why people living here had not thought of it.

After the morning break the temperature would climb very steadily. We did not dare to stop working with our sickles and hoes. The movements of our limbs helped us survive the heat. Our T-shirts became wet, dry, wet and dry again. Except for wiping sweat from our eyes, we did not worry about sweat any longer.

Lunch, though needed by everybody, was a battle. *Man tou*, soup, and stir-fry dishes, were all burning hot to the fingertips, the lips and the tongue. As there were no trees to provide the shade, we could only have our lunch in the big room. We would pick up a *man tou* quickly, bite off a mouthful and throw it on the plate. The tongue wagged the food from one side of the mouth to the other and drew short quick breaths of air. Our T-shirts were taken off, as were our trousers—we only wore our underpants. Sweat trickled down the face, the neck, the breast and the stomach like countless rivers. Standing up, the bricks we had sat on as our stools were as wet as if they had been in the rain.

Here I remember a story from *The Journey to the West*. It is about Monkey buying date cakes close to the 'Mount of Flame':

'There came a young man with a red cart. He stopped at the gate of the house, where Monkey's brothers, teacher, and himself were staying, shouting, "Date cakes for sale!"

Monkey pulled a hair from his tail, blew on it, and turned the hair into a coin. He went to the young man to buy cakes. The young man uncovered the baskets and gave Monkey a few steaming cakes. Monkey took the cakes in his hands. They were as hot as burning charcoal, like a burning red nail in the blacksmith's forge. He shifted the cakes between his two hands, and exclaimed, "Hot! Hot! Hot! Impossible to eat!" The young man laughed, saying, "Don't come here if you are afraid of the heat. Here it is forever hot!"'

Our farm was not the 'Mount of Flame'. Still the above description about Monkey buying cakes could be used to describe the hot weather of this place. The ambient temperature was about forty-two degrees centigrade—it might have been more but not less. We had a nap for several hours in the afternoon, to sleep off the noon heat rather than to sleep off our fatigue. Yet we had no electric fan in the room. The reed mats were too hot for our bodies to lie on. Once we lay down, the mat would be soaked through within minutes and we would have heat pricks. Most of the students did not worry about the pricks and they slept in pools of water, which was the accumulation of their own sweat. But I could not lie down. I felt intense heat from inside the breast, trying to find an escape. I just sat on two bricks, nodding. Sweat 'like waterfalls' poured down my face and body. My head, which my mother called a 'steamer head', emitted steam upward like that from a steamer on the cooking cauldron. I could sleep in any posture.

The weather was unpredictable. One afternoon, after mid-afternoon to be exact, clouds appeared. A cool breeze came, soothing our bodies and making us comfortable. Soon the clouds became as black as ink. The breeze became strong gusts of wind, creating one wave upon another in the green sea of wild jute. The whole sky was covered with dark clouds in a very short time, threatening to make a downpour.

The Deputy Team Leader suggested we go back to the Centre, immediately. Many others supported him. Looking at the clouds, I suspected there might be hailstones. It would be bad to be caught halfway to the Centre by the hailstones. I told them about my worry but they insisted on going back. I stayed behind. Nearly half of the students stayed with me and we raced to the awnings we made with wild jute. The other half had hardly reached two hundred metres away, when hailstones, as big as soybeans, pelted down. They started running back towards us. It was fortunate they returned to the awnings, for, a moment later, larger hailstones, as big as dates, shot down, just as they entered the shelters.

The shelters were good enough to protect us from the hailstones but not sufficient to protect us from the rain. When there were no more hailstones, I simply went out of the shelter to get a free drenching. Many others did the same. The rain took away our heat and we felt much better. The rain lasted for about twenty minutes. Then the sun came out, shining brilliantly, hotter than before the rain. The land became very sticky and we could not do much even if we continued to work, so we returned to the Centre.

A month or so later, we had a healthy suntan and our muscles bulged from our upper arms. We were relieved from the job and were called back to the Institute when the new term was about to begin. I was very sorry to leave the village at Wen-nan Wa, where, to borrow the words about Xinjiang—we were 'clad in fur in the morning, wore silk at noon and had watermelon around the burning stove at night'. Our school farm had a good harvest that year.

chapter 19

HUNGER

Hunger was always my shadow from birth. Try as I did, I was not able to shake it off. Hunger, through Chinese written history, was always the shadow of the poor Chinese peasants. Try as they did, they were not able to shake it off. I pitied my stomach for it was seldom filled, especially during the first three years of the sixties, when a shortage of grain, meat, oil, and other daily necessities was evident. This was caused by drought and human follies in the Great Leap Forward, which had taken the peasants off their fields and into the factories. Hunger gripped the Chinese people—the word 'hunger' evoking dreadful memories of those difficult years. Many people died from starvation in the countryside. This period was officially termed, 'the period of three difficult years'.

One Year Full Stomach

In 1959, our monthly boarding fee for each student was eight yuan and fifty cents. Eight students dined around one square table, two on each side. The bowls, basins, ladles, chopsticks and spoons, were washed by students on duty after every meal and were stacked and placed on the tables, which were numbered for each class and for each group. Each group had a student on duty every day and the duty was rotated. The student on duty fetched the dishes—two with meat and one vegetable, as well as soup, rice and *man tou* for the group.

Baskets full of *man tou* and tubs of plain steamed rice were placed in the middle of the dining hall. Placed side by side with them were big wooden barrels of the starchy liquid from the cooked rice—this served as the soup. Those who wanted to eat more could get rice or *man tou* as they wanted. There was no quantity limit for a student at mealtime. He could eat as much as his stomach could hold, which suited me well. I had a very big stomach, which seemed to have no bottom. At breakfast, I usually had a bowl of porridge and three *man tou* (each *man tou* weighed about two ounces) while each of my male classmates, who were mostly from the city, ate only one *man tou* and one bowl of porridge. I ate five or six *man tou* at lunch and the same number at supper. I seldom ate rice because I thought rice could not sustain me until the next meal.

All the students ate the dishes with chopsticks from the common basins. Everybody was healthy at the time and we never argued who ate dishes too quickly or who ate more.

There were strict regulations to guard against wasting food. Anybody, who was found throwing food away, would be punished severely. The punishment was to put that on record, which was regarded as humiliation. To punish those who wasted food was fair and just in my eyes. In a peasant home, if a child dropped some food on the meal table without picking it up, he or she would receive a slap from his or her parents. Food wasting was regarded as a sin and could not be tolerated. There was a well-known story from our area about this:

There was a city called Guang Jing City—an imaginary city, perhaps. It was said that this city was at the centre of the triangle enclosed by the Paradise Palace, Wolf Dog village, and the Four Dogs village. There were altogether three hundred and sixty-five families in the city and they were all very rich. Each day one family would pay for the municipal professional opera to entertain the whole city. They had meat and wheat flour pancakes for all their meals. Even their dogs ate much better food than the villagers around.

At that time toilet paper was not in use yet. The city's families didn't want to hurt the buttocks of their children so they used pancakes to clean their children's buttocks and then threw them away to the dogs.

Guan Shih Yin, the Buddha of Mercy, heard about the behaviour of the people in this city and came to investigate. She disguised herself as an old woman begging for food. She went into the first home and was turned away. She went into the second home and the owner was cleaning the buttocks of a child who had just stood up from a stool. 'Sorry, I just cleaned the buttocks of my child and I have no more food available at the moment,' the owner said to her. She went from door to door and received similar treatment everywhere until she had visited all three hundred and sixty-five families. She met a beggar in the street and the beggar offered her some food, which was some discarded cakes.

Guan Shih Yin made a toy boat with sorghum stalks and gave it to the beggar. 'Remember this. When there is catastrophe, get into the boat for safety. You must not save any human beings from this city. You are only allowed to save the animals. If you save even one person from this city, the boat will sink and you will be perished,' she told the beggar.

The beggar put the boat beside him and dozed off for the rest of the day. After Guan Shih Yin left, a white snake, which was called 'the junior white dragon', crawled along the street and passed by him. The snake then circled round the whole city. Before long there was a sudden big bang like that of a thunderbolt, but more threatening, more menacing, and more ominous. Water sprang from the ground and the city sank. The beggar's toy boat became a sailing boat and the beggar got into it. He realised that the lady was a Buddha and he obeyed her instructions. He saved only the dogs, pigs, chickens and ducks, but not any people. The boat carried him and the animals to the safe ground. He looked back and found the whole city disappeared with its people. This was the punishment to those who wasted food.'

Old villagers in our area knew this story well.

In our table group we never wasted any food. 'I can only have another half *man tou*, who wants to share the other half?' a student would always ask before going to fetch a *man tou*. This was willingly done.

To my classmates, the food we had might be what they had daily at home, but I was having the Spring Festival every day compared to them. I was as happy as a lark. I had endless energy to level our sportsground,to do exercises, and to study. My slim body grew into the shape of a robust young man, weighing sixty-two kilograms. That year I had a full stomach everyday!

Famine

In 1960, the changes came. Our boarding fee was increased to ten yuan and fifty cents per month. We still ate in a group of eight students around a table but the quantity for each student was fixed. There was no more unlimited eating.

The effect was gradually felt. At first our stomachs were all right, although they were not completely full, but then, the food of each meal was finished so quickly and our eyes and stomachs were still hankering for more. If one *man tou* looked a bit larger than the others; it became an attraction. One student in our group, at each meal, would stretch out his arm, arching a big circle over the table, saying, 'Let me take this big one,' and he took the largest. Somebody should have the comparatively larger one, anyway, but courtesy and thoughtfulness to others were still regarded as good virtue. His behaviour was not welcome.

When we had our composition class in Chinese, one of my classmates wrote an essay to ridicule his behaviour. His name was not mentioned, but the description was so vivid that a live picture of the person was presented to the whole class in just a few sentences. The composition, as per the standard, was so well written that our teacher read it to the whole class as the best story. The whole class laughed merrily and heartily.

'What's the joke?' the teacher demanded. Then he realised that the composition was modelled on a student of the class. The teacher apologised and as a result, the student became very considerate to others.

Soon later, the boarding fee was increased by another two yuan, making a total of twelve yuan and fifty cents per month. We no longer ate in eight-person groups either and the food allowance was further fixed for each individual—mine was thirty-seven catties a month; the highest of all students because I was regarded as the biggest eater. At the beginning of each month, students bought food coupons, which were printed on green or pink paper, from the General Service Department. One colour was used to buy *wo tou* and the other to buy *man tou* (the proportions were forty per cent *wo tou*, forty per cent *man tou* and twenty per cent rice). A coloured coupon could represent one ounce, two ounces or four ounces. Once coupons were bought, I, like many others, would cut them into individual pieces, and pin a weekly supply together—1.1 catty per day), which meant three ounces for breakfast and four ounces for lunch and dinner. The remaining three to four catties were used as flexible coupons, which could be used when I felt particularly hungry after a certain meal or on special occasions when I went out with my friends.

We had a few dishes for choice. I bought only the cheapest dish, very rarely touching those of a mixture of meat and vegetables. I could not afford to buy them. I had to save money for buying secondhand books—English books of course.

Dishes with meat became less available and then disappeared completely. Each student was given a coupon per month to buy half a catty of pork. A coupon was also given to buy half a catty of snacks (*dian xin*) per month. These were all carefully planned to serve as a meal. In winter, our heating stove in the dormitory was put to good use. Chao and I would buy half a catty of pork and five-cent soy sauce one Sunday per month. We would coat the meat in the soy sauce and cook it in an enamelled metal dish on the stove, adding water until it was cooked and the sauce was reduced to a sticky, thick broth. One *man tou* with the meat would make a very nice supper. I forgot who started this, but everybody in our dormitory did the same with his meat allowance.

Occasionally, on a late evening, now and then, somebody would suggest to buy some snacks from Di-an Men Street, normally soup or soybean curd and cakes. I had no money but I had more coupons than everyone else so I contributed a coupon. Two students in our dormitory would take a basin and a bag and climb out over the high wall to go to Di-an Men Street. They would be exempted from using a coupon or paying money because they were getting the food. Some of us would wait for them under the wall to receive the soup basin and cake bag before they climbed back inside from the top of the wall. The signal was clapping your hands three times.

But our hunger went from bad to worse. We were constantly hungry and our stomachs complained from right after breakfast, through lunch and dinner and all through the night. We became weak in the limbs. We seemed to be cars without sufficient petrol. We wished to play table tennis and other sports but we panted so much after a short time that we stopped playing completely. All physical activities were drastically cut. In classes of physical education, parallel bars, horizontal bars, basketball and volleyball were all stopped and we were taught ballroom dancing instead. Our teacher would demonstrate the foot-works while he counted 'one, two, three, four, one, two, three, four', again and again. He was, without exception, hungry but he had to teach. Students practised after him or just sat on the ground watching. On Sundays, except when buying lunch and supper, we would lie in bed, reviewing our lessons or reading aloud our English texts to conserve energy.

To help the students, somebody invented the 'quantity increase method' of cooking. *Wo tou* was cooked twice to double its size. It looked much bigger than the normal size, and wobbled like pudding. The stomach would be full, but very soon we would be hungry again. Rice was also cooked twice as long to increase the quantity. It filled one's stomach but made one hungrier later.

Sometimes, Chinese cabbage near the root would be cooked as a dish. It was not thoroughly cleaned and plenty of sand was in the dish. It was sold for two cents per small plateful. We boys would queue to buy it, even though we knew it was of poor quality.

One day Chao and I went to visit a classmate who was sick. We passed a restaurant at the Drum Tower Street and saw it selling vermicelli budding for twenty cents a piece, with each piece weighing about a quarter of a kilo. We could only buy a piece of budding if we also bought a mug of wine, which was about a quarter of a litre and of very bad quality. We had never tasted wine before but the budding was very attractive. Our stomachs complained and cried for it. We could not move our legs even for another step without eating the budding. So each of us paid fifty cents for a mug of wine and twenty cents for a piece of budding.

The budding was offered to me on a piece of paper and the wine was in an enamelled mug. The budding trembled in my hands. Manners, in front of hunger, were not something I paid attention to. Simultaneously with Chao, I raised it to my mouth and in a twinkling of an eye, I swallowed the budding, like a tiger swallowing a grasshopper! I looked at Chao and he was looking at me at the same instant. A burning desire for more budding flowed in our eyes. But we were not allowed to buy for the second time!

We looked at our wine, hesitating what to do. If we threw it away, we were wasting money, but if we drank the wine, we were doing something we should not do. Finally we decided to drink the wine. We gulped it down just like we drank cold water. We left the restaurant within ten minutes.

Happily we headed towards the house of our classmate. A few minutes later, I felt my face was on fire and I could not control my legs. I looked at Chao and saw his face was as red as a piece of light coffee-coloured cloth.

'Your face is very red!' I told him in great surprise.

'Yours is the same,' he blurted, swaying a bit on his legs.

We laughed together without knowing why. We laughed all the way to the house of our classmate, attracting many stares from passers-by. Our classmate was flabbergasted to see us like this. We had headaches afterwards, which was the effect of the inferior wine and the punishment of tasting what we should not, as students.

One Sunday, when we just got our coupons for the month, three of my friends came to see me.

'Why don't we have full stomachs today and starve later?'

'A good idea,' I agreed. I did need a full stomach!

It was already noon and the restaurants were open. We four: Chao, Jiang, Ha and I went to the first restaurant in Drum Tower Street. The regulation of the restaurant was that one customer was allowed to buy four ounces of *man tou* or rice or pancake and one dish. This was the regulation in all restaurants at the time. Each of us had four ounces of *man tou* and one dish, costing thirty cents in total. Out of the first restaurant we immediately went into the second, ordering four ounces of pancake and one dish each. Then out of the second we entered the third, eating four ounces of rice with one dish. Then, we entered another. Altogether we ate in six restaurants along Di-an Men Street that day. When we finished, it was already four o'clock in the afternoon. We felt very happy, patting our stomachs contently as we returned to our dormitory. But our happiness did not last long. The following morning we were hungrier than ever. One bowl of porridge and one *wo tou* went into my stomach. But they seemed not enough to fill even one small part of it. We had to tighten our belts to endure the scathing hunger.

Hunger! When could we say goodbye to it?

All the peasants in the countryside were short of food. My mother told my father, who, at the time, was working in the commune as a carpet weaver for forty-five yuan a month, 'Don't come back home and don't give us money. You just make sure you can survive!' My mother said to me, 'You have a food allowance and you have study aid. It is difficult for you. But there is no problem for you to survive. Don't come home and don't worry about us. We shall try our best to survive.'

Why did my mother say that to my father? Because my father had a big stomach. He had to spend all his money buying flour of grass seeds at two yuan a catty, and even then he had to come home to get a bag of grass seed flour from my mother.

'Your mother supported the whole family with a sickle,' my father told me. 'Your brother Chun-ling and sister Chun-mei were still very small, crying for food every day. Whatever food she got, she gave to the two of them first, then to your brother Xiao Bao. She would have whatever was left. I would go back home to get food now and then. Without her, our whole family would not have survived! She was sick after the bad years.' (Chun-ling and Chun-mei were born just a few years before the national famine. I seldom went home and I did not know their birth dates. I knew very little about them.)

'Since then, I never reasoned right or wrong with your mother,' my father added.

It was only then, that I realised the full magnitude of the famine. My mother's words alarmed me greatly and I spent the money I saved from not eating to go back to see her and my brothers and sister. I got off the bus at the terminal opposite our junior high school. I went to see my teacher before going home. She treated me to meat pies—her own supper. She advised me not to go back home, but I did not listen to her and went home before dusk.

My mother, my brothers Xiao Bao and Chun-ling, and my sister Chun-mei, all were having their supper. The so-called supper was grilled elm tree leaves and a bowl of porridge. I got a bowl of elm tree leaves to eat at the strong protest from my mother.

'Don't touch it! You will be sick!'

But I would not listen. I wished to taste and remember the life at the time. I was in tears. I went to sleep at my Da Ma's house and while there I had a chat with her. 'This is no worse than our life during the Japanese occupation,' she said. 'The cadres must work harder than we do but they eat the same thing as we do! The Party members work harder and eat the same thing as we do! This is only temporary. We shall have a better life very soon.' This was the opinion of my Da Ma, of my mother and of most people in the village. There were no complaints, or at least I heard none. There was no pessimism. The trust of the Communist Party held by the villagers had not decreased in the least.

But life was extremely hard. For the four members of my family left in the Paradise Palace: my mother, my two brothers and my sister, there was only six kilograms of corn kernels for the whole month! (one ounce a day for each person) That was crushed and used for porridge only—the reason why I could count the cornmeals in the porridge!

Elm leaves were rarely available—all edible leaves were. The Production Brigade used lime to soften the wheat stalks for food and succeeded in getting some soybeans. They used the beans to make very thin milk (a little bit better than water) for the sick villagers.

My second brother, Xiao Bao (whose official name became Chun-ming when he started school) was in his mid-teens during this time and attending junior high school. My parents could not afford to have him and me both in school—one of us had to help my mother at home.

'Xiao Bao,' my mother said to him, 'either you or your elder brother have to quit school to help me.'

'My brother is in senior high school and he gets school assistance. He can continue study without support from our family. If one must stop schooling, I will.' Xiao Bao told her.

Xiao Bao had an excellent memory—he was always above average in his studies though he had not much time to review his lessons. He had to help my mother after school. I was very sad that he could not continue studying and when I heard he had quit school I argued with my mother to let him continue. She refused to listen to me.

Xiao Bao and my cousin Xiang would travel four kilometres from our village to dig the roots of rushes. When they carried the roots back, they were so hungry and weak that they had to lie down on the roadside every hundred metres or so to chew the roots to soothe their stomachs and regain strength. Rush roots and elm tree leaves were the main edible materials to tide families over during the famine years.

My third brother Chun-ling was still not big enough to accompany Xiao Bao to dig rush roots, and like most poor children, he had a big stomach. He was always hungry. Hunger made him catch rats and he and my Da Ma would eat them. They were the only two people who dared to eat the rats. They were the only persons not suffering from dropsy. Meat was better than grass roots.

Hunger made my sister Chun-mei afraid of porridge. She was just a toddler. Though my mother and brothers wanted to save something good for her, they had nothing much to save. They could only let her have more porridge, because it was the only food made of grain. She cried every day for food. When the famine was over, she disliked porridge so much that she never wanted to look at or touch it again. Hunger made many families eat separately and each member ate his or her own allowance. Hunger hung over the head of so many people.

There are a few stories I recall from the famine years. This first story, a true story, happened sometime after our boarding fee was increased to twelve yuan and fifty cents per month. One of our classmates wrote to Marshal Chen Yi to complain about the poor quality of our food. In his first letter he said that he wrote to Marshal Chen because he cared very much about the students' welfare. He told Marshal Chen that the food at school was not satisfactory for the fee paid. He received no reply from Marshal Chen so he wrote a second letter, saying that he had not had a reply and thought this was probably because Marshal Chen had not seen his first letter. If Marshal Chen had seen the letter, he would definitely send a reply. He then waited for a reasonable period of time for a reply. Again none came. The student wrote for a third time, and this time his tone was no longer polite. He said Marshal Chen's reputation of caring for the students was in name only. There was no action from him. He said he was very much disappointed that the idol of his heart was only existing in imagination but not in reality. He said that now he would never write to anybody again.

It was said that Marshal Chen randomly selected letters from the people to read. The third letter was among them. Marshal Chen was very much displeased with the tone and demanded the former two letters. After he read them, he remarked that they were well written and the student was justified to criticise him. He said that as the people's Deputy Premier, he should give the student a reply and solve what he reported. It was said that Marshal Chen wrote on the letters: Return to the Ministry of Foreign Trade for satisfactory solution.

One afternoon, many cars came to our Preparatory Course! We were all surprised. It was said that the presidents of the Institute, the Minister of Foreign Trade, cadres of different levels from the Ministry, came to our school for a meeting with a student! We never heard the details of the meeting but one thing we did notice afterwards was that our meals changed for the better. For a couple of months this was the case, but gradually they slipped back to the old quality again.

We were already in the middle of the national famine years.

Life had become hard for everybody. A hard life made some students divert their attention to getting money and food. They could no longer concentrate on study. My second true story is about this.

One day in our English class Teacher Han told us, 'Students, let me tell you something that should not happen. In your friendship class in the senior grade, one student has studied English for three years. Do you know what he can recite? He can only recite "This is my family, my father, mother, brother, and I." That is all he can do after three years' study!'

The boys laughed noisily and the girls giggled.

'I am not joking!' Teacher Han spoke again in earnest. 'I am telling you the truth. The school has already persuaded him to quit!'

An audible exclamation rolled over the classroom.

'That student was not good at studying English,' Teacher Han continued, 'but he is very good at speculation and profiteering! He knew the prices of almost everything on the black market. He could predict what price would go up in the next few days. He gets roosters or hens or eggs from the countryside to sell in Beijing, and he gets things from Beijing to sell in the countryside. He said the profit was good. He stayed away from class frequently—study, to him, is a sideline! The pity is that he is not sorry to quit school.'

Later, in our dormitory, we discussed this. Everybody thought it was not right to do this. In those years, speculation and profiteering was something to be looked down upon and despised. I could understand why he did what he did, but I could not understand why he did it at the sacrifice of his schooling. I understood him because I thought the survival of his whole family might depend on his speculation and profiteering; depend on whatever he could earn. But such activities were illegal and could not last. Studying hard would give him a stable future. He sacrificed a stable future for temporary illegal profits. Why did he act like that? Was he trying to fill his stomach? Was he trying to win a battle of life and death?

My third story is about how my friends offered me the happiest New Year meal in the worst famine.

It happened on the first day of the Spring Festival in 1961. I could not go back home to see my mother, my brothers and sister, not only because my mother had nothing for the Festival but also because I didn't have the money to pay for the bus fare.

I was still sleeping on the morning of the first day of Chinese Lunar New Year. I had not the mind to get up. I had no need to hurry to the dining room because there would be no queues waiting to buy breakfast—and it was cold. Nowhere else was better than lying in bed, beneath the quilt. I had no idea yet of how to pass the seemingly gloomy day ahead for me.

'Hey, lazy bones!' a loud voice awoke me. 'See what I have brought here for you!'

I turned on my stomach and looked up. Jiang was by my bed, lifting a stack of lunch boxes in front of my face. He opened up each lid for me to have a look—meatballs, dumplings, black bean pork, and several other dishes. A gloomy New Year's Day now became a pleasant one, not only because of the good food he brought me but also because of the fact that

I was cared for. I jumped out of bed, raced out to get some water to brush my teeth and wash my face. 'Thank you for coming to see me,' I said to him, 'but you should pass the day with your family.'

'Rubbish,' Jiang retorted me, 'I cannot let you have the New Year's Day alone here! I told my mother and she urged me to stay here with you.'

Happily we sat down to enjoy the New Year's Day breakfast. Then a loud noise came.

'Chun-ying,' the familiar voice of Chao sang into my ears. 'We come to spend New Year's Day with you!' Then I heard the voice of Ha.

We stood up to open the door. We all laughed so much and spread the food the others brought on the table of our dormitory—a table full of good things. We had the best New Year's Day breakfast when the whole nation was struggling in the calamity and difficulty brought by Nature and the mistakes of human beings. I had the best and happiest New Year's Day breakfast of my life, but I knew my happiness was rendered possible at the sacrifice of their family members. I knew they had asked everything from their mothers. Mothers would do anything to please their son and their son's friend.

After breakfast we did not go out for a movie or other entertainment. Two of my friends planned to make snacks for our lunch. They brought with them flour, oil, sugar, and the other necessary ingredients to make the snacks. The real purpose behind this, I knew, was to keep me busy so that I would forget my loneliness—and I really thanked them in my heart.

One was making *you bing*, the kind of food one could buy from any restaurant in Beijing for breakfast. It was a piece of flattened dough fired in oil. Residents in Beijing loved this food. The other was making *you su dian xin*. It was a special snack, which was sweet and crisp. It was expensive and hard to get in the shops during the famine years. The cooking range was our heating stove. The pan used was an enamelled metal plate. Two wash basins were thoroughly cleaned for dough making. One piece of wooden board brought by one of them was used for kneading the dough. One soy sauce bottle in our dormitory was used as the roller. One pencil-sharpening knife was used to cut the dough into shape.

We started cooking at ten-thirty in the morning, leaving ample time to make up any possible clumsiness in making the snacks. I was helping and watching carefully. The skill I learned from them turned out to be very useful later in my daily life.

The *you bing* was made first. Ha added water, salt, alum and soda ash into the flour and mixed and kneaded them into the dough. He then waited for the dough to mature ('waiting for the dough to wake up' was our expression). Chao also started to make the dough. He mixed water, two eggs, pork fat and sugar with flour, also leaving it to mature. Ha used an enamelled metal plate, which was about six inches in diameter, to heat up the oil on the stove. He then used the soy sauce bottle to roll a small piece of dough into a thin sheet. He cut a few slits on the sheet and then threw it into the boiling oil. It soon turned out to be a professional *you bing*. Each one of us tasted a mouthful. We could not find the difference between that and the kind you find in restaurants. If there was any difference, our own was better—much better! I was helping to turn them in the oil. We made quite a big pile of *you bing*, all light brown in colour and very tasty.

Chao started to shape the *you su dian xin*. He rolled small pieces of dough into thin sheets, applied oil and brown sugar, rolled them up, flattened them out again and did the whole process again. Then he shaped them into round and flat circles and used an enamelled metal plate to grill them over the stove. They were well browned, crisp, sweet and fragrant. The colour, the taste, the quality—everything—was better than those from the shop.

Jiang and I were astonished by their skills and by the food they made. We enjoyed the food and played cards for a couple of hours before they went home with a promise to come back the following day.

Alone in the dormitory, I could not calm down for a long time. I missed my family. I worried about my mother, my father, my brothers and sister. I did not know how their New Year's Day had passed. I wanted to cry, loudly. But I also felt very happy and proud to have so many good friends. During the worst time of the famine, they saved from their own mouth something good to comfort their friend, to please their friend and to cheer their friend.

chapter 20

CORRECTIONS

In senior high school, students have more energy than they need for study. It is the teachers' responsibility to provide them guidance, to stop them going astray, and to spur them to concentrate on their studies. I am thankful that my teacher did her duty to give me timely corrections and suitable guidance.

Nipped in the Bud

Frequent physical labour and always being hungry did not dampen my zest for study. My thirst for more and more knowledge could not be hampered. I spent more and more spare time in the library reading.

One morning, at the beginning of Year Two, Jiang invited me to read English on the bank of the 'Rear Sea'. Looking around us he was sure we were alone.

'Chun-ying,' he said to me. 'I have a suggestion. When I finish, tell me whether you agree.'

I nodded my consent.

'If we study hard,' he said, 'we can go in for the examination one year in advance. If we can pass the university entry examination, we can go to a Military Engineering Institute.'

The suggestion was very attractive to me, not only because I could graduate from the Military Engineering Institute one year earlier, but also because I could go and learn technology.

'Are you sure we can be enrolled?' I asked, feeling that there would be no problem for us to pass the entry exam.

'Of course, but there is no free admission,' he explained. 'The introduction of an army general is essential.'

I was silent, for I didn't even know a soldier in the army, let alone a general.

'Don't worry about that. I can get two generals to be your sponsors and introducers,' he promised. 'As long as you are confident you can pass the exam, the other problems are mine!'

'In my opinion, there should be no problem for us to pass the entry exam. I am confident of that. And if we are not a hundred per cent sure a month before the examination, we can get a tutor to coach us a bit. The trouble is, what shall we do if we fail?'

'Continue our study in the Preparatory Course,' he replied outright.

'Agreed!' I made up my mind. We kept our plan a secret as we didn't want to attract criticism from our classmates.

I planned carefully so that I could put every minute to full use. I had to. It was easy to say that I was confident I could finish all the subjects one year earlier and pass the exam, but it was not easy to finish all the homework, recite all the English texts and maintain full marks in every subject, while pushing ahead in my study for the exam. I needed more time. I tried hard to squeeze more in—even time sitting on the toilet was used to memorise formulas!

Even though I was not much brighter than my classmates, I never went astray from my target. I persevered. I had a whip hovering over my head all the time called hunger, and the wish to graduate early so that my economic status could be improved. Chinese, English, chemistry, physics and algebra all progressed well on schedule. I was, in every respect, ready for the exam as the time drew near. So was Jiang.

We were trying to get a certificate stating we had finished senior high school study and were qualified for the exam. Just then, our secret reached the ears of our coordinator. I was called to her office.

'Chun-ying,' she said, 'I have heard that you and Jiang are prepared to go for this year's entry exam for another university.' She raised her hand to stop my protest before she continued.

'Are you sure that you want to go to another university? Do you still remember what your Dean said at the school ceremony for new students? He said "people always talked about the bowl of iron, but in foreign trade ours are silver and gold bowls!" Foreign trade is a good profession. Our country is still young. The blockade and embargo imposed by the United States of America will disappear some day. More and more well-trained young people will be needed for the profession of foreign trade. The future is good and you will have the opportunity to see the world.' She stopped, giving me time to chew on these words.

'You are still young and immature. You do not know what is really good for you yet. Listen to me and give up that idea.'

It was not a clever idea to be on bad terms with a teacher. It would be worse to be on bad terms with the authority. The school could do anything to me. If the school refused to certify that I was fully qualified to go for the early entry exam, I would not be able to do it. If the school stopped paying for my board, I would not be able to continue my study. I was not the rebellious-type—this kind of thinking had never entered my head.

'If you think I should follow the normal course of study, I will do it,' I told the coordinator earnestly. I then told Jiang what had happened and what my decision was. He was surprised that our secret was discovered. He was also surprised at my decision. However, he, too, dropped the idea.

Though my first ambition was nipped in the bud, I never regretted it, as it put me on a better footing. I no longer needed to spend more time on subjects other than English. I began dedicating more time and effort to my English study.

Using My Authority

In 1961, I was nominated by the school authority to be one of the two deputy chairmen of the Students' Association of the Preparatory Course (the Chairman was from the Institute). It was a new and bigger role for me. I was not clear about the range of my responsibilities and my authority—I just knew I had to do my best in the interest of the students.

During those days, our school often held social dances on Saturday night and public holiday evenings. Cadres and workers from the nearby companies and factories would come to dance with the students in our dining hall. Sometimes a few riff-raff would also come. The good and the bad usually came mixed.

It was found that love letters were being passed between the male and female students. This was regarded as something unacceptable, because it would distract the students' concentration on their studies. Yet the school did not intend to stop the dance parties because it thought it important for students to learn how to dance in order to attend social gatherings once working overseas. In response a security team was set up to keep out undesirable people from the dances. I had rather feudal ideas back then and I was reluctant to learn dancing. As a result I joined the security team. At each dance party, four or five security team members, each with a huge baton, would be at the entrance of the dining hall before the start of the dance to make sure that no riff-raff were coming into the hall. After the start of the dance, we would tour the whole area, ready to kick out those guests whose behaviour was sub-standard. We had to memorise their faces so as not to allow them to come back again. The arrangement was effective—no one was expelled from the dance. The presence of the security team alone was enough to ward off those who harboured ill intentions.

Our school band was very upbeat—it was probably the best one in our area—but their musical instruments, which had no proper maintenance, needed repairs. The head of the band had applied to the General Service Department time and time again for repairs, but his application had been rejected each time. The school could not afford such costs. As soon as I was elected as the deputy chairman, the head of the band and some of the other band members came to see me. 'Chun-ying,' he said. 'You should promote the interest of the students.'

'Of course,' I replied. 'Tell me straight what you want to say to me.'

'Many of the musical instruments need repair. The saxophone, the oboe, the flutes...all need repair,' they chorused.

'Why don't you go to the manager of the General Service Department?' I asked.

'We did,' they said, 'but he just refused.'

I was silent, but they, who were all my classmates in the same year, started to urge me to do something.

'I have no money to give,' I said finally. 'And you all know that. Why do you come to me?'

They started to smile mysteriously and exchanged glances with one another. I became alert and suspicious.

'Don't be suspicious,' they said to me. 'We know you have no money but we also know you have the authority to endorse our invoice for the General Service Department to pay. With your signature we can go to the General Service Department to get the money. The cashier will pay.'

It was the first time in my life I realised that as long as somebody took the responsibility, others would dare to do something. But no one liked to take such responsibility for fear of getting the blame if something went wrong.

'You just write: "It is hereby approved that sixty yuan be paid to the school band for repairing the musical instruments. Invoices of such repairs will be presented by the school band," and you sign as the deputy chairman of the Students' Association. If we cannot get the money, it will be our fault.'

'You mean that I have such authority?' I asked.

'Yes,' they said seriously. 'It is worth using your authority this once in the interest of the students.'

I was still hesitating.

'Don't worry. You are new in this position. Later when the manager of the General Service Department blames you, you have an excuse. You can blame him for not letting you know all the rules, regulations and authority of a person in your position. You definitely will not get into trouble—at most, all he can say is that you must not do such a thing again. With the instruction you make in writing, the cashier in charge will pay immediately—it is not up to him to worry about whether you can authorise it or not. When the manager of the General Service Department finds out, the instruments will have already been repaired. The millet is cooked!'

My classmates could not have such reasoning and logic. I suspected they had an adviser or advisers behind them. Maybe the cashier himself taught them the idea because he was a dance enthusiast.

Here was a quandary—when one wanted to do something, he would be pushed here and there and he still could not solve it. If somebody simply decided a task should be done, it could be very simple or very difficult. The repair of the instruments proved it.

I wrote the instruction for sixty yuan to be spent on repairs and, sure enough, the band got the cash and had their instruments repaired. The total cost was fifty-four yuan. I handed the invoices and the balance to the General Service Department. The cashier who released the money looked at me and smiled.

'Chun-ying,' the manager of the Department called to me. 'Come over here please.'

I did.

'Do you know who you are, and do you know what authority you have?' he asked me.

'Of course I do. I am the deputy chairman of the Students' Association and I have to promote the students' welfare.'

'Why did you write the instruction for payment of the sixty yuan for repairing the instruments?'

'Why?' I prolonged my pronunciation to show my surprise. 'The repairs were badly needed. If they had not been repaired now, much more cost would have been incurred later. Without proper instruments, it is hard for the band to play in the evenings.'

'Your authority is merely to approve for thirty yuan the whole term!' he told me.

'Sorry, neither you nor anybody else told me this limit. I will only authorise thirty yuan next time,' I replied.

'There is no next time this term. You have spent everything,' he said.

'All right, I will not write any instructions during my term, okay?'

'Naughty!' he grunted and dismissed me.

The full band was waiting for me in the courtyard. They laughed out a welcome to me. They were happy and I was happy, too. I gained a useful experience from the band and from the reproach given by the manager of the General Service Department. I had done something for the students that could not be done and for the first time in my life I discovered that it was not easy to do something that should be done.

Lecture or Movie?

One day, in the first term of Year Two, an army Divisional Commissar was invited to our school to give us a speech on 'The Long March'. He was introduced by his family name of 'Shih'. He was a veteran who had come through the Long March from the very beginning to the very end. His speech was a part of the revolutionary education to students, which was to train students to adopt the spirit of the revolution in order to strengthen communist ideology. The training consisted of three parts—attending speeches given by veteran revolutionaries, doing manual labour in the countryside, and learning communist theories and philosophy. This way, students would be armed with communist doctrines and theories and understand the sentiments of the workers and peasants.

We had read about the Long March many times and we could even retell the story ourselves. In 1934, the Kuomintang Army encircled the Red Army's central revolutionary base for the fifth time. The Red Army failed to break this stronghold and abandoned the base to start a five thousand kilometre march for another base in north Shaanxi. This march was later called the Long March.

In the dining hall, where the speech was given, male students from our class sat clustered together and the girls sat nearby. When attending meetings like this, and when I knew what a speaker was going to tell us, I would have half of my mind going through my new English words or texts, and I would listen to the speaker with the other half of my mind. Somebody was tapping my elbow and I looked back. It was Jiang.

'A Hong Kong movie is playing,' he whispered to me. 'A ticket has been bought for you already.' He thrust a ticket into my hand.

'Anybody else?'

'All the boys.'

'Don't wait for me, you go, one by one.'

I hesitated. I was the monitor, so I should stay behind.

'I will wait for you at the Drum Tower Street,' he said as he left.

One by one, the boys from our class left, all on the excuse of going to the toilet. There was nothing new in the speech and finally I surrendered to the attraction of the movie. I left, also on the excuse of going to the toilet.

Seven or eight boys were waiting for me at the Drum Tower Street and together we headed for the cinema, which was about half a kilometre away. We were just in time for the start. The movie was *Pity on the Hearts of the Parents on Earth*. It was not very exciting. We left the cinema halfway through and returned to school. We entered the lecture/dining hall, one by one. The speech was still going and the Red Army had not yet reached Yenan. We sat till the end of the lecture.

'Where were you during the lecture yesterday afternoon?' the grade coordinator asked me the next day.

'Listening to the speech.'

'Speech by whom?'

'By Divisional Commissar Shih.'

'What about?'

'The Long March.'

I was asked to give some details and I gave them. I was dismissed without any criticism. The coordinator walked into our classroom with me and she motioned Jiang, the youngest in the class, to come to her, and they left. Jiang came back very soon. He came over to sit by me and said, 'You confessed first, what else can I do?'

'What?' I said, surprised. 'I did not confess anything. Tell me what happened.'

'I was asked where I had been yesterday and I said I was attending the lecture about the Long March. She said I was lying because you had already confessed. Then I was asked to give her all the names of those who went to the movie. Then she told me to tell you all that if this happened again, we would all be severely punished,' he said. 'Because you never lie, not even white lies, I thought you had confessed and told the whole truth,' he added.

I was then called to the coordinator's office and was warned in real earnest.

'You are the monitor. You should lead your classmates to behave, not to break the rules! You must change for the better, right from this moment!'

I admitted that I was wrong and that I would never do such a thing again.

The Fans

The twenty-sixth world table tennis championship was being held in Beijing. It was a big event—a very big event for table tennis fans—and almost every student could be regarded as a fan. Prior to the commencement of the championship, students were busy buying tickets. Some tried like crazy to get tickets.

A package for attending all the events, from the opening ceremony to the closing ceremony, cost about 46 yuan—a month's salary for an ordinary worker. Some of my classmates bought these ticket packages and Jiang was one of them. The students were clearly told by the school that they were allowed to go to the matches only in their spare time.

Table tennis became the main and only subject during our daily chat. Those who had been to the stadium to watch the matches would tell us about Zhuang Ze-dong, Li Fu-rong, Xu Yin-sheng, Rong Gua-tuan, and Zhang Xien-lin—the best table tennis players in China. They also told us about the Japanese and Hungarian players, whose names were translated in Chinese. We only knew this and not their names in their mother tongue.

I had no money to buy tickets and nowhere to listen to a radio or to watch television. I could only read the sports news from the papers and pick up the news from those who had watched with their own eyes. I, too, lived in excitement.

The students watching the matches often returned to school late. By then the students all lived in a lane full of grand mansions. It was said that in one of the mansions lived the deputy chairman of China, Tong Bi-wu, and in another lived the high-ranking official Kang Sheng. I knew very little about Kang Sheng—only at the start of the Great Cultural Revolution did I realise how powerful he was as the head of the Cultural Revolutionary Group of the Communist Central Committee. Sometimes when we walked past those mansions, their gates were momentarily open. We would take a hurried look through the gates. The yards were very beautiful, but whether Dong and Kang lived there, I never really knew. Our living quarter was a very big compound with a gate of two huge leaves lacquered in red.

The watchman's room was just by the gate. The watchman was a tall, slim, old man. His face was long but not very wrinkled. He seldom spoke, but if he did, he spoke slowly. His face was kind and did his job very seriously. Unless instructed by the school authority to leave the gate open for somebody, he would close the gate at night on the tick of ten.

There was a two-foot gap between the bottom of the gate and the ground. The watchman placed two long wooden planks, one on top of the other, to fill up the gap to prevent animals or people from creeping into the yard. If somebody called for the gate to be opened, he would only do so when he was told clearly the name, class and grade and the reason for being late. Good table tennis players from our school were fans of the Chinese table tennis team. One evening, quite a few of them came back to the school dormitory very late—long after closing time. All the lights in the compound were out and quietness reigned.

The students did not want to wake the watchman in the small hours of the morning, and they did not want to be reported to the coordinator about their late return. They were clever and had ways to get into the yard. They got a few bricks and propped the wooden boards up, leaving enough of a gap for them to creep into the yard. With their backs against the ground and their heads in first, two or three of them were already heads, hands and chests through the gap under the gate when the board came gently down on their chests. Creeping in or backing out became impossible. An electric torch flashed on their faces.

The old watchman was a light sleeper. He would wake up at the slightest noise. In his sleep he heard somebody working at the boards under the gate. His sense of responsibility made him jump out of bed to check what was happening. He was just in time to see a few heads popping through the gap under the gate. He removed the supporting bricks and lowered the board onto the chests of the boys.

'Who are you?' he questioned, squatting down with a notebook and pencil in his hand.

'We are students,' they replied. 'We are late and did not want to disturb your sleep.'

'Come to my room to write down your name, class and grade.' He lifted up the board and opened the gate. They all trooped into the watchman's room to give their details.

'Off you go,' the old man said, 'but don't make any noise.'

When the quarterfinal and the finals of the table tennis competition drew near, these students seemed to be spellbound. I was also spellbound. It would be a great pity to miss the finals, but I had no way to see the finals and was resigned to a quiet evening's study.

'Chun-ying,' my coordinator came and spoke to me. 'How about watching the finals?'

I jumped up, too excited to say anything.

'Come with me, my friend's house is nearby and there is a very large TV in the house.'

We hurried there and were just in time for the group final between the Chinese team and the Japanese team. There were only four people in front of the TV—an old lady, a boy, my coordinator and myself. That was the first time in my life I saw a TV set. The TV itself was already an excitement for me, let alone the matches. It was the first time I watched a world match and it was the first match I watched during this table tennis world championship. The twelve smash hits by Xu against a Japanese player made it hard for me to breathe. The match between Rong and the Japanese player made me close my eyes. The last winning point of the last match finished before I opened my eyes.

Air Force Recruitment

The air force wanted to recruit pilots. All the teenagers in our Preparatory Course volunteered—actually, every male student had to be checked physically to see whether he was up to standard, though the word 'volunteered' was used. Those who could not meet the physical requirements would not be allowed to join the airforce and those who met the physical requirements had to join.

We were taken to an air force hospital for thorough health check-ups. We all sat in the corridor waiting for our turns for our examination. My turn came. I entered a room where doctors and nurses were in white gowns and masks—the great majority were women below thirty, and young girls.

'Take off your clothes,' the doctor at the first desk ordered. 'Only leave on your underpants.'

I obeyed. The doctor used a rubber hammer to knock at my knees, my feet and my arms. I was then ordered to stand up and straighten my arms to move them up and down. The doctor at the second desk checked my pulse, my heart, my teeth and ears. At the third desk, my height and weight were checked.

'Take off your underpants,' I was ordered by a very young female doctor at the next desk. I was very embarrassed to have to expose my naked body in front of a young female.

'Take off your underpants!' she ordered sternly for the second time.

Off came the underpants. She stretched her arm to take my groin into her hand, felt it with a gentle pressure and squeezed. I felt my face burning and I dared not look at the doctor. So far, I had never let my naked body be seen by a young female, let alone be touched by female hands. I felt humiliated for quite some time after the check-up. Thereafter, my eyes, ears and nose were checked and finally I was X-rayed in a dark room.

'Come back for a check-up if you get the notice,' I was told. I then put on my clothes and went out into the corridor, waiting to be taken back to school. The majority of us failed the first check-up because of our eyes, nose or ears. Everyone was given a cup of water and ten minutes later asked to provide a urine sample for checking. Some failed this too. I failed because of my nose and ears. By the time we were ready to enter tertiary education, some of us had had another check-up, not for the air force but for the infantry. Two of my classmates were chosen and joined the artillery corps.

Ginger Soup

Labour Day, 1 May 1961, approached. One late afternoon I was told that I had to go with some other students to paint the site for the celebrations at Tiananmen Square. We gathered at the gate of our dining hall after individual study evening classes. A truck picked us up, about five or six students and the manager of the General Service Department. We took with us paint, brushes and our midnight snacks. The manager of our General Service Department had a blueprint in his hand instructing how to paint the marks and where we had to paint them. With a pot of paint in one hand and a brush in the other we painted the square cement slabs according to instructions of the blueprint. At about two o'clock in the morning, we were each given two *man tou* and a piece of salted turnip as midnight snacks and we could have tea from a big enamelled container.

It was getting chilly. Although we were wearing our padded jackets, we still felt the biting chill, which kept our fatigued bodies active. The job finished at about four or five o'clock and our eyelids became leaden. I dozed in the cold when the truck took us back to school. We were dropped at the gate of our dining hall, where steaming egg flower noodles were awaiting us. We were not given any quantity limit and ate as much as we could.

It was about six o'clock when I crept into bed with a comfortably full stomach, which I seldom had that year. I was so careful about making any noise so that I did not wake up my friends in the same room. I was instantly asleep as soon as my head touched the pillow.

The morning hustle of my classmates did not wake me. When I opened my eyes, it was already noon. The door was locked. I had to jump out through the window, which was not too high for me. Then I washed and went to the dining hall to buy my lunch and supper.

Shortly after, my classmates came back to the dormitory. Everybody was wet and their lips were blue. My friend Chao carried back a basin of ginger soup, which was boiled water with a pinch of brown sugar and chopped ginger, to chase out the chills. Everybody was drinking and I was offered one bowl of it, too. I had my supper with the soup.

'How lucky you are,' my friends shouted to me.

'I know it has been raining but why you were all so wet?' I asked.

'Why?' Chao said. 'We all went to welcome the arrival of the Burmese Premier. It was raining all the time and we were soaked through. We walked all the way there and all the way back.'

A few sneezed. Soon everybody was in bed and we talked and joked in bed. Chills could not dampen our spirits as long as we boys were together.

To welcome the arrival of foreign dignitaries became the task of the students who had to line Chang-an Street all the way to the National Guesthouse. There were quite a few advantages in having the students line the streets to welcome dignitaries from overseas—production would not be affected as workers could remain in the factories and only classes would be sacrificed with students; and it was easy to provide effective security, as it was our responsibility to see that no outsiders were in our area. Students all knew one another so it was easy to pick any strangers. When I was growing up, I realised that students were used for many purposes.

chapter 21

MY TERTIARY YEARS

The words 'most beloved people', in my opinion, can be used to describe teachers, professors and experts. Unselfishly and with heart, they tried their respective ways to pass their knowledge on to the students. I began my tertiary years at the Peking Foreign Trade Institute in 1962 and would remain there until 1967. My teachers and professors were the 'most beloved people'.

My Teacher

My wish to continue studying English at university was satisfied. I was assigned to class one, English Department. There were twenty students in our class—six girls and fourteen boys. When the bell rang for the first class, in came a man aged about fifty. He was of below average height, slim and dexterous. His hair was black with not a single grey hair. His hair was oiled and combed. He wore glasses and was clean-shaven. He was clad in a black Mao-style suit.

'Good morning everybody,' he began. 'Do you wish me to introduce myself in English or Chinese?' he commenced his first class directly, with challenge in his voice.

'English!' we said in chorus. We had all studied English for three years in the Preparatory Course and every student had full marks in the entry exam in English. It would be a shame to let the teacher do it in Chinese.

'Good,' the man said. He started talking in English immediately, about himself, about the target for the first term and about the methods in English study. He talked non-stop until the bell for the finish of class.

From his self-introduction I learnt his name was Ho Shih-hou. He was our English teacher and he lived in the Institute dormitory with his wife and family.

The first two classes each day were dedicated to English lessons. Teacher Ho came into the classroom, stood on the rostrum, and spoke right away without wasting a minute.

'Take out your pen and paper,' he said. Write down what I talked about in the first class, preferably word for word. At least all the points I spoke about should be written down completely.'

This took us all by surprise. This was what we Chinese call 'an embarrassment given as one alights from horseback'—meaning an embarrassment at the start. In other words this was to curb our vanity and conceitedness and to let us know who we were and where we stood. This was to warn us to study English hard. The quickest student finished writing within half an hour and the majority finished just before the bell rang.

He was quite pleased with the papers we wrote and based on those papers, he drafted his teaching plans for each individual student and each plan was updated whenever a particular student progressed or slipped back. He was the only teacher I met in all my school years who made teaching plans for each and every student in his class.

One day shortly after, a young teacher came into our classroom when we had afternoon classes of individual English study. He sat at the desk on the rostrum and began speaking to us.

'Comrade students,' he said. 'I am your tutor to help you with your English. If you have any questions please come and see me.'

Notebook in hand, quite a few boys trooped to him in a queue, asking questions. He took the notebook from the first student, opened it and checked the questions. He checked them silently and after a few minutes raised his head.

'Sorry, I am not able to answer those questions.' He handed the notebook back to the student. He took the notebook from the next student, checked the questions, returned it back to the student, and said that he was sorry for he was unable to answer the questions. Then he signalled for the third student and repeated what he did to the first and the second students. He stood up from his desk.

'Very sorry, I am not able to answer your questions,' he announced and left.

'Boys,' Teacher Ho said to us the following day in his English class. 'How great, how brave and how proud you boys must be!' he sneered. 'You scared your tutor away! Now come to me with your questions. Let's see how difficult they are. If you can also scare me off, I will be very proud of you.'

He glared at us, but behind his stern voice I detected a dash of pride. He was proud to teach such students. Because I sat at the first row and just in front of him he called me first.

'Li Chun-ying,' he said to me. 'Come and give me your notebook.'

I obeyed. He took out his fountain pen from his breast pocket, marked about half of the questions and raised his head to speak to me. 'You have learnt similar phrases and sentences. You should be able to solve them yourself through careful thinking. I will explain the rest to you.' He began to give me detailed answers. He knew from what novel I got which phrase, expression or sentence. He told me which book I had to give up because it was too difficult and which book I should continue reading. He promised to give me a list of books to read—actually he gave a list of books to the whole class to borrow from the library.

I admired him. How many novels he must have read! He knew from which book my questions were taken. What an excellent memory he must have! What diligence he must have exerted in his quest for knowledge! One by one he called forward the boys and one by one he answered the questions and made suggestions. When he had answered all the student's queries, his position had been established in our hearts. He had won the admiration, respect and trust of us all.

He was personally invited by the president of the Peking Foreign Trade Institute to teach at the Institute. His English handwriting was beautiful and he wrote quickly on the blackboard, with no difference from the samples printed in the textbook. His Chinese handwriting was also excellent, similar to that in the calligraphy book. He had been a good interpreter during the peace talks in Beijing between the Kuomintang and the Communist Party, with the United States of America acting as an intermediary. He skated beautifully and he played violin as well as a professional.

At about the middle of the first term, he gave each student a copy of *The Invisible Man* by H.G. Wells. This became our textbook for individual study and the material had to be learned and studied in our spare time. Every morning, Teacher Ho would read a few pages to the class and then explain any new words, phrases and sentences. He read to us with emotion, like a storyteller. Sometimes he would demonstrate the actions of the hero of the book with his fists and feet to show us how the 'invisible man' hit the detectives. We were all fascinated. We had to review what he read to us in class and we had to read the book in advance so that we knew where we should listen carefully and what questions to ask. Sometimes he would read two whole chapters within the two classes of English in the morning. We had more new words and phrases to memorise and we had more grammar to analyse. The words, phrases and idioms had to be committed to memory. When we were examined on our translation from English into Chinese and vice versa, it would be either from the novel or something similar to what we had learned from the novel. Teacher Ho told us to treat *The Invisible Man* with due care, but we could read other novels for entertainment.

'Don't worry about new words or phrases in your first reading,' he explained. 'Just read through to grasp the story for entertainment, then read carefully for the second time, and check any new words in the dictionary. By doing this, your understanding of the novel will be more accurate.'

The novel taught in class, the books we read in our spare time, our textbook, our homework and our other subjects kept us busy all the time.

My Professor

Professor Yu Ho-luan, a stately-looking, beautiful, elderly lady, became our English teacher during our third year. At first glance she looked like the deputy chairman of our country—Madam Song Qing-ling. Her hair was a mixture of black and grey, which she combed back into a beautiful bun in an old style. Not a single hair was loose or in disarray. Her face, unlike other ladies of her age, did not have many creases. She was not on the slim side but had a bearing of high status. Her back was always straight when she walked. Her features were so well spaced and arranged that she looked at the same time candid, bright, honest and stern. Professor Yu was educated in China and, it was said, had never been overseas. Her oral English was so excellent that she aroused jealousy from an American lady of her age, who taught English at our Institute. Once a competition was arranged between Professor Yu and the American lady. Both had to speak into a tape recorder about a given subject. When the tape recording finished, the tape would be replayed and the speech printed out to assess who used more words, phrases, idioms in the same length of time; whose fluency and intonation was perfect; whose words, when typewritten, made a good essay; whose language, when typewritten, was more logical; and whose choice of words was more accurate.

The topic was new to both of them. The recording was finished within forty-five minutes and the results were that Professor Yu spoke one-third more than the American lady; Professor Yu's fluency and intonation was immaculate while the American lady faltered and stumbled a lot; Professor Yu's speech was very logical; Professor Yu's speech, when typewritten, was an excellent essay; and Professor Yu's choice of words was more accurate.

The winner, therefore, was Professor Yu. After the competition, the American lady would never see Professor Yu. If Professor Yu taught at the Institute, the American lady would go to the Preparatory Course, or vice versa.

A couple of weeks after she became our English teacher, Professor Yu came into the classroom at the ringing of the bell for the first English class of the morning. She sat down on her chair on the platform.

'Now listen to me reading an article from the *Peking Review*. I will read it three times and three times only. You must not take notes. Just listen to me.'

She started reading, not too fast and not too slow—just clear, emotional and comfortable to the ears. She read exactly three times, no more and no less. She then opened her briefcase and pulled out eighteen brand new exercise books. She asked the first row of students to pass them one by one to the last row until every student had one. (By now two students had quit our class, one due to sickness and the other being sent overseas.)

'Now write down the whole article. This article has fifteen hundred words. Any five mistakes such as incorrect spelling, omission of words or phrases or sentences, grammatical errors, and so on, will have one mark taken off.' At that time our full marks were only five points!

A deep sigh came from the students and then everybody was busy writing down the article from memory. I can't remember whether anybody did not make a single mistake, but I do remember that about five or six boys got full marks. In other words, five or six boys made less than five mistakes and I was one of them. Nobody made more than ten mistakes. Professor Yu was very pleased with the result.

'To be a good interpreter, your memory must be trained. You must be able to memorise quickly and clearly. Practice of this kind will be had now and then.'

'Each one of you must give an English word,' she instructed the class one morning, 'any English word.'

'Poor,' one student said.

'Shoes,' the second student uttered.

'Landlord,' the third student offered.

Fifteen more words were given and all eighteen words were completely unrelated. Professor Yu took from her briefcase eighteen new exercise books and distributed one to each student.

'Now write a composition of one hundred and fifty to two hundred words. All eighteen words must be included in your composition.' She looked at her watch and ordered us to start. 'I will give you fifteen minutes.'

Again she was very pleased with the result.

'You two come forward to the platform,' Professor Yu motioned to some students in the first row. 'You act as a Chinese business girl,' she told the girl, 'and you act as the interpreter to turn the words into English,' she instructed the boy. Then she instructed them to swap. She requested two students at a time to practise on the platform. When we were all finished she would ask the whole class to comment on each pair.

'Now paraphrase those phrases and paragraphs,' she told us, pointing at the phrases and paragraphs she wrote on the blackboard. As usual, she distributed new exercise books. She liked all the students' writings to look neat and in good order. She therefore bought notebooks with her own money, ready for use any time during class.

This practice was very frequently done with the view of training our ability to get over whatever difficulties we encountered at our posts after graduation. Everything was conducted in the form of an exam. Each morning we would have a short examination before she started to explain the texts. As a result the word 'examination' lost its pressure on our mind. Examinations, whatever, was just something very ordinary to us. Professor Yu's targets were to train her students' memory; to train her students' ability to interpret; to train her students' ability to overcome any possible difficulties in their future work; and to improve her students' ability at reading, writing, speaking, listening and spelling.

Professor Yu could not tolerate any careless writing, though she herself wrote hurriedly and without much attention to her writing style. If any student's homework was a bit of a mess, she would give each one a new exercise book and demand everybody do the homework again! She required us to write the letters from A to Z repeatedly, with the view of improving our handwriting.

Professor Yu encouraged us to make steady and gradual progress but she disliked anybody who wanted to 'jump before being able to walk'. She always spent some time in the afternoon English classes with students discussing their compositions. Once I wrote an essay called 'On English Self-study'. She gave me four plus instead of five marks. She spent one afternoon class each day for a whole week commenting on the essay, with my classmates also involved. I learned quite a lot from those comments. She had so many inventive ways in her teaching, we always wondered 'what will it be this time?' But we liked her and enjoyed her classes. She liked us, too. 'I have been teaching all my life but I have never had students as good as you!' she told us.

Thirty-six years have elapsed since she stopped teaching me, but in my mind's eye I still see the exceptional Professor giving us examinations in English. The air of her characteristic superiority, her elegant and cultured manners, and her ever-present confidence, all are vivid to me.

My English Expert

In 1964, Professor Yu taught us texts, another Professor who was the Dean of the English Department, taught us newspapers and magazines, and a third professor was our tutor during the individual study classes, and, we were told, an expert would soon come from London to coach us in oral English.

One morning when Professor Yu was examining us, a young blonde woman came to our classroom. She had one foot inside and one foot outside the door. Professor Yu was standing on the platform. Normal greetings were exchanged between the two and then with a short introduction, Professor Yu handed the class to the young girl.

'She must have lived in London for many years!' she remarked and that was her first remark about Professor Yu. When she learned that Professor Yu had never set her foot on any overseas soil, she was flabbergasted.

She introduced herself as Ms Holden. She was as old as most of the students in our class. Her long hair spread over her shoulders, which could not be seen among the Chinese girls during those years, because it was regarded as not revolutionary unless it was plaited. Her milky coloured face was oval and her two large eyes had very long lashes. Her nose, a Western-looking nose, was straight and much larger than that of the Chinese girls. She was dressed in Chinese clothing—the kind of clothing for boys. She noticed the difference from the girls in our class but did not realise why at first. Her height was not much different from that of the girls.

When the Chinese embassy advertised that an expert was needed to teach English at the Peking Foreign Trade Institute, she applied for the job and got it. She came to China by train, via France and several other countries and finally through Soviet Siberia. She was not familiar with the time zones and missed the meal times almost every day. She entered China from Man-zhou Li, which was a Chinese border town, bought an excellent breakfast, lunch and supper and arrived in Beijing, her destination, on schedule.

She was surprised to see so many colourful flags and banners fluttering and the drums beating very loudly as she set her foot on the platform. She thought people were welcoming a visiting president or queen or some important people and she looked around.

'But it turned out they were welcoming me, like a queen!' she told us, still very much excited. In those years, foreigners coming to teach or to help Chinese industry or to trade with Chinese companies were regarded as foreign friends. 'Foreign friends' was not just an expression, it was the feeling of the nation at the time. There were only two expressions for foreigners—'foreign friends' and 'foreign enemies', though in the Chinese language we were not short of expressions. Those who behaved themselves and did their jobs well were friends and were treated with hospitality. Those who could not bridle their tongues or who did something really detrimental to the country were regarded as enemies or spies.

Ms Holden was well paid. Her yearly salary was as big as the salary for an ordinary Chinese worker over one hundred and twenty-five years, or what any Chinese Assistant Professor in our Institute would make in thirty-five years.

'Living in China is so cheap!' she exclaimed to us one day. She said her parents lived in Australia and she was planning to pay for them to visit China.

Ms Holden did not like to be different from the girls in our class. With the help of the girls she bought clothes from a department store to look just like a Chinese girl. If her nose was not so big and if her eyes were not so blue, she would have looked like a Chinese girl.

Her method of teaching was completely different from Teacher Ho and Professor Yu. She had four classes over two afternoons a week. She applied from the school authority to have all four classes in one afternoon so that she could be together with her students for one whole afternoon. She got the approval. In her 'afternoon', she would take the whole class to the Purple Bamboo Park, which took its name from the clusters of purple bamboo in it. The park was only about one kilometre from the Institute.

Ms Holden would talk to us in turn and encouraged us to discuss anything with her. She would correct us whenever a word was not properly used. She was trying to create an English speaking atmosphere in which we could be trained without realising that we were being taught.

'I met Premier Zhou En-lai,' she told us one day in our oral English class. 'He even stretched out his hand to shake mine!' she exclaimed excitedly. 'And he thanked me for helping China!' Then she added, 'This is the hand he shook! I did not want to wash it so that I could always feel his holding it.'

She seized every opportunity to come to our classroom, whether it was her lesson or not. She would only leave the Institute for her accommodation after our two evening classes. She disliked being taken to her place by car from the Institute—she preferred to go back by bike. While this embarrassed the school authority, to her, China was a safe place and it was hard for her to see that there were any bad elements.

Two students would accompany her as escorts. She stubbornly complained about this and insisted that she would ride home by herself. But the Institute dared not risk having her harmed, even if the possibility was very small. She rode home alone later, but two students kept her in sight at a distance, without her knowledge. Ms Holden later realised that it was a burden to the students for her to ride home and she stopped doing it.

Sometime in the year, somebody in our class suggested turning *Uncle Tom's Cabin* by Harriet Beecher Stowe into a play. Six students from the class did the job. Each one wrote one act and thus the novel was abridged into a six-act play. I was one of the six to write an act, though I did not have much talent.

Ms Holden was very much surprised by this. 'What? Year Three students are re-writing a novel into a play!' she exclaimed in our class. 'How proud I am of you students!'

She gave her help wholeheartedly in correcting the writing. She helped direct the performance of the class to put the play on for the whole Institute. Every student in the class would play a character or two in the play. I was to act as the auctioneer. I had never seen an auction and did not know what one was. She explained and explained until I thought I started to understand a bit.

Advertisements about the play were pasted up. The Foreign Language Institute was advised of this performance. Experts from overseas were also advised by Ms Holden to attend the performance. The big classroom was fully packed in the evening of the performance. Professors, experts, teachers and students were all there waiting for the performance to begin. When it was my turn on the stage, I presented a bold face. I was auctioning Tom.

'One dollar, two dollar, three dollar, four,
Five dollar, six dollar, seven dollar, more!
More?' I shouted.

'One dollar more!' somebody shouted from the audience.

'Five dollar!' another shout was heard from the audience.

'More? Going, going, gone!' I shouted, striking the table with a wooden hammer.

Actually I was shouting without thinking. I forgot the audience and I forgot the stage. When I should strike the floor with the whip, which was our skipping rope, I caught the leg of 'Eliza', bruising her leg so much that she protested to me vehemently after the performance. When leaving the stage, nerves turned my head so much that I forgot to greet the slave-owner 'Henry' for him to start his speech. After the performance, I could not recall how I performed my part on the stage, though teachers and students commented that I performed very well.

The performance was exceptionally successful. The well-known Professor, Wang Zuo Liang, from the Foreign Language Institute praised our performance and said our writing and their writing could complement each other. Ms Holden presented us with a big basket of flowers and in her speech praised her students. Professor Yu, in her speech, said she was proud of Ms Holden for helping to achieve all this.

The abridged play, perhaps, may still be in the library of the University of Economy and Trade (which is the present name of the Foreign Trade Institute). After the play, Ms Holden no longer used my name; she just called me 'auctioneer'.

When she found out that we had no English newspapers or magazines, she bought some copies of *The Times* and gave them to our class to read. The newspapers did not stay long in our classroom—they were taken away for fear, I suppose, that the students would be influenced by Western ideals. I wonder whether Western countries were afraid of their students being influenced by Chinese ideals.

During the dancing at Tiananmen Square in the evening 1 October 1964, Ms Holden came down from the observers' stand for special guests as she saw the flag of our Institute. She joined the students of her class, and danced and talked happily with us under a night sky of splendid fireworks. When she left, two men in plain clothes came to us.

'Do you know the lady who just left?' they questioned us.

'Of course!' we chorused.

'What was she doing here?' they demanded.

'Who are you?' we demanded in chorus. Their tone made us resentful.

'The public security personnel!' they answered haughtily.

'Who is she and what is she?' they requested.

'She is our English expert and she teaches us English at our Institute. She came here to dance with us, her students,' we told them curtly.

'Did she do anything improper?' they insisted.

'What do you mean? Is it improper for a teacher to dance and talk to her students?' we asked.

They left but not completely convinced. But, without a doubt, Ms Holden, though very young, was a good teacher and a great asset to our Institute.

The Guards of Honour

During the October celebrations in Tiananmen Square, students from our Institute would be the guards of honour to head the whole parade with girls escorting the gigantic flower baskets and boys carrying huge slogans to march in the first three rows. For this purpose, as soon as the term after the summer holidays started, a busy drill of goose-stepping (a style of marching) would begin in the afternoons and during physical education classes. The male students would have the drill in pairs, and then in groups. The professor of physical education would demonstrate how we should walk properly and explain the goose step in detail:

The instep of the foot should be rigid.

The legs should be very straight.

The sole of the foot should be twenty centimetres from the ground and parallel to it.

The forearm should swing to the second button from the top and be parallel to the ground.

The head should be upright.

The eyes should look straight ahead.
The foot should strike the ground hard.
The upper body should be straight and not swaying.

When the drilled student became tired, the role of drilling and ordering of the students would swap.

In the afternoons such drills were scattered everywhere on the sportsground. All the students being drilled were from lower grades. In physical education, the professor would drill the students together. We would march from one end of the sportsground to the other and then about turn and marched forward again. At the finish, our legs became so sore that we needed to sit down immediately for a rest.

When 1 October approached, the Professor, like an army general, would have the students lined up to drill the march in the same way as they would when marching past Tiananmen. The drilling hours became longer and happened every day. Did the drill interfere with the students' study? It did to a certain degree, but because it was regarded as a political task, nobody questioned it. Students were able to find ways to make up for the time lost.

During my years at the Institute, I had personal experience of the parade only once, in 1964.

Clad in white uniforms, we were taken by trucks to Chang-an Street in the very early morning. We were positioned about two or three hundred metres from the eastern ornamental column (Dong Hua-biao) of Tiananmen Square. I was in the third row, which had altogether one hundred and ten students in its length. Six groups of girls were in front escorting the flower baskets. Girls from our Institute were flanking the three baskets on the Great Hall side.

It was cold and sitting on the asphalt surface of the wide street, we chatted and joked, and our teeth clattered. Steamed triangles (a wheat dough wrapping with brown sugar) and *man tou* and cold meat were distributed to us. We ate them immediately, but after regretted it, as we did not expect to be so hungry when walking the fifteen kilometres all the way back to our Institute.

We were to begin our march from outside the Ministry of Foreign Trade, to which, in all probability we would be assigned as interpreters after graduation. Its grey brick building did not have the magnificent and majestic façade I imagined it should have. Behind the walls and inside the building, to me at least, were things sacred, important and challenging.

It was the first time that I was in the parade and I was one of the guards of honour to march in Tiananmen and to be watched by Chairman Mao from the top of the Square. I decided to have a good look at him when we marched past and to salute him, of course failing to consider the distance between him and us marching along Chang-an Street.

The eastern sky gradually paled like a fish belly and the sun began to rise. Everything was brilliant now in the morning light. To the west at the very front of the procession, the national flag, which was surrounded by square formations of girls in beautiful white shirts and pink skirts, was fluttering in the morning breeze. Behind the flag and girls were three large flower baskets resting on timber frames which many male students in white uniforms would carry in the parade. They were so beautiful and colourful that I could not tear my eyes away from them. Still further to the west, Tiananmen Square was already fully packed with students, who, while holding different, colourful, artificial flowers in their hands, would raise them at a signal on a lamp post, to display patterns of different kinds. All the students were from the country's junior and senior high schools as well as from colleges and universities in Beijing, and were dressed in holiday costumes.

To our right and in our row, huge frames holding gigantic '1949 to 1964' signs (indicating communist China was already fifteen years old) were resting among the students, who would carry it through Tiananmen Square. From there to the east were huge slogans such as 'Long live Chairman Mao', 'Long live the Communist Party', 'Long live the great proletarian dictatorship', 'Long live the unity of various nationalities of China', and so on. All the slogans stretched from one side of Chang-an Street to the other. The slogans were carried by hundreds of students. Still further to the east were processions demonstrating the achievements of the country during the past fifteen years on all fronts. After them were the demonstrations of the workers, peasants and the masses, which I could not see clearly from our position.

At about ten o'clock, we were advised to get ready. The flag, the baskets and the slogans were raised up onto the shoulders. We lined up straight from the northern side of the street to the southern side of the street without the slightest curve.

'Now the parade begins!' somebody announced through the megaphone and this song came from the loudspeakers:

'In the breeze, the Five Star red flag is fluttering.
The song of victory is loud and clear.
About our great motherland we are singing,
She gets stronger and more prosperous from now.'

The music was filling the air, setting the speed of our forward marching steps. Our ranks started to move. The national flag fluttered further and further towards Tiananmen. The flower baskets moved forward with the escort of the girls, whose skirts swayed beautifully to the movements of their forward march. We started—one hundred and ten white legs lifted forward as one, all in line and all at the same distance from the ground. Our left arms swung backward and our right arms swung forward uniformly. The sound of our feet thumping the ground sounded louder than thunder—rhythmical and encouraging—eighty centimetres per step forward, we progressed to the pace the blaring music.

'How are you comrades?' Chairman Mao shouted from the rostrum of Tiananmen.

'Long live Chairman Mao!' we shouted back in unison. We did not shout the whole sentence—even numbers shouted 'Long live' and odd numbers shouted, 'Chairman Mao!' Because so many students shouted simultaneously to the music, it sounded like a continuous shouting of one voice.

'How are you comrades?' Mao shouted to the demonstrators again. I heard the words clearly. Those are the words uttered by the person who made it possible for me to have an education! Emotion filled my breast. I wanted to shout 'Long live Chairman Mao!' louder for him to hear. I was shouting, not only on my own behalf, but also on behalf of my parents, brothers and sister, to express our thanks.

When we were abreast of the entry gate to Tiananmen Square, all heads turned right and shouted 'Long live Chairman Mao!' At that instant I tried to make a longer stride so that I could get a glimpse of Chairman Mao, but the people on the rostrum of Tiananmen were merely tiny spots and I could not see him. I could only guess that the tiny spot in the middle was Chairman Mao. Our end of the line curved a bit forward, because, I was pretty sure, others also wanted to catch a glimpse of Chairman Mao. After months of practising goose-stepping, our row had a slight curve, both ends a bit more forward than the middle section, like that of a slight long swell of the sea.

Tiananmen receded and we continued without even an instant's delay. When abreast of the western alley of the Great Hall of the People, ten students from each row branched off as the street ahead was not wide enough for the whole row of students. The parade was over as far as those branched off through the alley were concerned. There was no bus, nor any other kind of transportation. I had to go westward parallel to Chang-an Street till I could cross it to the other side and walk all the way back to our Institute. The same thing would happen the following year. Whether our grade would still be required to march as the guards of honour, I did not know but I hoped that we would not be required to do it again.

chapter 22

THE SOCIALIST EDUCATION MOVEMENT

A party is doomed to corruption unless it keeps on cleansing its ranks conscientiously. A government is doomed to corruption unless it keeps on cleansing itself conscientiously. Mao wanted the Communist Party free of corruption. He wanted his government to be free of corruption. He wanted his cadres at various levels to be forever the servants of the people. He wanted the peasants to progress firmly along the road of collective farming and so he tried his best to cleanse the ranks of the cadres in the countryside. The Socialist Education Movement was such a cleansing action, which involved restoring ideological purity, instilling revolutionary fervor into the Party and intensifying class struggle. But opposition arose from the moderates represented by Liu Shaoqi and Deng Xiaoping who were unsympathetic to Mao's policies. To counteract this, Mao paired the Socialist Education Movement with another campaign for the people to learn from the People's Liberation Army (PLA). Mao introduced reforms on the school system, in the form of a work-study program, where classes were held around the work schedule of the communes and factories. Its purpose was to provide cheap mass education and for intellectuals and scholars to participate in manual labour, so they would to turn away from bourgeois influences. The movement did not achieve what Mao intended and so he started the Great Cultural Revolution.

Communications from the Countryside

In the early sixties, a great debate arose among the various Communist parties around the world. The Chinese Communist Party put forward, in succession, nine editorials dwelling on the doctrines and principles of Marxism and Leninism. One after another, each Communist party degenerated into revisionist parties. Mao worried that some day the same might happen in China. Consequently, he wanted the students to be educated in such a way that they would remain 'red' and 'expert'. For this purpose, he requested that all students, after their graduation, go to the countryside or the factories for one year to live, eat and work with the peasants or workers. He wanted them to understand the peasants and workers—to understand their worries and their joys.

Meanwhile there was a tendency in the countryside to go 'private', that is, the cadres give land back to the peasants and let them manage it their own way. Some cadres in the countryside were corrupt and China was at a crossroad of keeping the red colour or becoming revisionist. (Actually Mao knew the idea of going 'private' existed in the Party's Central Committee.) Many cadres were infringing the rights of peasants, embezzling public funds, raping girls and promoting private farming. Consequently, with the arrival of the students into the countryside as part of the Socialist Education Movement, the 'Four Clear Ups' began, which encouraged students to clear up the politics, economy, organisation and thinking of the villages. For the sake of continuing collective farming, Mao advocated the 'Four Clear Ups'.

In 1964, all the third year students of the Peking Foreign Trade Institute were sent to the countryside to take part in the Socialist Education Movement. They were sent to Shaanxi Province, and among them were some of my friends. When northern China was in the depth of a severe winter, my friend, Chao, wrote to me saying that the villagers were very poor, so much so that teenage girls could not venture into the village street because they had no winter trousers. In some families there was only one pair of winter trousers. Whoever went out wore the trousers. When he did the 'visiting the poor and the desolate' in the evenings, he had to sit on the *kang* with the whole family, old and young, male and female. Everybody would stretch his or her legs on the *kang* and a quilt would be spread over the legs to keep everybody warm. There were no dishes except salted vegetables to go with their three meals (the Chinese meal has two components—the dish and the staples. For example, *wo tou*, *man tou* and plain rice are the staples. For people who could not afford stir-fry dishes to accompany their staple food, they had salted vegetables). It was forbidden, Chao said, for any student from our Institute to go into a restaurant to have a better meal, or to ask their parents to post biscuits or good food of any kind, for fear that would generate bad opinion about the students among the peasants. The only opportunity, for Chao, or for anyone else to taste something better, was when he or she was on a business tour in Xian, where he or she could order some '*mo* in mutton soup' (*mo* is the local name for a kind of bread, which is two centimetres thick and twenty centimetres in diameter. It looks similar to an English muffin). 'I never imagined peasants could be that poor,' Chao told me when he returned to the Institute, 'and it is already fifteen years after the Liberation!'

'Why is it that the peasants remain so poor?' I asked him.

'The cadres!' he said. 'The peasants said "Mao's doctrines are good, but the local cadres did not recite them well".'

'Some of the cadres are really bad. They eat wantonly from the funds accumulated by the brigade for further production. They ill-treat the peasants, worse than the village council during the Kuomintang regime. They must be punished, otherwise the colour of the countryside will soon change.'

Then I received a letter from my other friend, Quan, who was my classmate in junior high school. He was studying at the Hebei Beijing Teachers' Institute. He and his classmates were sent to Yong Nian County in Hebei Province, to take part in the Socialist Education Movement. He wrote to me that he and his classmates had to pay visits to poor peasants' families in secret, otherwise nobody would dare to tell them anything. He said that the villages were under 'white terror'—the cadres of the production teams were worse than the bad village heads had been before Liberation. They feasted frequently by spending the revenue income of the production brigade. He said that one production brigade leader raped girls, had sex with a widow, and possessed the wife of a peasant as his own...and that the peasants dared not complain. My friend said that some of the villagers wrote to the cadres at higher levels to report the bad things in the village. Consequently that brigade leader arranged to have those peasants tortured after he learned from the senior cadre above him about the letter. They were referred to as 'local kings' in the villages.

'Those villages are not under the socialist system. They are under the "white reign"! The Socialist Education Movement is absolutely necessary!' was his conclusion.

Then one day, we were organised by the school authority to visit an exhibition called the 'Achievements of the Socialist Education Movement in the Countryside' held in the Forbidden City (a walled part of Beijing consisting of a group of palaces, shrines and halls occupied by former Chinese emperors). The exhibition had statistics, written reports and documents exposing the bad things committed by the cadres of the production brigades or the production teams from various places. They were 'shocking at a glance'! In Yong Nian County, a man declared himself a king to the peasants. He had many wives by forcing girls to marry him and he treated the villagers like slaves. He had a small handful of stooges to keep watch, who later reported to the higher levels of his activities to expose him. Villagers lived under constant terror. Yong Nian County was so near to Beijing that it seemed amazing that such a thing happened. What would it be like without this Socialist Movement?

Then I went to see my parents.

'Chun-ying, what shall we do?' A few neighbours asked when they came to see me.

'What about?' I replied.

'Six thousand kilograms of rice disappeared from the storeroom! We know the cadres of the brigade stole it. We six poor peasants reported this to the county. Do you know what happened? The county sent some cadres to our brigade to investigate. The brigade cadres treated them with a banquet and they returned to the county. We reported the theft again, and once more cadres were sent to investigate the brigade. Nothing has been done about it so far.'

'How many cadres have become crooked?' I asked.

'Just a few,' one said. 'But most dine frequently in the name of entertaining cadres from the upper levels or in the name of entertaining sales people on business here. They have spent all the funds of the brigade! Our year's payment becomes less and less.'

So, I thought to myself, the Socialist Education Movement in the countryside was necessary because the bad cadres had to be punished and replaced so that the peasants could have a better life.

The Skin and Fur Processing Factory

In 1965, our whole grade, at the beginning of the first term of Year Four, was sent to Tianjin to take part in the Socialist Education Movement, which, by then, was called the Four Clear Ups. My class was sent to the skin and fur processing factory in Tianjin as part of this campaign. Mao had turned his attention from the countryside to the cities, and ordered students to work in urban enterprises and factories to continue the Four Clear Ups there. We were the first to do the Four Clear Ups in the city. I supervised workers to have group discussions, I read documents to them and I listened to their confessions and reports. I never asked myself whether it was necessary to do this in the factories or companies, for it was unthinkable to query a decision of Mao. To me, whatever he decided was correct and should be done. I was worried about my studies, but I could only worry in my mind without telling anybody.

The skin and fur processing factory was situated by the New Crescent River, in the eastern suburbs of Tianjin. The factory was surrounded by paddy fields and had no neighbours. Over the railway and down the slope, the short-cut to the factory zigzagged through the paddies with two right angle corners. The path was only about one metre wide and when careless, one might ride his bike into the paddy. I did this quite a few times, not only because I was careless, but because I was learning to ride a bike.

The factory was fairly large—at least it was in my eyes. It had about fifteen hundred workers and staff, and seven or eight workshops, each having its own office building and management. The head office alone was as big as a single factory or company, having all the necessary offices, such as a general manager's office, an accounting department, a personnel department, a security department, Party and Youth League offices, a Union office, a militia office, and so on. The environment of the factory was not bad, though it was on fairly alkaline ground. But it constantly had the bad smell from the raw sheepskins, cat skins and skins of other animals. The smell was everywhere and it stuck to one's clothing. However, 'when one stays too long in a room of iris, he fails to catch the fragrance. When one stays too long in the fish market, he fails to catch the stench.' After a few weeks, we were, or at least I was, no longer conscious of the presence of the peculiar stench.

The eighteen students of our class were divided into a few groups to join the work in different workshops or in the head office. When we arrived, the Service Department of the factory, judging by the name on my luggage, thought, as other careless people had, that I was a girl, and sent it to the girls' quarters. This made me very embarrassed.

One of my classmates and I were assigned to the group taking part in the work of the seventh workshop, the workshop of finished products. We had five members in our group with the group leader being a high-ranking manager from an Import and Export Corporation. The group leader was a guerrilla before Liberation. He was an educated man, about fifty years old and his square face was always well shaven. He spoke in a low and kind voice and he never flared up, a quality pertaining to high-ranking managers.

The group stayed in the same dormitory, which was on the second floor of the seventh workshop's office building. It was the room by the eastern end of the two-storey building and it also served as our office—this was what we called 'a man with a bald head becoming a monk', a compromise good for both. In the same building and next to our office was the office of the workshop's general service man. The general service man was old, well, old in comparison with the others coming in and out of his office, robust, and of medium height. He came from a village in Shandong Province, and like most men from Shandong Province, he was a man of few words and slow in expressing himself. He would provide our needs such as paper, notebooks, ink and glue, as well as help us to fulfil our tasks. He was a factotum for the seventh workshop. Three teenage girls, who were clean as far as politics were concerned, and who could be spared by the workshop without affecting the production, were his assistants. The four of them tried to synchronise the progress of the Four Clear Ups between our group and the workshop.

The manager of the seventh workshop was in his mid forties. Although he only had a few years schooling in primary school, he was exceptionally good at calligraphy. When slogans had to be written, he would organise to have whole pieces of blank paper, each one-and-a-half metres long and one metre wide, glued to the walls. Then with a small pot of ink and one well-worn broom (not a writing brush), he would climb onto the ladder to write one character on one piece of the blank paper just as casually as a calligrapher wrote at a desk. All the characters, each about one metre by one metre, looked so beautiful, that they seemed to be magnified characters from famous calligraphers. Nobody else in the factory, including all the staff, workers, or those doing the Four Clear Ups could do brush writing nearly as well as he did.

Among the workers in our workshop we had many classed as category six, seven, or eight. Their knowledge about skins and furs was very comprehensive. One day when I took part in physical labour in the workshop, I took up a piece of very soft sheepskin with wool to a level seven worker and asked him to tell me about it. He took the skin and felt it with his right hand.

'This skin was produced from Ning Xia Province,' he told me. 'The sheep was taken out of its mother's belly about ten days before it was due. It was still alive when it was taken out. It was a fine day. There was no big wind that day but there might be a very soft breeze.' I thanked him and without arousing his suspicion, took the skin to another worker who was in the eighth (the highest) category. And I was told exactly the same thing. I was so surprised and asked how it was possible for them to know that.

'From experience! Thousands and thousands of sheepskins have passed our hands and so the feel of our hands can tell everything—the origin, the time of dissecting the mother, whether the lamb was alive or dead when taken out of its mother's belly, and the weather, are all written on the skin itself.'

I secretly conducted such tests among different skilled workers, for I suspected that they might have heard each other's analysis. Finally I had to admit that their skill was real—they really did have detailed knowledge about Chinese skins and furs.

Because many workers were highly skilled, most of them were from the old society, and might have a checkered history. Among them was an escapee from the Communist-led Eighth Route Army. He deserted during the difficult times under the Japanese occupation and when the Japanese Devils were 'mopping up' the guerrillas. He deserted from fear of the Japanese and did not do anything against the people or the guerrillas and he had no criminal record. There was one homosexual, who was a young man with a family. His wife was very beautiful and he had a son. I could not understand why he preferred to be gay. But the most serious was an old man, who had a history of raping women, from young girls to his aunts and grandmothers (not his own grandmother, but the grandmothers of his cousins, who in China, were also called 'grandmother'). But he committed all those cases before Liberation. Another man was said to be backward in thinking. He had been an expert furrier sent to Mongolia to help in the processing of their sheepskins during the late fifties. He had many friends and students there. When he returned home they gave him so many garments as gifts that he had to store them in gunnybags and he wore good clothes all the time, which, I am sure, made other workers jealous of him. That might be the reason why he was considered backward in thinking, for I sometimes chatted with him and I could not find anything wrong with him as far as his thinking was concerned. There were several old men who had small businesses before Liberation. We had to decide whether to classify them as self-employed workers or as capitalists. All those people were considered 'dead tigers', a term used to describe people who had a criminal past. They would be re-checked at this time. There was no new 'target' yet in that workshop, that is, there was no one suspected of having any criminal activity.

The staff from our workshop were divided into quite a few groups. Every afternoon we would conduct group meetings to study Chairman Mao's works and to volunteer confessions of wrong thinking by the workers. I joined a group and read Mao's works to them. When it came to discussion, I found that each of them was very patient when waiting for others to speak. The meeting place was always in the workshop around their desks. Each group sat around a big rectangular-shaped desk. The more one urged them to expose their own problems or to expose the problems of the cadres in the factory, the more perfect their poker faces were. They never looked at me. I could not catch the eyes of anybody. The Chinese saying was 'never open your mouth unless it concerns you. Shake your head to say "no" whenever you are asked.' That was what they did during the group meetings. The policy in the movement was 'Those who confess will be treated leniently while those who refuse to confess will be treated strictly.' But people were always sceptical to this policy. Some joked, but not in front of us Four Clear Ups members, that 'Those who confess will rot in prison and those who refuse to confess celebrate the Spring Festival at home with their families.' The joke sounded ludicrous but it did reflect the truth. This probably was the reason why nobody wished to speak or confess.

'Anything new?' my group leader would asked me and I would shake my head. I had nothing to report. However, I was not asked to press the workers so that I could hit upon something to report about.

But outside the meetings, the workers liked to talk to me or teach me. When I worked in the workshop, I was taught how to hold the knife, how to suspend my wrist, and how to cut the sheep skin without severing the wool on the skin. The knife should be handled nimbly and skilfully as an Innuit handled his knife to cut and eat raw seal meat. I was also taught how to sew two skins together to make them look like one complete skin. I was taught how to check fur or sheepskin so that one day, when I wanted to buy a sheepskin jacket or a fur jacket, I would not be taken in.

'Don't look down upon this profession,' they told me. 'Everything concerning this industry is "gold"—the furs, the skins, and even the waste water.' I believed what they told me, but I did not imagine I would be involved in this profession some day in the future. The workers also told me stories that happened in the factory. The head of the Factory Militia Organisation was after a girl who did the broadcasting in the factory broadcasting room. One day the man came into the room to have sex with her on a revolving chair. The girl forgot to switch off the megaphone and the whole factory heard the details of their conversations, their moans, their laughter and giggles. They became the laughing stock and the factory punished them.

A member in our group created, with his pen, a model worker from all the workers in our workshop. I used the word 'created', because, in my opinion, there is no perfect worker in actual life and a perfect worker can only exist under a flowery pen. 'The flower bloomed within the wall but looked redder outside the wall.' In the eyes of his fellow workers, a model worker was not as great as in the eyes of the outsiders who read about him or her.

A real model worker was elected by the Four Clear Ups group at the skin and fur factory. He was a good man, in his early forties, donned a monk hairstyle, was sun-tanned like a peasant, and was strongly built. He had bushy eyebrows, a high-ridged but fleshy nose, and a square firm jaw. He was a silent man. He was a level six worker with a fairly good salary but because his wife was sick and his children were in school, his life was hard. He was honest and did not flatter people. In our group political study, he was, like all the others, silent all the time.

If any person with counter-revolutionary ideas or a criminal record was exposed by a Four Clear Ups team, it was called an 'achievement' of that group. It was an 'achievement' if a person confessed his criminal activities under the pressure of this policy. None of the Four Clear Ups groups had had much achievement—the only 'big achievement' was made by the head office, where through political education, an accountant had confessed his criminal ways. The accountant was, it was said, greatly moved by the Socialist Education Movement, and so he confessed to embezzling money from the workers. The account books were immediately checked but nothing could be found—everything was neat and in good order. Finally, the Four Clear Ups team had to ask the man to explain himself. He said that when workers asked for leave, in some cases there would be no pay. Every worker understood that and everybody, he was sure, kept a record of his non-pay leave. But the account book was triplicate. He therefore made the first copy to reflect the true situation with everybody, but he made the second and the third copies all full attendance. This meant that everybody was fully paid. The full payment of a worker minus the actual payment was what he kept for himself. The first copy was cut into strips and given to every worker at the time of payment—only the second and the third copies remained for checking. That explained why nobody could find anything wrong about the accounting books.

The total sum of money he got was about eight hundred yuan. He was not ordered to pay everything back because the money was already spent and he was not given any other punishment because he confessed. He was not capped as a 'bad element'. His case was used to educate others though. A time limit was set and anybody who confessed to a crime within the time would be treated leniently. If one made no confession at all but was found guilty after the time limit, the punishment would be severe. This was called 'knocking the mountains to warn the tigers'. To the timid person it was a very effective method, but to those who really had problems, it was of no use. This method was frequently used but the result was doubtful.

English Study and Visiting the Poor

Professor Zhi-wei Li, who was assigned to teach us *Eden's Memoir*, accompanied us to the factory to do the Four Clear Ups. He was a really good teacher—he received his doctorate in America and was one of the translators to turn Chairman Mao's military writings into English. He was very fit because he played Tai Chi shadow boxing every morning. He argued with the authorities and succeeded in having us attend one hour of English study every morning before we went to our respective jobs as a member of the Four Clear Ups team. Whatever happened, that one hour should not be affected. 'A pugilist must not stop practising boxing and a singer must not stop practising singing,' so a language student should not stop studying language. To our professor, study was the only thing a student should do. He followed the decision of our Institute to do the Four Clear Ups with the students, but what actually occupied his thinking was how to teach the students English. He could not stop the students being ordered to do the Four Clear Ups but he could try to make up for the students the lost study hours to a certain degree.

He distributed to each student of our class a copy of *On the Accomplishment of a Communist* by Liu Shaoqi, as our textbook. (Liu Shaoqi, in the fifties and early sixties, played an important role in all aspects of public life, especially as chairman and head of state of the Chinese People's Republic (1959–68). He was attacked during the early stages of the Cultural Revolution as the 'number one capitalist-roader'. Liu was stripped of power in 1968.) The professor demanded that we study the book by carefully comparing the Chinese and English versions. To be future interpreters, political phrases, political terms and political expressions would need to be constantly translated and so studying the book carefully would help in our future work. He supervised our studies and answered our questions. He would not let anybody go a minute early unless it was urgent and necessary.

One Sunday, it was very quiet in the factory. After breakfast, everybody from our group was gone—they either went back home or to the city to do something. The whole building, where our office and dormitory was situated, was empty, except for myself. I had no money to go to the city, so I remained in the dormitory to read English. I sat and compared, as instructed by the professor, the English and Chinese versions. I checked the meaning of each new word and looked for examples of how the word was used. Very soon my full attention was on my book, because I expected nobody to come to my dormitory.

'You are concentrating so hard!' Just as I stretched my arms and raised my head from the book, a voice sounded behind me. I was startled. I looked back and found out it was our professor.

'I have been here watching you for almost half an hour!' he said, 'but you did not hear me. You were so immersed in your study. Now I understand why you always get full marks. You do not need anyone to push you in your English study.'

'Sorry, Professor,' I apologised. 'I did not expect you.'

'In the whole factory you and I are the only people remaining,' he said. 'I have been into all the dormitories and none of our students remain.' Then he added, 'When I was in primary school, I was taught "if a son has no manners, the father is to blame for not teaching him. If a student does not study hard, the teacher is to blame for not giving him the urge to be diligent." That has been my motto my whole life as a teacher. Now I think the self-motivation of a student is also important!'

'I'd like to go to the movie, too, if I could afford it,' I confessed to him. He laughed because of my honesty. We sat across the table and had a chat until it was time to soothe our stomachs. Descending the stairs, he told me that if I did need to leave early in the mornings I could. He said he no longer worried about me.

Soon after, our English class ceased because when study and politics clashed, politics would prevail. The one-hour English study could not be maintained because the students, which comprised just a small part of the team, would be absent from the workshop during the one hour of study. Consequently, the other members could not sit in the office waiting for us to finish. The English class was especially difficult when visiting the poor was conducted daily, for we had to start early. 'Visiting the poor' meant that the team members had to visit those families whose living standard was bad, either because there were too many members in the family to be supported by the worker in our factory, or because somebody in the family was sick. We visited them to see whether they needed help and to check whether it would be fair for the factory to give them help.

Our group head, the high-ranking manager whose job in the Import and Export Corporation was taken over temporarily by his deputy, liked me to accompany him on such visits. He knew the city well and so would put three or four families together for us to visit in one day. We would start early, right after breakfast, because the factory was far from the quarters where the workers of the factory lived and because I was a bad bike rider and he had to ride slowly to allow me to keep up with him.

I enjoyed his company very much, listening to his witty chatter, and in particular his adventures during his guerrilla days in the Japanese-occupied area. He was not talkative but his words were witty, humorous and colourful. It was a pity that I could not fully appreciate some of his expressions due to his local dialect.

He had an easy approach to the wives and older people of a worker's family. It was handy for him to slip into their dialect—probably a skill picked up while in the guerrilla team, when he had to mix with the masses. From him I learnt to appreciate the life of the workers; to understand the life of the workers; to communicate with the workers; and to be on the same level with the workers. In most cases he used his lips and I used my ears during such visits. I could not take notes with my pen, for that would make the housewife nervous and stop answering our questions. I was reluctant to open my mouth, for I was not familiar with their vocabulary. I might be doing what is described by the Chinese as, 'to call the mother-in-law as sister-in-law', meaning to attempt a conversation without proper and suitable words or to attempt a conversation without content or meaning. Another reason was that an older man of high rank would not like a young man doing the talking.

To me such visits were just one kind of learning—pleasant and not difficult. To him, sometimes, it might mean he had to rack his brains to find out what we wished to know.

A little before lunchtime he would lead me through side streets and lanes, where I could be spared the worries of getting through the heavy traffic to his house. It was a normal flat-roofed three-room house in a big compound. He probably had other houses in the compound, for he had to accommodate his children. His living room was simply decorated with one scroll of Chinese calligraphy, in the style of a famous calligrapher. Offering me a cup of jasmine tea on the tea table by the sofa, he would ring his wife to come back to cook lunch for us. His wife would return in five to ten minutes, being not very far from home. His wife was as beautiful as a flower. She was at least ten years younger than him. After entering the large cities, lots of the Communist cadres divorced their wives to marry young girls. The father of the only Party member in our class did that, too. Very few men in high positions could resist marrying a young girl at the sacrifice of the old wife.

His wife was nimble and dexterous. Like a magician, she would have the table laid with a few nice dishes, two tiny alcohol cups and a bottle of white alcohol. The dishes were delicious and the alcohol was sweet, sticky to the tongue, and burned down the throat. I just dared to have one cup, which, every time, made me nap soundly for an hour or so. After lunch, the two of them would disappear into their bedroom to have a dream of 'the female god meeting the King Xiang of Chu', eager like a newly married couple after a week's separation. (During the Warlord States period in China between 403–221 BC, Song Yu, an official of the time, wrote a poem. In the preface, he wrote that he and the king 'Xiang' of Chu State visited Yun Meng Lake. While there, the king ordered Song Yu to create a poem about Gao Tang (a beautiful village built on a lake). That night the king 'Xiang' met the female god in his dream. She and the king went to bed as husband and wife. Later, when describing the love of a man and a woman, it was always said that 'King Xiang was meeting the female god'.)

When refreshed by an hour's nap, we would visit another one or two families before we rode back to the factory. 'Everything learned about the world is knowledge.' I enjoyed acquiring knowledge with him during those days, however, I always thought that the Union of the factory should be conducting such visits. It was not necessary for high-ranking cadres and university students to do such things. To me it was like 'hitting the mosquito with an anti-aircraft machine gun'—just wasting time.

An Interpreter

Between 5 and 15 October 1965, a group of forty-eight British companies would come to Tianjin to present an industrial exhibition. Five students from our class would be chosen as interpreters at the exhibition and, in 1965, I was one of them. I was very pleased to have the opportunity to see whether I could do the job well and to find my weak points in English.

The exhibition site was Er Gong (the Second Palace), where we five students would stay right through and after the exhibition until we had written the report on our activities there.

Students from Nan Kai University and technicians from different factories were also invited to work at the exhibition. Every day, once in the morning and once in the afternoon, we would divide into groups to study the rules and regulations guiding our conduct with the English people, whom we termed as 'foreigners' or 'foreign friends'. We also 'armed' ourselves through studying Chairman Mao's works.

The Second Palace was a huge beautiful park. My accommodation was in a compound courtyard at the north-east corner of the park. It was very quiet from the evening to the early morning. Flowers of many kinds were grown in the courtyard. In the morning, the air was filled with a mixture of beautiful fragrances. Pushing open the door and taking a few deep breaths of the air in the morning, I would feel very energetic. Outside the walls of our courtyard were many flowers and a variety of trees, which were all beautiful and majestic. When the gate closed, our yard became an independent world. I called the courtyard the 'park within the park and the palace within the palace'. I had never imagined that one day I could live in such a place that I had only read about in novels like *The Journey to the West* or *The Dream of the Red Chambers*.

It was my habit to get up early every morning to read my English texts loudly, a practice I have never given up. I read while wandering in the park for pleasure and enjoyed the environment while reading. I would stay in our corner where there were no early risers, to do various morning exercises. Elsewhere I would be distracted from my reading by the fascinating activities done by other people before breakfast.

The most fascinating sport in the morning was shuttlecock kicking. About fifteen to twenty men of different ages, formed a circle and moved slowly round and round as if dancing all the time. It looked like when Mongolians circled the ring before wrestling. Every participant would try hard to display his skill and style when the shuttlecock came to him. One would catch the shuttlecock with his forehead, stabilise it in the middle of the forehead, jerk it in the air, and kick it to another person in the circle. The receiver would try to get the shuttlecock falling on his chest, jerk it off into the air, and kick it to the next person. The other person might jump high, turn 360 degrees and catch the shuttlecock with the sole of his right foot, send it into the air, and kick it to another person. Nobody allowed the shuttlecock to fall onto the ground, and if somebody did, all the players would make a disgruntled sound.

Anybody could join in as long as he was sure he could play as well as the other players in the circle. From their clothing I could see that there were workers, cadres, clerks and students. During the week, they played for just a short time, but on Sundays, they would play for quite a few hours at a time. When the numbers of players in a circle grew too big, somebody would pull out from his pocket a shuttlecock to start a new circle. Sometimes there could be five or six circles happening simultaneously. The players in each circle would try to demonstrate the best skills and tricks to attract the onlookers. Competition, though not declared, would be heated among the circles. This was the most civilised, the most inexpensive, the most co-operative, and the healthiest sport.

On Sunday mornings, the park was crowded with clusters of people. Some groups were males of all ages showing their bird cages and birds to one another, hanging their cages from tree branches and listening to the twittering competition between the birds. Some groups were doing Tai Chi led by a teacher, for the purpose of keeping fit. Some groups of males and females were singing Beijing opera accompanied by volunteer musicians. Some groups were dancing, some were Mongolian wrestling.

Scattered almost everywhere in the park were individuals practising different styles of Chinese shadow boxing.

Not far from our accommodation were three people attracting many onlookers. One was an old lady, who was small, very slim, with silver hair. Her feet were 'three-inch golden lilies' and although her face and hair showed she was in her late seventies, her eyes had the lustre and brilliance of a teenage girl. She wrapped four bricks in one piece of white cloth called the wrapper, and then holding the cloth with both her hands, doubled backwards with her upper body parallel to the ground. Her arms stretched at full length over her head, also parallel to the ground. The bricks hung in the white cloth from her hands about twenty centimetres from the ground. Her feet seemed to be piles driven into the ground. She would stay like this for about two hours, like a statue. Her feet remained firm without moving, her legs remained straight without trembling or shaking, and her body remained firm without the slightest indication of movement. When she straightened up, her face was not crimson from the exertion. She just kicked her legs a few times to relax and walked away.

An old man with a silver beard was playing Chinese boxing, not far from the old lady. His hands clawed half way into his fists. His hand struck out Shaolin style at the start, changing to Bagua halfway and then becoming Tai Chi in the end. With each movement of his arms or legs he would display a few styles of Chinese boxing. His face had plenty of wrinkles but was red in colour. Like the old lady, his eyes had the lustre and brilliance of a teenage man.

'Have some baked horse beans!' the old man shouted when he saw the old lady, and the two would share the horse beans surrounded by onlookers.

'Both of them are over eighty now,' an old man remarked. 'I have been in their audience for at least forty years.'

I was shocked by this and I realised then and there the importance of exercise in the morning, for whether it was boxing or not, what they were doing was, for sure, a kind of morning physical exercise.

Then there was the third. It was a man in his mid-forties. He was taller than average and looked strong. He came to the same spot at the same time every morning. He bared his upper body, hung his jacket on a tree branch and started practicing Ba Gua boxing. Not far away from him an old man, who was a cripple, was watching him.

'Your style could be improved a bit,' the old cripple said to the young man. The cripple actually meant to give him some guidance, but the man took it as being looked down upon.

'Mine needs improvement,' he said to the old cripple, 'you think you are better. All right, let's have a fight next week to see who is better.'

The old man was flabbergasted. He wanted to explain but the young man would not give him the opportunity.

'Let's sign a life and death agreement,' the man insisted. 'If you kill me, my family will not claim against you. If I kill you, your family should not claim against me.'

'Tell your teacher my name. Tell him I want to speak to him. I know your teacher well,' the old cripple said.

But the man would not listen to him. When he was pushed away by the onlookers, the cripple shook his head and left.

The following morning I went to the spot to see what happened. The old cripple was sitting at his old spot. The middle-aged man was practising at his usual spot. Two children, a boy about eleven years old and a girl about nine, came to the old cripple and bowed. 'Good morning, grandpa,' they saluted him.

The boy put his school bag beside the old man and started, with the permission of his grandpa, to practise Ba Gua boxing. Many onlookers came over to them. Gradually, the man who had quarrelled with the cripple stopped practising. He stood there watching the boy. When the boy came to the finish, the girl started practising sword dancing in the Ba Gua style (sword dancing has many styles, such as Tai Chi, Wu-dang, Ba Gua and Qing-cheng, which were all created by different people from various Chinese provinces). Her movements were beautiful and fast. The onlookers could hardly see the movements of the sword—it seemed everywhere, wrapping the girl in the middle! When she was halfway through, the man picked up his jacket and left. Up until we left the Second Palace, I never saw him at the spot again.

On 5 October 1965, all the interpreters and technicians were at the front of the exhibition hall waiting for the British businessmen to arrive and the opening ceremony to begin. A cadre from the municipality made a short speech before he and an Englishman held a piece of red silk ribbon and cut it into two pieces jointly. The English businessmen, the interpreters and the technicians were all at our posts. I was assigned to do interpreting for the industrial plastic products. Although this was the first time I was an interpreter, I was not nervous, for I already had experience with English people through our expert Ms Holden. In addition, I was fully prepared for such jobs by Professor Yu in the previous year.

The work of an interpreter was not very difficult. The technician with us could explain all about the plastic film-extruding machine. Questions about the polyethylene granules, about the feeding box, the tapered screw, the film, and so on, were all frequently asked by visitors. I just needed to ask the British manager and translate once for the questioner and thereafter the technician would be able to explain to other visitors. She tried her best to give me more time to talk to the manager from a British company. He was quite young and liked to talk, joke and debate. Perhaps he was trying to help me improve my oral English through more use. Then somebody from his group, the head of the delegates, cautioned him not to do that. That was within my earshot and I could hear them clearly, though they talked undertones.

When there was nobody around except the technician, who could not understand English, the manager told me why. 'You have your rules and regulations and we have ours. We are not allowed to joke or argue or debate with an interpreter, for fear that we might be misunderstood and thus have the business affected. We are not allowed to embrace or kiss a Chinese girl because that is not tolerated in China. We are not allowed to discuss sensitive political topics because you Chinese put politics before business. Altogether we have eight things that we should not do.'

I was very surprised about this but I could understand and appreciate it. To the Chinese, politics came first; to Western people, business came first. To please the Chinese and carry out business well, in my opinion, the Japanese were the best. They knew how to lip the Chinese policies in exchange for favourable business.

'I find you can understand me well and I find you appreciate jokes,' he further explained, 'that's why I liked to joke, discuss and debate with you. I enjoy your company.'

'That's also my attitude,' I assured him. So when neither the British businessmen nor the Chinese interpreters were around, we talked happily.

Later, when I did become an interpreter, I found the Chinese rules and regulations were dogmatic, general and never specific. The rules and regulations were itemised in a booklet, which was called *The Rules and*

Regulations for People Dealing with Foreigners. It totalled twelve points and sometimes was referred to as 'The Twelve-point Rules and Regulations'. They seemed to cover everything! No matter how hard an interpreter did his work, those who did not understand English could use the rules and regulations to criticise him or her. The rules for foreigners, contrary to those of the Chinese, were specific rather than general, updated according to the situation in China. The rules for foreigners were much more effective in helping them to do business with the Chinese.

At the end of the exhibition, the group of forty-eight British companies gave a dinner party in Tianjin Hotel. The buses assigned to take the delegates and the interpreters to the hotel were running late. Our British friends became impatient and began singing:

'Why are we waiting?

Why are we waiting?

Why are we waiting?

Why? Why? Why?'

The singing made the organiser from the government very embarrassed. Here was the difference between the Chinese and Western people. When we Chinese had to wait, we just waited. We were patient enough to wait for anything!

The dinner gave me my first opportunity to step into a first class modern hotel. It was also the first time in my life that I sat at a banquet table with people from the West. It was the first time in my life that I used a knife and fork to eat my food. I was not a bit at home. I again adopted my usual tactic of 'wait and see'.

The first course came. It was a large piece of beefsteak on a large plate with sauce and topping. I copied the British, holding the fork in the left hand and the knife in the right. I pressed the steak firm with the fork and cut a small piece off. I disliked the taste of the sauce, but I was worried about the waste if I refused to eat it. One piece of beef was worth more than a day's allowance for a peasant. My immediate neighbour, the technician, whispered to me, 'If you don't like it, you can tip it onto my plate.' I did. Immediately, a waiter came up to me and whispered to me, 'Don't give your food to other people. If you don't like a course, just leave it there and I will take it away.'

I blushed, but did not know exactly whether etiquette or table manners forbade this. I decided to learn some table manners for dinner parties.

The exhibition came to the close and we had two more days in the Second Palace to report about what we did and how we behaved. Then I said goodbye to the beautiful environment and went back to the stench of the skin and fur processing factory.

First Tour of Investigation in the Countryside

There was no end of investigation tours. If a person was to be promoted, people were assigned on a tour to check his family. To check a family meant to investigate whether they had any criminal dealings or whether they were a landlord, rich peasant, reactionary or rightist. If a person who was in contact with foreigners through his work and was to get married, people were assigned to investigate the family of his fiancee. If a student was to be assigned to a post dealing with foreign countries, people were sent to check his family. If a person had problems, people were assigned to collect evidence. There were many occasions that required an investigation tour.

I was a member of one Four Clear Ups team, which also included one of my classmates, a student from another university, a cadre from the bureau of public security and a cadre from an import/export corporation. In the factory, there were a total of nine such groups. The students and cadres who were deemed clean were sent to carry out the investigations. Everybody was investigated regardless of whether he or she was suspected of unlawful conduct. This was in contradiction to the purpose of the Four Clear Ups. The original target was to see whether executive cadres managed the factory according to the Party's policy—whether their thinking was politically correct, whether they were corrupt, and whether the account books were correct and in good order. Now everybody was investigated and the spearhead of the Four Clear Ups was pointed at the masses. Somebody was trying to get the Movement astray. But at the time I could not see it so clearly. Even if I could, I would not dare to comment. My friends and I were assigned to do these investigations. We did not have the power to make the final classification of a person; we just sent our recommendation to the team office for them to make the decision.

China had been liberated for seventeen years and the famine was already four years in the past. It was difficult to imagine what the vast countryside was like now. I had not much personal experience about it except from my own village, before I began my tours of investigation. During the tours, I saw what it was like in governmental motels and I was seeing places other than the Paradise Palace.

It was between three or four o'clock one Monday morning in late February or early March in 1966 and I was alone in the dormitory. All the others had gone home for Sunday and had not yet returned to the factory. I was still fast asleep when my bed shook violently.

'Don't be naughty,' I protested. 'I am still very sleepy.'

But the bed shook more violently. I raised my head to see who was joking with me. Nobody was in the room. I looked under my bed and nobody was there. Just then the bed shook so violently that it moved about six inches away from the wall. 'Earthquake!' The idea flashed across my mind and I got dressed immediately and ran down the stairs into the open. It was still dark. I stood alone in the yard for some time before I went back to my bed again. My response to the quake was not immediate. I didn't imagine it could be serious.

During office hours we learned that it was a disastrous earthquake and the epicentre was around Xing-tai in the Hebei Province, which was several hundred kilometres away from Tianjin. That explained why we only felt the violent shaking. Many houses in the vicinity of the epicentre had collapsed and there were some casualties.

Shortly after the quake, I was chosen to accompany comrade Lou Qiang, the head of the security office of the factory, to the countryside in Hebei Province, not far from the epicentre, to investigate the problems of some workers from the factory. Lou gave me a train ticket but did not tell me any details of what we were going to do and what our target was. People like Lou Qiang, who had something to do with 'security', preferred to keep things to themselves, for the sake of 'security' or for the sake of making them seem mysterious.

Our first stop was the county town of Heng Shui. We went to the county department of the Communist Party Organisation. Lou showed the person on duty our letter of introduction, got a letter of permission or his stamp on our letter of introduction, and then we were led for the night to the County Reception Centre for our accommodation.

The Reception Centre was actually a hotel run by the county government. Such a centre was for people with letters of introduction from a factory, a company or a local government. With the allowance they got, they could only stay at such centres because the accommodation and food at the centre were cheap.

The Reception Centre was actually composed of dugouts—pits three metres deep. The top of the dugout was covered with corn stalks over timber rafters. The entrance of the dugout was a slope leading into the pit and at the bottom of the slope, the end of the entrance and the beginning of the pit, was a curtain made of jute bags to provide privacy and to protect the guests from the cold wind. The floor was covered with a thick pile of corn stalks with reed mats on top to serve as a bed. The 'bed' vibrated up and down as I sat on it, like a spring mattress. There were no tables, no chairs and no wardrobes. The pit walls were just earth. During the night we had to use our bags as pillows—a measure to guard against theft. We had to spread our clothing over the quilts, for nowhere else could we place them. In one such dugout, five or six people would be accommodated. It was very damp inside. The payment for the night was one-and-a-half yuan per person, the same fee as when one stayed in a house.

Heng Shui was not very far from the epicentre of the earthquake and as it was considered not safe to stay in a house, the dugouts were the best alternative. It was primitive but safe. So nobody complained about the poor conditions.

The following day we hired two bikes as transport to go to the villages. Bikes at the Reception Centre were all homemade. The cross bar, the fork, and the handlebar were all welded water pipes. Only the chains, the wheels and the foot pedals were bought either from factories or from wholesalers. The bike looked just like a horse without a saddle or a bridle. It also had no brakes. When one wanted to stop, he had to use his own foot pressing hard against the front wheel. When somebody was in the way, I had to say, 'Lao jia, rang wu guo qui.' (Let me pass, please), as the bikes didn't have a bell. Almost all the roads were unpaved, bumpy country roads so we could not ride fast and it was easy for us to brake any time it was necessary.

The first thing we did that day was to go to a prison to check the dealings between a prisoner and an employee in our factory. I asked the name of the staff member and what kind of dealings he suspected. Lou did not reply to my questions nor did he tell me what he intended to get from the prisoner.

'Prisoners are very shrewd. If a prisoner knows what you want him to tell you he will not tell you about it at all. You just take down whatever questions I ask and every word he answers, word for word and in question form. You just put 'question' before each of my queries and 'answer' before each of his replies. At the end of the interview, you will write on the bottom of the paper, 'the above has been read to me word for word. Everything is true to what I said. Signed.' I felt I was just a pawn on a chessboard, being moved here and there but without my own will.

The prison was not very far. We went to the guard on duty, showed him our letter of instruction and were shown into an office.

'Please wait here, I will fetch the prisoner for you.'

The guard came back with the prisoner within five minutes. The prisoner had no handcuffs or leg shackles.

'Sit down!' The guard ordered, while pointing to a stool in the middle of the room about two metres away from our desk. 'Answer their questions honestly. Don't try to be evasive or play tricks!'

'I will, I will,' the prisoner answered obediently.

The guard left us alone with the prisoner.

'You must tell me the truth,' Lou told the prisoner.

'Yes, Monitor,' the prisoner replied. He could only call us Monitor. The word 'comrade' could not be used to refer to us, because a prisoner was not a comrade. He wore a black padded jacket and was about fifty years of age. He stole glances at us now and then, perhaps trying to see what we were. His stealthy glances were shrewd and shifty.

'Your name?' Lou started questioning.

'Peng Hua-tou.'

'Your age?'

'Fifty-four.'

'Your profession before coming here?'

'Skin tanner.'

Then Lou started to bombard him with unrelated questions, which seemed pointless. The prisoner answered them but kept silent when the question seemed to be serious.

Lou warned him quite a few times to keep answering.

'You are playing with me now. If you don't answer me sincerely and truly, I will report you to your prison authority. You know it will not be good for you.'

'I know, Monitor,' he answered meekly.

It was like a chess game. Both read the mind of his opponent and weighed his own moves carefully. Lou tried hard to ask irrelevant questions with his real question mixed in. The prisoner answered in such a way that he had enough time to guess what Lou really wanted.

I watched with interest. It would have been very difficult for me, or for any inexperienced young person, to question such a crafty prisoner and get what I needed to know. Two hours later, the 'battle' was over.

'Now listen carefully to the reading,' Lou ordered.

'I will, I will,' the prisoner assured him.

I clearly and slowly read my neatly written notes, the record of their questions and answers.

'Is this clear.'

'Yes.'

'The answers are the same as your replies?'

'Yes.'

'Sign!'

The prisoner signed on the appropriate spot. The prison guard came in to take him back to his cell. We got our record stamped by the prison office, thanked them for their help and left.

'When we investigate business dealings, we must not ask questions directly to the point.' Lou said to me. 'When a prisoner is tried, he might conceal some major details for fear of getting a more serious punishment. What we want to know might be what he has concealed. It is not easy for him to divulge such things from his own mouth. We have to outwit him through mixing important and unimportant questions.'

We rode along a narrow country road towards a village about ten kilometres away. Along the way, Lou looked over some of my notes.

'Look at this one we just questioned,' Lou continued. 'He's shrewd, very shrewd! I could not ask directly. I could not let him guess what I wanted. If I did, he would give me false answers!' He smiled and then continued, 'We have got the clues we wanted.' He laughed complacently. I reviewed minutely the questions and answers given by him and the prisoner but I could not find any material that could be of importance. From the beginning to the end of the trip, Lou had not asked anybody we contacted a thing that might link to the answers of the prisoner.

We were about halfway to the village, when my bike's steel piece connecting to the handlebars and the fork, which controlled the direction of the front wheel, broke. I could no longer control the movement of the front wheel and instead of riding the bike, the bike now rode on me. I carried it over my right shoulder and walked along with Lou. Fortunately, we came across a roadside repair shop and had the bike repaired.

The unexpected delay was bad for us. When we finished our investigation in the village, which was to see whether a worker had any criminal activities in the past, it was already dark. The village party secretary showed us a short cut to the County Reception Centre.

'Be careful, it might not be safe at night,' he warned us. We said goodbye to him and set out along the short cut.

'Remember this,' Lou said to me as we rode along the country path zigzagging through the fields. 'If somebody stops us, don't panic. Just watch what I do.'

'All right,' I agreed. 'We can stage a fight, anyway.'

'If he does not have a gun, but has a knife, our bike is our weapon,' he said.

We were not familiar with the path, which was only a metre wide at most. Lou rode fast and I had to race behind him to catch up. I did not want to lose him in the dark in a strange place. When the path cut its way through a small wood of willows, he suddenly disappeared from sight. I was on the point of calling when all of a sudden I was tumbling down a two- or three-metre steep slope, nearly falling on top of him, who was panting at the bottom of the ditch.

He stood up. 'If you support me, I will climb up first,' Lou said.

'No, not this side,' I stopped him as he was ready to climb up the bank. 'The other side please.' He laughed and we carried our bike to the other side.

I propped my bike against the slope. Lou stood on top of the seat and tried to reach the top—he was still a bit short, so I had to push him higher with my hands. He lowered his belt to get the two bikes up first and then lowered the belt for me. When we reached the Reception Centre of the county, it was already past midnight. We were hungry, tired and dirty.

To have a bath was out of the question. We could only wash our hands and face with cold water before we could get some cold food from the kitchen. The person on duty was an old man. He did not grunt when we woke him.

'Don't be so late next time,' he told us. 'Bad things happen on the road nowadays.'

Thus with me riding in his wake, Lou and I travelled from county to county and from village to village. One day we came to County Meng, which was an autonomous county of the Hui people (the Chinese name for Muslims). As soon as we went through the paperwork at the counter in the Reception Centre, we were led to our respective individual bedrooms. I put down my bag, sat on the only chair at the only table in the room. A woman in her late fifties came in with a basin half full of lukewarm water and a brand new towel.

'Comrade, wash your face, please,' she said to me with a smile. I thanked her before I started washing. I had hardly finished, when she came in again with a thermos full of boiled water, and some jasmine tea bags.

'If you wish to have your supper, it is ready now in the dining room,' she advised me.

I called Lou to go for supper. The food was very cheap and of a better quality than anywhere else we had travelled so far. The *man tou* was pure white, big, puffy and resilient. The stir fry mutton strips with onion was fragrant, tasty and delicious. The burning hot mutton soup was exceptionally good and nourishing.

Back in my room I had the time to have a look around. All four walls and the ceiling were immaculately whitewashed. On the wall facing my bed, which was a single bed placed north and south, was a framed picture of Chairman Mao. The only table and chair were positioned in the centre of the wall opposite my bed. On the table was a tray with one thermos, two mugs with lids and a printed sheet of 'notice to guests'.

My bed was made of wooden boards supported by two benches, one placed near each end of the bed. A padded mattress was spread over the boards, and a snow-white sheet was over the mattress. The quilt was what the Chinese called 'the three-new' quilt, meaning it had the lining, then cotton, and the surface cover, which was brand new. In those years, the motel management was not clever enough to use quilt covers.

That was the only proper motel we had during the whole investigation trip. I was so happy I fetched enough water to have a good scrub, so as not to soil the new sheet and quilt, for it was not an easy job for the old woman to wash and sew.

'We can have a nice clean sleep tonight,' I told Lou in his room. We sat in his room to jot down the details of the day, such as from what time we were on the road to what time we were investigating in the village, and when we returned to the Reception Centre. Every day we had to do this carefully, because our travel allowance would be paid according to the details we supplied—one yuan and twenty cents for staying at a place and two yuan and forty cents for the time spent on the road during a journey.

'Don't be overjoyed yet,' he cautioned me. 'When you are not wakened by the lice before midnight, then you can enjoy the sleep.'

'You are too pessimistic!' I objected.

'Let's hope for the best,' he said, shaking his head and smiling. 'I still suggest you put your clothing on the chair, and push it away from the bed. If you leave your underpants on, don't forget to check the seams in the morning.'

I did not agree with him, but I did put my clothing on the chair and pushed it away from my bed. I went to sleep in a relaxed mood, ready for a beautiful dream. As I switched off the light and was nearly asleep, I felt I was itching all over my body. I sat up and switched on the light. I turned the quilt lining upwards to find under each exposed stitch a louse as big as a large sesame seed with their red bellies betraying them. Lice were no cleverer than ostriches—they just hid their heads but did not mind their backs. I had the quilt completely upturned and under the light, the red backs of the vermin lay there in neat rows, as if they were being inspected by a president!

Immediately, I launched a devastating attack on those invaders. Carefully, so not to soil the lining of the quilt, I slaughtered them between my thumbnails. Each pop of a louse between the nails was sickening and made me nauseous. When I had killed the last one from the last stitch, my thumbnails were covered with a thick layer of darkish red blood.

'Now, I can have a good sleep,' I said to myself. I crept into bed with a happier heart. I was just asleep when I was wakened again by the burning itching of my body—lice! The word flashed across my mind and immediately I sat up and switched on the light. I once again turned over the quilt and sure enough under each stitch I found more red bellies, only smaller this time. The slaughter finished within fifteen minutes with my nails again thick with sticky blood.

For the third time I crept into bed and tried hard to remain awake, waiting for more attacks, but I was tired and fell asleep. I cannot remember how long it was before the itching of my body awoke me again, for the third time. I switched on the light and turned over the quilt. This time it was not so easy to catch the vermin. They were very tiny, and so I could only see tiny red dots under the stitches. If I were just a little bit careless, I would have missed some. I had to check each row of the stitches to make sure none were overlooked.

Now that the whole lice clan—grandparents, sons, and grandsons—were all wiped out, I could possibly grab a few hours' sleep. There might be 'guerrilla' attacks but 'massive army attacks' would be out of the question. I slept confidently this time, vowing that even if there were further attacks I would not bother to do anything. I slept undisturbed this time, partly because I was awfully tired and partly because the lice attacks were sporadic. When I got up in the morning, I made a final check of the quilt and found a few lice—three generations and all with bulging bellies. I made a final lice-killing campaign before I had my morning ritual of washing my face, brushing my teeth and combing my hair.

The Reception Centre had nice rooms, nice service and nice food—why didn't they buy some chemicals to eliminate the lice? It became a puzzling question in my head but I could not ask any of the management. Lou looked worse. He seemed to have had no sleep at all, shaking his head to me all through breakfast but too tired to tell me his story about the lice. I suspected that he was too lazy to kill the lice and he did not sleep well.

'Even an emperor or a queen may have a couple of royal lice!' was the usual excuse.

We finished our investigation and returned to the factory. What is the result? We got nothing important as far as I can remember. That some workers were classed as 'clean' was the only achievement.

Second Tour of Investigation in the Countryside

A week later after my first tour with Lou in Hebei Province, I was instructed to do another investigation. This time it was Shandong Province and my companion was Si instead of Lou. Si was a seventh grade skilled worker from our workshop. He was a man in his mid-thirties, a bit tall and his hair, cut short, was always well maintained in the style of a young man. His eyes shone, revealing a very brilliant inner strength and wisdom. He was a member of the Communist Party and thus could be entrusted to conduct investigations, though he did not have much schooling. I was nominated for the job because I was a member of the

Four Clear Ups team and because I was only a student and it would not matter much if I knew the secrets of some of the workers.

China had at least thirty million cadres at the time. This figure would keep investigators on endless tours all year round. This perhaps added to the crowding on the Chinese passenger trains, which were already filled to capacity most of the time. So Si and I were two more investigators making the train a bit more crowded. Unlike Lou, Si briefed me on the purpose of the trip. He gave me only a sketchy description, leaving the details to be discussed on the train. 'There might be ears on the other side of the wall' so little discussion was held in the factory. This was a precaution to prevent the secret of a worker or cadre from being divulged.

On 1 April 1966, we embarked from the West Station, which was as crowded as any other time. Inside it was also full, but we had our seats reserved and had no problems. We did not take the sleeping coach, for the food allowance when travelling in a sleeping coach was only half of that when taking a hard bench seat.

It was a night trip and we had nothing to see on the way before we arrived at Ji-nan in the morning to change for the train taking us to the peninsula. We had plenty of time before the connecting train was due. The idea of visiting the famous springs in the city did not come to our mind, so we looked for a restaurant near the station to have a hot breakfast. I ordered two bowls of long soup. When the soup was served on my table I was exceptionally surprised. The bowls were large, a size usually for holding long soup for families in northern China. The noodles were homemade with the oil and chopped spring onion floating on the surface. Slices of pork were also mixed in with the noodles or floated on the surface. The quality of the noodles, the meat, and the spring onion, was definitely good.

Si changed his mind and asked the waiter to give him the long soup as well. In Shandong Province, long soup was the most convenient food one could order almost everywhere.

'The quantity is big, the quality is good, and the price is cheap,' Si said to me.

'We could not get the same thing in Beijing or in Tianjin, even if the price were three times higher,' I commented.

That was my first impression of Shandong Province. It was the neighbour of Hebei Province but I seemed to be in two different countries. Hebei seemed always poor and Shandong had a better quality of life, though we did have more stories about the poor people of Shandong abandoning their homes for Manchuria to make a living before the Liberation.

We arrived at our first stop, County Yie, after a lengthy bus ride. From Weifang through to County Yie was the plain of this peninsula. Fields were grown and trimmed like manicured gardens—green everywhere without wasting even a small piece of land.

At County Yie we rented bikes from the County Reception Centre. The bikes were nearly brand new and their green enamel paint glistened in the sun. The bikes were all made in a factory in Qingdao and were not homemade like those in Hebei Province. The bikes had new bells as well as effective brakes. They were called 'the reverse brakes' and worked when one foot reversed the foot-pedals and trod hard.

The road here was also different. Everywhere the roads had a cement surface with fine sand spread thinly over its surface. These were called roads for home defence. The wheels swished when we rode quickly over the road, making me happy and reminding me to be careful not to fall.

Our first stop was Ping Li-dian, where we stayed for one day and one night in order to investigate workers at Cao Jiafu and Chunyu. Then we rode north-east to Xiao Lang-jia. Afterwards we visited Bao-li, Teng-jia, Hou-po, and Feng-mao. Next we stayed at Xing-cheng and visited Qiu-jia. From Xing-cheng we separated for two days—I rode to Zhao-yuan County to conduct investigations in a village and Si went elsewhere to investigate another village.

I started early, carrying several pancakes and a bottle of water in case I did not come across any place on the way to have lunch. It was fortunate that I was prepared, for there was not a single restaurant until I got to the county. The road at the start was flat and the weather was good. Later, a strong wind rose. I was riding up a slope against the wind. I felt thirsty every now and then and soon my water was finished. My throat was dry and itching and I needed water badly. Fortunately, I passed a building by the roadside and begged for water.

The people there told me that I had to ride at least another twenty-five kilometres up the mountain road before I would have ten kilometres down slope to the county town. I was dismayed but I had to ride on. The wind roared and tried to push me back. It was cold but I shed my padded overcoat. When it was approaching noon, I stopped by the roadside to have a pancake and water. Just then a junior high school student rode by.

'Hi, have a rest,' I called at him.

He looked at me, hesitated for a second and then rode to me and alighted from his bike.

'Where to?' I asked.

'The County Junior High School,' he said as he sat by me. I passed him a whole pancake and he accepted it without hesitation. That was the natural behaviour of Shandong people, no unnecessary politeness or pretentious shyness.

'What's in the bag?' I pointed to his bag on the saddle bed of his bike.

'Sweet potato chips,' he replied, 'my food for this month.' This was not what I expected. To me the life of the people here was much better.

'I thought you would have corn or wheat flour at school,' I commented.

'Our county is poor and our life is poor,' he replied. I experienced a sudden surge of emotion. I seemed to be back to my junior high school days. My eyes became moist.

'One more pancake?' I offered him when he finished the first one. We chatted while we ate and drank. I gave him a third—my last pancake.

'I have already had enough,' he said.

'Keep this one for supper,' I told him. And he put it into his school bag, which was hanging from his shoulder.

'Let's go!' he said. 'It will be quite late when we get to the town.'

I looked up and found the sun was already on the descent and I still had at least fifteen kilometres up the slope of the mountain road before me.

We started to go together. The wind showed no sign of abating. My legs and ankles were sore and weak. I exerted myself but could not get my usual strength back. My bike seemed to be progressing at the speed of a snail crawling.

The story of a general in Song Dynasty came to my mind. The general's name was Cao Wei, who was also called Cao Nan-yuan. Nan-yuan was the title of his position given by the emperor. Once he took an army to fight the enemy. When they came to a place that he thought advantageous for his army to use as a battlefield, he ordered them to halt, rest and to cook their meal. When his army was fed, rested, and energetic, the enemy army arrived. The number of the enemy soldiers tripled his own. He sent his messenger to the general of the enemy.

'Dear general,' the messenger said,' my general has instructed me to tell you that it is not fair to fight now because after a long ride your soldiers and horses are tired. Take an hour's rest and then we shall start fighting.'

The enemy's general agreed and chuckled. 'Everybody says General Cao is an able general, but I think he is an idiot. My army is three times stronger than his army and he lets me rest my army for one hour!' He ordered his soldiers to rest. Officers and soldiers alighted from their horses and sat on the ground to rest.

After exactly one hour, General Cao sent his messenger to the enemy's general to tell him it was time for the battle. The enemy was defeated, nearly wiped out. Officers under Cao asked how they won so beautifully. He replied, 'After a long journey and a rest, people will not be energetic enough to fight. Their legs, arms and ankles will be weak. That's why they were defeated.'

I could not get back my strength to ride fast. After a while the student looked back and found he had already been far ahead. So he waited for me to catch up.

'Now, let me haul you up the hill,' he said to me. He untied his belt, which was a long piece of white cloth. He tied his trousers around his waist with a short thin string. He tied the cloth to his cross bar under the seat and tied the other end to my cross bar under the handlebar.

'You just pedal your bike as usual,' he said to me, 'but make sure not to fall!'

We started up the slope against the wind. He seemed not to be exerting himself much, but the speed was faster than I could manage myself. When we finally arrived at the top of the mountain, we got off the bikes and untied the cloth rope.

'Thanks,' I said to him. He just smiled shyly.

'Come to see me at school when you have time,' he told me. 'Be careful riding downhill. Many people fall due to carelessness. Keep your bike braked.' He got on his bike and rode away, fast as an arrow.

The down slope was much steeper. I had to reverse the pedal and press my right foot hard on it to control the speed. I did not pedal even once until I reached the foot of the mountain, a fifteen-kilometre slide. I became relaxed and careless and fell.

Upon reaching the town, I went straight to the County Reception Centre, where I was able to have a hot bath and a good supper. It was late and I was tired. I went to bed early without thinking of lice or bed bugs or fleas. I just slept.

I started early the following day for my destination, a small village in the mountains, but it was in a flat place high up on the mountain and people had land to till. My purpose was to talk to a peasant who was a business partner of a worker of our factory. I arrived in the early afternoon. The brigade leader of the production team was still in the field, working. I had to wait for him in his yard. He was called back about mid-afternoon. I told him my mission.

'Don't be in a hurry,' he told me. 'I will take you to the person you need to see. I think he will be back around supper time.'

He went to cut a big armful of spinach, which was half a metre high and very tender. Then he told his wife to make pancakes and spinach soup.

'You have supper with our family. My son will be back from school soon.' The sun was setting early, probably because we were in the mountains. His son, a boy of six or seven, came back, skipping into the yard, stopped at the sight of me and timidly walked past me. I said hello to him but he just bit his fingernails, stared at me and ran into the house to his mother.

'Village boy,' the man said. 'No manners.'

The man was about thirty years of age, not very tall, but strongly built. Like other Shandong peasants, he looked honest and trustworthy. His head was clean-shaven in the monk style. His eyebrows were very bushy, and as black as Chinese ink. His eyes flashed brightly. His nose was fleshy and his neck thick. He was very sun-tanned. He was not very skilful in expressing himself but he spoke from his heart and he spoke about his heart.

'Supper is ready,' his wife called.

I was surprised because she made a big pile of pancakes as well as a large quantity of spinach soup, but no other dishes. I was wondering how the four of us could consume the pancakes and soup. The boy was elated at the sight of the pancakes and soup, just like I was at the sight of good food when I was his age.

'I reserve the flour for special occasions,' the man told me. 'Today is a special occasion. You have come so far from Tianjin to our small village.'

His wife, who was a beautiful peasant woman, smiled and passed me a pancake and a bowl of spinach soup. The size of the bowl was so big that I was wondering if I finished the soup whether I would still have room for the pancakes. I, the big belly student, was now afraid of not being able to finish the soup!

'We have nothing better to offer you,' the wife said. 'Please forgive us.'

'The food is very good. I am also from a peasant family and if you were a guest in our house, my mother would not be able to treat you with such good food!' I replied.

'I like you very much,' the man said. 'No more such ceremony. Eat as much as you can!' I really exerted myself and I finished one whole pancake and nearly the bowl of soup. My stomach was very full. I put down my chopsticks to wait for them to finish their meal.

'Finished?' he asked. 'You really have had enough?'

I patted my belly and assured him.

'You eat like a kitten,' he laughed. 'I haven't dared to eat yet. I was afraid that there might not be enough for you!' Then he added, 'You eat even less than my son does.'

I was surprised he used the same expressions my father often used such as 'to eat like a kitten'.

Like a whirlwind clearing the remaining clouds, the pile of pancakes and the soup all dwindled quickly. When they finally put down their chopsticks, the pancakes and the soup were gone.

'See? How we peasants can eat!' he told me. Then he laughed like a musical bell.

I loved this family from the bottom of my heart.

After supper, the production team leader took me to the man I wanted to see. He was the party secretary of the village. I asked him all the questions I wished to know about the worker at our factory, read my record of the conversation to him, and showed him where to sign. According to him, the worker had no criminal past, had never changed his name and was a loyal son to his parents. The party secretary pressed his right thumb on the inkpad and then on the place I showed him on my paper. This was the usual way for a peasant to sign.

It was already late and the moon shone brightly in the eastern sky.

'You should stay for the night in our house,' both the party secretary and his wife spoke in unison. 'It is not safe to be travelling so late.'

'I must get up early and join my friend at Xing-cheng,' I told them.

The whole family saw me off to a hilltop.

'Be careful,' the man said. 'This is the short cut. It is seven *li* to the foot of the hill. Then about five or six *li* and you will be in the commune office.' I thanked them wholeheartedly before I mounted my bike.

The moon shone above me and I could see the road clearly. The road was cut off the hill slope, not very wide, but wide enough to allow a single horse cart to pass. On the left side was the steep wall of the cleft hill and on the right was a deep valley. There was still room for a person on foot to pass a cart, but if a cart came from the other direction, there was no way for the two to pass. One had to back off to the very end of the road. It was so quiet that the rushing sound of my bike stirred fear in my mind. Then in the middle of the road was a rock, blocking my passage. When I noticed it, it was already too late for me to avoid it. The front wheel bumped it and I was thrown onto the ground. Fortunately, I was thrown to the side of the hill, not to the side of the valley, which was so deep that I could not see its bottom.

My right hand was bleeding near the bottom of my forefinger. My left knee was also hurting. I found it hard to get up, but I had to move on. The front wheel was out of alignment. I held the wheel between my legs and I took hold of the handlebar to twist it back to normal. I mounted the bike and slid faster and faster, forgetting to brake hard. Before I realised the danger, I was already at the foot of the hill. The road turned parallel to a highway and I failed to notice it. My bike headed directly to the steep side of the highway and I was thrown into the air.

I lay on the slope for some time, my bones seemed to be shaken loose. I looked at my bike, wondering whether I could get it back in alignment. I was about two metres from the highway. I took off my belt, tied it to the handlebar of the bike, and climbed up to the highway. I examined the bike and, thankfully, the damage was not serious, not as serious as the damage to me.

The office of the commune had a light on and I felt relief. I went into the office. A young man on duty, who was practising his brush writing, raised his head and asked me what he could do for me. I handed him my letter of introduction.

'Take a seat,' he pointed to a chair. 'And have a cup of tea.'

I thanked him.

'Your calligraphy is so beautiful!' I remarked as I looked at his writing. His calligraphy was exceptionally good, hard for me to tell the difference between the model writing and his own. He was very pleased.

'Not as good as you think,' he modestly replied. 'Just to pass the time.' Such a reply was the Chinese way of responding to praises by other people. This did not mean he actually denied the quality of his writing.

'You are too modest,' I told him.

'You are so brave to travel during the night,' he said. 'It is not as safe in the night as in the day. Don't be on the road so late at night.'

'The reception centre is by the highway.' He wrote an instruction note, 'Not far, just about a hundred metres or so from here.'

I said goodbye and left. In a couple of minutes I was there. The centre was similar to the motels in our area, which were mainly for carts and drivers. The gate was not locked and there were a few carts in the yard.

'May I have a single room?' I asked when the man in charge came to me.

'Of course,' he replied. 'If you dare do it.' He then took me to a lean-to shed. It had no front wall, but there was a cart inside. He propped the cart with a bench and put some corn stalks inside it. 'You can sleep here. Twenty cents for a quilt if you wish to have one,' he said to me.

'Lice?' I asked.

'No guarantee!'

I did not rent the quilt. I climbed onto the cart and considered what to do. I had a padded overcoat to keep me warm, but what should I do about my letters of introduction and money? I had more than seven hundred yuan in my bag, and that was a fortune! Finally I buckled the leather strap handle of the small bag onto my belt, turned it flat on my breast, buttoned my overcoat and lay face upward in the cart.

My body was aching and all my joints seemed to be falling apart, but I was soon fast asleep despite the aches. It was already morning when I woke up and got ready to ride to join Si about fifty kilometres down the highway.

At County Yie, we returned the bikes and booked bus tickets for County Hai-yang. The Reception Centre did not charge me extra for the damages to the bike. The bikes were for the convenience of the cadres doing investigations and, in any case, the damages were not very serious.

The bus, at about sixty kilometres per hour, moaned forward in the mountains. The local passengers as well as Si dozed to the rocking of the bus. I told myself not to doze off for 'travelling ten thousand *li* is as good as reading ten thousand books' and I wanted to see more with my eyes.

Here and there along the road, I saw small groups of people sieving the pebbles out from a strip of land. Wherever there was soil, pebbles would be sieved out for grain growing. I often saw darkish green wheat growing well in plots of soil about the size of a wash basin. Everywhere on both sides of the road was green—the green of awakening wheat and early vegetables. No soil was wasted. Mountain slopes, covered with terraced fields, looked like potted landscapes!

We arrived at Hai-yang County, tired and fatigued from the shaking of the bus. The sight of the beautiful county town cheered me up, and I insisted that we go for a walk. However, this was not very easy, for we had to either go up hill or down hill all the time.

Everywhere on the peninsula, in county towns and even in villages, we saw beautifully constructed monuments. They silently told people how many good sons and daughters sacrificed their lives in driving out the Japanese invaders, in driving the Kuomintang to Taiwan, and in fighting in North Korea. Exaggerating slightly, I could say that every family had one or more martyrs.

Every county town on the peninsula was much more beautiful than any found in Hebei Province. A gate, a small imitation of the Arc de Triomphe, would welcome a visitor to the town. The towns looked like small-sized cities.

When we entered a restaurant for lunch, each of us would be offered a basin of cold water and a towel to wash our face and hands. Then we would be offered a pot of boiled water and two cups, but not tea. Tea had to be ordered. This I had never come across except on the peninsula.

Two days later, after completing our investigations of several factory workers from the area, we went to Lai-yang County to catch the train to leave the peninsula. It was midnight. We decided to stay in the waiting room of the railway station to sleep a few hours, instead of going to the local reception centre, in order to save money for the factory. Around two o'clock in the morning, two militiamen with guns came to question us:

'Where are you from?'

'Tianjin.'

'Why don't you go to the county reception centre?'

'To save money.'

'Do you know this is a border area?'

'No.'

'Your identification!' they demanded.

We gave them our identification cards.

'We suggest that you go to the reception centre, about a hundred metres from the station.'

We did not go but remained in the waiting room. We were the only occupants. An hour later, another two fully armed militiamen came patrolling into the waiting room. The questions and answers were repeated. If Si and I were to stay in the waiting room, more pairs of armed militiamen would come and repeat the questioning. We were afraid we would meet some unreasonable militiamen and felt we were asking for trouble, so we went to the county reception centre for a few hours sleep.

On our journey back to Tianjin we disembarked at De-zhou to change for the slow train to Wu-qiao, which was our last stop on this trip. We arrived at De-zhou around noon and the train for Wu-qiao was not due until the late afternoon. We each had a piece of famous De-zhou roast chicken, which we ate with discomfort among the stretching arms and open palms of beggars around us. Until now, we had not seen one beggar in the Shandong peninsula.

We decided to find some other transport to get to Wu-qiao. There were many peasants at the station offering to take people to different destinations with their bikes, which were called 'second class vehicles'. The bike owner secured another seat in place of the saddlebag, which the passenger sat on. This was an alternative way to get to Wu-qiao County, which was about twenty kilometres from De-zhou. However, there were many rumours about this type of transport. It was said that the rider could control the seat at the back and if he released a particular mechanism, the seat would tip to one side, leaving the passenger's feet skyward and head earthbound. The rider could then rob the passenger, who was in a helpless position.

Two such riders were negotiating heatedly with Si—'Only ten cents for half a kilometre, very cheap!'

The two riders were strongly built, had stern eyes and muscular faces, which were not seen in real peasants. They tried to persuade Si with sweet words to take the transport. Si was hesitating, he might agree at the price any minute.

'Si, we can wait for the train,' I said to him. 'Anyway we cannot do anything today. It doesn't matter much if we wait for a few more hours for the train!'

He immediately understood my real intention and stopped negotiating with them. Young as I was, Si respected my words and trusted my decision.

The two riders stared at me hard, full of venom and hatred. Had there not been such a big crowd around, they surely would have staged a fight with me. That made me more determined not to travel by 'second class vehicle'.

We arrived at Wu-qiao at six o'clock that evening. The man on duty in the county Communist Party Organisational Department sent us to have our supper at the post office, where, according to him, the food was the best in town. The post office did have the best food of our whole trip, because it was the only place where people offered us pies made from Fu-qiang flour—the whitest wheat flour in China during those years. In Shandong Province, only normal wheat flour was offered at each reception centre.

After supper, the man on duty suggested we deposit our letters of introduction, cash, and other valuables in the department with him. He then recommended an inn for us to stay in. It was not far and it did not take long for us to get there on foot. The management of the inn arranged for us to share a common room with about thirty others, all men and all doing business like us.

At first I thought I was in a common bathroom, because many men were wandering around naked. I was taken aback that cadres should be naked like that and without the least sense of shame. I doubted whether we had come to the right place. I turned to look at Si, and what did I see? He was already naked and was wandering the floor like the others!

When I finished washing my face and feet, I went to the place allotted to me for the night. The neighbour on my right side suggested I should be naked.

'I would like to suggest you take off your clothing and underpants,' he said to me. 'See the basket above your head? It is to hold your clothing. Pull the string and the basket will come down. Otherwise you will carry lice back home!' To show me he pulled his basket down. The basket was secured to the ceiling with rubber bands as wide as the width of a finger and as thick as half a match. They were, I suspected, cut from the used inner tyres of a bike. Lice could not get into the baskets, for sure. They were not as clever as ants and therefore could not get from the wall via the rubber band into the baskets.

My neighbour then explained, 'When you are naked, lice have no place to hide. As long as you make sure that there are no lice hiding in your "bushes", you are safe!'

Si nodded to me to confirm this.

I was still hesitant.

'You are not a teenage girl, are you? What are you ashamed of? Everybody is naked and everybody has the same thing,' my neighbour said as he winked at me jokingly.

In the morning it was a sight. I looked around and found everybody sitting up on the bed parting his pubic hair to check for lice, just like monkeys grooming themselves. Then they would slip off the bed immediately before they pulled down their baskets to get dressed. Once completely dressed, everybody looked like a respectable, gentlemanly cadre. Everybody walked out as if he had not had such an experience. Like everybody else, Si and I thoroughly checked our bodies, dressed, and walked out of the inn like our old selves again.

I could not understand why the management did not try to eliminate the lice with pesticide. It would not cost too much to buy a few bottles of pesticide. I could not understand why Chinese travellers could tolerate the lice without complaint and why no authority had ever checked the sanitary conditions of the inn.

This tour of investigation took us half a month, during which I had seen more of the country and we had collected several dozens of duly signed papers to prove the workers and cadres we investigated were 'clean'.

Ending into a Beginning

The Four Clear Ups steadily approached its ending. Cadres were 'taking a lukewarm bath and descending the stairs'. This meant that the cadres at various levels in the factory were encouraged to raise their political consciousness so that they would confess any wrongdoings they had committed (that is taking a lukewarm bath), and once he had opened up and was considered to have confessed thoroughly by the Four Clear Ups team, as well as by the masses of factory workers, they would descend the stairs and be a normal cadre again. Unless a cadre was exceptionally bad to the workers, it was not very difficult for them to reach this stage. Once descended the stairs, the cadre would have no more burdens or worries.

Meanwhile, all the workers were assessed and divided into groups according to whether they had no, slight or serious economic and/or political wrong doings. The group of workers with a bad past were the most active group. Each one wanted to show that he was politically active by exposing others in the group—such a group was organised by the 'prisoner against prisoner' method, which was invented by a man in our group who came from the Public Security Bureau. When this stage finished, I thought, the Four Clear Ups would come to an end.

Sometime about March 1966, long articles of criticism appeared more frequently in the *Ren Min Ri Bao* (*People's Daily*). Articles called 'Criticising the Three-household Village', 'Criticising "The Deposing of Hairui"', and so on began to occupy full pages of this official newspaper.

'When mountain rain approaches, the wind fills the tower'. My friend Zuo and I felt that a greater political movement loomed over us. We paid more attention to the articles carried in *Ren Mi Ri Bao*, trying hard to understand what was happening. There were always two trends in a movement—one to target the cadres and the other to target everyone. There was some kind of struggle behind this. Then Madame Jiang-qing (Mao's third wife) and Madame Wong Guang-mei (Liu Shaoqi's wife) each respectively put forward their experiences in the Socialist Education Movement in the countryside. The conclusions of the two reports were different, with each opposing the other.

On 2 June, the Central Broadcast Station aired an article by Nie Yuan-zi, a cadre of Beijing University, and her friends. This heralded a new political movement—the Great Cultural Revolution. On 13 June, without completely finishing our task as the Four Clear Ups, we were taken back to the Institute. As far as we were concerned, the Four Clear Ups ended with the commencement of the Great Cultural Revolution.

chapter 23

ACTIVITIES IN THE GREAT CULTURAL REVOLUTION

Mao tried his hardest to make the cadres and members of the Communist Party, as well as the officials at various levels in the government, servants of the people. He continuously cleansed the Party and the government in order to keep China red. For the same purpose, Mao began the Great Cultural Revolution in 1966. The Great Cultural Revolution was designed to destroy the culture of pre-Communist China, and to shake up the ranks of the party cadre from their positions of privilege, to punish cadres and intellectuals who would not proceed along the socialist road mapped out by Mao. Leaders such as Peng Zhen, Liu Shaoqi and Deng Xiaoping all suffered, as did intellectuals and those who didn't fit within the grand plan of Mao. Mao's power and popularity peaked during this period when a cult of personality was born in the symbolism of a little red book consisting of his quotations, buttons that bore his portrait, and statues edifying him in front of significant public buildings. However, silent opposition was too big for him to overcome and the comrades he chose to direct the Cultural Revolution were wrongly selected—they could not possibly put Mao's thinking into practice. Mao failed and his ideals about cleansing the party and the government were disposed of after his death in 1976. His thinking of keeping China red was also destroyed.

Stopping Classes to Carry out Revolution

On 13 June 1966, our grade was driven by truck back to the Peking Foreign Trade Institute, which was warm, cordial and welcoming, but at the same time as unfamiliar as a stranger. Something foreboding was in the air, like the calm before the storm. In the entrance hall of the office building, two big character posters attracted my attention. (During the Great Cultural Revolution, students wrote political posters with very large characters or 'Chinese words'. Such posters were called 'big character posters'.) High on the right wall was one saying:

'Comrade Kang Sheng said: After investigation, we confirm that there was a February military coup.'

High on the left wall was another poster saying:

'Comrade Deng Xiaoping said: After investigation, we confirm that there was no such a thing as a February military coup.'

These two examples of 'big character posters', which did not arouse much attention at the time, showed clearly the two opposing forces in the Great Cultural Revolution—those who allegedly followed Mao's policies and those who opposed them. It was believed the former wanted to keep China red, to follow the socialist road, and to respect workers and peasants as masters of the country, while the latter wanted China to go along the capitalist road and return to the private system, which in the past had exploited workers and peasants.

A work team from the Ministry of Foreign Trade was already at our Institute to lead the Great Cultural Revolution. A work team was made up of all levels of cadres from the Ministry of Foreign Trade, and each member was responsible for directing the students of one class in studying Mao's works and in criticising their own selfish thinking for not writing big character posters exposing cadres who were pro-capitalist. Classes were ceased and every day we studied Chairman Mao's works and wrote posters to expose the bourgeois reactionary educational line of the Party Committee of the Institute. My friend, Zuo, and I jointly wrote a big poster called 'From the Chinese Textbook to See the Bourgeois Reactionary Educational Line of the Party Committee of the Institute'.

In the corridor of the office building there was a poster exposing the 'crime' of the president of our Institute. In 1958, at the order of the Party Committee of Beijing, he wrote the *Report on the Life of Peasants in the Countryside*. In the report he said that every peasant was a thief and that each peasant was fat from eating sweet potatoes. It was said that such reports were prepared to use against Mao at the Lu Shan Conference, a gathering for government officials to learn the lessons of the Great Leap Forward.

Another 'crime' was conducted by the deputy president of the Institute—a specialist in economy. He hung a scroll of his own calligraphy of the poem by Lu You called *In Praise of the Plum Flower*. It reads:

'By the dilapidated bridge nearby the courier station,
It bloomed lonely, unnoticed.
Lonely and sad in the evening twilight,
Wind and rain added to its sorry plight.

Harbouring no intention to vie for the spring,
   She tolerated the jealousy of the beauties.
   Flower petals fell off, were crushed into dirt,
   But the fragrance still lingered.'
   (Lu You '1125–1210' was a famous poet in the Song Dynasty 960–1279 AC. This is my own translation of the poem.)

This was criticised as being 'dissatisfied with the Party'. The deputy president lost his position and was forced to do physical labour.

Soon, the targets of criticism became the professors and teachers who were labelled as bourgeois rightists. Posters denouncing them all covered the walls of the teachers' building. The professors and teachers were called 'oxen demons' and 'serpent spirits'. They were forced to do the cleaning in the Institute and they lived in the common dormitory, which was called the Ox Shed. Everywhere were posters such as 'The Red Skinned Turnips Bai Hong', meaning that although Bai Hong, a young teacher, looked like a red expert on the outside, he was actually a 'white expert', and 'Small Reptile Peng Ming', meaning that the young teacher, Peng, who was a candidate for promotion, was an opportunist.

One day a few men, among them the deputy president of the Institute, were pushed onto the stage in our dining hall. Each one had a tall paper funnel hat on his head and a small heavy blackboard hanging from his neck. Behind each of them stood a student.

'Lower your heads to the people!' the students below the stage shouted.

Most of the men on the stage lowered their heads. Sweat dripped from their faces due to the weight of the blackboards and their bending backs and heads. Only one man refused to lower his head. He was of middle height, strongly built and his square face was coffee-coloured. I heard somebody say his name was Lu Gang.

'Lower your head!' the students shouted.

'No! I am not a counter-revolutionary! I cannot lower my head!' he shouted back.

The student behind him tried to press down his head, but he stiffened his neck and struggled to keep his head high. Two more students came over to hold his arms to force him to bend his back and lower his head. He again refused and struggled to keep his dignity. Tempered through wars and coming from Yenan, he definitely regarded himself as totally revolutionary.

On another day, I was wandering in front of the office building, reading the posters. Suddenly, some students surrounded a professor who had a goatee.

'Confess your anti-party thinking!' someone shouted from among the crowd.

'I've never had any anti-party ideas and thinking,' the professor replied. Confusion was clear on his face. It was said that he had lived overseas for many years and he now lived in China because Premier Zhou had wanted him to stay to coach young teachers.

'Why did you refuse to translate Mao's poems?' somebody shouted from among the crowd again.

The professor took off his glasses to wipe off the sweat from his brow.

'Down with Hu Tu!' students shouted. 'You cannot fool us. You must confess!'

'Dear students, I really have nothing to confess. Please don't criticise me. I will translate a few of Mao's poems for you. I guarantee the translation will be much better than the ones you already have,' he pleaded.

Then the students started to surround another professor who, it was said, was a schoolmate of Liu Shaoqi. Such incidents became more and more frequent with each passing day.

Immediately afterwards, the spearhead of criticism was directed at the students. Posters between students against one another appeared on the walls. In our class a few of my classmates were manoeuvring to label me a 'white expert'. I had no idea why they wanted to do this but I did know that if I was labelled this, it would be impossible for me to be assigned posts in foreign dealings. Posters also started to appear, accusing Jiang of harbouring reactionary thoughts. The 'task of criticising those authorities within the Party who followed the capitalist road' was forgotten and heated debates and arguments about the 'ideals' of certain students arose between groups of students. Fortunately, the work team was regarded by the Party's Central Committee as implementing a reactionary capitalist line and was withdrawn from the Institute. Consequently, students stopped writing posters against one another and nobody had the mind to accuse me of being a 'white expert' anymore.

'Dragon gives birth to dragon and phoenix gives birth to phoenix.' 'A rat's offspring can only make underground tunnels.' Such couplets were posted on the sides of classroom doors and caused many debates and criticism. They were regarded as reactionary and occurred everywhere and everyday! The noise of heated arguments and debates filled the corridors and antagonism belched from the eyes of the two sides—those who supported the work team and those who opposed them. The study of Chairman Mao's works took up less and less time in the classroom—it was difficult for students of the same class to even sit together. The day when normal classes would resume seemed far away. I dreaded that the day would never come until it was time for me to leave the Institute. I felt very indignant at heart.

818 Red Guards and Maoist Red Guards

My First Big Character Poster, by Chairman Mao, which was subtitled 'Bombarding the Headquarters', was published and broadcast. For the first time it was revealed to the whole nation that within the Communist Party there were two headquarters—one was Mao's and the other was Liu Shaoqi's and Deng Xiaoping's. Liu Shaoqi and Premier Zhou were directing the daily routine of the Party's Central Committee. When the Great Cultural Revolution broke out in the universities in June 1966, they sent work teams into the universities to control its orientation. This was regarded as a measure to extinguish any revolutionary flames in the universities. Mao ordered to pull the work teams out of the universities and demanded Liu and Zhou to make a self-criticism. We did not hear whether Liu did so, but we did listen to the broadcast from the station of our Institute to the self-criticism of Premier Zhou En-lai, from his tape-recorded speech.

The work team in our Institute began conducting self-criticisms in front of the entire student body. 'During the fifty-two days since our arrival at the Institute, we, the work team, have made mistakes in direction and line.' The head of the work team, a deputy minister from the Ministry of Foreign Trade, uttered those exact words slowly and clearly at each self-criticism. He was described by Western countries as thinking while speaking. No matter how much the students shouted slogans, he never changed a word.

'What kind of mistakes in direction and line?' the students questioned him, shouting from below the stage. He still used the same words. He never mentioned what 'direction' or what 'line' was.

On 18 August 1966, Chairman Mao interviewed representatives of the Red Guards from universities in north-east China. This meant he acknowledged the Red Guards. The Red Guards was an organisation of student revolutionists that soon spread to all the universities, high schools and primary schools. They pledged their loyalty to Mao and the socialist road. The Red Guards despised anything foreign and old and broke into the homes of cadres, teachers and writers to destroy or seize old books and artworks. They orchestrated many denunciation meetings where they jeered and humiliated accused intellectuals for their bourgeois thinking. It was very simple to form an organisation of Red Guards. A group of students of the same opinion just selected their leaders, made and wore the red membership armbands, which had the name of their organisation printed on them. Each member also adopted a revolutionary name—mine was Xiao Bing meaning 'little soldier'.

To show loyalty to Mao, the 818 Red Guards were formed in our Institute, the members of which were those who supported the work team and the authority of the Institute. Whenever students shouted that the work team should make further self-criticisms, the 818 Red Guards would make a greater noise to drown out their voices. The 818 Red Guards were thus called 'The Royal Protection Section', meaning that they, being the great majority at the time, protected those in power.

Another smaller group, which included the son of a deputy mayor of Shanghai as its head, was demanding the work team make further self-criticisms. This group was called the 'minority group'. To distinguish themselves from the 818 Red Guards, they adopted the name 'Maoist Red Guards'. Helped by the 818 Red Guards, the work team withdrew from our Institute.

The Maoist Red Guards was formed to protect Chairman Mao, to protect the Central Committee led by Mao, and to protect the Socialist road. They demanded that the work team come back to the Institute for self-criticism and to answer questions. The demand of the Maoist Red Guards was not treated seriously, and as a result, some sixty students, who were its members, went to the Ministry of Foreign Trade requesting that the work team return to the Institute. About five or six students from our class, who shared the same opinion of this minority group, joined the Maoist Red Guards when it was formed. We were also present among the peaceful sitters and I was one of them. There was no response from the Ministry at the time.

The students refused to leave the yard of the Ministry and a 'peaceful sitting' was staged. Each member spoke explaining why the work team should be back at the Institute. People working in the Ministry came to listen to the speeches of the students. Office hours had long finished and the evening deepened into a starry night. The air became cold but we all sat there, singing:

'Taking up our pens as knives and rifles,
People of the whole country are smashing the black gangs.
Workers, peasants, soldiers, students, and merchants rebel together,
We must be the vanguards of the Cultural Revolution.
Sha! Sha! Sha!'

We made speeches, regardless of whether people from the Ministry were present or not. Cold and hungry, we were in high spirits. The thought of protecting Mao's Headquarters was firm in our hearts. Suddenly, some people from the Ministry became active, but no important people appeared. They came to us with hot water. Midnight passed. The air became colder, but the sitting and speeches continued.

The acting minister of the Ministry of Foreign Trade came out at last. It was said that he was a guard of Zhu De, one of the initial members of the Communist Party's standing committee, and that he had completed the whole of the Long March. He was a veteran revolutionary. It was also said that he suffered from poor health.

'Comrade students, it is cold here. Please come into the building,' he spoke to us persuasively.

'Thanks,' students chorused. 'We are quite all right here!'

'If you don't come in, I will stay here to accompany you!' the minister said. Overcoats were taken to the spot to protect us from the cold and the ensuing speeches by the students became emotional with many weeping and crying out.

'Dear minister,' some students said as they stood up to speak, 'please go back home and sleep. We know you old revolutionaries are caring for us. But you are not young, and if you become sick, we shall feel very bad!' Our affection moved the minister so much that he went back into the building.

During the small hours of the morning, it got terribly cold. The minister came back and spoke to us affectionately again. We remained unmoved and our demand remained unchanged. The work team had to come back to the Institute to answer questions from the students.

The Ministry asked the students to send representatives into the building to negotiate. Ten students were selected to do the job, including me.

'Your name please,' a secretary said as he was ready to jot down the names of the representatives.

'Our names do not matter much,' we replied. Nobody gave his name.

'But I have to keep a record,' the secretary said.

'Record? For what?' we asked.

Just then the attendants from the Ministry entered with the deputy minister. An agreement was made in the end, after lengthy negotiations. It was agreed that the work team would return to the Institute to conduct self-criticisms and to answer questions. The contents of the negotiation were not to be disclosed and no personal physical harm was to happen to the work team members. The peaceful sitting demonstration would end immediately after the agreement took effect. Later we learned that students from other universities also made 'peaceful sitting' demonstrations at the same time.

We returned to the Institute and the work team came back as well. The 'great debate' was held in front of the classroom building.

Things changed quickly. A conference for establishing the headquarters of the Maoist Red Guards was convened at the Great Hall of the People in Beijing. Madam Mao spoke at the meeting. She announced the establishment of the second headquarters of the Red Guards and told the Red Guards that General Liu Zhi Jian was nominated as their commander. (The first headquarters of the Red Guards was that of the 818 Red Guards. Very soon a third headquarters was set up. Red Guards in the universities were divided into sections of 'tian' (meaning 'sky') and 'di' (meaning 'earth'). Mayor Peng and the deputy mayors of Beijing were criticised in front of tens of thousands of students. Vivid stories like that described in novels were told about how Mayor Peng was taken away for criticism. His face became swollen from the beatings inflicted upon him. The deputy mayors were criticised and manhandled in front of the masses. Posters insinuated that Peng and a deputy mayor kept girls in a hospital in Beijing for sexual pleasure. I felt confused and flabbergasted. I decided to just worry about what happened in our Institute.

'The Sunshine of the Communist Party Illuminates the Road of the Proletarian Cultural Revolution' was published in an editorial in *Ren Min Ri Bao* (*People's Daily*). The political views of the Maoist Red Guards proved to be in line with Mao's policies. Its orientation was considered to be the right one. The Maoist Red Guards became the great majority and have remained so ever since.

House Searching

One day, the Maoist Red Guards from our class were called to check the property of a professor of our Institute.

'He has been suspected of being a spy,' a man from the Public Security Bureau hinted. 'He might have a radio transmitter in his house. Make sure you dig it out.'

About ten boys and girls were taken to the house by a truck. It was a typical Beijing compound house of grey bricks, with a date tree in the middle of its small yard. On the walls were expensive pictures and scrolls of calligraphy from well-known calligraphers.

The professor was a sick old man with a pale face. His eyes were very large and his features still showed that he had once been a handsome young man. His wife, a small lady, was Japanese. Both of them stared at us with wide eyes—so wide that I feared that they might split at the corners. Great fear showed in their eyes, which looked like the eyes of scared, timid animals. We asked them questions but their lips quivered so violently that their answers were impossible to understand. We advised them not to be nervous, but nothing we said to them could calm them down. We put two chairs in the yard and asked them to sit there. They obeyed, resignedly watching.

'Please, somebody, keep a record,' I suggested. My friend, Zuo, immediately sat by a desk to write all the items that were moved out of the house into the yard. Rolls of fabric, such as silk, wool, velvet and twills were piled into the yard first. Then their clothes were moved out, again piled high in the yard. Next came washing soap, twenty or thirty boxes, all so dry that I doubted whether they could still be used. Next were boxes of toilet soap. When beautifully painted fan coverings were bundled out, the man spoke—he had at last found his voice.

'Please do not damage them. If they are sold to a foreign country, each can bring at least five to ten US dollars.'

We knew that. In China, pictures, calligraphy scrolls, and fan coverings could maintain their value. People with money always stored these things. Many had not recovered from the fear of the shortages they had suffered during the famine years and kept these 'treasures' in case they could be sold for an emergency. The couple was already old and had no children. I could not understand why they stored up so many things, which they might not need to touch for many years to come. I thought that although they had money and knowledge, they lacked the practical knowledge needed in everyday life.

We tried our best to look everywhere inside the house for the radio transmitter suggested by the man of the Public Security Bureau. We knocked on the walls, probed each and every brick of the floor to see whether anyone could be concealing a secret chamber. Nothing was found except a certificate issued to him by the Kuomintang authority as an interpreter of Senior General category. Whatever we tried, we could not locate any radio transmitter. I never trusted a word from the Public Security Bureau from then onward. We put everything back in its original position, following the list we had made. The lady, from the beginning to the end, never uttered a word. Her wide eyes watched us with melancholy. I was sorry that I was among the searchers.

My Only Visit to Zhong Nan Hai

One day I was wandering in front of the office building of the Institute, reading the posters, which, by then, were glued onto reed mattresses rigged up on the walls. Somebody called to me loudly, 'Chun-ying, please come here.'

I looked up and saw a minibus with a few students in it.

'Come! Be quick!' Somebody gestured to me from the bus.

I ran over and no sooner had I jumped into the bus than it closed its door and moaned away, out of the school.

'Where to?' I asked.

'Deputy Premier Li Shian-nian is to see us in Zhong Nan Hai,' somebody advised me. I was immediately excited about this. Zhong Nan Hai is west of the Forbidden City in Beijing and is where the leaders of the Chinese Central Government and Party work and live. It contains many gardens and houses and is protected by high brick walls. It was another world to me and I never dreamed that I would set foot there. Now the opportunity fell upon me from Heaven and I could not find any suitable adjectives to make a comment.

The minibus ran swiftly towards the city. I was remembering the first time I saw Li Shian-nian from a distance in the dining hall of our Institute. Li had come to make a speech and when he talked about Mao's age, he made this comment:

'Everybody shouted and wished that Mao live for ten thousand years. This is merely wishful thinking. This is merely a good wish. Whoever can live ten thousand years? From my heart, I do wish that Mao be able to live a hundred and twenty years. Thus he can lead us into doing lots of revolutionary deeds.' Just then, a piece of paper was passed from hand to hand onto the stage and then into his hands.

'Please read the paper out!' some students shouted from below the stage.

'We all wish that Mao live ten thousand years, you alone wish that Mao live a hundred and twenty years. Aren't you opposing Mao?' he read.

'I am not against Mao. I support him without reserve. I just used that as an example to explain that we should seek truth from the facts!' Li explained.

'Li Shian-nian opposes Mao! Down with Li Shian-nian!' broke out from the audience. It became impossible for Li to explain further. He was escorted off the stage and left quickly.

The minibus stopped just inside the rear northern gate of Zhong Nan Hai, just in front of the guards' shed. A soldier, his waist holding a pistol, came directly to us.

'Line up and follow me,' he spoke with a solemn face. He started to walk, army style, without any other words. We followed him in single file, and at the end of the line another soldier, similarly attired and armed, escorted us. We walked about thirty metres to a door, opened from a high wall on the right side. We were told to go through the door, where two men in plain clothes were awaiting us. When the last person was inside the door, the two soldiers left for their shed at the gate. Inside, it was a normal courtyard with high walls on each side. A normal northern Chinese house which was quite old and faced south.

Li Shian-nian was waiting for us at the door, on top of the steps. One of the two men who waited for us at the gate came forward a few quick steps, raised the curtain for the Deputy Premier, and for us. Deputy

Premier Li, with a smile on his broad face, shook hands with each and every one of us and then ushered us into a room with a gesture of his right hand.

It was a large conference room with a curtain to conceal another room to our left, which I thought was Li's office. We were asked to sit around a big long rectangular table with immaculate white cotton sheets spread over the table. An ordinary porcelain mug filled with jasmine tea was placed in front of each of us. The chairs had arms, also covered with white cotton. Secretaries and shorthand recorders were sitting under the window all along the bottom wall. No recording machine was to be seen anywhere in the room. Standing at the window side, not far from the door, were girls ready to serve tea. The droning of passing buses or trucks and the honking of cars could be heard now and then. The Deputy Premier's office was not far from the street—even a deputy premier was not exempt from noise pollution.

'Xiao Song,' the Deputy Premier started speaking, 'how is your father?' (Song was the son of a deputy mayor of Shanghai.)

'I have not heard from him in a long time,' Xiao Song answered.

'Xiao Liu, how is your father?' Li asked a dark-skinned girl with a round face.

'Very well,' the girl answered, 'thank you.' (The father of Miss Liu was a high-ranking commander.)

He then asked the name of everybody, only without the small talk due to unfamiliarity.

'Now let me check whether I have got the names correctly,' a secretary said. He then read the name and the position of the seat corresponding to the name.

'The purpose of bringing you here,' Li began after he knocked at his cup with a spoon, 'is to listen to you talk about the Great Cultural Revolution in your Institute. One will speak on your behalf and others can make amendments.' He leaned back against his chair, ready to listen to the report by the student's speaker. His face had an expression of concentrated attention. Song, being the head of the Maoist Red Guards of our Institute, began reporting. Now and then Li would ask a question or two. Like most of the ten students present, I kept silent during the whole meeting, which lasted about fifty minutes. I was terribly surprised that the Deputy Premier should allocate such a long time to listening to the students. He had so much to deal with every day. 'Why?' I asked myself. This only showed that the Great Cultural Revolution was of particular importance. Deputy Premier Li, to assess the situation in the universities, had to know what was actually happening there so that he could always adjust his own orientation.

'Thank you for letting me know so much. Thank you everybody. If there is anything you wish to let me know, just give my secretary a call.' Li stood up from his chair.

Li saw us off to the step of his house, waved goodbye to us and we were then escorted, one soldier at the head of our single file and one at the end, to our minibus. When our bus started to leave, the soldiers saluted us by putting their right palms to their hat rims. They stood at attention until our bus exited the gate.

Becoming Inactive

A liaison cadre was positioned in our Institute by Premier Zhou to report to him about the development of the Great Cultural Revolution in our Institute. The name of the liaison man was Shih. I also heard that Jiang Qing (Mao's third wife) also positioned a liaison cadre in our Institute, but I did not know his name. Similarly, liaison cadres were positioned in all universities in Beijing.

One night we were already asleep when we were woken to make posters in the street. The head of Dong Fang Hong Commune (the headquarters of the Maoist Red Guards) told us that Jiang Qing requested us to make the posters. She had advised our Institute that Yang Cheng Wu (a well-known army general), Yu Li Jin (also from the army), and Fu Chong Bi (a high-ranking officer in the army), all were reactionaries. We had to post up 'Down with Yang, Yu, Fu!' slogans quickly in support of her.

A few rubber-wheeled pushcarts were already loaded with huge tubs of homemade glue (cooked starch), bundles of paper and brooms, ready for us to set out. Many students were already waiting in front of the office building for other students to come. About thirty students set out immediately with pushcarts, glue, papers and ink. Our group started from the outside wall of the zoo. I was applying glue to the wall with a broom, like a few others, and some girls were attaching paper, pieces as large as one metre by one-and-a-half metres, to the wall. Some students who could write with a beautiful hand started to paint the words on the glued paper. Others also used big brushes and ink to make circles with vertical crosses on the names meaning they were already knocked down. Groups of students from other institutes and universities also came to write the same slogans. They branched off to the other main streets. We returned to the Institute in the small hours of the morning, but I could not sleep.

Lying in bed I was thinking about what I had read from *The Journey to the West*. Monkey was fighting monsters, demons and devils of various kinds, but where did those monsters, demons and devils come from? Some were from Buddha, some were from Heaven, and some were from the gods. In the Great Cultural Revolution, who brought the news to us, always so timely? Who were the activists in the different Red Guard organisations? Most of them, if not all of them, were the sons and daughters of high-ranking officials in the government offices or in the army.

I recalled what Lewis Carroll wrote in his complete works about a man standing on a balcony with a green flag in one hand and a red flag in the other. Down below, there were two lines of people extending to far away distances. When he raised the green flag in one hand, one line would wriggle like a snake and shout vociferously. When he lowered his green flag that line would immediately stop shouting and moving. When he raised the red flag in his other hand, the other line would start wriggling and shouting instantly. He thus alternated his flags to control the two lines. This vividly describes how the Party supporters and Party handlers operated. Yes, Mao inaugurated the Great Cultural Revolution because he wanted to root out the capitalist line within the Party. But now everybody labelled him or herself as raising high the red banner of Mao. Who was to be believed?

At best I could only be an unknown and unimportant helper to people I did not know. I was only one of the students of the Red Guard, helping somebody to dispose of others for their own personal interests. I seemed to be, as every student was, a puppet. I could not see what would happen and I could not predict the outcome of the Great Cultural Revolution. I could not see who was really working for the benefit of the people while everyone labelled themselves as servants of the people. The Red Guards were like huge guns that were always used by people to reach their aim. I did not want to be part of this gun, yet I had to be a Red Guard, to support or oppose according to instructions. One's performance in the Great Cultural Revolution would be decisive in their assignment to different posts at the time of graduation. I could not openly show my dislike of being manipulated—the zeal I had felt at the beginning of the Great Cultural Revolution began to die away. With two *man tou* in my pocket, I would go into a nearby field each day and sit under a big tree to read my English novels. I was in constant fear of being found out by other students. I was not keen to carry out the revolution and only interested in reading English. This would endanger my graduation, even endanger my assignment to certain posts if anyone found out. To study, I had to be like a thief!

However, as far as I was concerned, the Great Cultural Revolution had lost its attraction, although at heart I was convinced that it was necessary. Without self-purging and self-purifying, the servants of the people would soon be lords over and above the people. I could see Mao could not attain his original goal because the people he appointed to lead and guide the Great Cultural Revolution were seeking their own power. In my mind I compared the struggles of the Great Cultural Revolution to the struggles of the old dynasties between the good and bad officials. I did not believe any of them would really carry Mao's target to the end. But I, unknown and unimportant, was insignificant and could do nothing about it.

As an Interpreter at an Exhibition

One of my classmates became one of the heads of the Dong Fang Hong Commune. He said to me one day, 'Belgium will have an industrial exhibition in Beijing very soon. Will you agree to be an interpreter?'

I agreed instantly. Three or four from our class and from our Red Guard organisation were also chosen to be interpreters there.

In a day or two, I was notified to undergo policy training in the building of the Foreign Trade Promotion Committee. The contents of training included learning the twelve rules and regulations for those who had dealings with foreigners, answering questions such as 'how did you come here to be an interpreter?' But mainly we learned policies about Taiwan, Tibet and the Great Cultural Revolution.

The Foreign Trade Promotion Committee shared a huge building with the Ministry of Aquatic Products—a majestic building on the western end of Chang-an Street. We got in and out of the building with a temporary pass. The room for our policy study was on the eighth floor.

One mid-morning, our training was interrupted by chaotic cries from below the building, outside in the yard. We ran to the window to see what was happening. We just caught sight of a man dangling on the power line and then falling to the roof of a small building, dead. I pulled my head in immediately, feeling sick. The man was a cadre from the Ministry of Aquatic Products. He jumped out the window to end his life. At that time, those who committed suicide were mostly those, as I saw it, with problems. They either wore the 'rightist' hat or were men of authority. In our Institute, a teacher working in the printing office jumped to his death from the roof of the office building, which was six storeys high. The president of the Institute also jumped to his death, not from the office building but from the teachers' building. The president was a revolutionary and had worked in Yenan for many years before 1949. When I heard about his death days later, I found it hard to accept the cruel fact. He was such a kind, educated, good mannered old man when he 'ordered' me to sit by him on the riverbank, where he liked to fish, to have a chat. He told me jokes and asked me to tell him a joke or two. He laughed so heartily he had to take off his glasses to mop his eyes. This was so vivid in my mind that I simply could not accept that he was dead.

The site for the Belgium Industrial Exhibition was in the Agricultural Exhibition Hall on the other side of Beijing—the eastern side. We were taken there for the night. We were paid twelve yuan per day per head—the highest salary at the time. The money would be paid to the Institute, but where the money really went, I did not know.

I was in charge of the Control and Automation Section. The boss was called Mr William. He was busy every day lecturing on automation to the Chinese experts and specialists. He seldom came to the site but attended seminars while he entrusted the work at the site to an engineer called Michael and myself. Michael was an honest and interesting man. Whenever I needed his help, I could not say, 'Hello, Mr. Michael, would you please come over and help me?' If I said this, he would invariably reply, 'Sorry, I am busy.'

One day it was too difficult for me to explain or to answer the questions of the visitors. I was so frustrated that I forgot the proper etiquette. I beckoned Michael to come over and help me. Beads of sweat on his forehead, he scurried over to me and asked for my instructions. He made some very comprehensive explanations and the visitors seemed very pleased and satisfied. Michael himself was also very happy to answer all the questions.

Later I resumed calling him Mr. Michael and again he rebuffed me. Then I tried the informal way again, just to call him over to have a cup of coffee, and he hurried over to me right away.

'Michael,' I once asked him when we were sipping coffee in our office at the site. 'Why are you displeased when I am polite with you and happy when I am very informal with you?'

'Simple,' he replied. 'When you are polite you are treating me as a capitalist. I am not a capitalist. I am just an engineer—an employee. But when you are informal with me you are treating me as one of your own comrades. That's why I am happy.' Then after a while he added, 'So don't "Sir" me and don't "Mister" me in the future. Just treat me the way you do your own friends.' I agreed. We became friends and, at the call of an old man who made coffee for us, we sat together with our coffee and had a short chat during the morning and afternoon break. The old man making coffee was very tall and had an honest and kind face. He told me that all his life he had been working in embassies of foreign countries in China. If either Michael or I was in the office, he would never sit down. I asked him to sit down several times but he never did. He said he had no right to sit while Michael and I were there. I told him we were equal but he just smiled and went busily about his work.

On the last day of the exhibition, Mr William was to entertain managers and the interpreters.

'C.Y.' he spoke to me, 'can you organise a banquet for about forty people on my behalf?'

'Yes, I can.' I told him. 'How much per head do you want to spend? And where would you like to have this banquet?'

'How much do you think will be all right? I want it to be better than the one you Chinese treated me to. It must look very good,' he said. He was very happy because he had received some business orders from the Chinese. 'How about the Beijing Duck Restaurant?' he suggested.

'The restaurant is all right. What about twelve yuan per head?' I asked.

'Enough?'

'I must check.'

'I will be available within one hour. Ring my hotel by then.'

I checked with the Beijing Duck Restaurant at Qian Men Street as to how much it cost per head for a good banquet for forty people. I was told that if it was for a Chinese company, it would be twelve yuan per head. If it was for a foreign company, the price was double. I told them that I was arranging the banquet in the name of a foreign friend and I wished to have good food at a reasonable price. The man who answered the phone told me he would make sure I was pleased about the food at twenty-four yuan per head. I rang Mr William and he was exceptionally happy with the arrangement.

Mr William met me at the restaurant on the day of the banquet. He thanked me for my efforts in managing his section at the exhibition and asked that I sit next to him. After the hosts and the guests were seated, he whispered to me, 'I will not speak to you before you have eaten enough. Don't worry about me or about any other people, just eat and let me know when you have had enough.' I thought Mr William was so considerate to me because he was pleased with my work during the whole exhibition.

Four waiters came in, each with a big fat duck on a tray. They bent their backs to show them to us and then left.

'The waiters are showing which ducks will be prepared for us,' somebody explained.

Next the soup and entrée came which looked beautiful and tasted marvellous. Mr William tried his best to let me eat a comfortable meal. We interpreters were not allowed to have food in the mouth when interpreting for people. Therefore frequent interpreting would make an interpreter hungry. When the Chinese acted as hosts, interpreters could, after the banquet, stay behind to have a meal without worrying about any interruption. When foreigners acted as the hosts, if they were not considerate, the interpreters had to go home with a half-filled stomach. I was taught not to eat fish nor to eat pork with bones, but just to have something I could swallow instantly if I was spoken to.

Boisterous conversation was rolling on at the other three tables, but our table was very quiet. We just concentrated on our food. Mr William and I did not join the conversations. When the duck was finished, I looked up and questioned him with my eyes. He opened his eyes wide to question whether I was really ready to interpret for him. I nodded slightly. Instantly he put down his fork and knife and became lively with chatter. Just then, each of the waiters served another dish at each table. I had never entered the Beijing Duck Restaurant before and I did not know what the dish was. I shook my head when Mr William looked at me. Nobody explained what the dish was.

Michael, who sat at another table, was back to back with me. He turned his head and touched my shoulder.

'C.Y.' he whispered to me, 'what is it?' I whispered back, 'I have no idea. I have never had Beijing duck before.' He turned to the normal position at his table. He picked up one half from the small plate and put a piece into his mouth. He was so bold that, like 'Columbus finding the new continent', he had to have a try. He bit down hard on it but could not wrench even a small bit off it. He was not successful after several more tries. He then put it into an ashtray.

'Michael,' a Chinese manager said to him, 'it is the beak of the duck. When the beak is served on the table, it means the duck is already completely finished.'

'Oh!' Mr William said. 'Our Michael has not had a meal for three days since he was advised about this dinner party.'

Rowdy laughter broke out. Instantly Michael's face turned red. The joke, I thought, was a bit too much.

Mr William would not let his tongue rest, even for a minute. He started to chat and talk and joke with everybody around the table. I was busy interpreting non-stop, but I no longer worried about having food in the mouth. I thanked him for letting me have an untroubled meal. He patted on my shoulder and said, 'I have to thank you, my dear friend. You have done so much for me.' Then he hugged me goodnight.

The exhibition came to an end. The Chinese Foreign Trade Promotion Committee arranged a farewell party at the Xin-qiao Hotel. On all three sides of a big hall were very long tables, which had food of various kinds—chicken cooked in different ways, roast duck, cooked pork, mutton, beef, fish, dim sum, cakes, and so on. In the middle of the hall and encircled by the tables with food were about forty round tables. Ten chairs were placed around each table, for guests to sit on.

The administration department of the exhibition requested that an interpreter sit at each table. Everyone wanted to squeeze to the front tables to catch the eye of the reporters' camera. I preferred to have a peaceful meal, so I took a seat among the last ten. No Belgians would want to sit at such a table, away from the important Chinese officials. My judgement was correct. At our table was a man from the Ministry of Construction Industry, a reporter from *Ren Min Ri Bao* (*People's Daily*), a reporter from Xinhua News Agency, a reporter from *China Reconstruct*, and a friend of mine from our Institute who was interpreting in French. We had no interpreting work to do the whole night.

At the close of the exhibition, we had one week of group discussion to sum up the work. Every day we had to talk about the great victory of Mao's thinking, about the success of the Great Cultural Revolution. This became the formula for our life for many years.

The 'Long March'

Students were encouraged to kindle and spread the 'fire of revolution to all parts of China'. As the railway was overburdened, students were called upon to do the 'liaison' on foot. This was termed the 'long march'.

The autumn of 1966 deepened. The sky seemed higher and the air fresher. Willow trees in the yard had already completely shed their leaves, and their long twigs no longer looked like the long sleeves of dancing girls on stage. The poplars, like a girl from Heaven scattering flower petals, dropped their red and yellow leaves to the ground, mixing up with wind-torn old posters, rolling aimlessly in the yard.

In front of the office building, the members of the two Red Guards organisations—the 818 Red Guards and the Maoist Red Guards, argued and debated in low tones and hysterical shouts, about the rights and wrongs of the work team. Everywhere one could hear students ridiculing the two ninety-five per cents—that ninety-five per cent of the cadres and ninety-five per cent of the masses were good—as advocated in a speech by a man named Ku, a young teacher at the Institute and a member of the 818 Red Guards.

After lunch, the sunshine became warmer. Teachers and students, who were deemed revolutionary, became tired from the morning's debates and returned to their respective dormitories to have their afternoon naps with their hands resting contentedly on their bellies.

Wandering along the walls, which were erected for the sole purpose of showing the posters, I felt disenchanted, frustrated, confused and angered. Disenchanted, because I thought by then that the Great Cultural Revolution was a drama, which was being played by two antagonistic groups in the arena of all universities and schools. Frustrated, because I was at the same time no longer interested in the movement and afraid of being unable to graduate due to my non-active performance. Confused, because, in my mind, I had believed that from the very moment that classes and states came into existence, all governments were doomed to corruption and bureaucracy. Mao initiated the Great Cultural Revolution,

I believed, to cleanse the government and the Party of undesirable elements in order to make the cadres real servants of the people. Yet, I intuitively felt, none of the two opposing sides followed Mao's requirements—none was progressing in that direction. I felt angered because I could not find any way out. I could not see how I would finish my study since I could not see an end to the movement.

It was broadcast that Mao had received the Red Guards who had come to Beijing on foot from the north-eastern provinces. Mao liked the idea and called upon other students to follow suit. This news, which brought a solution, gladdened me immensely. I decided to organise about a dozen friends to make a 'long march'. If the team was too small, there might be dangers on the way and if the team was too big, it would be too hard to solve the problems met on the way. So I decided just to organise about a dozen friends or so.

A 'long march' offered quite a few opportunities for us: seeing the daily life of the peasants in the countryside far away from Beijing; seeing the landscape of the country; seeing the different habits and customs of rural life; increasing our ability to solve problems and overcome difficulties; and broadening our scope of knowledge. But above everything, I could win the love of the girl I regarded as my ideal choice by organising a 'long march'. I regarded her as my ideal, without having an actual face to face meeting and without even knowing her name, because of her beauty and the prospect of tall children. I was short and did not wish my children to be so. It was selfish thinking, but I could not help but entertain it.

The first time I saw her was at the sports day of our Institute, when she was competing as a high jumper. Only two girls remained to conquer the last height. She knocked down the bar and fell into the sandpit, her hands and legs pointing to the sky. When she got up to walk out of the pit, I saw she was tall and beautiful. 'How happy I will be if she will be my girlfriend!' I thought to myself.

The second time I saw her was shortly after the sixty students staged the peaceful sit-in in the Ministry of Foreign Trade. The Red Guards were criticising a teacher. She was present to watch. Somebody suggested she be the note taker. 'Anybody got a pen?' she asked. Nobody replied. I had a pen with a broken stem. I felt it, but hesitated lending it to her, even though it was a very good pen. 'Does anybody have a pen?' she asked again. I then offered her mine. 'Not good looking, but writes well!' she commented to me. I left the sit-in well before the end of the criticism. I was not keen to get the pen back. When she had the pen with her, she could not find me and when she did see me, she did not have the pen with her. She apologised and I told her each time not to be too serious about it because it was only a pen with half a stem. I was not in a hurry to get it back. The longer the pen was in her hands, the more she would wish to find the owner to return it. The pen with half a stem actually became the 'matchmaker' in the end.

The third time I had a face-to-face talk with her was when she stopped me in front of the dining hall. 'Xiao Bing,' she called me from behind. I turned to look. I was surprised and elated because I did not know how she came to know my new name and because she had offered me an opportunity to speak to her.

'You should not have embarrassed the head of our Red Guard with so many pointed questions the other day.' She was referring to a speech I had made during the peaceful sit-in. She gave me lots of reasons, but I did not take them in. All the time I was watching her face, which looked very beautiful. Then she was conscious of me staring at her face, blushed and excused herself.

I only knew her new so-called revolutionary name, not her real name. She announced that she was called Du Xiu ('Du' meaning to stop or to prevent and 'Xiu' meaning revisionism. Eventually she stopped using Du Xiu and changed back to her given name, Lu Huan-qin. But between her and me, she was Mountain Rose, and I often just called her Rose). She meant that she would dedicate herself to prevent revisionism from appearing in China. When I knew her well and was intimate enough, I joked with her and said that Du was the family name and Xiu was the given name. I meant that the person with the family name Du was a revisionist. She laughed and said she did not think that way.

I decided to invite her to join our team for the 'long march'. I did not expect her to join but I wished to try my luck. She accepted my invitation instantly.

To form a team was much easier than I had imagined when talking to my friends. It was formed within a couple of days and had eleven members—six males and five females. Three were from our class and all were from our Red Guard organisation.

Quickly we made our preparations. We obtained coupons and money from the General Service Department. We obtained letters of introduction from 'Dong Fang Hong'—the Red Guard's office. We made a red flag and cardboard posters of Mao's quotations. We were making them in the room inside the teacher's building, near its entrance. Everyone had one on his or her bedding roll for the person behind to read during the march. All the preparations were finished within a couple of days. We decided to set out on 15 November 1966. Our destination was Jing Gang Mountain, which was the base of the Chinese Red Army of the Workers and Peasants under the leadership of Mao and the cradle of Chinese revolution. We meant to be politically educated there by our visit and to become revolutionaries ourselves.

The 15 November greeted us with a clear blue sky—so blue that it seemed to have just been washed. There was a breeze but it was just strong enough to unfurl our not-very-large red flag, on which was embroidered 'the conquering army'. The air was a bit cold and dry but the sun was beaming.

With our bedding rolls on our backs, all eleven of us lined up in front of the office building to embark on our journey. We looked like a team of well-trained soldiers. A board made of cardboard, about two feet by two feet, was attached to each bedding roll and on each were written quotations from Mao, such as 'make up your mind, fear no sacrifice, surmount all difficulties, and strive for victory'. This was to encourage the person walking behind.

I was elected the team leader. I gave the order to set out. There was a crowd beating drums and cymbals to see us off. We set out in high spirits. 'Lofty, lofty is the Jing Gang Mountain', I began the first sentence of the song and ordered the team to begin. With the singing loud and echoing in the air, we marched out of the gate of our Institute:

'Lofty, lofty is the Jing Gang Mountain.
It nurtures and nourishes the First Steel Company.
Representative Mao is at the head of the line.
We came from Nanchang City,
We came from both banks of the Xiang River.
To safeguard the red political power,
We are fighting a life and death against the white bandit army.'

We turned west to march along the road in front of our Institute to Huang Zhuang, which was the next closest village. Every member sang heartily. Fatigue and tiredness did not enter our heads and when the first song came to the end, somebody started another:

'Revolution is not a dinner party,
Nor writing a composition.
It cannot be that refined, that gentle, that moderate.
Revolution is an uprising,
A violent action of one class to overthrow another.'

We turned south from Huang Zhuang to Feng Tai. We had planned and mapped our route along the highway running parallel to the Beijing–Kuang-zhou railway line. Our voices became hoarse so we stopped singing. Our shoulders started burning and aching, but our spirit was still very high. Shortly before noon we passed Feng Tai. We soon came to a small village bordering the highway and stopped under a big tree at the head of the village to have our lunch and 'liberate' our shoulders.

Children from the village, with fingers in their mouths, came and watched us with interest. Some women came to us and asked, 'where are you going?'

Our *man tou* was cold, as were our water bottles. We kindled a fire and were on the point of using our enamelled wash basin to warm our water, when a woman voluntarily lent us a metal kettle for the purpose. To most of the team members, though eating under the curious eyes of children and women, the experience was exciting—an experience they could not get in the city.

After eating our lunch, thanking the village woman who lent us the kettle, and waving goodbye to the curious children, we resumed our journey. By three o'clock, we arrived at the Lu Gou Bridge, the place where the Chinese government army fired the first shot of the formal anti-Japanese war on 7 July 1937.

The bridge was constructed over Yong Ding River, which was called Lu Gou River during the Jin regime. The construction of the bridge commenced in 1189, and was completed in 1192 under the Jin's rule. It was reconstructed during the Qing Dynasty. The bridge was a stone construction of eleven arches. It was two hundred and sixty-five metres long and eight metres wide. It had stone railings on both sides, on which were 485 carefully carved lions of various shapes and sizes. They were so cleverly arranged and hidden by the artists that it was very hard to get the actual figure when counting them. I counted three times and each time got a different number. All the team members counted the lions many times. No two people got the same number and no one got the same number in their numerous counts. No one reached the figure of 485. It was easy to count the big lions, but the artists hid the smaller ones in the eyes, ears, paws and mouths of the larger lions. Almost everyone in China knew about Lu Gou Bridge and we were proud of the opportunity to do so.

By the eastern bridge head was a beautifully carved marble tablet placed on the back of a huge marble turtle. On the marble tablet was an inscription by Emperor Qian Long (1736–1796) of Qing Dynasty (1644–1911), called Lu Gou Xiao Yue (Lu Gou's Morning Moon). This stele had witnessed how the river had threatened the lives of the peasants living alongside it and how they had tried to curb it and make good use of it, and how the Chinese army fought the Japanese invaders here.

A team member bought a few persimmons, one for everybody, to mark the occasion. Though the persimmons puckered our mouths a bit, we still enjoyed them. The short rest not only increased our knowledge but also boosted our morale.

We reached Chang Xin Dian, our stop for the night, in high spirits. When we entered the reception centre, Red Guards from different schools, colleges and universities, crowded into the yard, talking in high tones, shouting greetings to students they knew, and joking or complaining. Team leaders were busy looking for staff to arrange accommodation and meals. Red Guards, who held bowls of porridge, scattered everywhere in the yard, eating supper. Some Red Guards were washing their feet in their own wash basins, also in the yard. This commotion added more pressure to the already over-burdened staff. Our accommodation was free for the night.

The males in our team were led to a big makeshift dormitory, which, I thought, was something like a classroom. Throwing our bedding rolls at our allotted spaces we started doing the pre-supper washing. I reminded my friends not to leave their valuables behind in the room. Everyone was ready for supper at the same time and we squatted in a circle in the yard to enjoy our first supper in our 'long march'. Before we were halfway through, somebody came to advise us that we should attend a report at the 7 February Revolution Primary School. A simple sketch was given to me to serve as a map to show us the address.

We were very tired, yet at seven o'clock that evening, our whole team went to listen to the report on the General Railway Strike all along the Beijing–Hankou railway line. The strike began on 4 February and ended on 9 February 1927. On 7 February, Wu Pei-fu (a warlord) ordered the strike to be suppressed. More than forty workers were killed, and a further forty were imprisoned. The well-known lawyer, Mr Shi Yang, was also killed. This strike became part of the education of students about the history of the Communist Party.

The speaker was an old worker, a survivor of the general strike. He was an eloquent speaker and seemed to be telling us the events as if they had just happened the previous day. One moment his anger seethed, the next excitement rose high, and then he was in tears. His emotion changed continuously when he described different scenes. One moment we felt indignant, then angry, and the next we became excited. Our emotion rose and ebbed with his emotion.

On our way back to the reception centre, we discussed the report heatedly. Everyone commented that it was worthwhile making the 'long march'. In my heart, I was thinking that the lecturer, though a worker, must have stopped working for years. His job had become telling visitors about the strike! Otherwise he could not be so eloquent.

On the second day, Zuo became lame and Tong-tong got blisters on her feet. On the third day Zuo became more crippled and sweat was on his temples all the time. By the mid-morning break, everyone threw down their bedding rolls on the ground to lie on the corn stalks by the roadside. I warned them not to do so for fear that they might catch a cold, but nobody heeded my words. At noon we reached a place called Xian Po (Fairy Slope), where we were divided into two groups to have our lunch in two poor peasant homes. The host of the house was a kind peasant woman in her fifties. She treated us as she did her close relatives. She made noodles with sweet potato flour. The noodles were so tasty that they seemed to slip down our throats of their own will. The woman apologised that she was not able to give us better food. Then I noticed that she and her family had food much worse than what she offered us. Their life was still very difficult. My friends were so moved that they were all in tears. Such was the Chinese peasant families' hospitality. They treated their guests with whatever good food they had while they themselves dined on food of inferior quality! The peasants just tried their very best to survive and never complained. Unless it was impossible for them to survive, they would just struggle along with the greatest tolerance. Xian Po was not far from Beijing and we were already in the latter half of 1966. Yet their life was still so poor! Why? That's what the Great Cultural Revolution intended to answer and solve. They just needed good cadres to lead them forward in real earnest.

Before sunset we reached the city of Zhuo Zhou. People from the reception centre were waiting for the Red Guards at the city gates. A woman took us directly to her house. She gave us a very warm welcome. She put the boys in her house and led the girls to stay in another house. She was kind and hospitable. She told us that many heroes, who undertook the Long March, had fought in the anti-Japanese war, the Liberation war and the Korean war, had stayed here in the city to enjoy their old life or to enjoy their well-nursed and well-cared-for new life. She told us that if we wished she would arrange for us to meet an old hero from the Long March.

We needed a pause of one day before resuming our own 'long march' for two reasons—we wished to listen to a hero who personally took part in the Long March, so to be educated; and we wished to let our members recover from their lameness and to treat their blisters.

The Red Army hero lived in a secluded house specially constructed for him and his family. It was a red brick peasant-style house of five rooms, including the middle kitchen room and two bedrooms on either side. The house faced south and was enclosed with patterned fences. The courtyard was unpaved but swept very clean. The rooms on one side of the kitchen were turned into a living room to receive visitors. The living room had a picture of Mao on the wall, a square table and two chairs with arms. On the table sat a teapot and a few cups and a thermos flask.

The old hero had survived all the wars: the ten-year land revolutionary war, the Long March, the anti-Japanese war, the Liberation war and the Korean war. He wore neatly ironed cotton suits of Mao style. His hair was grey and his face was a bit pale. He was not talkative but he tried hard to make us understand him. He tried hard to dwell on Mao's tactics and strategies in military affairs. He vividly described the battles he had experienced. He talked about the Long March and he taught us how to carry on in our own 'long march'. He told us this story which happened prior to crossing the grassland:

'Some units had already entered the grassland, a very vast swampy land full of quagmires. It was uninhabited. To shake off the enemy, the Red Army had to cross it. The Red Army units tried their best to acquire more food before entering the grassland. There was nothing left, not even wild vegetables, for their unit to collect. The battalion mess officer was ordered to procure food for the battalion. He set out to look for food with two soldiers. They tried to get food from a few locals, who had not even enough food for their own families to survive, let alone to spare something for the Red Army. They looked for wild vegetables but they were all gone. The three of them were hungry, tired and irritable.

The sky became overcast and it started to rain. They came across a temple and hurried into it for shelter. They kindled a fire to keep warm and to dry their clothes. The mess officer looked around and saw the smiling Buddha. The smiles of the Buddha looked like sneering grimaces to him.

"You sneer at me?" he shouted angrily. He stood up, took the Buddha's arm and intended to break it. The arm became bent but did not break. The officer was surprised and called at the two soldiers.

"Come over and help me!"

Jointly they ripped off the arm. The arm seemed be made from a sticky mixture of clay, rice and other materials and it was not hard. He threw it into the fire intending to get more warmth. A moment later, the smell of burnt food filled the air. The three of them sniffed and suddenly realised that the smell came from the arm in the fire. The officer snatched it out of the fire, wrenched a small piece off the arm and tasted. He offered some for the soldiers to taste.

"Real food made of grain!" they exclaimed.

They were ecstatic. They dismembered the Buddha and carried it back to the battalion. It was not sufficient but it served the purpose. Immediately soldiers were dispatched to look for more Buddhas in different temples. The food thus obtained did not taste like corn, nor did it taste like rice or millet. But it was better than cooked wild vegetables and better than their own cooked leather belt, which many Red Army units did.

We got through the grassland in a better bodily condition. We all said jokingly that "Buddha saved the Red Army". Later we learned that in this region, Buddha was made with a mixture of sticky rice and clay.'

Four hours elapsed without our noticing it. Every member of our team was pleased. Such talks were more interesting than the ones we heard in our political classes.

We pressed forward. Comradeship permeated the whole team. Each one wanted to give a helping hand to the other. Carrying something for other members, or trying to save some food for others, was done willingly by everybody.

On 20 November, we came to a village called Zhu Ji in the late afternoon. We decided to pass the night in the village. The production team leader of the village was a young man named Kwo. He had finished his term in the army just a couple of years earlier. His posture, his gait, his gestures and his speech was that of a soldier. He welcomed us warmly and begged his mother to ask several other families to accommodate my team members. Another male, called Ju, and I stayed in Kwo's house to share the same *kang* because he was unmarried. When Kwo woke me in the morning, breakfast was already ready. I did not notice him getting up, nor did I hear his mother cooking.

'Don't worry about your coupons and money!' he told me. 'Eat as much as you can.'

I did, for I felt as if I was in my own home.

As per the regulations, we each gave him a quarter-kilo coupon and twenty cents. Kwo would not accept this, insisting that he did all this for friendship. I told him that we wanted to train ourselves like soldiers and that we had to obey the discipline. He gave in to that.

We arrived at Bao Ding on 22 November. We were surprised when we passed a high wall, the top of which had barbed wire connected to electricity. Very big Chinese characters were written on the wall, which read 'The Heavenly Number One Prison'. We had our lunch in a restaurant on the edge of the city where the girl I was interested in, jokingly smeared a little condiment sauce on my face. This joke left a good memory. I took it as a good omen.

We did not leave to continue our march until 24 November. During those two days, we had a meeting and decided to see more villages and more peasants so as to propagate Mao's thinking and to learn more from the peasants. Also we relaxed by seeing the city. Just one week away from Beijing, we seemed to slip back to being just peasant boys or girls.

'Where to?' the conductors of the bus asked the girls who were out sightseeing.

'The busiest and liveliest place in the city,' the girls replied, forgetting even to say 'downtown'.

All the other passengers and the conductors looked at them with surprise, wondering, perhaps, why the girls did not know where they wished to go to.

Two male members and I went for a walk along the street. We came to a shop selling cooked meat and *mo* soup. Each of us bought an extra *mo* and sat on the bench to have the soup.

'It is different from what I had in Shaanxi,' Chao commented. 'But it is tasty, anyway.'

We two agreed.

'Why don't we buy some coin meat?' Zuo suggested.

'What is coin meat?' we asked.

'Look over there,' he indicated some meat on the butcher's table.

The meat had a hole in the middle and looked similar to chicken loaf in shape, colour and thickness. The grain of the meat looked very fine.

'What's that?' we asked again, loud enough to be heard by the butcher. It was too late for Zuo to stop us.

'This meat?' the butcher asked. He replied when we nodded our confirmation. 'It is the male donkey's penis!'

We thought he was joking but Zuo nodded in confirmation.

'The best meat!' the butcher told us.

Again Zuo nodded to confirm. I did not know how he knew this.

We bought a quarter of a kilo to try. We inserted the meat into a *mo* each and started eating on the spot. I should admit that the meat tasted better than any other cold meat I had ever eaten.

Village after village, county after county, we walked and walked. The customs in the villages were very different from where I came from. When we walked through a village during lunchtime, we found by the gate of each house, a man—the master of the house—would stand with a big bowl of porridge in his left hand, chopsticks in his right hand, eating his lunch. His shoulder was against the gatepost, one foot hooked to rest against the heel of the other. In his left hand was also a small saucer of salted vegetables, one or two pyramid-shaped *wo tou*, and two or three pieces of sweet potato. I did not see anybody with *man tou*. Life was still hard in the countryside.

In other villages it was again different. The master of the house usually carried to the gate a handled basket, which contained *wo tou*, sweet potato and preserved vegetables. He would squat at one side of the gate, as if to make way for people to pass, and carry out a conversation with his neighbours.

On 25 November, we stopped at a village called Yu at the invitation of the commune secretary, who asked us to watch a performance of a group of students. The students eagerly sang and danced in front of us, as if they were performing on stage in front of a large audience. I do not know why I thought the secretary was fishing for his own fame.

On 28 November, we met a ten-year-old girl on the way to Xin Le (meaning New Laughter or New Joy). She had a small bedding roll on her back and walked happily northward, alone.

'Where are you going to?' the girls from our team asked.
'To Beijing,' she replied.
'Do your parents know?'
'No.'
'Why don't you go with friends?'
'We are too young to be allowed by our parents!'
'But why do you still go?'
'I want to see Chairman Mao.'
'Do you know how to get to Beijing?'
'Of course,' she smiled, ' I just follow the railway line.'

The girls advised her repeatedly to join a north-bound team, for safety's sake. Looking at the small girl I thought they could do anything once they hit upon an idea of some kind and had their minds made up.

'Xiao Bing,' Du Xiu whispered to me. 'Would you like me to sing a song for you?'

'I'd be greatly honoured!' I whispered back, trying to guess whether she had already suspected I was interested in her.

'The north wintry wind blew the whole night. The wind is blowing over Ke Mountain.' She began, like the soft twitter of a bird, singing for my ears only. Nobody else paid any attention to us. Everybody was busy talking to everybody else. Her voice was beautiful but she very seldom sang.

On 30 November, we arrived at Shi Jia Zhuang. We approached the Municipal Cultural Revolution Group for help, for we were short of meal coupons, money and clothing.

'All right. One, you need meal coupons. Two, you need a map. Three, you need four padded jackets and four, you need money,' the man from the Municipal Cultural Revolution Group said to us. 'I have got your points clearly and I will see it done by tomorrow. Now go back to the reception centre.'

We were already familiar with the formalities at the reception centres, in other words, we had become 'experts'. It did not take long for us to have everything arranged. We then went for a bath, in a common bathroom of course.

The Municipal Cultural Revolution Group was quite efficient. The following morning, a man came to our room and handed to me what we wanted—money, four padded Mao-style jackets, and meal coupons, which were like certificates. We could buy food according to the quantity printed on the coupons.

'Xiao Bing,' Du Xiu said to me one morning, 'would you please have a walk with me? My parents once lived here and I wish to have a look at the place.' I went with her for the adventure. Again I was trying to decide whether she already knew my intentions. Du Xiu knew the district but she could not remember her parent's old address. We combed the lanes but could not find the place. I wondered whether she using this as an excuse to have a long walk with me? In my heart my hope of approaching her became a bit stronger and more realistic.

After Shi Jia Zhuang, dissension arose among the team members. Some wanted to change destination, some wanted to go by train and others insisted in going to Jing Gang Mountain. The difference grew with each passing day. When we reached Bo Xiang County it was no longer possible to stay together. I called a meeting to see whether it was still possible for the team not to split. Everyone voted to break up. I felt very sad but could not save the team. We had left the Institute to see and learn. I could not force everybody to stay together. There was no regulation demanding that we stay together. We formed the team democratically and now we disintegrated the team democratically. There was no animosity among us and we bore no grudge against each another. The following day all the members set out in new groups. Each was of a different size and going to different destinations.

'Xiao Bing,' Du Xiu said to me. 'I am going home and I will not continue the march.' She left and I went after her, asking her to talk. We walked side by side. I wanted to hold her waist but I dared not, because I suspected she was a bit conservative with slight feudal ideas. If I held her waist with my right arm, she surely would refuse to have a walk with me. I just tried to push her forward with a very light nudge. I wanted to know whether she would become my girlfriend. I had to know for sure, for I feared that once the team disintegrated I would not have the opportunity to get together with her. It was cold and we needed gloves to protect our hands. When the team members went shopping in a small village Du Xiu bought a pair of gloves.

'Du Xiu,' I said to her in a whisper. 'May I swap gloves with you?'

'Why do you wish to swap gloves with me?' she asked me, loud enough to embarrass me and make me sweat. She thrust her gloves in my hands and snatched mine from me and walked away. That night I could not sleep. I was wondering whether she understood the old saying, 'it is hard to deny the relationship once a girl and a boy exchange something'. I hoped she understood.

The sun was big and round as it set. Its orange glow tinged everything. We sat on a ridge of a paddy field not far from the village, facing the sun. Her face looked more beautiful.

'My home is not far from here. It is just fifty kilometres away. I want to go and see my parents,' she began.

I could not let her end the march like this. If she walked away, she would never be attainable. I was trying my hardest to persuade her to continue the march with me. 'In my opinion it is not good for you to leave us like this. First, it is not safe for a girl to cover fifty kilometres alone. Secondly, the team is disintegrated but the "long march" can still be conducted.'

She remained silent. Her head lowered without looking at me. She was writing at random with a stick on the ground.

'Since we have left the Institute, we must see the world. This is part of our performance in the Great Cultural Revolution.' I was using all the reasons I could think of to persuade her to continue the 'long march' with me.

She would not break her silence. I was at the end of my resources. But she would not help. Her silence made it harder and harder for me. Finally, I ventured a proposal.

'Why not continue the march with me and one or two other members of our team?'

'Let me consider this during the night. I will let you know in the morning.' In the morning, she was ready to continue the march with me!

My group, including her, totalled three. The other was Zuo. We decided to continue on foot. More and more Red Guards hurried along the road, either in small groups, in pairs or alone. We pressed on, easier and quicker than we had when the whole team was together. One day we reached Yong Nian County and stayed at the reception centre. When supper was over, Du Xiu and I had a walk. The street lamps, which were spaced quite apart from one another, lit up the dark night dimly. We dared not go too far away from the lamp.

'Xiao Bing,' she began. 'I cannot continue the march like this. I will return to Beijing tomorrow by train. If you have anything to say to me, tell me now.'

I hesitated. It was still a bit too early for me to let her know that I loved her. But if I did not make it clear that I did, there would be no excuse for me to see her later. If I just told her I wanted her to be my girlfriend, it might not convey my full intention.

'I love you and I wish you can accept my love,' I blurted out after long hesitation.

Her eyes showed surprise. She seemed to be thunderstruck and blushed. She just stared at me. It was clear that it was the very first time she had heard such words.

'But you don't know me yet. I am living with my aunt. Don't commit yourself to anything without considering it carefully,' she finally began.

'What else is there to consider? I think I have the ability to take responsibility,' I told her.

How could she know that she had occupied my whole mind? When I went to bed, my last thought was of her, and when I woke to a new day my first thought was of her. A word, a gesture, anything from her would make my heart thump.

'Let me reply to you in the morning,' she said to me, and we parted for our dormitories.

She did not give me any verbal reply in the morning but she did not return to Beijing. She continued to head south with Zuo and I. We ended our march at Xin-xiang, where we stayed for a few days because Zuo was sick. When he recovered, we took the train to Zheng-zhou, where we stayed for a month or two to take part in the Great Cultural Revolution in the Foreign Trade Bureau. At Xin-xiang, she had stayed in the same room as a young girl from Beijing. The girl was the Commander of a Red Guard Organisation. Letters became our means of our communication. I wrote to her almost daily. At first, she signed her reply 'your comrade-in-arms'. I joked with her and told her that I did hope for the day when she was my comrade in my arms. Then she began to sign her letters as 'Mountain Rose'. I began calling her Rose.

Xin-xiang was not big enough for us to stay in, so we started to move to Zheng-zhou.

Our Activities in Zheng-zhou

Zheng-zhou was situated on the south bank of the Yellow River. It was the junction of the Beijing–Kuang-zhou railway line and the Long-hai railway line. We arrived at Zheng-zhou from Xin-xiang by train in the latter half of December. From the railway station, we began asking our way to the Zheng-zhou Foreign Trade Bureau. We were directed onto a thoroughfare that was lined on both sides with empress trees (*Paulownia Imperialis*). When we walked along the street to the Foreign Trade Bureau, the thick trees were bare apart from some fruit-like round yellow balls covered with prickles dangling from the twigs. The thoroughfare had not seen many Red Guards yet.

The Bureau had several buildings—the office building and the dormitories. We two boys were accommodated in one room inside the office building, which was also our office. Du Xiu was accommodated in the female dormitory. Another girl from our Institute was already in the bureau before we arrived.

We were just in time to see the 'rebels' (the employees) grab power from the Bureau. The 'rebels' were not in great numbers and they came to us for support. We followed them to give them support, because we regarded ourselves as revolutionary rebels, too.

'Hand over your authority.' They demanded the general manager as they stormed the office. 'Give us the company stamp!'

'From now on,' they said to the general manager, 'the authority is in the hands of us rebels.'

Both sides looked at each other like real 'enemies'. The faces of both the 'rebels' and the 'authority' were red. Sweat covered their foreheads.

'This is a child's game,' I thought. But no sooner had the idea crept into my head than I turned it down. In Chinese history, the stamp had always been the symbol of authority, even after the new China was founded.

In *The Journey to the West*, before the monk Tang Xuan Zhang, who went to get the Buddhist Canon, was born, his parents went to a post where his father would be an official. When they took a boat to cross a lake, the boat owner, who turned out to be a pirate, killed his father and forced his mother to be his wife. The pirate carried the stamp to the post and became the official for many years until the monk, Tang, went to his grandfather to expose the pirate.

A letter of introduction, without the company's stamp, would not be accepted. Grabbing the power by taking over the stamps was not a child's game! Like the wind the 'rebels' swept through almost all the offices. When they arrived at the security office, the door was locked and somebody wanted to stop them. The rebels argued with them, using quotations from Chairman Mao. Then a rebel broke the glass of the door with his elbow. The door opened and the rebels thronged into the room. They stopped in front of the weapons, not knowing what to do for a moment. Then somebody suggested sealing the room with a piece of paper on which was written the date, month and year. Nobody dared to touch the weapons.

Thus the rebels took over. This occurred simultaneously throughout China.

Business was still going on. People regularly came to the rebel's office to ask for the use of the stamps. It was very inconvenient for the managers at various levels and it was also very awkward for the rebels. The managers were in the position to carry out business, but they had no authority, while, the rebels had 'authority' but were not in a position to carry out or direct business. Like fighting roosters, both sides were ready to 'kill', yet both had to co-operate, though unwillingly.

The 'wind of power grabbing' swept the whole country. The 'wind' originated from Shanghai, and was called the 'January Revolutionary

Storm'. Chaos arose in most places, hence the 'Revolutionary Committee' was created as well as the 'Revolutionary Group'. The Revolutionary Committee was the name for a company's authority. The Revolutionary Group was the name for the department's management. Those names have been in use ever since.

Opinions about the use of power in companies differed greatly. Heated debates arose among the staff and the rebels.

'I suggest that we not debate or argue with the staff face to face in the corridor or in the dining hall,' I said to the other two of my team. 'Let's speak with our pen.' So, after discussion, we posted on the door of our office 'The Speedy Boat on the Rough Sea' as the name of our group. We signed all our posters with that name.

'To debate with comrade Yin' was our first poster. In this we spoke for the rebels. We argued that there was no doubt the action of the rebels was a revolutionary action. Yin put up a poster to dispute our claims. We wrote a second one to refute his points. Then we wrote a third to strengthen our views. Effectively, our third poster silenced him. Every day we wrote posters that greatly influenced the opinion of the people in the Bureau. Zuo was very happy about the achievement, but I was not. I was very angry with myself. I had left the Institute to get away from doing such silly things and now I was in the same atmosphere, doing the same things again. I mentioned this to Rose but she only partly agreed with me. She was more revolutionary than I was, though she had a very gentle nature.

Were the rebels really right? Weren't some of the leaders in the Bureau really bad? In a place far from Beijing, how would I know? The cadres, who had blackboards hung around their necks or who were ill treated by the masses, were in one way or another alienated from the people. They needed to be corrected—but should this be done by the rebels?

As a result of my confusion, I became less active in writing the posters. I wanted to study English so as not to waste time. But even here, the 'revolutionary' atmosphere would not allow me to do it. To fill the days I found my way to the kitchen to help the cooks. Every day I helped prepare lunch and supper. I found consolation in seeing Rose and visiting the city as well. The rebels always came to our office to talk or exchange information about the movement elsewhere. During such meetings, I would adjust the mirror in our office to such an angle that I could watch Rose's face without looking directly at her. Occasionally she looked into the mirror and caught my burning eyes and she blushed profusely. The mirror became our means of communication and we spoke to each other with our eyes.

More students from our Institute arrived and they all supported the 'rebels'. More posters were written in support of them, but still the products of the 'Speedy Boat on the Rough Sea' topped everyone else—both in quality and quantity.

Rose was told to move into a room in the reception centre. I helped her move her luggage there—it was in the evening after supper.

The centre was full of Red Guards mainly from primary schools and high schools. The high pitched voices of Red Guards debating filled the air so that the place seemed like a mad house. Rose was put in a single room at the end of the corridor on the second floor. Her room was 'an oasis in a desert'.

Before leaving her room, I had a sudden desire to kiss her. I became very excited but was afraid that if I voiced my wish she might regard me as vulgar. But I did not wish to leave without kissing her.

'New Year is just three days away,' I stammered. 'May I ask you to satisfy a wish of mine?'

'What is your wish?'

'I will let you know when you tell me "yes".'

'How can I say yes if I don't know what it is?'

I realised that she might think that I was trying to ask her for something she could not agree to. So I mustered my courage to tell her my wish.

'I wish you and I could spend New Year's Day together.'

'But other people will see us together. It is embarrassing.' She persisted in saying that we should not let anyone see the two of us together. She did not want other students to know she was in love. It was still the time when girls did not want to be exposed to sex before marriage.

'If you cannot do that, I wish to kiss you today,' I blurted out and I caught her shoulders. Her face and her neck became red instantly. Suddenly she became too weak to refuse my kiss. I kissed her on the lips and as my tongue tried to enter her mouth, she doubled her tongue between her teeth, putting up an effective resistance.

'Please go back to your dormitory,' she said as she pushed me away after a minute or two. Her eyes were very, very bright.

I left obediently. My face was burning. I stayed under a tree by the street opposite her room. Perhaps she knew I was there. She opened the window and looked out. She waved me goodnight.

More Red Guards arrived and told us of their journey. Only then did I learn that the majority of Red Guards were accommodated in the reception centre and that was why the Bureau seemed comparatively quiet and peaceful.

The rebels from the Bureau expanded the scope of their contacts and formed an organisation called the 'February Seventh Commune'. 'We shall join!' a rebel from the Foreign Trader Bureau, who was a graduate from our Institute a few years' earlier, told me. (The name was after the February Seventh General Strike of the railway workers along the Beijing–Hankou railway line in 1923.)

Then students started to talk about the February Adverse Current. In other words, it was called the Ten Veteran Generals Making a Noisy Row in Huai Ren Tang (the name of a house in Zhong Nan Hai). It was also said that somebody was organising to have Premier Zhou En Lai overthrown because they regarded him as anti-Mao. The generals could not remain silent any longer. They went to Huai Ren Tang to protest to Mao. It was said that one marshal was so indignant and angry that he banged on a table and broke his small finger—this later was labelled as the February Adverse Current by their opponents. The people who were directing the Great Cultural Revolution accused them of sabotaging the Great Cultural Revolution.

'What's the use of following the movement?' I said to Rose. 'We'd better go back to Beijing.'

If even Zhou was not spared, who was safe?

Life was unsettled and rumours ran amok. 'The son of Lin Du (probably a made-up name, as many were in the rumours circulating) was beaten by the opposition. He has a head wound! His life is stake!' somebody said. 'Violent fighting is in some cities.' 'Comrade Jiang Qing said "we prefer peaceful struggle but we do valiant self defence!"' 'The gate of the Military District Office has been surrounded by rebels!' Such stories could be heard now and then.

I decided to leave for Beijing. Rose agreed with me. Zuo had already returned to Beijing to see a doctor, to witness the development of the Great Cultural Revolution in our Institute, and to get money. We heard Zuo came back to Zheng-zhou again after we were back at the Institute.

We had booked a morning train and were at the waiting room about two hours before the train was due.

Killing in the Countryside

The huge waiting room was overcrowded. Red Guards and travellers occupied all the benches. Watermelon and sunflower seed peddlers, nearly all children, elbowed, squeezed, and zigzagged among the crowds, howling that their seeds were for sale. Seed skins and fruit peel covered the floor.

Young people from Xin Jiang Province were dancing in a corner. Many people waiting for the train were sleeping on the floor. The station cleaner, an elderly woman holding a dustbin handle in her left hand and a broom handle in the right, swept the floor slowly. Her broom touched a few strokes here and there. She watched the dancing for a few minutes; she looked at other passengers for another few minutes. She was interested in anything and everything, except sweeping the floor.

'Passengers, the number two train to Beijing is further delayed for at least two hours!' the loud speaker announced. More sighs and more curses arose. Noon had already arrived. We dared not leave our spot on the bench. One would guard the bedding rolls while the other went to buy food, fetch water, or go to the toilet. If our seats were left vacant and unwatched, others would occupy it instantly.

Night came and it grew cold in the waiting room. There was still no sign of the train. Nobody knew when it would arrive and nobody left in case it came.

With our arms resting on our bedding rolls, we sat against each other, chatting. As long as Rose was with me, I did not worry about waiting.

The train finally arrived and after strenuous squeezing and elbowing, we got onto it. By now it was the small hours of the morning. The compartments were so crowded that we just managed to have enough space in the corridor between two compartments to sit on the floor.

'Why did the train arrive so late?' I asked a man crowded in the corridor with us.

'Rebel workers and Red Guards lay on the rails to stop the train. The negotiations took many hours!' From then on, trains could not keep to schedules for many years!

It became very cold as we were headed northward. I opened my quilt and arranged half of it on the floor for Rose and myself to sit on and folded the other half over our legs to keep us warm. Wafts of fetid air came to us through the doorway whenever it was pushed ajar by people or by the swinging motion of the train. The train was delayed at each stop where more Red Guards squeezed onto it. Even the toilets of the train were full of Red Guards.

The next morning, we were back in Beijing. I was happy that I had organised the 'long march'. I had begun it with two goals and I returned to Beijing with one of them fully realised—by getting the girl of my dreams. The other goal, though not fully realised, was more than half achieved—I had enriched my experience. To a certain degree, the 'long march' was a success for me.

To my surprise, Rose took me directly to her aunt's place when we got out of the railway station. Her aunt was very nice to me and made me stay for the night after a delicious supper.

'You have got my aunt's approval to be my boyfriend,' Rose told me in the morning. 'Aunt seemed very fond of you.' I could see and feel that myself.

'Come to see us whenever you have time,' her aunt told me when she left for work in the factory. I said goodbye to Rose and decided to return to the Paradise Palace to visit my family. It was just three days away from the Spring Festival.

'Ma,' I shouted as soon as I arrived at the gate of our yard, announcing that I was back home to see her and my father and to pass the Spring Festival with them.

'Is Chun-ying back?' my mother asked loudly and came into the yard to meet me. She beamed broadly as she saw me.

'Have you had your breakfast?' she asked.

'Not yet,' I replied.

We went into the room. My mother started cooking. It was already time for her to cook lunch. My Da Ma came in. She looked at my mother in surprise but did not say anything. She just spoke to me. My father came back for lunch. He also looked surprised at my mother, who was still cooking, but he did not say anything. My father just greeted my Da Ma and spoke to me.

At lunch, when my mother had had enough and sat back against the windowsill, my father spoke.

'What happened?' he asked her. 'This morning you were still very sick!'

'Ah, yes,' my mother replied. 'When I heard Chun-ying calling me, I just got up to cook for him. I forgot I was sick.'

Then my father told me that my mother had been sick for over a month. She was not even able to get off the *kang*. My Da Ma had to come over to help with the cooking every day.

'Yes,' my mother said. 'We always heard about the Red Guards being killed. I became worried about you and I suddenly became sick,' she told me. I was moved in tears.

My father said that it was not unimaginable for my mother to be sick, having heard what happened around our district. And then they started to tell me what had occurred.

'Your cousin Wei living in front of our house is the party secretary in Fu-zhuang Commune. Some time ago he was sick and came back home to get treatment. During his absence, in Fu-zhuang village, the militia head called the landlords and their families, the rich peasants and their families, and the reactionaries, to a big house for a meeting. The house had high walls.

'Wu Da-tou [a landlord], come out please,' somebody called at the door and Wu came out. 'Somebody is waiting for you outside.'

'Wu started to walk towards the gate. A militiaman stealthily put a garrotte around his neck and carried him to a well and threw him into it. One by one men were called out and strangled with a garrotte and thrown into the wells. Then the women and children were treated the same way.

'There were two students studying in the universities in Beijing. Each of them received a telegram telling them that their mothers were seriously sick and that they should come back home immediately. Upon their arrival at the village, militiamen of the village met them at the entrance of the village, greeting them. When they headed into the village, nooses were placed around their necks from behind. They, like their family members, ended up in the wells.

'Three wells were full of bodies and filled with earth.'

The total of killings in that village was one hundred and three. Another village had fifty-three murdered. Then my father told me about a third village in which a massacre occurred. The third village, which was called 'new village', had thirty victims.

The situation in the surrounding villages became tense. Militiamen posted armed checkpoints at village entrances. Entry into a village was not hampered but the exit from the village was strictly controlled. Fear also appeared on the faces of the families of landlords and rich peasants in our own village.

'How could such killings happen?' I asked my father.

'Because during the 'White-necks' terror before 1949, poor peasants were killed by the landlords in those villages. The children of those poor peasants had never forgotten, and they wanted to take revenge on the landlord families. I think you know the saying "it is not too late for a gentleman to take revenge within ten years". Now the Great Cultural Revolution has begun and there is no authority in each village. So they have made use of this rare opportunity to take revenge on the landlords and rich peasants' families,' my father explained. 'Our village had no killings by the White-necks and so the hatred for the landlords and rich peasants is not so deep. That's why the poor peasants did not kill the families of landlords and rich peasants in our village.'

'Everybody carries a knife when working in the field now,' Chun-ling told me.

'Why?' I asked.

'Because the killed have relatives and the relatives want revenge!'

'If this goes on, there will be no end to the killings,' I commented.

'The army has been positioned in those villages now,' Chun-ling said.

'The situation is improving,' my father interjected.

True, the killings did not spread and were stopped quickly. Malice should be dissolved, and not harboured. Once the fathers have passed hatred to the next generation, it is hard to wipe it from the hearts of their descendants. Compromise is the best thing in solving wrongs between individuals, groups of people, and even between countries. It would be very cruel for the fathers to pass hatred down to burden their sons or grandsons.

chapter 24

AN INTERPRETER AT THE GUANGZHOU TRADE FAIR

The 1967 Spring Guangzhou Trade Fair came when the Ministry of Foreign Trade had been taken over by the rebels. The rebels, with ex-managers and a Deputy Minister nominated as their advisers, were entrusted to run the fair. Amidst anarchism nationwide, the fair was a success.

The Reception Centre of the Fourth Military District

The Spring Guangzhou Trade Fair of 1967 was approaching. Most of the students studying various languages in our year were chosen to be interpreters at the fair. We all belonged to the same Red Guards organisation—the Dong Fang Hong Commune—the actual authority of the Institute. The presidents were in the 'shed of ghosts and serpents' and the Party and Youth League organisations (the former authority of the Institute) had ceased operation.

As was the practice, we were called to stay at the reception centre of the Ministry of Foreign Trade in Beijing to study the policies, rules and regulations in dealing with foreigners before heading out to Guangzhou.

The reception centre of the Fourth Military District in Guangzhou was situated at the foot of Bai Yun Shan (White Cloud Mountain). The gate was still guarded by soldiers with bayoneted rifles. The one-storey buildings were scattered in patterns in a huge yard. A sportsground had all the necessary equipment for physical activities. The dining hall was in the middle of the buildings and meal times were strictly adhered to.

We were all given single rooms—an honour usually bestowed to the high-ranking officers in the army. Each room was neatly furnished with a double bed, from which hung a mosquito net. Two overlapping halves of the mosquito net at the front of the bed served as the entrance. Two pairs of sandals were lined neatly under the bed, out of the way but handy for the feet. A desk with a chair was placed under the window.

It was the first time in my life I had seen such a bed, but when I crept into it to sleep, I reserved my opinion. The sheets felt half-dried and cold to the touch. It was very uncomfortable. The bed, made from woven palm fibre, was like elastic and I would hunch my body up and sag it back to feel the up and down swinging motion of the bed before I settled down to sleep.

In the morning I would be intoxicated by wafts of a pleasant fragrance. I traced it to the bushes lining both sides of the entrance road to the reception centre. Tiny snow-white and pale purple blossoms densely covered the shrubs. This was my favourite place to read English every morning while I stayed at the reception centre.

After breakfast, the mornings were mainly passed by the group study of Chairman Mao's works or by studying the rules and regulations of dealing with foreigners or by studying policies concerning the Great Cultural Revolution. All kinds of questions a foreigner might ask about the Great Cultural Revolution were considered and proper answers were prepared. The afternoons were spent playing sport such as basketball, volleyball or mountaineering along stepped ways, not by climbing up cliffs.

At the beginning, the cooks did not know what we students from northern China preferred. They cooked jasmine rice with every meal, which was dry and hard to chew. My stomach rejected it and I was determined to find alternative food. One day I told the cooks that I was sick, so food for the sick was prepared for me. It was noodles with a kind of green vegetable, which we nicknamed 'seamless steel pipe'.

The following day, more students became 'sick', and more noodles with 'seamless steel pipes' were cooked and served. By then the mess officer seemed to smell a rat. He investigated and learned that students from Beijing did not like rice. So noodles, *man tou*, and twisters were prepared for lunch and supper, as well as rice to please students from southern China. The mess officer, the cooks and stewards all felt happy to see smiling faces at every meal. At that time, serving the people was still something to be proud of.

In the morning of 15 April 1967, small red books containing quotations of Chairman Mao, called *The Little Red Book*, were piled high on a desk in front of us. (*The Little Red Book* was used by the Red Guards during the Great Cultural Revolution, and helped create the cult of Mao. Often, Mao's quotes were not clear and people could easily get out of trouble simply by using a quote from the book to explain their false behaviour.)

We were considered ready to receive visitors from overseas countries.

'Red Guards from Beijing come out to the bus, please,' somebody shouted urgently.

'Red Guards from Beijing, pass your work at hand to others, come to the bus urgently,' somebody else repeated.

Surprised, we immediately entered the bus, whose windows had drawn curtains to hide who was travelling inside.

'What's the matter?' everybody started asking when we saw a number of students from our Institute and from the College of our Institute present in the bus.

'Reception by an important leader,' they told us, smiling mysteriously.

'Which leader?'

'You will know later,' they replied. 'You can make a guess.'

There were only two possibilities—Jiang Qing or Zhou En-lai. There were no comments from the ten students who had come to Guangzhou on the same plane as that leader. For the safety of the leader, they would not disclose the name, though I thought it was unnecessary for them to keep silent.

As soon as the last student jumped into the bus, it shot forward with a jerk. I had no idea which direction the bus took, but before long, we were on a suburban road. The bus finally stopped at the front entrance of the Zhu Jiang Hotel (Pearl River Hotel).

'Come to the small hall, please!' a man in a white steward uniform said and led the way.

The hall was already full of cadres from the Ministry of Foreign Trade and members of various import and export corporations. We arrived late so we could only sit on the benches in the back rows.

By then we knew that Premier Zhou En-lai, the man we longed to see some day, was to give a lecture. I took a seat by the aisle and tried hard to think about how to get a better position to see him.

'Note takers of this meeting come forward please!' some people shouted from the front row.

I dashed all the way from the back to the front, sitting at a desk in the middle just behind Comrade Lu, the Deputy Minister of Foreign Trade. My friends, a second or two later, realised what I had done and raced in my wake to the front row. All the other attendants looked at us, surprised.

'Are you the note taker?' the Deputy Minister turned around to speak to me.

'Of course,' I replied.

'Cheeky!' he smiled understandingly.

Just then thunderous applause arose. I stood up immediately, like a tree in a forest, and caught the sight of Zhou being escorted by a few army commanders and officers. Zhou came to the centre of the row of tables facing the audience. He gestured the applauding audience to sit down with both hands. His eyes swept over the hall, making everybody feel as if the Premier was looking at him.

'Lao Lu,' Zhou said to the Foreign Trade Deputy Minister when everybody sat down. 'Have you relayed the telegram from the Central Committee of the Chinese Communist Party, the Cultural Revolutionary Group, the Central Military Committee and the State Council?'

'Not yet,' Lu replied.

'Our Comrade Lu was always slow in doing things. I am already here and he has not told you about the telegram yet!' Zhou said. 'Now let me read it to you myself.'

Sweat appeared on the forehead of Deputy Minister Lu. Zhou stood up to read the telegram to the revolutionaries working at the Trade Fair, but I did not hear it. I was trying too hard to get a look at Zhou, a legend to the whole country, and the rest of the world.

His hair was black, glossy and well trimmed. His eyebrows were thick and black and his eyes, when looking in your direction, looked like beams of flashlights. They seemed to see the very bottom of one's heart. His handsome face looked darkish from the roots of his whiskers, which added to his masculine charm. His face was a bit thin, though it glowed with a radiance of strength and determination.

Zhou was wearing an army suit, which added authority to his stature. The Chinese say 'a man depends on his clothes and a horse depends on its saddle'. In this case I would say that the clothes depended on the man wearing them. I was about two metres away from Zhou, with only one row of tables between us. When Zhou finished reading and explaining the telegram, I was calm enough to listen to him talk.

'Huang Yong Sheng,' Zhou turned to the man sitting on his right side. 'You must support the revolutionary rebels!' The man called Huang Yong Sheng was the Chief Commander of the Guangzhou Military District. He had a square face and his eyes were like slits. He appeared to be dozing as Zhou read and explained the telegram. He agreed to do as Zhou asked. Zhou then warned the students not to break into the Military District because here was the front line.

'Now Taiwan and the United States of America are trying to work out what I am doing here. They said that I am here planning the liberation of Taiwan! Let them think that. Let their nerves strain,' Zhou remarked.

Next he told us, 'When dealing with overseas friends, there are no trivial things. You must treat everything with your utmost attention. I am expecting the fair to be a success!'

'Comrade Xi Piao-ha,' Zhou spoke to a rebel student from our Institute who was in charge of the fair with the help of people from the Ministry. 'I expect only success, not failure, of this trade fair. If anything goes wrong, I hold you personally responsible for it!' Comrade Xi Piao-ha was a member from the Red Corps of Rebels, which was a Red Guards organisation split from the Maoist Red Guards. It was stationed in the Ministry of Foreign Trade—that was the reason why he was in charge of that 1967 Spring Guangzhou Trade Fair.

When Zhou finished speaking, flanked by army commanders and officers, he was escorted out of the hall. The applause continued long after his exit.

I could hardly believe that I had had the opportunity to sit in front of him and listen to him talk for nearly two hours. To Zhou that was just one more speech in his political life, but to me it was an important meeting, remaining with me throughout my whole life.

In the small hours of the following day, we were summoned to the hall of the fair to be security guards to Premier Zhou. He was visiting the exhibitions at the fair. We stood in two lines about one metre apart, from the eighth floor (the top floor) down to the ground floor of the building. We were told not to initiate a handshake with him, unless he stretched out his hand to shake ours, because he was too tired.

Zhou slowly came down the lane lined with us students. Though he looked a bit tired, having had no rest between meetings, conferences and visits for over forty-eight hours, he was still energetic, alert and vigilant. His eyes still darted and swept with the intense light of wisdom, clear insight, and great strength.

I did feel very proud to have Zhou as our premier.

An Interpreter for the Fair

Business visitors from Western countries encountered difficulties, which also affected their business talks.

Quotations by Chairman Mao from *The Little Red Book*, were given to every visitor before the start of business talks.

'May I leave this?' one visitor asked. 'I got one from the airport and one from the hotel. Two little red books are enough for me. You can give this one to another visitor.' He was very honest to tell us this, but one of my colleagues felt indignant. He wanted to include him in the category of 'not loving Chairman Mao'.

'It's natural for him to want only two,' I said to him.

'He can give the other one to a friend at home,' my colleague said.

'He has no obligation to do this. What if he had not told us and later thrown it away?' I retorted.

That visitor never learned why he could not get good treatment at the fair.

I was interpreting for foreigners in general things, not in business talks. We accompanied visitors on calls, during shopping or to go to see a doctor during the day. During the night, each time an interpreter was called up, he or she would get forty cents extra pay.

The Revolutionary Model Opera, which performed operas such as 'Cleverly Taking the Ferocious Tiger Mountain', 'The Surprise Attack on the White Tiger Regiment', and 'The White Haired Girl', came to perform for the visitors. The actors and actresses sweated profusely, although most of the theatres had air-conditioning. When accompanying a foreign friend to see 'The Surprise Attack on the White Tiger Regiment', my friend and I were seated in the middle seats in the third row from the front. I could see sweat trickling down the faces of the actors, smearing their oily make-up. Their jackets were wet.

'C.Y.,' the rebel student in charge of the fair said to me one day, 'let's go to instigate a revolt on "The White Haired Girl" troupe.'

'Why do we want do that?' I asked.

'The leader of the troupe came to ask for an air-conditioned theatre for them to perform in, air-conditioned single rooms with bath facilities for them to stay in. They are full of bourgeois thinking.'

'We watched their performance and we were sweating. They have to dance on the stage, so they would sweat profusely even with air-conditioning!' I said. 'It's also reasonable for them to ask for air-conditioned single rooms with bath facilities. If they are not able to sleep well, how is it possible for them to perform well the next day?'

'I still think they ask too much.'

'Comrade Xi Piao-ha, don't forget what Premier Zhou said to you,' I warned him. 'The Premier expected only success, not failure. You personally are responsible. It was said that there are two opposing sections in the troupe. If you take some Red Guards to stir trouble there and the troupe cannot perform, it will not go well for you!'

Then I added, 'I will not go to the troupe, anyway.'

Nobody agreed with him so he gave up his idea of instigating a revolt in the troupe. I was happy that I succeeded in stopping the rebellious action.

One day I was instructed to take a Western friend to see a doctor. The doctor gave him a thorough check-up, a prescription and then told us a story:

'A few days ago, an interpreter accompanied a Western man here. I checked the man and then asked, "How is your appetite and bowel movements?" The interpreter did not translate at once. He hesitated for a while and then asked the patient, "How are your imports and exports?" The patient was surprised, looked at the interpreter confusedly and replied with displeasure, "My imports and exports are my secrets." The interpreter's face became red. He knew he was misunderstood. He remedied the situation immediately by pointing his forefinger to his open mouth with vigorous emphasised speech, "Your imports!" Then he motioned his forefinger to his back along his thigh, stressing, "And your exports!" The patient looked perplexed for a short instant, then his face lit up, and he laughed so heartily that tears came into his eyes. "Doctor, thank you, I am all right now." With that he and the interpreter stood up to go. "Are you sure you are all right?" his interpreter asked. "Quite sure."'

As I translated this story to the patient I accompanied, he laughed very much and said to me, 'C.Y. after laughing so much, I also feel worlds better now.' Still, I suggested he take the prescription, and he did.

Here I recollect a story told to us by our professor about a witty interpreter. At a diplomatic cocktail party, an American diplomat and a Chinese interpreter met.

'What "nese" are you—Japanese, Chinese or Pekinese?' the American taunted the Chinese interpreter sneering.

'What "key" are you—monkey, donkey or Yankee?' the Chinese interpreter retorted proudly. The American diplomat blushed and moved away.

One day I was asked to interpret for a business talk. The foreigner was from New Zealand and he was at the fair to purchase violins and other musical instruments.

'Let's read quotations from Chairman Mao,' the Chinese negotiator suggested as soon as we sat around the table. Everybody, including the man from New Zealand took out *The Little Red Book* to read after the negotiator. At the finish, the New Zealand man suggested we read the paragraph about equality and mutual benefit.

The atmosphere was warm and pleasant and the talk went smoothly. A price was agreed upon, as were the terms and conditions of the contract. Both sides were ready to sign when a man suddenly came in, thrusting a telegram to the Chinese negotiator.

'Sorry,' he said, 'we have to change the price.'

'What? Change the price?' the New Zealand man asked in disbelief and surprise.

'Yes, we have just received a telegram from our head office telling us to reduce the price for violins by one and half shillings per piece. So the contract has to be amended.'

'C.Y. please translate once more,' the man from New Zealand said in great urgency.

I did.

'Unbelievable,' he said. 'This would never happen in Western countries. The price and terms and conditions were all agreed upon and I was ready to sign the contract. Then the price is reduced! How honest the Chinese people are!' he commented.

Another day I was instructed to accompany a man to purchase antiques. The man chose some painted plates of the Tang Dynasty, and a vase from the Qing Dynasty. His taste told me he knew Chinese history and antiques well. He spent quite a large sum of money and his face shone.

'Mr Boss,' he spoke to the old man in charge of the shop. 'Can you check the stamps on the articles for me?'

The old man adjusted his glasses and examined carefully the articles his customer had bought. His hands were not steady, due to his age. 'They are genuine,' he said before continuing. 'We are in the Great Cultural Revolution. People are hurriedly selling antiques instead of buying them. It is a good time for you to buy. If you come next year, you may have to pay double the price to get the same thing.'

The man nodded. When the articles were packed and paid for, he extracted a stack of ten-yuan notes.

'Here's your tip,' he said to me.

I was taken aback. It was my duty to interpret for him and the fair authority paid me eighty cents per day.

'Sorry,' I shook my head.

He doubled the stack in his hand.

'You have done a good job,' he said. 'I think there are at least four hundred yuan or so, isn't that enough for you?'

'Thank you very much for your kindness,' I said. 'But I can't take your money.'

'Why?'

'We have rules and I can't take tips.'

'Only you and I know. There is no worry,' he said.

'Sure,' I replied. 'But the sky and the earth know. My own conscience knows, too. I don't want to do anything against the rules and harbour a guilty conscience for the rest of my life.'

'This is the first time that my offer has been rejected by a Chinese interpreter,' he said as he shook his head. 'As far as I know, this money is at least a half a year's pay for a graduate from the university, in your country. And you don't want the money.' He shook his head again. When we were approaching the building of the hotel, he spoke again.

'You are so honest!' Then he added, 'I wish some day I could have you working for me.'

I smiled at him and we shook hands warmly before we parted.

Venture to the Well-known Snake Restaurant

The interpreters from various Guangzhou Import and Export Corporations told us that there was a well-known restaurant in the city that sold dishes of snake meat. 'It's a pity if you are here and do not try the snake dishes,' they said, trying to persuade us northerners to eat the snake meat.

When we had a quiet morning, three or four friends, including me, obtained leave and embarked on the road of adventure. To explore Guangzhou, we thought, was similar to exploring a city in a foreign land.

'Excuse me, please tell me how to get to the snake restaurant,' we spoke to a nicely clad old man. He shook his head and talked in the local dialect to us. We could not understand, because it was very strange to our ears. To me, it could have been any language.

'Let's try students,' I suggested, thinking that they studied Mandarin in school and should be able to speak to us. I was right and we found the directions.

We arrived at the restaurant we were looking for.

'Don't go in yet,' one of the friends suggested, 'let's see the processing first.' We all agreed and went into a snake shop opposite the restaurant. Inside, against the three walls were boxes stacked high, like drawers holding herbal medicines in a pharmacy. All the boxes were labelled with the names of a various snakes. On the floor near the boxes were roosters or hens with their legs bound for sale.

A round wooden tub full of water was in the middle of the floor. A couple of dirty-looking bowls were placed on a dirty-looking table near the counter, where a girl was receiving payment.

Three or four elderly women and two or three elderly men were clustered around a girl, who was the snake butcher. The girl was, at the most, in her early twenties, and had a round face and plaited hair. She had a long plastic apron on, which also looked dirty. In her hand was a tool used like a knife, but it did not look like a knife.

She was handing a parcel to a woman when we entered the shop. An old woman spoke to her in a queer voice, which was in Cantonese. The butcher-girl approached the boxes, opened the lid of one, and swept her right hand over and above it. Immediately, numerous triangle-shaped, poisonous snake heads appeared, popping out of the box, their pinkish tongues shooting out of their mouths vibrating menacingly. My eyes widened. I was worried the girl might get bitten by one of the big snakes in the box, but she was not worried at all. She quickly caught a snake just under its head with her right hand, which was unprotected. The snake immediately coiled around her right arm.

The girl slipped the snake coil off her arm with her left hand and pressed it firmly to the floor with her right foot. The snake, now stretched straight like a piece of rope, was over one metre long and as thick as a hen egg. She opened the snake at its lower part and got something out and threw it into one of the dirty wooden bowls. It was greenish-blue looking. The elderly woman took it and gulped it down her throat. Breakfast nearly escaped from my throat, but with an effort I held it back.

'The snake gall-bladder,' one of my friends whispered into my ear.

Then the girl cut a slit in the snake and dripped the blood into another dirty bowl. When the blood stopped dripping, that elderly woman drank it all. This time I was really nauseous, yet curiosity forbade me from leaving the shop.

Now the girl circled the snake's neck so quickly that I did not notice what she was doing. With her right hand holding the snake's head hard and her left hand holding its body, she ripped off the head. Then, like removing an arm from a sleeve, she pulled the snake's skin off in one piece with a hard pull. The naked pinkish flesh of the snake coiled around her left arm. She threw the skin and head into a heap already piled on the floor and she brushed the snake body off her left arm into a wooden tub. The whole process of selecting the snake, getting the gall bladder, draining the blood, skinning the snake, all took at most ten minutes!

The headless and skinless snake, with its front body raised high above the water, swam and wriggled around the tub swiftly. The sight sickened me so much that I dashed out of the shop, doing my utmost to swallow hard and comfort my protesting stomach. My friends came out shortly after me. Without a word of discussion, we retraced our steps back to the hotel.

'How did you like the snake dish?' our Cantonese friends asked.

We simply threw ourselves into bed, not bothering to answer them.

'You did not have enough courage to try the snake dish!' they exclaimed. 'We can see it from your faces.'

I sat up, feeling my stomach with my right palm.

'The snake dish is nice, really nice,' one of them said. 'Now let me tell you about something you will not dare to touch.'

My comrades, the few boys who shared the same room gathered around him. Curiosity compelled me to listen too, though my stomach still complained slightly.

'There is a dish called *san zi*. *San* means three and *zi* means squeaks,' he began. 'They are mice just born, without hair and with their eyes not yet opened. They are considered the best and most nourishing dish.'

'But why call it *san zi*?' somebody asked, which was also on the tip of my tongue.

'When you pick it up with chopsticks, it squeaks—that is the first *zi*'. When you dip it into the sauce, it squeaks again—that is the second *zi*. When you crush it with your teeth, it squeaks yet again—that is the third *zi*! That is why the dish is called *san zi*.'

'Cruel!' we chorused. 'Have you ever tried it?'

'No, the mice are not easy to get!' he replied, a bit regretful that he had not the opportunity to taste it.

'Cruel?' another friend put in. 'Let me tell you about a diet that is *really* cruel.'

Silence fell while everybody listened.

'Of course, I am just telling you the story, because I myself have never seen, let alone eaten it,' he added.

'This comes from the traditional idea that "whatever one eats, the corresponding part of one's body is strengthened". For example, a dog's penis or a tiger's penis to enhance a man's libido. So people ate what I am now telling you to enhance their brain.

'I heard that only special restaurants could provide this food. People ate around a specially designed table with hinges and a round hole in the middle. You must wonder what that table was used for? Don't be impatient for an answer. Let me tell you gradually.

'When the diners sat around the table, the steward would place saucers and spoons in front of them. Then the steward would distribute a variety of sauces and spices into their saucers. By then and only by then, the thing they were going to have was taken to the table. What was it? It was a live monkey!

'The monkey, timid as a small boy in front of the strangers, looked at each and every face of the diners, seemingly trying to understand why he was taken here.

'The steward unlocked the table, fitted the monkey's neck to the hole of the table, and had the two halves of the table fastened securely together. Now only the monkey's head was above the table with his body and limbs were under the table, out of sight.

'All the time the monkey was too frightened to cry or scream. It looked at the steward with large watery eyes. Intense fright was in its eyes. The monkey's eyes were pathetically pleading for release.

'The steward would fetch a basin of warm water and soap to shave the monkey's scalp. Then he would use a small hammer to knock at the skull to break it. Then he would use a sharp knife to cut the skin and lift up the skull to expose the brain.

'The diners would then, at the signal of "please help yourself" by the steward, start spooning brain from the head. The monkey screamed crazily at the touch of the first spoon but remained silent after that, forever!

'Not everybody had the courage to dine on monkey's brain. Those who dared perhaps thought they were not clever enough unless their brains were enhanced through eating the clever brain of a monkey! Also, ordinary people can never have the opportunity to taste it because the price is so exorbitant that only rich people can afford it.'

'What about the dead monkey's body?' somebody asked.

'It was baked and the meat was sold.'

I thought what the man told us was merely a story, hearsay, or a cruel joke. I hoped it never happened in real life. Unfortunately, one day, when I was walking along the street in Guangzhou, I did catch sight of a baked monkey in the display counter of a restaurant! My heart was wrenched and the cruel story haunted me there and then. I ran back to our hotel.

chapter 25

THE END OF MY SCHOOLING

In China, Mao said that if any country tried to invade China, all the Chinese, men and women, young and old, would become soldiers. The invaders would be drowned in the sea of soldiers comprising the whole nation. In an effort to guard against any future attack, we all had to partake in military training. In 1968, all the students graduating were longing for assignments to different posts. We relied on the Institute to place us in our future employment. While we waited for our graduation, 'combating selfishness and criticising revisionism' through studying the selected works of Chairman Mao became our daily political routine. Neither the Red Guards organisation, the Worker's Propaganda Team, nor the Army Representative checked what we actually were doing, so this period was termed 'the idle period'. 'Xiao-yao Pai' (the idle students) became more and more common.

Militia Training

From the Preparatory Course until graduation from the Peking Foreign Trade Institute, I remember clearly two military training occasions. The first was after the border war between India and China and the second was during the Great Cultural Revolution.

The first time we were trained with wooden sticks in the shape of rifles. There was a joke about using a stick as a rifle:

'Comrade militiamen,' the commander addressed the militiamen loudly. 'Today, you will be given rifles!'

Applause arose from the militiamen like thunder.

'One rifle for each person,' he continued. Applause again. When the applause died down he completed his sentence, '…is not possible.'

A sigh of disappointment was heard from the audience.

'One rifle to be shared by two people,' he said. Applause rang out again. It was not bad to share one rifle between two people, but again he finished the latter half of the sentence, '…is not possible.'

The militiamen became more disappointed.

'However, one rifle to be shared by three militiamen is possible,' he stopped without completing the sentence. Applause broke for the third time. It was not bad even to share a rifle among three people. 'But the rifle is a wooden model of a real gun!'

The disappointment was real this time.

We were trained with such wooden rifles. The thickness of the 'rifle' was that of a real gun and its length was the total length of a real rifle including the bayonet.

The training included learning all the fighting skills. We were taught to stand with one leg in front and one behind so that we could thrust the bayonet forward into the enemy's chest or move backwards to ward off the enemy's thrust. We were taught how to twist our wrists to knock the rifle out of the enemy's hands. We were taught how to thrust the bayonet forward with a loud shouting of 'Sha!' We learnt how to turn and knock the chin of the enemy with the butt of the rifle and how to confront a crowd of soldiers single-handedly.

One day, heroes from the Sino–Indian border war were invited to our Institute to demonstrate how to fight with a bayonet rifle. One hero who came to our class was a man below average height. He was robust and full of strength. He had an air that would destroy the morale of any enemy.

'Who wishes to fight me first?' he said to us. Nobody answered.

'I will not attack you. I will just defend myself,' he said again. Still, nobody volunteered.

'Everybody has a try in turn!' the trainer officer ordered.

'Think of me as the enemy and thrust your bayonet at me!' the hero said to the first boy.

'Sha!' the first boy attacked. The hero just twisted his wrist and his 'rifle' caught the tip of the boy's 'rifle' and knocked it to the ground.

One by one the 'rifle' of each boy was knocked to the ground. His knocking was hard. It made one's 'tiger mouth' ache—the web of skin between the thumb and forefinger. If one did not release hold of his rifle, his 'tiger mouth' would bleed!

He then told us about the deeds of heroes in battles. He became a hero because he killed seven enemy soldiers with bayonets during combat without being wounded.

We heard the story about a regimental commander during the Chinese civil war. It happened during the Huai-Hai Campaign from 6 November

1948 to 10 January 1949. The regiment had a bayonet fight with the Kuomintang soldiers. The regimental commander had already killed twenty-seven enemy soldiers with his bayonet. The twenty-eighth thrust his bayonet into the regimental commander's stomach.

'Pull your bayonet out!' the commander shouted.

The soldier panicked and pulled the bayonet out. Then the regimental commander thrust a bayonet into the chest of that soldier.

When the two soldiers faced each other with rifles fixed with bayonets, he who was the bravest would win.

The second training session during the Great Cultural Revolution was different. This time we were all given real rifles. Each rifle had a long triangular bayonet, which could be easily secured into fighting position with a clip. But this time we were not taught about combat with a bayonet—we were taught about how to protect ourselves while killing the enemy. We were taught how to lay and avoid a mine and how to attack. Then we were instructed to practise for an emergency. The boys from my class lived on the fourth floor and were commanded to get to the sportsground with our rifles within three minutes after hearing the emergency bugle.

One day, in the small hours of the morning, the emergency bugle blared. I was awoken from a sound sleep. We had ten boys in our dormitory, all from the same class, and we hurriedly put on our padded clothing, socks, and shoes to get to the sportsground. We ran down the stairs with our rifles.

In just three minutes everybody was queued at the nominated place.

'Comrades,' the army commander in charge of the training spoke, in solemn low tones. 'We are instructed to round up a handful of counter-revolutionaries. Nobody should make a noise or speak during the march!'

He then instructed us to set out. We walked silently along the 'sheep runner path', narrow and uneven. My classmate, Hu, who walked in front of me could not walk properly. His two hands were always under his jacket a bit above the buttocks adjusting his rifle. The butt of the rifle pointed forward while the bayonet tip was about half a metre from my face.

'Get your rifle right, you are threatening my face!' I told him in a very low voice.

'Don't be impatient. I cannot do it at the moment,' he replied.

'Quick march,' the order came through the line. We had to walk faster and all the time I had to pay attention to his bayonet.

About two hours later, we were given a short break near a village. There was a toilet nearby and Hu dashed to it. A while later he came out, all smiles on his face.

During the break he whispered to me what had happened. Because he was on the upper bunk, when he came down to put on his shoes he put the right shoe on his left foot and his left shoe on his right foot. He had no time to put on his socks. What was more, he put on his padded trousers with the front at his buttocks. All the way he was trying to button up his trousers. Now he had everything all right but I told him he would have a cold due to changing in the toilet. He did have a cold on getting back to the Institute.

'Don't let anybody know. I don't want to be a laughing stock,' he cautioned me.

He was not the only one. Some boys had no time to put their socks on and therefore had frostbitten feet. Some could not find their glasses and suffered on the winding path.

'Just a practice? It is a practice to spoil our morning sleep!' we complained when the commander announced that it was a practice for an emergency and it was a success.

Diversity of Activity

When I returned to the Institute from the Spring Guangzhou Trade Fair of 1967, the zeal and zest shown at the beginning of the Great Cultural Revolution by the students had disappeared. Many left the Institute to travel around China to 'liaise' in name but to sightsee in reality.

The students were full of energy and had to find something to do.

As students, they should study hard to gain knowledge, but the professors and teachers were brushed aside and classes were stopped. If they persisted in self-study, they were in danger of being labelled 'bad performers in the Great Cultural Revolution' and thus risked their after-graduation assignment.

As required by the Great Cultural Revolution, students should be active in writing posters and support or oppose lines within the Party. Members of the 818 Red Guards organisation had joined the Maoist Red Guards organisation by the end of 1966, after reading the editorial 'The sunshine of the Party lights the Great Proletarian Cultural Revolution' in *Ren Min Ri Bao* (*People's Daily*). Some Red Guards were not happy with the absorption of the 818 Red Guards into the Maoist Red Guards and formed an ultra leftist group called 'The Red Rebel Corps'. Yet students lost interest in the activities of the Red Guards. The students could not just twiddle their thumbs to while away the time—they had to be active. Students who now belonged to the Maoist Red Guards, now had two opposing sides—the Maoist Red Guards and the Red Rebel Corps. If one side was in the classroom, the other side was in the dormitory. They would not mix. Each side, superficially, would study Chairman Mao's works, which was the proper thing to do during the Great Cultural Revolution.

Students still wandered around reading the posters that were at least a week old. Fresh posters still appeared on the walls, always bearing the familiar signatures of the most prominent activists in the Institute. The posters now took a new turn, and began targeting leaders intensively.

The huge loud speakers of the different Red Guards' organisations, blared noisily from morning till night. The representatives of workers and army units found it hard to bring students of the same class together, and when they were brought together in the classroom, heated arguments would start. I remember I was nominated to 'liaise' by an army representative, because both sides accepted me. I called the whole class together. The army representative told us to discuss the Great Cultural Revolution. The two sides started debating at once and two students stood up, each with a chair in his hands, ready to fight. The army representative asked me what to do. 'Dismiss the class. Instruct everybody to study Mao's works in the dormitory!' I suggested. He accepted my suggestion and the whole class never came together again until graduation.

The energy of most of the students found new outlets. Quite a few male students made transistor radios, which were as big as a soapbox. They would fill the dormitories with the singing of the Model Peking Opera.

One would hear them sing along with the actors, some were so informal that they always wore their underpants and only got dressed to come down from the dormitory to eat their meals.

Some practised calligraphy. Their progress was surprising. Once when I looked at the writing of one friend I could not believe my eyes—his writing was so similar to that of the model stone script! (Printers made model copies from stone stele for students to copy. This was called stone script.) But swimming was the most loved sport. About two hundred metres to the west of our Institute the Beijing–Miyun Canal flowed slowly down south. About eight hundred metres of its banks beside our

Institute were paved with cement slabs, serving as a swimming section. Students from nearby schools, workers and cadres from nearby factories, all came here to swim, but mainly the swimmers were from our Institute.

Some students were bold in spirit and strong in body. They stayed in the canal from morning to night. Broad-shouldered male students, about ten or so, would patrol both banks, ready to plunge in to save those in need. They were good swimmers and they sacrificed a few hours a day to protect the beginners. They could only jump into the canal for a swim when their patrol was over.

The canal would get so crowded that it was 'like boiling the dumplings'. One or two male students would, with a line in hand, walk along the bank to help girlfriends by pulling in or pushing out the line at her order. The other end of the line was tied to the waist of the girlfriend learning to swim. Such docile 'servants' would now and then be scolded by the screaming girls in the water, never worrying about their embarrassment in front of the crowd.

Rose also came to swim in the canal. As soon as she saw me in the river she would warn me not to swim near her. She did not wish to be seen by her classmates and friends. In the canal we were like strangers, though at heart I wished I could swim side by side with her.

One early evening after supper, students, singly or in pairs, were sauntering along the eastern bank of the canal for a leisurely walk. A few girls were still swimming in the water. A few had just come out of the changing room, which stood next to our Institute. Two girls, each about ten years of age at most, were playing with a ball near the change room. One girl failed to catch her ball when it bounced into the enclosure.

'There is a man inside!' the girl screamed.

Three or four female students went in to check.

'There is nobody inside!' they told the small girl.

'Yes, there is!' the small girl insisted.

The big girls went in to check again and still insisted there was nobody inside.

The small girl would not budge.

'There is a man inside. Let me show you!'

'You boys go in to check!' the girls spoke to the male onlookers.

The small girls, a few big girls, and a few male students, all went in together. Nobody was there.

'Over there!' one of the small girls pointed at the mat-wall, in which was a hole as big as a small fist.

A male student walked to the hole and looked into it.

'Yes, there is a man inside!' he said aloud.

A few more boys clustered around to have a peep into the hole.

'A naked man!' they confirmed. At the word 'naked', the girls evacuated the changing room. The man lay in the dark interior provided by the double reed walls looked deadly white, and still, as though it was a corpse.

'A murdered victim!' somebody commented.

'Murder or no murder, victim or no victim' a student, who grabbed a shovel inside the enclosure, said, 'let me cut him with the shovel!' He made the hole bigger with the shovel and was ready to strike.

'Don't hit me!' the corpse-like body shouted.

'You damned hooligan!' a few students swore.

The man crept out, naked.

'What are you doing here!' the student with the shovel demanded and hit him with it on his back. He fell flat on the ground.

'Put on your clothes!' someone else ordered.

He pulled his pants from inside the hole and put them on.

'Look! An imported camera! Clothes and a wooden board! You dirty skunk! You hid there to take pictures of the girls!' the student hit him with the shovel again.

'Take him to the office of Dong Fang Hong Commune!'

He was escorted out of the enclosure. Two carried his clothing and camera.

'Kill him!' the girls shouted in one voice, very angrily.

A slap on his face sounded clear and loud. A kick landed on his buttocks. The shovel smacked his back.

'Don't kill me! Don't kill me!' he begged.

Somebody pushed him forward with a jerk and he fell to the ground. Kicks landed upon him. He crept up and was pushed forward again.

'Stop hitting him!' an army representative came and stopped the beating. 'Take him to the office.'

I did not follow to the office but later I learned that he confessed that he had been sent to study overseas and had just come back from overseas to take part in the Great Cultural Revolution. He said he loved the natural beauty of girls and he wanted to get pictures of them naked. He found out that the girls change room was double-walled and that the gap between the two walls was big enough for him to hide in. He brought food and drink with him and got into the gap before sunrise. He started to take pictures when the sun was descending into the afternoon to provide good light. He had been there three times. Several reels of film had been used. The film in his camera was destroyed then and there in the office, so as not to embarrass the girls, who had swum that afternoon.

There were also accidents at the swimming area. Only one death occurred. One day, boys, like bears shaking trees to demonstrate their strength to the females, dived from the bridge by the end of the up-river end of the paved swimming area. A male student from our Institute dived from the top of the bridge. The water became red after a while and he failed to come up. Help was called and the patrolling students got him up. He was laid flat on the bank, blood gushed from a hole on top of his head. He was already unconscious. The doctors and nurses from our Institute were called and he was sent to hospital. He never woke up. The water was only two metres deep and he had dived in without taking any precautions. The top of his head hit a rock at the bottom.

Every afternoon I liked to swim for a few hours, too. But, being a very poor swimmer, I preferred to swim during the rain. When it rained there were just a few students in the canal. When it rained hard, your body felt warm in the water.

'Love-talking', by now, was popular. 'Like bamboo shoots after the spring rain', the sportsground as well as the fields near our Institute became an arena for more and more love-talking pairs. They milled around the sportsground for hours, trying to get to know more of each other, to express each other's lofty ideas for the future, to joke and to gossip.

During this period of time, up to the very day of marriage, love was strictly limited to only talking, and with no obscene or salacious language either. To put it politely, a loving couple never discussed or mentioned sex. At the time one's virginity was highly regarded so that the most daring body language would be, under the cover of the night sky or in a secluded place, hugging each other or kissing each other. Even this could only happen when the girl was sure that a boy was definitely to be her husband in the future.

When night fell, couples sauntered in the woods, the fields, or along the banks of the stream, or the canal. Once I heard a couple advising another that a dog was in the direction from which they came. 'Be careful, there's a dog over there.'

'If the dog did not bite you, why would it bite us?' the couple pressed forward without worrying at all. The joke was not appreciated. So the other pair who offered the information laughed awkwardly and headed in the other direction.

Some soldiers, who were in the Institute as the Army Propaganda Team, could not stand these liaisons. Once the head of the Army Propaganda Team spoke to the whole Institute.

'If a bomb falls, many pairs would be killed.'

Probably by the combined ideas of the Army and Worker Propaganda Teams and the Dong Fang Hong Red Guards organisation, or on its own initiative, the Dong Fang Hong Commune organised the students to help the peasants harvesting. First the students went to help harvesting wheat in the Sino–Korean Friendship People's Commune, then to Chang Xin-dian (a suburban town not very far from the outer edge of the city) to help harvest rice.

At Chang Xin-dian, the male students were accommodated in the storehouses for the night. Lying on the mattress spread over the floor, I could see the naked roof, without any beams, rafters or girders, just bricks crowded into the shape of an arch. The bricks squeezed tightly against one another and none would fall.

At noon it was very hot and I did not like to have my nap in the room. I would stay in the shade of a tree, fighting hard with my drowsiness to read *Pride and Prejudice*, not the translated version, of course.

We had three young peasants to lead and supervise our work. On the very first day, they suggested competing with us boys. I could not keep silent about this, for if we lost, the peasants would despise us as 'worthless'.

'Who has experience in rice cutting?' I asked my mates.

'I do!' five or six responded simultaneously.

'Now let me explain to you,' I said. 'We must not lose—we cannot lose! Let's do it this way. Let's form two groups with three members in each. Everyone will cut eight rows, as the peasants do. But the one in the middle of each group will cut twelve rows and those on either side of them will only cut six rows. Don't look back. Just press ahead. Thus very quickly, the peasants will lag behind the four of our harvesters in our groups. When the four are sure that they will get to the other side of the paddy ahead of the peasants, then each of you cut ten rows. Thus the two in the middle will catch up quickly with you. But the morale of the peasants will be destroyed.'

I then told two girls to get six more sickles and showed them how to sharpen them. Whenever we reached the other end of the paddy, we would change for the newly sharpened sickles. The peasants' sickles would gradually become blunt. Their speed would become slower and slower.

'We will win,' I told my mates.

Work progressed as I predicted. By the end of the morning, all six of us were far ahead of the three peasants. They could not believe it and wanted to pick our faults. However, our trails were at least two or three times cleaner than theirs, with less littered rice behind. Finally they accepted defeat.

'You must have been helping in the fields at home,' they commented. They never staged another challenge to us boys till the very end of our stay there.

Thereafter, more and more students went for 'liaison' all over the country, though there were a lot of stories about the violent fighting between opposing workers' organisations. There was a lot of talking about the chaos created by the Red Guards. I remember Premier Zhou had proudly spoken about it.

'We have fifty million Red Guards having free travels, free accommodation and free boarding all over the country. They went to factories and villages to spread the fire of revolution. Tell me which other country in the world can do this or dares to do this? Does the United States of America dare to allow fifty million of its young people to do the this and instigate revolution?' our Premier Zhou said.

Time to Say Goodbye to the Institute

Gradually, 1967 idled into 1968. All the students graduating were longing for assignments to different posts. Students from the same class still could not sit together, but the relation between students from different classes of the same year returned to the normal, no matter which Red Guards organisation they belonged to. 'Combating selfishness and criticising revisionism' through studying the selected works of Chairman Mao became our daily political routine. Neither the Red Guards organisation, the Worker's Propaganda Team, nor the Army Representative checked what we actually were doing, so this period was termed 'the idle period'.

'Xiao-yao Pai' (the idle students) became more and more common.

Finally word spread that our year was approaching graduation and jobs were to be assigned. One day, our former coordinator struck up a casual conversation with me.

'C.Y.,' he asked, 'what's your opinion about the assignment of jobs?' 'Do you wish to have trouble in the future or do you wish it to go smoothly?' I asked.

'Is there a difference?'

'Definitely.' I replied.

'Tell me both.' he said.

'If you want trouble, assign the students according to which Red Guards organisation he or she is in.'

'Why would we have trouble later?'

'Because,' I smiled, 'the Great Cultural Revolution is about solving the struggle within the Party to go along socialist or capitalist lines. Don't forget Mao has said, "Long live the Red Guards!" Chairman Mao did not discriminate against the Red Guards.'

'What about the other way?' he asked.

'Do you remember the "poplar poem" about job assignment in our Institute?' I said.

'What is it?'

'Assign the couples to the farthermost places.

Assign those with burdens near their homes.

Assign single students to places in between.'

He laughed.

'My opinion is,' I continued when he stopped laughing, 'that behaviour in the Great Cultural Revolution should be taken into consideration. But it should only be as a reference. The class origin of a student should be taken into consideration but not as the only consideration. It should be, again, a reference. Results of study should also be taken into consideration but not as the sole consideration. Thus everybody will be happy when the assignment is announced.'

He remained silent. We then chatted about other subjects and then parted.

Summer was already half over, and the inside of the dining hall was too hot to eat lunch in. I liked to have it under the shade of a tree in the yard. One day four of us from the same year were having lunch in the shade of a tree. Our former coordinator was accompanying two young ladies to the dining hall. They stood in front of the dining hall, talking for a while. For some time during their brief conversation, the coordinator was pointing in our direction. We noticed this but did not give it any thought.

'Coordinator,' I asked him one day, 'where am I being assigned to?'

'A job of similar nature to that of your brother,' he replied.

At that time my brother Chun-ming, a soldier of the ground service of the airforce, was in North Vietnam 'assisting Vietnam to resist the US'. I thought that I could not be positioned overseas. There was no precedence. Probably I was assigned to a company to deal with foreigners.

Finally the assignment of all students were announced. The four of us, who had lunch in the yard that day, were all assigned to the Ministry of Transport. Some were sent to farms as 'cadres in storage'. It was said that language students should not all be assigned permanently. Some should be ready to meet the expected requirements of interpreters after China was admitted back into the United Nations.

Now that I was soon to leave the Institute, Rose and I seized every possible opportunity to walk together, pledging to each other that even if the 'sea dries and the rocks decay' our loyalty to one other would not change. The fascinating thing about love is that at heart the boy always wants to touch the girl, and yet he is always afraid of being rejected. This state of mind is poignant, sweet, irritating, and exciting. I was no exception. I finally got an opportunity to caress Rose when we visited Jing Shan Park. I was reading a chapter from *The Hatter's Castle* to her. When I came to the paragraph where Dennis traces a vein from Mary's neck downward, and he suddenly takes hold of Mary's breast, a sudden urge took me and I did the same. With her breast held in my hand, Rose's face and neck became red. She gave me a light slap on the face. She did admit that she was fully and desperately in love with me.

Soon, I was notified to get my certificate of assignment from the Institute. It was just a card on which it was written: Report to China Ocean Shipping Company, Shanghai Branch on the 6 October 1968. Goodbye from the Peking Foreign Trade Institute.

EPILOGUE

The Chinese saying 'accepting the drop of water from other people, while paying back a gushing spring' aptly describes the attitude of the majority of Chinese peasants. Because the Chinese Communists led by Mao gave the peasants land, the majority of the peasants offered Mao and his Communists unreserved support, which accelerated the collapse of the Kuomintang regime and enabled the newly established Communist regime to be firmly rooted in China. Because the Communists led by Mao intended to lead them to a better life, the peasants forgave the mistakes and blunders committed by the Communists in 1958. During the national famine of the early sixties, the peasants harboured no doubts about the Communists, even though in their stomachs were merely grass roots, tree leaves, or wild vegetables.

I was born at a time when China was torn by war and bogged down by natural disasters. I spent my childhood and teenage years during a time when China was moving from a private system to socialism. My life in the countryside, in school and university carried the stamp of that era.

From 1949 until 1968, political movements in China had never stopped. However, because I was only a Chinese peasant boy, who could not understand the full magnitude of each and every political movement, I can only try to reflect them from the incidents and events I actually lived through.

What I have tried to do is to convey the customs, traditions and the everyday life of peasants. How students were trained in primary school, junior and senior high school, and in university. Physical labour and political movements occupied a large part of our time in school.

'Water flows always down but a man climbs all the way up.' Through overcoming one difficulty and hardship after another, I finally succeeded in graduating from the Peking Foreign Trade Institute in 1968 and immediately started the life of a sailor. Rose and I married in 1970.

CHRONOLOGY

Year	Author/ Family	National/Local
1941	I am born on Lunar 26 July.	Japanese soldiers frequent Paradise Palace and the district 'looking for flowery girls and gold ingots'.
1945	My mother and I run for safety when guerrillas ambush a Japanese tank.	Japan surrender on 15 August but not to the guerrillas.
1946	My second brother, Xiao Bao is born. I begin baby-sitting.	First land reform in Paradise Palace and in the district by the Communist guerrillas. Kuomintang organise 'Home Return Corps' called locally 'The White-necks'.
1947	I am still baby-sitting.	Seesaw between the Kuomintang and the Communist guerillas.
1948	I witness the redistribution of moveable belongings.	The second land reform and the redistribution of moveable belongings. Young men joined the PLA.
1949	I begin my primary school years.	Beijing peacefully liberated. Reorganisation of Kuomintang 49th Army in the Paradise Palace. People's Republic of China established on Lunar 1st October. Mutual aid groups form among the peasants.
1950	Yang-ge dance, the flower stick dance, introduced to our school.	Suppressing the counter-revolutionaries. 'Resisting US, Helping Korea, protecting home and motherland' by the volunteers.
1951	I try to get my own fees for schooling.	Proclamation of the rules in suppression of the counter-revolutionaries.

1952	Killing flies and mosquitos against the US 'germ war' by us pupils.	Success of the suppression of counter-revolutionaries as a nation-wide movement.
1953	Teachers wear flowery shirts made of fabrics imported from USSR.	Junior co-operatives established. Grain selling under government control. Peasants buy grain with a book.
1954		Sale of edible oil and fabrics under government control.
1955	I become a peasant for one year.	Senior co-operatives established.
1956	I get into junior high school.	Digging reservoir to solve irrigation problem.
1957	I self-support my schooling.	Launching of the 'agricultural satellite'.
1958	I learn steel making.	The Great Leap Forward begins. The establishment of the People's Commune. Nation-wide steel making on a large scale.
1959	I get into the Preparatory Course of Peking Foreign Trade Institute.	
1960	I intend to graduate one year earlier.	Students feel nation-wide natural famine.
1961	Digging soil in Wong Jun Tan.	Nation-wide natural famine continues.
1962	I am enrolled into class one, first English department, Peking Foreign Trade Institute. Labouring in Wen Nan Wa.	Last year of the natural famine. 'Red and Expert' is debated among students.
1964		Start of the Socialist Education Movement in the countryside.

1965	I take part in the 'Four Clear Ups'.	Socialist Education Movement is called the 'Four Clear Ups'.
1966	My classmates and I are trucked back to the Institute to take part in the Great Cultural Revolution. I organise a 'long-march'.	The Great Cultural Revolution begins.
1967	I am an interpreter in Guangzhou Spring Trade Fair.	The Great Cultural Revolution continues.
1968	I am assigned to the China Ocean Shipping Company, Shanghai Branch.	The Great Cultural Revolution continues.